Explorations of the Syntax-Semantics Interface

Jens Fleischhauer, Anja Latrouite & Rainer Osswald (eds.)

d|u|p

Hana Filip, Peter Indefrey, Laura Kallmeyer,
Sebastian Löbner, Gerhard Schurz & Robert D. Van Valin, Jr. (eds.)

Studies in Language and Cognition

3

Jens Fleischhauer, Anja Latrouite & Rainer Osswald (eds.)

2016

Explorations of the Syntax-Semantics Interface

d|u|p

**Bibliografische Information
der Deutschen Nationalbibliothek**
Die Deutsche Nationalbibliothek verzeichnet diese
Publikation in der Deutschen Nationalbibliografie;
detaillierte bibliografische Daten sind im Internet
über http://dnb.dnb.de abrufbar.

© düsseldorf university press, Düsseldorf 2016
http://www.dupress.de
Einbandgestaltung: Doris Gerland, Christian Horn, Albert Ortmann
Satz: Friedhelm Sowa, LaTeX
Herstellung: docupoint GmbH, Barleben

Gesetzt aus der Linux Libertine und der Linux Biolinum
ISBN 978-3-95758-000-9

Table of Contents

Introduction 7

THE SYNTAX-SEMANTICS INTERFACE AND LINGUISTIC THEORY

Linguistic Categories and the Syntax-Semantics Interface: Evaluating Competing Approaches
Gisa Rauh 15

Why Verb Meaning Matters to Syntax
Eunkyung Yi & Jean-Pierre Koenig 57

Representing Constructional Schemata in the FunGramKB Grammaticon
Ricardo Mairal & Carlos Periñán-Pascual 77

Multilingualism, Multilectalism and Register Variation in Linguistic Theory – Extending the Diasystematic Approach
John Peterson 109

RRG and the Exploration of Syntactically Based Relativistic Effects
Caleb Everett 149

CASE STUDIES OF THE SYNTAX-SEMANTICS INTERFACE

Head-Marking and Agreement: Evidence from Yucatec Maya
Jürgen Bohnemeyer, Lindsay K. Butler & T. Florian Jaeger 169

Degree Expressions at the Syntax-Semantics Interface
Jens Fleischhauer 209

Volition in Grammar and Lexical Representation of Verbs: The Case of Kabardian Involuntative
Ranko Matasović 247

Direct versus Inverse in Murik-Kopar
William A. Foley 265

Shifting Perspectives: Case Marking Restrictions and the Syntax-Semantics-Pragmatics Interface
Anja Latrouite 289

Notes on "Noun Phrase Structure" in Tagalog
Nikolaus P. Himmelmann 319

Integrated and Non-Integrated Left Dislocation: A Comparative Study of LD in Avatime, Tundra Yukaghir & Whitesands
Dejan Matić, Saskia van Putten & Jeremy Hammond 343

Introduction

The origins of this book go back to a colloquium on 'Exploring the syntax-semantics interface' which took place at Heinrich Heine University Düsseldorf in May 2012 in honor of the 60th birthday of Robert D. Van Valin, Jr. Most of the papers collected in this volume grew out of talks given at that occasion.[1]

Van Valin is widely known as the principal developer of Role and Reference Grammar (RRG), a linguistic framework that combines insights from cross-linguistic syntactic analysis, lexical semantics and formal pragmatics in a way that makes it equally attractive for theoretical linguists, field linguists and psycholinguists. The range of languages and linguistic phenomena discussed in this volume, and the variety of perspectives taken by the authors in their analyses, nicely reflect both, Van Valin's systematic but open-minded approach to the study of grammar and language, and his emphasis on taking seriously the typological variation among languages. Several papers aim at extending the coverage and scope of RRG, e. g. by describing in more detail the interaction between syntax and semantics of specific constructions, or by proposing new constructional schemata for pragmatic and discourse-level phenomena. Other papers sharpen and challenge specific assumptions of RRG, e. g., the syntactic status of referential phrases in head-marking languages. Again others discuss more fundamental issues such as the type and the amount of syntactic information in the lexicon.

The book is divided into two parts. The five papers of the first part, entitled 'The Syntax-Semantics Interface and Linguistic Theory', address a number of general questions concerning the relation of meaning and its syntactic encoding as part of a theory of grammar, much in line with Van Valin's overall goal to disentangle the interaction of syntax, semantics, and pragmatics. The contributions of this part investigate, for instance, the predisposition of lexical items to occur in

---

[1] The colloquium and the production of this volume have been financially supported by the Collaborative Research Center 991 'The Structure of Representations in Language, Cognition, and Science' funded by the German Research Foundation (DFG).

certain syntactic environments and its consequences for the information stored in the lexicon. A closely related issue is the connection between argument realization and lexical representation and, in particular, the common semantic basis of verbs which show a similar valency alternation behavior in the syntax. Further topics discussed in the first part are the representation of discourse-level and code-switching phenomena within the syntactic framework of RRG and possible extensions of the latter.

The second part of the book, 'Case Studies of the Syntax-Semantics Interface', contains seven contributions whose focus is on specific grammatical phenomena in a number of typologically diverse languages. The investigated languages include, among others, Yucatec Maya, Kabardian, Tagalog, Murik-Kopar, Avatime, Whitesands, Yukaghir, and various Indo-European languages. The topics range from the syntactic realization of arguments and degree modification to the structure of noun phrases and the encoding of information structure. Several papers are concerned with issues of argument realization including: morphological operations that affect the valency pattern of a verb by cancelling parts of its semantic structure, as exemplified by the involuntative in the Caucasian language Kabardian; the non-standard argument realization patterns in Murik and Kopar, which show an inverse actor-undergoer ranking; and differential object marking in languages like Tagalog and its consequences for a theory of argument linking. Another common theme shared by several of the papers is to test and, if necessary, to extend and modify the predictions of RRG about how the syntactic position of different kinds of constituents can be explained in terms of semantic and pragmatic properties. Among the cases discussed are the structural positions of argument noun phrases in head-marking languages and of adverbials that express gradation. A related topic addressed are the pragmatic functions associated with dislocated constituents, and their specific syntactic integration across different languages.

Overview of the contributions

The opening paper 'Linguistic Categories and the Syntax-Semantics Interface: Evaluating Competing Approaches' by **Gisa Rauh** examines how different linguistic theories characterize the relation between syntactic and semantic properties of words in the lexicon and beyond. The author compares Chomsky's

Standard Theory, Head-Driven Phrase Structure Grammar, and traditional Construction Grammar with Neo-Construction Grammar and RRG. While the former approaches assume that the syntactic and semantic properties of words are specified in their lexical entries, the latter approaches regard the syntactic properties determined to a large extent by the syntagmatic environment of the word in phrases and sentences. Rauh evaluates the plausibility of the interface between the syntactic and semantic categories of words in the selected linguistic theories and concludes that a certain amount of syntactic information in the lexicon seems to be the empirically plausible option and that the counterexamples discussed in the literature often just reflect the inadequacy of traditional part of speech classifications.

The paper 'Why Verb Meaning Matters to Syntax' by **Eunkyung Yi** and **Jean-Pierre Koenig** is concerned with the question why verbs that show the same patterning in diathesis alternations tend to be semantically similar to each other. The authors propose the hypothesis that such a semantic clustering is triggered by one or more "semantic anchors", that is, by one or more frequent verbs that come with certain syntactic frames and lead speakers to use the same frames for semantically similar verbs. They consider two variants of the hypothesis: "global semantic anchoring" in which a single semantic anchor is responsible for the coherent syntactic behavior, and "local semantic anchoring". The authors provide corpus-based and psycholinguistic evidence that the global semantic anchor hypothesis may be true for the verb *give* and its impact on the spread of the ditransitive frame. In other cases, such as the material object frame of the locative alternation, they suggest that several anchors need to be assumed, each representing a different semantic subclass of the alternating verbs.

Ricardo Mairal and **Carlos Periñán-Pascual**'s paper 'Representing Constructional Schemata in the FunGramKB Grammaticon' describes the format and integration of constructional schemata in FunGramKB, a multi-purpose natural language processing system. The authors propose to represent constructions by "constructional nodes" in the syntactic representations, thereby extending the layered structure of the clause traditionally assumed in RRG. This approach allows them to codify not only argument structure constructions but also non-propositional elements of meaning that have been of concern in pragmatics and discourse analysis. To this end, the authors distinguish four levels of constructions: argumental, implicational, illocutionary, and discourse constructions. In their model, the layered structure of the clause is configured as one or more argumental constructions, which are recursively arranged, and is enhanced by nodes for constructional schemata belonging to the other three levels. The paper concludes with a brief description of how a parser can cope with the extended syntactic structures.

In his contribution 'Multilingualism, Multilectalism and Register Variation in Linguistic Theory – Extending the Diasystematic Approach', **John Peterson** addresses the challenge that multilingualism and intralingual variation represent for models of language theory. In the light of studies showing that all of a speaker's languages are simultaneously activated in production and should not be viewed as strictly discrete systems, Peterson develops a model of multilingual speech in which grammatical structures of all types are either language-specific or unspecified for both register and language. He integrates his ideas into RRG and shows how the principles developed in his model can be applied to bilingual speech data and extended to intralingual variation.

The first part of the volume concludes with the paper 'RRG and the Exploration of Syntactically Based Relativistic Effects', in which **Caleb Everett** pursues the question whether syntactic variation has an influence on cognition and may cause disparities in non-linguistic thought. Pointing to the fact that RRG and the notion of macro-role transitivity has been fruitfully used to explain test results regarding the differing conceptualisation of situations in unrelated languages, Everett argues that RRG provides an ideal basis for the development of empirical tests with respect to the influence of syntax on non-linguistic thought.

Part two of the volume starts with a paper by **Jürgen Bohnemeyer**, **Lindsay Butler** and **Florian Jaeger**, entitled 'Head-marking and Agreement: Evidence from Yucatec Maya', which critically examines a recent proposal of Van Valin about the syntactic positioning of noun phrases (or reference phrases) in head-marking languages. According to Van Valin's proposal, syntactically optional reference phrases, which co-refer with the argument marked at the head are to be analyzed as taking a core-external position, that is, they are immediate daughters of the clause. The authors challenge this assumption based on data from Yucatec Maya, which seem to indicate that reference phrases are in fact constituents of the core. They base their analysis on two observations: The first is the apparent core-internal position of a shared reference phrase in a core cosubordination construction. The second observation is that plural marking in the presence of a reference phrase can be analysed as an agreement phenomenon.

The paper 'Degree Expressions at the Syntax-Semantics Interface' by **Jens Fleischhauer** is concerned with verb gradation. The goal of the paper is to show that different types of verb gradation – degree gradation on the one hand and extent gradation on the other – are realised in different syntactic configurations. Degree gradation is expressed at the nucleus layer, whereas extent gradation is realized at the core layer. The paper extends RRG's approach on adverbs and presents a cross-linguistic analysis of a type of adverbial modification that has received comparatively less attention in RRG but also in other frameworks.

In his paper 'Volition in Grammar and Lexical Representation of Verbs: The Case of Kabardian Involuntative', **Ranko Matasović** focuses on the status of lexical rules in RRG. His analysis is based on the involuntative in the north-west Caucasian language Kabardian, which is used for expressing that an action is performed unintentionally. The involuntative is analysed as a lexical rule that cancels the agentivity of the base verb. Broadening the picture, Matasović raises the question why such a rule is less widespread and less often grammaticalized in languages than the inverse rule expressing that an action is performed volitionally. This finally results in the question why certain types of lexical rules are attested more often in some languages than in others.

In his paper 'Direct versus Inverse in Murik-Kopar', **William A. Foley** discusses the direct-inverse inflectional system of two particular Papuan languages – Murik and Kopar, which both belong to the Lower-Sepik family. Inverse languages are built on a role hierarchy, which generally ranks the higher argument (= actor) over the lower argument (= undergoer). This ranking holds for the well-known Algonquian languages but not for Murik and Kopar, which reverse the hierarchy. In this regard, the two languages exemplify an unusual inverse system. The author discusses the linking system of these languages in detail and aims in developing a theoretical analysis of inverse marking that can be applied to languages showing such an unusual inverse system.

The paper 'Shifting Perspectives: Case Marking Restrictions and the Syntax-Semantics-Pragmatics Interface' by **Anja Latrouite** deals with differential object marking, and voice and case marking exceptions in Tagalog. Latrouite focuses on actor voice sentences with specific undergoers and argues that the description of the licensing conditions for these sentences requires the recurrence to three different levels: the level of referentiality of the respective theme argument, the level of event semantics, i. e. the question of whether a verb is actor- or undergoer-oriented, and the level of information structure. The fact that multiple layers need to be evoked to provide an account of case marking restrictions and exceptions is taken as evidence that a multi-layered theory of language as provided by RRG is clearly to be favored over syntactico-centric approaches.

The subsequent paper 'Notes on "Noun Phrase Structure" in Tagalog' by **Nikolaus P. Himmelmann** gives an overview of referential phrases in Tagalog, demonstrating that the complements of the phrase-marking clitics *ang*, *ng*, and *sa* crucially differ in nature from their equivalents in European languages. Himmelmann furthermore finds that the distribution of the three markers differs to an important extent. He suggests that the two former markers should be analysed as determiners and heads, even though the internal structure of the phrases they are heading is shown to be quite different from standard X-bar conceptions of determiner phrases. Importantly the two determiner clitics mark complementary syntactic functions of referential phrases. While *ang* marks topics, subjects and predicates, *ng* marks non-subject complements and possessors. In contrast, the marker *sa*, which may also head a referential phrase, is given a very different analysis. In addition to determiners, demonstratives are discussed in some more detail as they seem to be poly-functional.

The final paper, 'Integrated and Non-Integrated Left Dislocation: A Comparative Study of LD in Avatime, Tundra Yukaghir & Whitesands', by **Dejan Matić**, **Saskia van Putten** and **Jeremy Hammond**, investigates the similarities and differences of left dislocations (LD) in three unrelated languages. The authors show that in all three of the languages, LDs allow for iteration, for noun phrases as resumptive elements, for LDs similar to Chinese-style topics and for the violation of island constraints, suggesting that these elements are not easily analysed as integrated into the sentence. On the other hand, they observe that the languages differ in important structural and functional ways which indicate that we may have to distinguish different levels of integration. For example, LDs in Avatime may appear in unexpected environments, like embedded clauses, suggesting a higher degree of integration (loosely integrated LDs). Moreover, Whitesands has developed specialized pronominal forms to indicate LDs, which is also viewed as a sign of a higher level of integration.

The Syntax-Semantics Interface and Linguistic Theory

Linguistic Categories and the Syntax-Semantics Interface: Evaluating Competing Approaches

Gisa Rauh

1 Introduction

Words have meanings, which provide the basis for semantic categories, and words occur in particular positions in sentences, which categorizes them syntactically. What I will be concerned with in this paper is how the semantic and the syntactic properties of words are related or – to be more precise – how linguists assume that these are related and describe this relationship. In other words, the crucial questions are how various linguists describe the interface between the syntactic and semantic categories of words and how plausible their positions are. It is the goal of this paper to provide an answer to these questions.

According to the traditional view, words are specified for syntactic and semantic properties in their entries in the lexicon. However, more recently this view has been criticized. One central argument is that various languages allow the same form with the same meaning to be used either as a verb or as a noun, for example *walk*, *drink* or *sleep* in English, indicating that syntactic categorization is fixed not in the lexicon but rather in the syntax.

In what follows I will first take a look at how the relationship between the syntactic and semantic properties of words is described in selected approaches that conform to the traditional view. These include two representatives of the generative-interpretive approach, the Standard Theory and the Theory of Principles and Parameters, followed by Head-Driven Phrase Structure Grammar and

Construction Grammar. After briefly discussing the general characteristics of the interface conception in these approaches – including a discussion of the criticism leveled at them – I will turn to others which claim that syntactic specification is not part of lexical entries but rather a matter of syntactic (or morphological) structural environments. Here I will take a look at Neo-Construction Grammar and Role and Reference Grammar. Subsequently, the plausibility of the interface conceptions of these various approaches will be investigated. The paper will end with a discussion of controversial views on cross-linguistic differences concerning the noun-verb distinction and the consequences these can have for interface conceptions.

2   Generative-interpretative approaches

In this section, aspects of the description of the interface between syntactic and semantic properties of words in the Standard Theory (henceforth ST, cf. Chomsky 1965) and in the Theory of Principles and Parameters (henceforth PPT, cf. e. g. Chomsky 1981, Chomsky & Lasnik 1993) will be considered.

The grammatical model of the ST consists of a generative syntactic component, the interpretive components of semantics and phonology and a lexicon. The lexicon is considered to be a list of lexical entries which specify all the idiosyncratic properties of a given language. It is language-specific.

Lexical entries for words are claimed to include a phonological representation (a phonological matrix), intrinsic semantic properties and syntactic properties. Of these Chomsky himself only specifies syntactic properties, namely a categorial specification, e. g. N, V, A, etc., strict subcategorization determining the number and syntactic category of complements, e. g. —NP, —NP PP, and selection restrictions specifying intrinsic semantic features of the complement(s) and the subject. The following provides an example:

(1) (*sincerity*,[+N, +Det—, −Count, +Abstract, ...])
    (*frighten*,[+V, + —NP, +[+Abstract], Aux — Det [+Animate], +Object-deletion, ...])
                                                              (Chomsky 1965: 107)

It should be noted that one phonological matrix may be associated with more than one set of syntactic properties and/or with more than one set of intrinsic semantic properties, resulting in various readings (cf. e.g. Katz & Fodor 1963). In these cases there is more than one lexical entry.

Syntactically, the ST distinguishes two levels of representation, deep structure and surface structure, which are derived by phrase-structure rules and transformational rules respectively. The syntactic categories of words, i.e. their distribution, are then described by the interaction of lexical-syntactic properties with phrase-structure rules and transformational rules.

The semantics of sentences in this framework, as worked out by Katz & Fodor (1963), interprets deep structures via projection rules, which start out with the lexically specified semantic properties of the words, which are inserted into deep structures and then amalgamated to form larger semantic units.

In this approach then, the idea is that the relationship between syntax and semantics at word level is described by means of lexical entries, which therefore can be identified as representing the interface between the two. Syntactic categories are determined on the basis of shared syntactic properties of various lexical entries and semantic categories on the basis of their shared semantic properties.

Like the ST, the PPT distinguishes between a lexicon and grammar in the narrow sense, the latter here called the 'computational system'.

As in the ST, the lexicon of the PPT is a list of lexical entries which specify all the idiosyncratic properties of a language, and it is language-specific. Here as well, the lexical entries for words at least are claimed to combine phonological, semantic and syntactic specifications.

Whereas the phonological and semantic specifications are basically as in the ST, syntactic specifications here include a categorial specification based on feature combinations of [±N] and [±V], with [+N] – according to Chomsky & Lasnik (1993: 517) – expressing the "traditional substantive" and [+V] the "predicate", an argument structure specifying how many arguments an item licenses and what semantic roles they receive, strict subcategorization if this cannot be predicted by general principles, and Case-assignment properties. The feature combinations [±N] and [±V], which describe nouns as [+N, −V], verbs as [−N, +V], adjectives as [+N, +V] and prepositions as [−N, −V], are more flexible than the corresponding category labels N, V, A and P in that they allow for generalizations over particular features. Thus, for example, [−N]-categories are identified as Case-assigners in English and [+N]-categories as Case-receivers.

The PPT distinguishes four levels of representation: d-structure, s-structure, logical form (LF) and phonological form (PF). Of these the first two are clearly syntactic representations, whereas LF and PF are characterized as interfaces to other, 'external' systems with which they interact, LF as an interface to the conceptional-intentional system C-I and PF to the articulatory-perceptual system A-P.

The computational system consists of various general and parametrized principles such as the Projection Principle or the Principle of Full Interpretation and those of the modules of X-bar Theory, Theta Theory and Case Theory, and the operation Move α. Starting with lexical representations, sentence structures are then derived by interaction between the various principles, which finally identifies the syntactic categories of words.

As in the ST, the idea in this framework is that the syntactic and semantic categories of words are intimately related since syntactic and semantic properties are claimed to be combined in their lexical representations, which therefore, in principle, function as an interface between the two. However, except for argument structures, no suggestions are made concerning the kind of semantic representations, and their interpretation is not discussed either. All that is said is that LF interacts with the 'external' conceptual-intentional system, 'conceptual' in this case referring to semantic issues and 'intentional' to pragmatic issues.

3 Head-Driven Phrase Structure Grammar

Just like the two approaches considered above, Head-Driven Phrase Structure Grammar (henceforth HPSG) distinguishes between a lexicon and grammar. However, the lexicon is not just a list of lexical entries which specify idiosyncratic properties of words but consists of lexical entries with various degrees of generality determined by constraints related to a hierarchy of lexeme types, by additional constraints – e. g. the Specifier-Head Agreement Constraint or the Case Constraint – and lexical rules, e. g. inflectional rules. Lexical entries of type *word*, the building blocks of syntax, are the most elaborated and specific lexical entries. There are numerous variants of HPSG. The characterization below relates to the classical version developed by Pollard & Sag (1994), which forms the basis for subsequent variants and overviews.[1]

---

[1] Cf. e. g. Sag et al. (2003), Levine & Meurers (2006) and Müller (2010, chap. 8).

Linguistic Categories and the Syntax-Semantics Interface

The information provided in lexical entries is modeled by a system of typed (or 'sorted') feature structures, which are described by feature descriptions with the format of attribute-value matrix (AVM) diagrams expressing constraints on well-formed feature structures. AVM diagrams of words include descriptions of a phonological matrix, of syntactic properties such as categorial specifications and specifications of grammatical arguments, including inflectional specifications, as well as of semantic (referential) properties such as the word's context-independent contribution to the semantic interpretation of a phrase and – where necessary – context dependent (pragmatic) information relating to indexical properties, presuppositions or conventional implicatures (cf. Pollard & Sag 1994: 22). In addition there are tags, represented as boxed numerals, indicating structure sharing of attributes or values. The example in Figure 1, which presents a lexical entry of the finite verb *gives*, illustrates this.

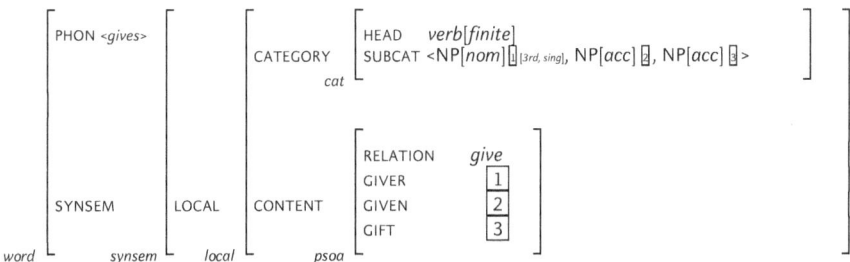

Figure 1: Lexical entry of the finite verb *gives*, adapted from Pollard & Sag (1994)

The AVM diagram describes a feature structure of type *word* with the attributes PHON(OLOGY) and SYN(TAX)SEM(ANTICS). The PHON value *gives* indicates the phonological matrix of the word. The SYNSEM attribute includes a complex of integrated syntactic and semantic information. Its value is a structured object of type *synsem* with the attribute LOCAL, whose value, *loc(al)*, contains the information relevant in local contexts,[2] described in Figure 1 by the attributes CATEGORY and CONTENT.[3] The CATEGORY value is an object of type *cat(egory)* which contains the attributes HEAD and SUBCAT(EGORIZATION). The HEAD

---

[2] In addition, the value of *synsem* may contain the attribute NONLOCAL, in this case describing information relevant to the analysis of unbounded dependency phenomena.

[3] CONTEXT is a possible additional attribute describing pragmatic properties, which play no role here.

value specifies for *gives* the part of speech *verb* with the feature *finite*. The SUB-CAT value specifies a list of three NPs describing constraints on well-formed grammatical arguments of the verb. The NPs are marked by tags, [1], [2] and [3]. NP [1] is specified for the case feature *nom(inative)* and in addition for the person feature *3rd* and the number feature *sing(ular)*. The other two NPs are both specified for the case feature *acc(usative)*. The CONTENT value is a structured object of type *psoa* ('parametrized state of affairs') with the attributes RELATION, GIVER, GIVEN and GIFT. The RELATION value *give* describes the kind of state of affairs that the word *give* refers to. The attributes GIVER, GIVEN and GIFT describe the roles of the participants in this state of affairs. Their values are specified by the tags [1], [2] and [3] respectively, which correspond to the tags of the argument NPs, with identical tags indicating structure sharing. This describes that the first argument NP in the SUBCAT list and the GIVER role share the same structure as their common value, and so do the second NP and the GIVEN role and the third NP and the GIFT role.

The sample AVM diagram of a lexical entry in Figure 1 illustrates that in HPSG syntactic and semantic properties of words, represented by the attributes CATEGORY and CONTENT and specified by their values, are described as one complex of integrated linguistic information represented by the attribute SYNSEM|LOC.

The syntax of HPSG consists of principles such as the Head Feature Principle (which requires that the HEAD value of any sign is always structure-shared with that of its phrasal projections), the Valence Principle (which replaces the earlier Subcategorization Principle[4]), or the Immediate Dominance (ID) Principle and schemata representing the Head-Specifier Rule, the Head-Complement Rule, the Head-Modifier Rule and finally Linear Precedence Rules. The semantics of HPSG includes the Semantic Compositionality Principle and the Semantic Inheritance Principle. The principles and schemata or rules interact with the features in the feature descriptions of words to derive feature descriptions of phrases and sentences with integrated syntactic and semantic properties. There is just one representation containing phonological, syntactic, semantic and information structural constraints at the same time. This is in line with the general claim of HPSG that language is a system of signs intimately relating form and meaning (cf. e. g. Pollard & Sag 1987: 15 ff., 31; cf. also Rauh 2010: 169 ff.).

---

[4] This is discussed by Pollard & Sag (1994: 348).

In this approach then, just as in the previously discussed approaches, syntactic and semantic properties of words are determined by the information spelled out in lexical entries. Unlike these approaches, however, lexical semantic properties are not accessed for the purpose of interpreting independently derived syntactic structures but they are integrated with syntactic properties in lexical entries as well as in syntactic structures yielding single integrated syntactic-semantic representations. As a consequence, in one respect, no interfaces between syntactic and semantic categories of words can be identified because syntactic and semantic properties are described as sharing feature structures and thus forming one integrated complex of linguistic information. In another respect, however, it could be claimed that it is the feature structures of the attribute CATEGORY and of the specifications of its value on the one hand shared with the feature structures of the attribute CONTENT and of the specifications of its value on the other – as described in the lexical entries of words – that function as interfaces between these types of categories.[5]

4 Construction Grammar

There are several variants of Construction Grammar. The one considered here is the version developed by Fillmore and Kay (henceforth CxG, cf. e. g. Fillmore & Kay 1993, Kay & Fillmore 1999, Fillmore 1999, Kay 2002).

CxG does not strictly distinguish between lexicon and grammar. Representations of lexical items and phrases or sentences have the same construction format and differ only with respect to their internal complexity. As in HPSG, representations of lexical items can be of various degrees of generality, the more specific ones here being related to the more general ones by particular lexical constructions (e. g. the Pluralization Construction, the Count ≫ Mass Construction, cf. Figure 6 below) or by grammatical constructions (e. g. Linking Constructions). And as in HPSG, lexical items as well as phrases and sentences are described by means of feature descriptions consisting of attribute-value matrices.

Feature descriptions of words include a description of the lexeme and – in fully specified lexical entries – the form of the lexeme (e. g. write vs. *writes*), syntactic properties including categorial specifications such as *n*, *v*, etc. and morphological

---

[5] Cf. Kuhn (2007) for a discussion on interfaces in HPSG and other constraint-based theories.

properties such as specifications for plural, tense or voice, specifications of maximality (of projections) and lexicality and particular syntactically relevant specifications such as 'proper' in the context of *n*. In addition they include semantic properties such as the conceptual or notional specifications 'configuration' (cnfg), 'boundedness' (bounded) and 'number' (num) in the context of *n*,[6] the specification of conceptual frames or scenes evoked by verbs, for example, *read, put* or *shout*, and the specification of the number of participants involved in particular frames, i.e. two participants in the case of *read*, three in the case of *put* and one in the case of *shout*. Furthermore, valence properties are specified, including the specification of the syntactic category of valence elements (e.g. np), their semantic value, which is unified with a frame-specific participant (expressed e.g. by #1[...]), the specification of the grammatical function of valence elements (e.g. gf subj(ect)) and the specification of the theta-role of valence elements (e.g. θ exp(eriencer)).

Of the valence properties only the specifications of the theta-roles are part of the general minimal valence entry (e.g. Figure 4). The specifications of grammatical functions and syntactic categories of theta-roles, which are part of fully specified lexical entries (e.g. Figure 5), are the result of the interaction of an inventory of theta-frames determining possible combinations of theta-roles as well as a distinguished argument role, the subject principle and linking constructions. The latter in addition determine voice properties. Figures 2 to 5 represent examples of lexical entries taken from Fillmore & Kay (1993).

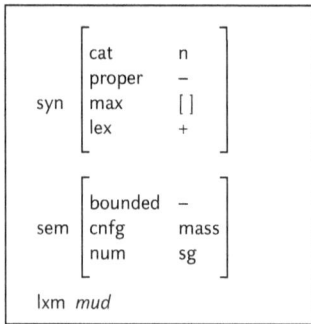

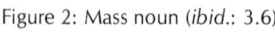

Figure 2: Mass noun (*ibid.*: 3.6)

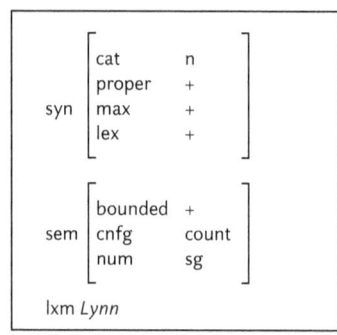

Figure 3: Proper noun (*ibid.*: 3.6)

---

[6] According to Fillmore & Kay, 'configuration', 'boundedness' and 'number' are attributes representing the three dimensions of semantic variation which apply to lexical nouns and nominal constructions (cf. Fillmore & Kay 1993: 3.1 ff.).

Linguistic Categories and the Syntax-Semantics Interface

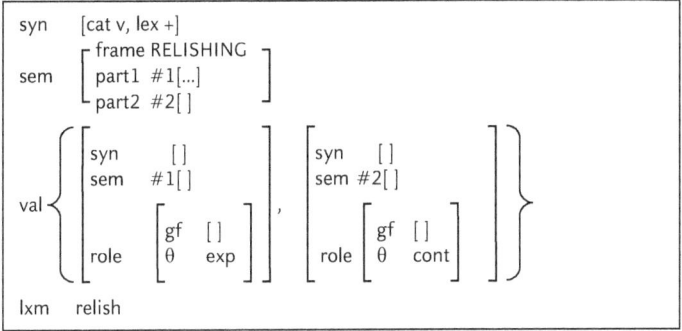

Figure 4: Minimal entry (*ibid*.: 5.1)

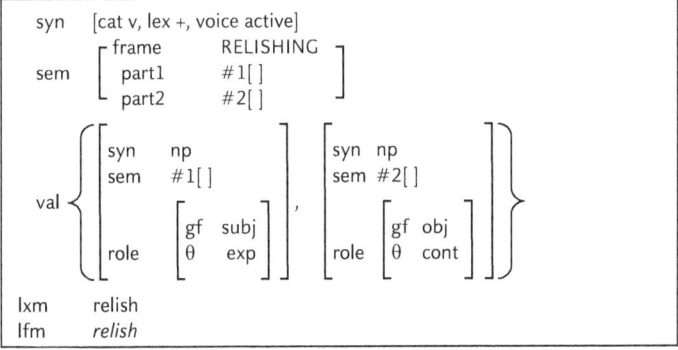

Figure 5: Fully specified entry (*ibid*.: 5.1)

The fact that lexical items specified as count nouns may be used as mass nouns and vice versa and that proper nouns may be used as count nouns is described by means of particular lexical constructions such as the Count ≫ Mass Construction, shown in Figure 6.

In CxG phrases and sentences are licensed by the unification of fully specified lexical entries with grammatical constructions of various kinds, such as the Left Isolate Construction, the Subject-Predicate Construction, the Verb Phrase Construction, the Modified Nominal Construction, the Determination Construction, Coinstantiation Constructions or Ordering Constructions and their interaction with general principles such as the principles of instantiation and semantic integration.

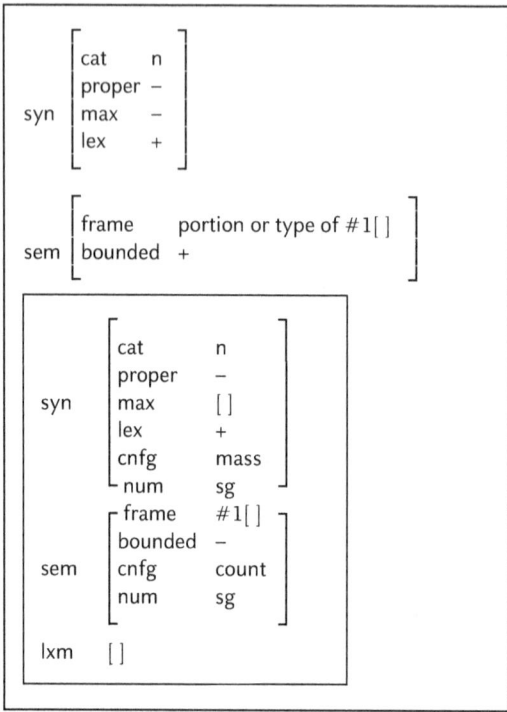

Figure 6: Count ≫ Mass Construction (*ibid.*: 3.28)

As in the previously discussed approaches, the syntactic and semantic categories of words in Fillmore and Kay's version of CxG are determined by syntactic and semantic properties specified in their lexical entries. Different syntactic and semantic properties result in different lexical entries. As opposed to the approaches discussed in section 2, but to a certain extent similar to the HPSG approach characterized in section 3, the role of the interface between syntactic and semantic categorization in this approach is played by their corresponding representations (cf. syn and sem in Figures 2, 3 and 6, and in addition by syn, sem and the role of valence elements in Figures 4 and 5).

5 Intermediate considerations

So far, four different approaches with different specifications of the syntactic and semantic properties of words have been considered. These different feature specifications as such would no doubt be worth more detailed discussion. In this context, however, I will concentrate on what these approaches have in common.

In all of them the syntactic and semantic properties of words are specified – or are claimed to be specified – in their lexical entries, implying that the semantic and syntactic properties are lexically specified and represent two sides of one and the same thing. The syntactic specification in each case includes a specification of what is known as a part of speech, such as a noun or verb. It also includes contextual syntactic properties described as strict subcategorization, selection restrictions, syntactic argument structure or syntactic valence.

Specifying syntactic properties like these in lexical entries has been criticized on various grounds. One is that in many languages, including English, the same phonological form with more or less the same meaning[7] can represent different syntactic categories, for example *walk, boat, form, fringe* or *dog*, which can be used as nouns or as verbs. Furthermore, many forms can be used with various and sometimes unexpected argument structures or valences. An impressive example of this is given by Clark & Clark (1979: 803):[8]

(2) a. The fire stations sirened throughout the raid.
    b. The factory horns sirened midday and everyone stopped for lunch.
    c. The police sirened the Porsche to a stop.
    d. The police car sirened up to the accident.
    e. The police car sirened the daylights out of me.

Providing each phonological form with all its potential categorial specifications and argument structures or valences would result in listing a number of lexical entries for each form which some linguists consider uneconomic or even redundant and therefore unnecessary.

Another criticism is that parts of speech are not universal and therefore the syntactic categoryhood of lexical items in many languages cannot be identified in isolation but only in the context of phrases or sentences.[9] This has been claimed

---

[7] 'More or less' here is intended to express the fact that the meanings are closely related and yet different in that one of them is verbal and the other one nominal. This difference is not without consequences for the approaches discussed in the following, as will be shown below.

[8] This example is also quoted by Borer (2003: 40), but with slight differences.

[9] Note that this criticism overlooks the fact that parts of speech as such do not represent syntactic categories, which will be discussed in section 8.1.

by, among others, Swadesh (1939) for Nootka, by Hengeveld (1992), Bhat (2000) and Hengeveld & Rijkhoff (2005) for Mundari, by Mosel & Hovdhaugen (1992) for Samoan, by Schachter (1985), Gil (1995) and Himmelmann (2008) for Tagalog and by Van Valin (e. g. 2008) for various languages.

These two aspects have led some linguists to conclude that syntactic specification should not be part of lexical entries. In the following, two approaches will be discussed which are in line with this conclusion and yet very different, first Neo-Construction Grammar and then Role and Reference Grammar.

6 Neo-Construction Grammar

Neo-Construction Grammar (henceforth N-CxG), as developed by Borer (2003, 2005a,b), does not include a lexicon which describes lexical entries as sets of information combining phonological, syntactic and semantic properties. Instead it distinguishes two distinct reservoirs of linguistic items, an encyclopedia on the one hand and a functional lexicon on the other.

The encyclopedia contains encyclopedic items (EIs), also called 'listemes', which are arbitrary sound-meaning pairs not associated with any information concerning syntactic category and argument structure. 'Meaning' here refers to conceptual information of some sort (see below), and 'sound' to abstract phonological representations (cf. Borer 2003: 34).

The functional lexicon includes grammatical formatives represented as head features such as <p(a)st> or <pl(ural)> or as independent grammatical formatives such as <*the*,[+def]>, called '*f*-morphs'. In addition it includes category-labeled derivational morphemes such as -*ation*, -*ize* or -*al*.

The categorization of listemes is achieved in two different ways – either by the phrase structure of functional projections or by a morphological structure.

In the first case, listemes forming a conceptual array are inserted into an unmarked and unordered lexical phrasal domain (L-Domain, L-D), providing the set of listemes from which a sentence is constructed, yielding, for example, [$_{L-D}$ listeme$_1$, listeme$_2$, listeme$_3$]. The L-D is then merged with an item from the functional lexicon, e. g. <pst>, which specifies one of the listemes with the categorial label V after it has moved and merged with <pst>. If the grammatical formative is a determiner, e. g. <*the*,[+def]>, then the listeme merged with it is categorized as N.

Leaving out further details, N-CxG in essence claims that there is a fixed set of structures determined by functional nodes and their order which is the same for all human languages and thus universal. Merged with particular functional items and occupying particular positions in these structures, uncategorized listemes become categorized via the properties of the functional nodes dominating them. The following structures and their instantiations – taken from Borer (2005a,b) – provide illustrative examples.

(3) and (4) represent assumed structures for proper names and the definite article (Borer 2005a: 80, (28a and b)) respectively:

(3)
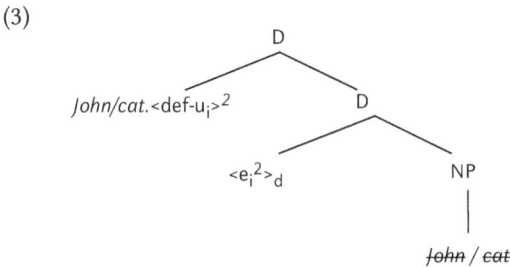

(4)
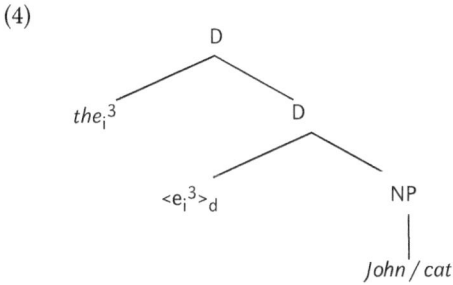

In (3) and (4) proper names and the definite article are analyzed as specifiers of the empty head of D, with the specifiers determining the range of the head. Co-superscription indicates range assignment, whereas the subscripts designate a binding relationship via indexing (cf. *ibid.*). The specification 'def-u' is short for 'definite and unique' (cf. *ibid.*: 72).

(5) represents an assumed structure for count nouns (Borer 2005a: 109, (27)) and (6) represents one for mass nouns (*ibid.*: 110, (28)):

(5)
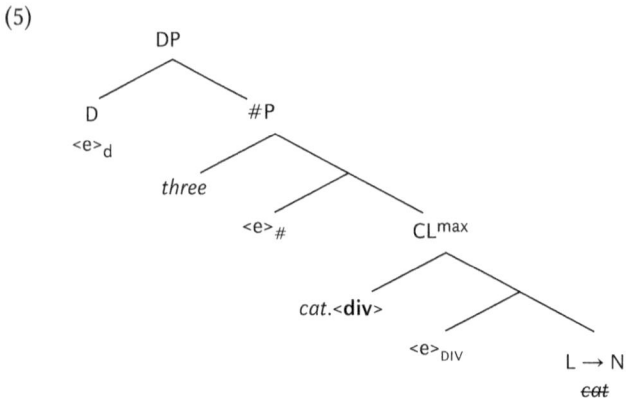

(6)
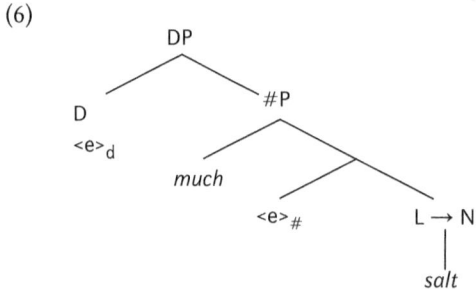

In (5) and (6) #P represents a Quantity Phrase, which is responsible "for the assignment of quantity to stuff or to division of it" (*ibid.*: 96). CL^{max} represents a Classifier Phrase. According to Borer, CL^{max} and #P are optional. If there is no CL^{max}, this gives rise to a mass interpretation; if there is no #P, the result is a non-quantity interpretation (cf. *ibid.*).

(7), (8) and (9) represent unaccusative (Borer 2005b: 84, (15a)), unergative (*ibid.*: 84, (15b)) and quantity transitive (*ibid.* 85, (17)) structures respectively:

Linguistic Categories and the Syntax-Semantics Interface

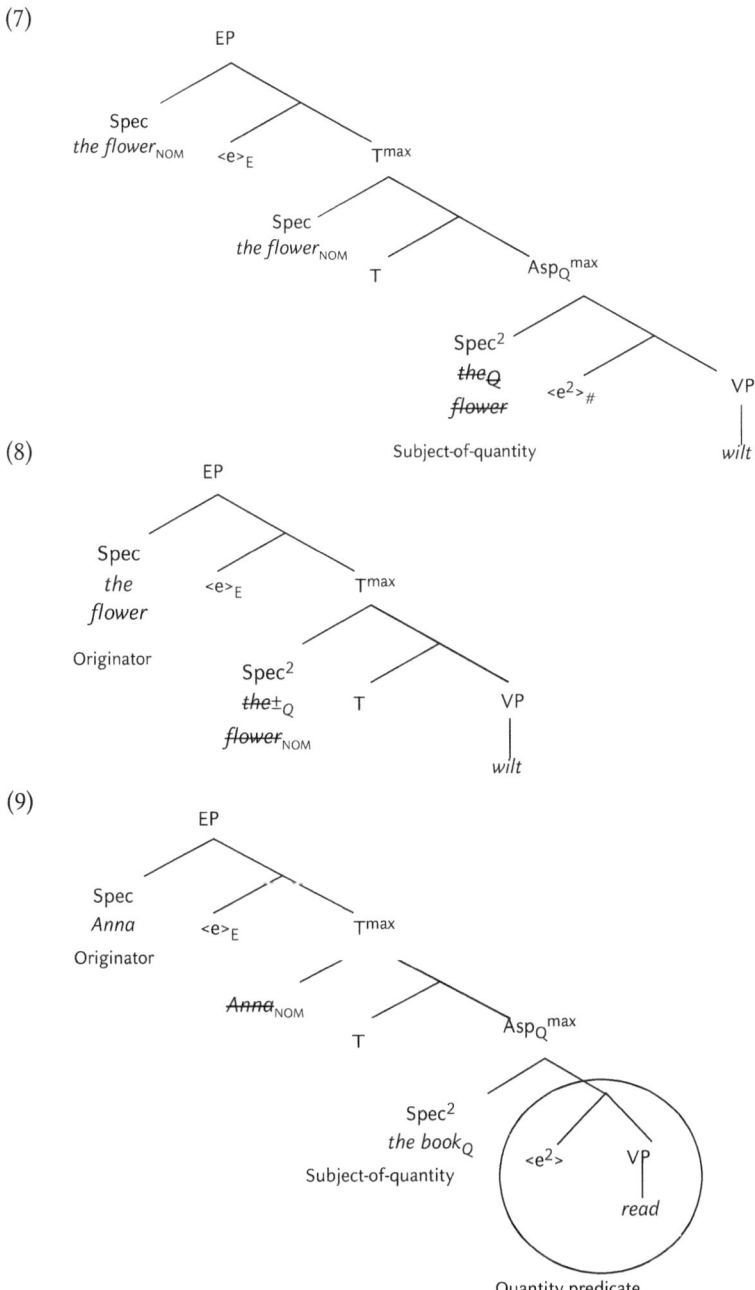

In (7) to (9) EP is an Event Phrase denoting types of events such as states and telic or atelic events. Asp$_{Q(uantity)}$ is the syntactic projection for telic interpretation. The DP 'Subject-of-quantity' in the specifier position of Asp$_Q$^{max} is roughly characterized as the 'subject-of-structured change' (cf. *ibid.*: 72). The DP 'Originator' designates any event participant in the specifier position of EP "which is not otherwise assigned interpretation" (*ibid.*: 83), i. e. "as subject-of-quantity, or through the mediation of a preposition" (*ibid.*).

The examples show that one and the same meaning-sound pair or listeme may show up in different structures which then determine whether it is categorized as a proper name or a common noun, as a count noun or a mass noun, or as an unaccusative, an unergative or a transitive verb. In addition, what is categorized here as a verb could just as well be categorized as a noun and vice versa, depending simply on what position and in what structure the listeme occurs. There are no predictions formulated in the encyclopedia.

Categorizing listemes by a morphological structure is accomplished in the following way. In the functional lexicon category-labeled morphemes such as *-ation* or *-al*, representing morphological heads, are not only specified for a category of their own but their entries in addition specify the category of the listemes which they take as their morphological complements. Thus, *-ation* and *-al* are specified as in (10), representing structures such as those instantiated in (11) for example (cf. Borer 2003: 36 f.):

(10) a. -ation, N, [[v] _N]
     b. -al, A, [[N] _A]

(11) a.   b.

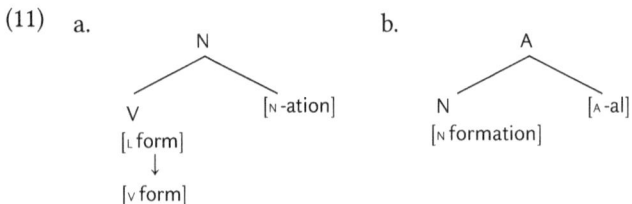

(11a) illustrates the categorization of a non-categorized listeme. In (11b) the listeme is already categorized. In cases like this, the specification of the category in the entry of the morpheme serves as a restriction on word-formation.

As regards the relationship between the syntactic category and the semantic category of a word, the basic idea of N-CxG is that this is not lexically fixed. Instead there is a general concept, such as BOAT or FORM or DOG, paired with a phonological representation to form a listeme which is syntactically categorized in the syntax. But what is a general concept, what is the meaning that count nouns, mass nouns and various verb types share? Whatever this may be, one important implication of this approach is that it is not only the syntactic category of a listeme that is determined by the syntax (or by morphological structure). In addition, whatever distinguishes the meanings of items associated with more than one syntactic category must also be determined by the structure in which they occur. For example, the mass-noun meaning of *dog*, its count-noun meaning or its transitive-verb meaning must be contributed to its listeme meaning by the particular structure.

As a consequence, N-CxG claims that the particular meanings of words are determined by the meanings of their listemes, by the structures they occur in and by the positions they occupy in these structures, with the latter also determining their syntactic category. The interface between the syntactic and semantic categories of words in this approach is thus syntactic structure. This applies to words that are derived from listemes and distinguishes them from items from the functional lexicon, which, in line with the traditional view, are lexically specified for their (grammatical) meanings as well as for their syntactic properties.

7 Role and Reference Grammar

Role and Reference Grammar (henceforth RRG) was developed by Van Valin and Foley (Van Valin & Foley 1980, Foley & Van Valin 1984) and refined by Van Valin (e. g. 1993, 2005, 2008, 2010, Van Valin & LaPolla 1997). One of the central goals of RRG is typological adequacy. This determines the design of both its grammar in the narrow sense, i. e. of its syntax, which is semantically based, and of its lexicon. The lexicon contains lexical entries for items attributed to lexical, not syntactic categories, and lexical rules deriving morphologically related words or describing grammatical generalizations.

As opposed to the approaches discussed in sections 2, 3 and 4 above, and only in this respect similar to Borer's approach, in an RRG lexicon lexical entries do not specify any syntactic properties, i. e. neither a syntactic category nor strict subcategorization. There is only a semantic representation in the format of logical structures (LS). These differ, depending on whether they represent items assigned to the 'lexical' categories of verb, noun, adjective, preposition or adverb.

LSs of verbs analyze them as *Aktionsart* classes, as represented in Figure 7:

Aktionsart class	Logical structure
STATE	**predicate'** (x) or (x, y)
ACTIVITY	**do'** (x, [**predicate'** (x) or (x, y)])
ACHIEVEMENT	INGR **predicate'** (x) or (x, y) or
	INGR **do'** (x, [**predicate'** (x) or (x, y)])
SEMELFACTIVE	SEML **predicate'** (x) or (x, y)
	SEML **do'** (x, [**predicate'** (x) or (x, y)])
ACCOMPLISHMENT	BECOME **predicate'** (x) or (x, y) or
	BECOME **do'** (x, [**predicate'** (x) or (x, y)])
ACTIVE ACCOMPLISHMENT	**do'** (x, [**predicate$_1$'** (x, (y))]) & INGR **predicate$_2$'** (z, x) or (y)
CAUSATIVE	α CAUSE β, where α, β are logical structures of any type

Figure 7: Van Valin (2005: 45)

(12) provides some examples of English verbs and their LSs:

(12) a. Bill knew the answer.   **know'** (Bill, answer)
     b. John drank beer.   **do'** (John, [**drink'** (beer)])
     c. Bill snored.   SEML **do'** (Bill, [**snore'** (Bill)])
     d. The ice melted.   BECOME **melted'** (ice)
     e. The sun melted the ice.   [**do'** (sun, ∅)] CAUSE [BECOME **melted'** (ice)]

The representation of the LSs of nouns follows suggestions made by Pustejovsky (1991a, 1995) in that it gives their qualia structures including the Constitutive Role, the Formal Role, the Telic Role and the Agentive Role of the referents of the nouns. Van Valin provides the following example adapted from Pustejovsky (1995: 85f.) and translated into his own formal representation of LSs (cf. Van Valin 2005: 51):

(13) **novel** (y)
     a. Const: **narrative'** (y)
     b. Form: **book'** (y), **disk'** (y)
     c. Telic: **do'** (x, [**read'** (x, y)])
     d. Agentive: **artifact'** (y), **do'** (x, [**write'** (x, y)]) & INGR **exist'** (y)

Linguistic Categories and the Syntax-Semantics Interface

According to Pustejovsky (1991a: 426 f., 1995: 85 f.) and quoted by Van Valin (2005: 51), the various roles are characterized as follows. The Constitutive Role is concerned with "the relation between an object and its constituents, or proper parts", specified as material, weight and parts or components of an object. The Formal Role characterizes "that which distinguishes the object within a larger domain", which includes orientation, magnitude, shape, dimensionality, color and position. The Telic Role captures the "purpose and function of the object", specified as "the purpose that an agent has in performing an act" and "the built-in function or aim that specifies certain activities". The Agentive Role characterizes "factors involved in the origin or 'bringing about' of an object", specified as creator, artefact, natural kind and causal chain.

Adjectives are described like state predicates, and so are (predicative) prepositions, whereas adverbs are assumed to represent one-place predicates that modify parts of LSs, with temporal adverbs, spatial adverbs or manner and aspectual adverbs modifying different parts.

Semantic representations of sentences are constructed in the lexicon on the basis of the semantic representations of words.

Syntactic representations of sentences are constructed by combining semantically motivated syntactic universal templates, basically consisting of a PREDICATE plus arguments, which form the CORE, and non-arguments, which form the PERIPHERY. These universal templates are complemented by language specific templates stored in a syntactic inventory. Each of the templates represents a partial structure. The universal templates represent the layered structure of the clause, identifying the NUCLEUS, the CORE and the PERIPHERY. Arguments are represented by RPs, i. e. as referential phrases replacing the former NPs. Figure 8 provides an example of an English instantiation of such a structure.

RPs themselves are described as layered structures as well, as shown in Figure 9. The same holds for predicative PPs, which however, are not universal.[10]

One important aspect of RRG syntax is the claim that phrases need not be or are not endocentric. $CORE_R$ and RP, for example, are not projections of the item that instantiates the NUC_R, and NUC, CORE and CLAUSE are not projections of the item that instantiates the PRED. NUC_R and PRED, as well as all the other categories in the syntactic structures, represent syntactic categories, and items

---

[10] Figure 9 is constructed on the basis of Van Valin & LaPolla (1997: 57), replacing NP by RP, however.

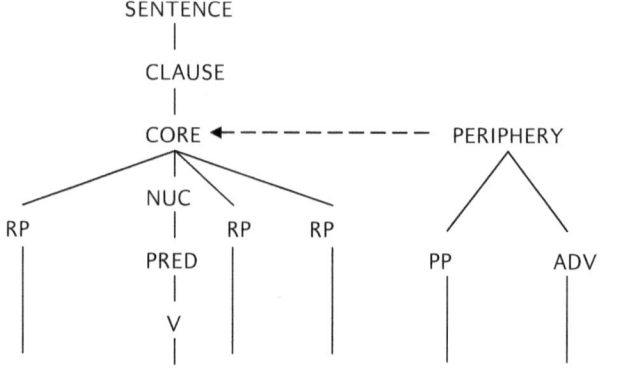

Figure 8: Van Valin (2010: 707)

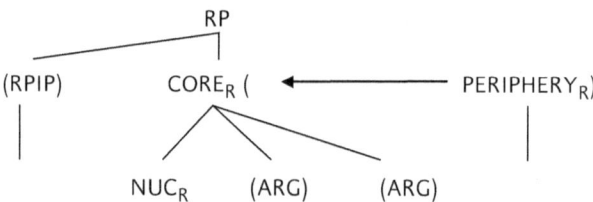

Figure 9: RPs as layered structures

instantiating them are syntactically categorized on the basis of their positions in these structures. There is no corresponding syntactic specification in the lexical entries. As was shown above, lexical entries specify lexical categories such as noun or verb and represent these semantically in the format of LSs. This is intended to capture the claim that for languages like Nootka, Mundari, Tagalog and others the lexical specification of words does not determine their syntactic properties. That is, for example, the same lexical item can instantiate either NUC_R, corresponding to a traditional 'syntactic' noun, or PRED, thus instantiating a traditional 'syntactic' verb.

The question then is how the semantic and the syntactic properties of words are united. In RRG this is achieved by means of a bi-directional linking system that links semantic representations and syntactic structures of sentences, on the one hand mapping semantic representations onto syntactic structures and on the other mapping syntactic structures onto semantic representations.

In both cases a linking algorithm gives the individual steps with general principles being supplemented by language-specific constructional templates or 'schemas' (Van Valin 2005: 131), which impose language-specific restrictions on otherwise very general principles.

One general principle governing the linking algorithms is the Completeness Constraint, which requires that all of the arguments explicitly specified in the semantic representation of a sentence must be realized in the syntax, and that all of the expressions in the syntactic representation of a sentence must be linked to something in the semantic representation of the sentence (cf. e. g. Van Valin 2010: 732).

Language-type-specific or language-specific aspects of the linking concern the introduction of morpho-syntactic specifications such as finite-verb agreement, case assignment or preposition assignment, which may be formulated as rules or, in case of idiosyncratic language-specific features, represented as constructional schemas.

A prerequisite for the linking is the assignment of macroroles to the arguments in the LS in lexical entries, which provides the basis for deciding which semantic argument is linked with which syntactic argument. Two macroroles, ACTOR and UNDERGOER, are distinguished. Where there is idiosyncrasy, the assignment is specified in a lexical entry. Otherwise it follows the Actor-Undergoer Hierarchy (AUH, cf. *ibid.*: 717).

Another prerequisite for the linking is the determination of the 'privileged syntactic argument' (PSA), often corresponding to what otherwise is called the 'subject'. It is defined as "a restricted neutralization of semantic roles and pragmatic functions for syntactic purposes" (*ibid.*: 720).

The linking of a semantic representation to a syntactic representation is described as follows: On the basis of the LSs of lexical items, the semantic representation of a sentence is constructed in the lexicon first. After assigning the macroroles and after determining the PSA selection and assigning morpho-syntactic properties including preposition assignment, an appropriate syntactic template is selected from the syntactic inventory. Finally, elements from the semantic representation are linked to the appropriate positions in the syntactic representation (cf. *ibid*: 735).

When a syntactic structure is linked to a semantic representation of a sentence, the syntactic representation of the sentence, including its morpho-syntactically specified phonetic instantiations of the terminal nodes, is the starting point, with the structure being produced by a parser. The linking algorithm then first extracts the morpho-syntactic information and retrieves the LS of the instantiation of the NUCLEUS from the lexicon. Where possible, the arguments of the LS are assigned macroroles. Finally the syntactic and semantic arguments are linked (cf. *ibid.*: 736).

Clearly, in this approach the interface between the syntactic and semantic categories of words is provided by the linking algorithms. In lexical entries words are specified for a semantic category but not for a syntactic category. The latter is assigned to them only in the syntax.

8 The interface between the syntactic and semantic categories of words: lexical entries, syntactic structures or linking rules?

The major concern of this paper is to evaluate the plausibility of the description of the interface between the syntactic and semantic categories of words in selected linguistic theories. In the preceding sections it has been shown that the theories discussed differ in that they assume that the interface between the two categories is provided either by lexical entries of various types (ST, PPT, HPSG and CxG) or by syntactic structures (N-CxG) or by linking rules (RRG).[11] The present section is concerned with the plausibility of these positions. To begin with, the position that lexical entries provide the interface will be discussed, followed by a discussion of the position that it is syntactic structures, and finally that it is linking rules.

8.1 Lexical entries

The approaches discussed in sections 2, 3 and 4, i.e. the ST, the PPT, HPSG and CxG, all elaborate the traditional view, which assumes that syntactic and semantic properties are combined in lexical entries and thus determine the syntactic and semantic categories. The lexicon thus specifies whether a particular form can be used both 'nominally' (i.e. as the head of a referring expression) and 'verbally' (i.e. as the head of a predicate), and whether in such a case the meanings asso-

---

[11] Of course the approaches differ in other respects as well, as was indicated in the previous sections. This, however, is irrelevant for the present discussion.

ciated with the two uses are related in predictable or unpredictable ways or not at all. This also applies to uses of the same form as a mass or a count noun or as a transitive, unergative or unaccusative verb, and as items of other categories. In all these cases, a syntactic variant of a lexical form and the particular meaning associated with it can be – or is at least supposed to be – described appropriately, and overgeneration or over'construction' is restricted because categorial variability is described only where attested. This restriction is justified because lexical knowledge first and foremost comprises the actual words of a language, leaving the 'lexicalization' of potential words to creativity in accordance with – or sometimes violating – lexical rules.[12] In addition, forms belonging to particular inflectional classes that display features such as gender, declension and conjugation, which are syntactically relevant because they correlate with appropriate or inappropriate syntactic environments, are – or can be – lexically specified as well. According to this view then, it is the lexical entries themselves which provide the interface between the syntactic and semantic categories.

It was shown in section 5 above that two essential criticisms have been leveled at this general approach. First, specifying all the possible syntactic variants and consequently syntactic representations of words in the lexicon requires a large number of lexical entries for many lexical forms, produces redundancies and is therefore uneconomic. And second, parts of speech are not universal and therefore in many languages the syntactic categoryhood of words cannot be identified on the basis of parts of speech in the lexicon, i.e. in isolation, but only in the context of phrases or sentences.

An answer to the first point is that redundancy as such need not be problematic, especially where lexical (rather than syntactic) knowledge is concerned. It is even less so given the fact that in HPSG as well as in CxG the lexicon is not just a list of isolated lexical entries specifying only idiosyncratic properties, but contains entries of various degrees of generality or specificity related by lexical principles and rules, constraints, schemata or constructions formulating gener-

---

[12] Here I completely disagree with Barner & Bale (2002), who – defending the approach of Distributed Morphology, which shares essential properties with N-CxG – claim that overgeneration is not a problem because "theories of grammar are designed to account for the set of possible grammatical utterances, and nothing more" (*ibid.*: 777). Whereas this holds for the syntax of utterances it does not hold for lexical items. This is the reason why the lexicon is considered to be the place where idiosyncratic properties of languages are described. And this is the reason why morphologists since Halle's seminal paper (1973) distinguish between actual and potential words.

alizations concerning the various relationships between lexical items. These can include generalizations concerning zero conversion wherever they are observed, thus avoiding or at least reducing redundancy as well as overgeneralization.

The second point is only valid if parts of speech do indeed represent syntactic categories. But this is a wide-spread misunderstanding, as I have pointed out in various publications (e. g. Rauh 1999, 2000a,b, 2002b, 2010). The syntactic category of words is determined on the basis of shared distribution. A grammar should describe this distribution by means of principles or rules or constraints or constructions and the like which place each word in appropriate positions to construct syntactically well-formed sentences. According to the view underlying the approaches discussed in sections 2, 3 and 4, a grammar can do so only if words are lexically specified for syntactic properties that can be accessed and activated by the principles, rules, constructions, etc. of this grammar. Labels such as N, V, A, etc. used in the lexical entries of these approaches represent neither the traditional parts of speech[13] nor syntactic categories but are cover terms for particular sets of (morpho-)syntactic properties which determine syntactic categories only when supplemented by contextual properties, as is illustrated by the examples in (1) and Figures 1 to 6 above. These supplementary properties include the specification of selection restrictions and strict subcategorization (1), valence and syntactic argument structures (Figure 1) and syntactically relevant specifications such as 'proper –' or 'proper +' for nouns (Figures 2, 3 and 6) and syntactic, semantic and role-based specifications of valence for verbs (Figures 4 and 5). This shows that the lexical representation of the syntactic categories of words includes syntactic properties of the phrases and sentences that can contain them and does not categorize them in isolation, as it does in the case of parts of speech.

Thus, the two criticisms leveled at approaches like those discussed in sections 2, 3 and 4 are at least considerably weakened. As concerns the second criticism, its being weakened is confirmed by the fact that it is a controversial issue among typologists whether there are languages that do not specify words for syntactic properties in the lexicon but only in the syntax, as is claimed for Mundari,

---

[13] This is obvious considering, for example the fact that prepositions in the PPT, following Jackendoff (1973, 1977) and unlike traditional prepositions, are items that can be intransitive or select PP or sentential complements and not always NP/DP complements. Note as well that the infinitive marker *to* in HPSG is analyzed as representing type *verb* (cf. the discussion in Rauh 2010: 180 ff.).

Linguistic Categories and the Syntax-Semantics Interface

Nootka, Samoan, Tagalog and others[14] (cf. e.g. Evans & Osada 2005, Peterson 2005, Hengeveld & Rijkhoff 2005). I will come back to this in section 9. And what is more, it turns out that approaches which suggest that words are lexically specified for syntactic and semantic categories, with their lexical entries providing the interface between the two, avoid problems that N-CxG and RRG are faced with in assuming that syntactic categories are assigned to items only in the syntax.

8.2 Syntactic structures

Considering N-CxG first, it was shown in section 6 that this approach distinguishes between functional items stored in a functional lexicon and listemes stored in an encyclopedia. Functional items in addition to their (grammatical) meanings are specified for syntactic properties whereas listemes are described as meaning-sound pairs with no syntactic specifications. It is thus predicted that each listeme can occupy any position in a sentence structure that identifies mass nouns, count nouns, proper names, unergative, unaccusative or transitive verbs (and possibly even others), and is syntactically categorized accordingly. The sentence structures themselves are claimed to form a universally fixed set determined by functional nodes and their order. The meaning of a listeme is characterized as a general concept which is associated with the various words that result from the syntactic categorization of the listeme in sentence structures. Particular structures, in turn, contribute to the general concept thus deriving the particular (nominal and verbal) meanings of the various words. In this approach then, it is syntactic structures which provide the interface between semantic and syntactic categories of words.

There are various problems which weaken the appropriateness of this approach. To begin with, it is empirically at least problematic to assume that the meanings of nouns and their verbal counterparts are the same except for aspects contributed by the structures that syntactically categorize their shared listeme. Not only is it entirely unclear how to identify shared 'general concepts' of nouns and verbs, but one prerequisite for the appropriateness of this assumption is that the contribution of a particular structure to the meaning of a listeme is constant. This however is not the case, as the following examples of the simple transitive construction illustrate:

---

[14] Needless to say, this does not mean that it is controversial whether these languages specify words lexically as members of the traditional parts of speech. There is no doubt that they do not.

(14) a. They boated everyone.
   b. They dogged everyone
   c. They formed everyone.
   d. They snailed everyone.
   e. They mothered everyone.
   f. They fathered everyone.
   g. They uncled everyone.

The reason is that the semantic relations between the nominal forms of the items and their verbal counterparts are very different and cannot be predicted by the transitive construction as such. The following possible paraphrases show this:

(14) a'. They transported everyone by boat. / They got everyone on the boat.
   b'. They rushed everyone as dogs do.
   c'. They got everyone into form.
   d'. They removed snails from everyone. / They threw snails at everyone.
   e'. They treated everyone like a mother does.
   f'. They caused everyone to exist by acting as their fathers. (= They begot everyone.)
   g'. They called everyone 'uncle'.

The semantic relationships between nominal and verbal forms must therefore be determined lexically. They may either be idiosyncratic for a particular nominal-verbal pair or be shared by unpredictably restricted sets of such pairs. An impressive number of forms exemplifying this have been gathered and analyzed by Karius (1985). Evans (2000) furthermore shows that in various languages the verbal use of kinship terms is restricted to only a few and that these in addition are related to their nominal uses in very different ways. Examples which he gives include *to mother*, *to father* and *to uncle*, with interpretations like those in (14e'), (14f') and (14g'), which follow his suggestions (cf. *ibid.*: 107 f.).

Another point is that this approach in principle claims that listemes could occur in any functional context. Remarks concerning the fact that there may be certain preferences and that these may be specified in the encyclopedia are of little relevance since Borer at the same time points out that these preferences may be overridden in the syntax (cf. Borer 2005a: 77, 106). As it stands then, the grammar to a large extent over'constructs', i.e. a vast amount of sentences that are not acceptable are constructed in addition to sentences that are.[15] As an illustration, consider the sentences that according to Borer (2005a: 29) can derive from the L-Domain [$_{L-D}$ dog, boat, sink]:

(15) a. (The) *dog boat*(ed) (three) *sink*(s)
 b. (The three) *sink*(s) *boat*(ed) (some) *dog*(s)
 c. (The) *sink*(s) *dog*(ged) (the) *boat*
 d. (The) *boat*(s) *dog*(ged) (the) *sink*
 e. (The three) *dog*(s) *sank* (the) *boat*
 f. (The) *boat sank* (the) *dog*(s)

Borer claims that the unacceptable sentences are unacceptable only for reasons of world knowledge, not for grammatical reasons (cf. e. g. Borer 2005a: 11 f.). However, there are cases where grammaticality is indeed involved such as when a verb requires a particular syntactic environment, meaning that it is idiosyncratically determined as unaccusative (like *arrive*), unergative (like *dine* or *bark*) or transitive (like *see*) but is inserted in a structure that does not provide that environment:

(16) a. *The boys arrived the house.
 b. *The dog barked the cat.
 c. *Bill dined the food.
 d. *The crowd saw.

Contrary to fact, N-CxG would have to identify these constructions as grammatically well-formed. It should also be noted that examples (14c) and (14f) above are telic, whereas (14b) and (14e) are not, and (14a) and (14d) are telic only in one of their interpretations. But according to N-CxG, any of the verbs may occur in a structure like (9) describing telicity.

Another rather serious problem can be seen in the fact that in numerous European languages such as German, the Slavic or the Romance languages nouns are specified for gender. This property is not attributed to listemes in particular syntactic environments but is an idiosyncratic and mostly unpredictable property and thus a typical example of lexical specification. Similarly, there are various

---

[15] Note that a similar criticism is leveled at Goldberg's version of Construction Grammar by Boas (2008). Goldberg's (cf e. g. 1995, 2006) version differs from that of Fillmore and Kay in that she claims that constructions have meanings, predicting that the verbs of a semantic class can all occupy the same position in a given construction and thus assume the meaning of the construction, which Boas shows not to be the case.

languages in which verbs belong to particular conjugation classes and nouns to particular declension classes. Again, these are properties intrinsic to a linguistic item and thus lexical and not the result of syntactic environments.[16] This means that being categorized as a noun or as a verb at least in these languages is not a matter of syntax. It is determined by properties of the kind mentioned which must be specified before these items enter the syntax. And this renders implausible Borer's assumption that a lexicon of the more traditional kind can be replaced by two reservoirs, a functional lexicon and an encyclopedia, with the latter merely listing meaning-sound pairs with no further specifications.

There are additional problems which I will only mention briefly. Prepositions are classified by Borer as members of the functional lexicon and thus as *f*-morphs (cf. Borer 2005a: 49). However, as pointed out by Rauh in various publications (e. g. 1997, 2002a) and by others, prepositions do not form a homogeneous class. Some of them represent a lexical category comparable to the categories noun, verb and adjective, whereas others behave syntactically more like items of a functional category. Also, what about items subject to processes of grammaticalization that are changing from lexical to functional items and exhibit an intermediate state? As it stands, neither of the two reservoirs is designed to accomodate them. And finally, morphologists are well aware of the fact that word-formation by affixation is subject to various restrictions, which are not captured by the simple specification of a base to which an affix is attached as N, V or A (cf. e. g. Baeskow 2002: 18 ff.; Plag 2003: 59 ff.).

The conclusion to be drawn from this discussion is that assuming with N-CxG that it is syntactic structures that provide the interface between the syntactic and semantic categories of words is less plausible than assuming that it is lexical entries, as suggested by the approaches discussed above.

8.3 Linking rules

Turning now to RRG, the discussion in section 7 has shown that a distinction is made between lexical and syntactic categories of words, the former including lexical verbs and lexical nouns, the latter including syntactic predicates (PRED) and

---

[16] Aronoff (1994) and others discuss the lexical character of properties like these. Cf. also Don (2004), who on the basis of Dutch illustrates that there are morphological and phonological properties of nouns and verbs which distinguish items of these two categories lexically and that the relationship between the forms in question is not bi-directional. As a result, he claims that this relationship has to be described as (zero) conversion either from noun to verb or from verb to noun.

referential expressions (RP with NUC_R as its head). Lexical categories are represented by logical structures (LS) in lexical entries, with different representations for verbs (*Aktionsart* classes) and nouns (qualia structures). Semantic representations of sentences are assumed to be constructed in the lexicon, and syntactic representations of sentences, i.e. category-labeled tree structures, to be the result of a parser combining universal and language-specific templates. Bi-directional linking rules, subject to the Completeness Constraint, are designed to link the two types of representations, thus in effect assigning syntactic categories to lexical items, which up to this point lack any syntactic specifications. One reason for this is to allow for both lexical verbs and lexical nouns to instantiate either PRED or NUC_R and accordingly correspond to a 'syntactic' verb or to a 'syntactic' noun. In this approach then, it is the linking rules that provide the interface between the semantic and syntactic categories of words.

The advantage of this approach is to be seen in the fact that in various languages, but not most European languages, words are – or are claimed to be – lexically underspecified and as such (syntactic-) category neutral before entering the syntax, where they may combine with verbal tense markers or with nominal definiteness markers, for example, and thus be syntactically specified as verbs (= syntactic predicates) or nouns (= nuclei of referential phrases). This is where RRG is similar to N-CxG. RRG differs from N-CxG in that it does not assume an encyclopedia listing meaning-sound pairs, with the meaning part representing general concepts claimed to be shared by listemes which are categorized in the syntax either as nouns or verbs. Instead it includes a lexicon with lexical entries distinguishing lexical categories such as N or V by representing LSs of Ns as qualia structures and LSs of verbs as classes of *Aktionsarten*. It also differs from N-CxG in that it formulates linking algorithms with specific requirements, among them the Completeness Constraint, which reduces overgeneration. Furthermore, RRG operates with a wide range of semantic and syntactic categories, including operators of various types. As a consequence, certain problems of N-CxG are avoided here, but there is one crucial problem to be discussed.

This problem relates to the linking of semantic and syntactic representations and to the claim that lexical verbs may occupy NUC_R or RP positions and lexical nouns PRED positions. It is thus central to the present issue. The problem has various facets. Some of these will be discussed here.[17] The first is the following.

---

[17] Additional facets are discussed in Rauh (2010: 380 ff.).

Although both are represented as LSs, lexical verbs and lexical nouns are represented differently. Lexical verbs are represented as *Aktionsart* classes on the basis of logical predicates and arguments, with the latter corresponding to syntactic arguments to which they can be linked accordingly. Lexical nouns are represented as qualia structures which specify a set of roles that characterize the relationship between an object and its constituents on the basis of logical predicates and arguments, with the latter not necessarily corresponding to syntactic arguments and thus violating the Completeness Constraint. The following examples illustrate this. In the first example the PRED position is linked to a lexical verb. Van Valin (2010: 715) analyzes sentence (17a) as an active accomplishment, providing it with the semantic representation in (17b):

(17) a. Carl ate the snail.
    b. **do'** (Carl, [**eat'** (Carl, snail)]) & BECOME **eaten'** (snail)

In this case *Carl*, instantiating the argument x in the LS of *eat*, is assigned the macrorole ACTOR, selected as the PSA (= SUBJECT) and linked to the syntactic argument RP preceding PRED (= *ate*) in the syntactic representation of (17a). *Snail*, instantiating the argument y in the LS of *eat*, is assigned the macrorole UNDERGOER, selected as the OBJECT and linked to the syntactic argument RP following PRED in the syntactic representation of (17a).

In the second example the PRED position is linked to a lexical noun. Imagine a situation where John thought that his life would provide a good story for a novel and he did what is expressed in (18), with *novel* as an instantiation of PRED:

(18) John noveled his life.[18]

As (13) – repeated here for the reader's convenience – shows, the lexical noun *novel* is described as a qualia structure specifying four roles, the Constitutive Role, the Formal Role, the Telic Role and the Agentive Role.[19]

(13) **novel** (y)
    Const: **narrative'** (y)

---

[18] According to RRG, this sentence should be well-formed. To the speaker of English, though, a more appropriate verbalization of *novel* would be *novelize*, yielding: *John novelized his life.*

[19] It should be noted, though, that according to Pustejovsky not all of the four roles need be specified.

Form: **book'** (y), **disk'** (y)
Telic: **do'** (x, [**read'** (x, y)])
Agentive: **artifact'** (y), **do'** (x, [**write'** (x, y)]) & INGR **exist'** (y)

The question that has to be answered is how this structure is linked to the syntactic structure of the sentence in (18). One might assume that the specifications of the four roles are conjoined to form one LS and that the logical arguments x and y, in a way similar to the process discussed above with respect to (17), are assigned the macroroles ACTOR and UNDERGOER, are selected as SUBJECT (= PSI) and OBJECT, and are linked to the syntactic argument RP preceding PRED (= *novel*) and to the one following it in the syntactic representation of (18). However, this would not correspond to the interpretation of (18), because y in (13) refers to the novel (cf. **novel** (y), **book'** (y), **read'** (x, y), **write'** (x, y)) and not to *his life* which – rather than *novel* – instantiates the syntactic argument RP following the PRED *novel* and is interpreted as the UNDERGOER. But there is no semantic argument in the qualia structure of *novel* designed to semantically represent *his life*. This shows that there is a semantic argument y which cannot be linked to a syntactic argument, and there is a syntactic argument *his life* which cannot be linked to a semantic argument. In both cases the Completeness Constraint is violated. It is also at least questionable whether specifications of the Constitutive Role, the Formal Role and the Telic Role should be part of the LS of the syntactic predicate *novel*, especially if comparable information is not part of the LS of lexical verbs. One might therefore assume that it is only the Agentive Role that characterizes *novel* in this case. But this would not solve the problem pointed out above. The Completeness Constraint would be violated in just the same way. In addition, in either case a lexical rule would be required to derive the LS of the syntactic predicate *novel* from its nominal qualia structure, which indicates that it is in fact not the case that lexical nouns – as represented in the RRG lexicon – can occupy the syntactic PRED position. Furthermore, this kind of examples raises the question why lexical nouns used as instantiations of PRED and thus syntactically equivalent to lexical verbs in these positions should not be classified and represented like these, i. e. as belonging to one of the *Aktionsart* classes. The uses of the lexical nouns *bottle, fringe* and *lecture* as instantiations of PRED in (19) show that they express an active accomplishment, a state and an activity respectively:

(19) a. They bottled the wine in less than four days.
　　b. Grass fringes the creek.
　　c. The professor lectured for hours.

The question seems especially justified because, as Dowty (1979: 55 ff.)[20] demonstrates, membership of a particular *Aktionsart* class not only specifies semantic properties but in addition determines various syntactic properties. And finally, why should qualia-structure information not be relevant for the interpretation of sentences if a lexical verb instantiates NUC_R but be relevant if it is instantiated by a lexical noun?

Another facet of the same problem has to do with the fact already pointed out in connection with the N-CxG approach above, namely that many European languages – and not only these, as Aronoff (1994) shows – distinguish various conjugation classes of verbs and various declension classes of nouns as well as various gender classes of the latter. Classification in all these cases is lexical. Unlike the N-CxG approach, RRG can handle this by specifying the relevant information in the lexical entries, which distinguish between lexical verbs and lexical nouns anyway.[21] Nevertheless, a problem remains because particular conjugation classes determine the selection of particular morphological tense markers, and particular declension and gender classes determine the selection of particular morphological case and plural markers.[22] The problem that remains shows up where a lexical verb is linked to a NUC_R and a lexical noun to PRED. In the first case the lexical verb determines the selection of a particular tense marker, which is not required in this position, but no case or gender marker, of which at least the former is necessary for syntactic reasons. And in the second case the lexical noun determines the selection of a particular case and gender marker, which is not required in a PRED position, but no tense marker. The question that arises here is what determines which particular case and/or gender marker is associated with

---

[20] Dowty (1979: 60 ff.) in addition demonstrates that contrary to Vendler's (1967) assumption it is not verbs that express *Aktionsarten* and can therefore be analyzed as *Aktionsart* classes but rather verb phrases. Cf. also Pustejovsky (1991b). Van Valin captures this fact via lexical rules (cf. Van Valin 2013).

[21] This however requires a reformulation of the following statement by Van Valin (2001: 211): "The lexical entry for each verb and other predicating element contains its logical structure, and for most that is all that is required."

[22] Examples of the selection of these markers in various languages are presented and discussed by Aronoff (1994).

lexical verbs in NUC$_R$ positions, and which particular tense marker is associated with lexical nouns in PRED positions, and where and how this is determined.

Furthermore, in a language such as English it is not the case that just any lexical verb can instantiate NUC$_R$ and that just any lexical noun can instantiate PRED, as is predicted by RRG. And finally, like N-CxG, RRG is faced with the situation that nominal and verbal syntactic uses of lexical nouns differ in meaning in ways that cannot be explained by the structures in which they occur. The same holds for nominal and verbal uses of lexical verbs.

It seems then that what at first sight appears to be an advantage of RRG, namely that it distinguishes between lexical and syntactic categories and allows items of various lexical categories to be linked to the same syntactic position turns out to cause a problem, at least for the present conception of this approach. One way out would be to formulate lexical rules that convert lexical representations of nouns into those of lexical verbs to fit the semantic and the syntactic requirements of PRED, and to convert lexical representations of verbs into those of nouns to fit the semantic and the syntactic requirements of NUC$_R$. And these rules should apply only if the particular conversion is attested. But this would not conform to the general ideas of RRG because one result of including these rules would be that the syntactic categorization of words – or at least its pre-determination – is in fact accomplished in the lexicon and not just a matter of syntactic structures. As it is, the problems pointed out weaken the RRG approach considerably.

8.4 Conclusion

In sum then, it turns out to be empirically more plausible to combine syntactic and semantic categories of words in their lexical entries, which provide the interface between the two, because these categories are more intimately related than is assumed in approaches like N-CxG and RRG. As a result the approaches discussed in sections 2, 3 and 4 are more plausible in this respect than N-CxG and RRG. However, it must be noted that there are essential differences between these approaches. Whereas those discussed in section 2, i. e. ST and PPT, describe the relationship between the syntactic and semantic categories of words only in theory but not in practice, since there is not really any description of semantic properties,[23] this is different for those discussed in sections 3 and 4, HPSG and

---

[23] To a certain extent, Katz & Fodor (1963) can be considered an exception for the ST, and Higginbotham (1985) and Zwarts (1992) for the PPT.

the Fillmore and Kay version of CxG. As far as descriptive adequacy of the interface between the two types of categories is concerned, these approaches are superior to the others. This is due not least to the fact that in these approaches the lexicon is not simply a list of idiosyncratic properties of lexical items but includes lexical rules or constructions that capture generalizations relating lexical entries of various kinds.

9 Cross-linguistic differences?

Predictable criticisms of this discussion and the conclusion suggested above are that my argumentation is based only on English and properties of (mostly) Indo-European languages[24] and that this does not hold for languages like Mundari, Samoan, Nootka, Tagalog and the like, which do not lexically specify the syntactic properties of words, which therefore can be used in either 'nominal' or 'verbal' syntactic contexts, for example. The first criticism is true, but the second needs to be discussed. Not having a native-speaker like knowledge of any of these languages nor even having studied parts of them, I can only refer to and rely on published views. And as revealed by the controversial discussion of the Austronesian language Mundari, which is spoken in India, there are doubts about the claim that languages like this one do not lexically specify forms that can be used nominally, i. e. as heads of referring expressions, or verbally, i. e. as heads of syntactic predicates. Contrary to previous claims, Evans & Osada (2005) argue that they do, whereas Peterson (2005) as well as Hengeveld & Rijkhoff (2005), commenting on the paper by Evans & Osada, defend previous claims and argue that they do not.

Evans & Osada (2005) base their argumentation on three criteria which have to be fulfilled to classify a language as 'flexible' in the sense of Hengeveld (e. g. 1992) and thus as not distinguishing verbs and nouns (and in addition adjectives and adverbs, an aspect which is not discussed here) in the lexicon. These criteria are (1) distributional equivalence that is fully bi-directional, (2) explicit semantic compositionality for arguments and predicates, and (3) exhaustiveness. The first criterion requires that members of a 'flexible' class must have identical distribu-

---

[24] Note though, that Aronoff (1994) includes Arapesh and Yimas, two languages of Papua New Guinea, and also various Semitic languages in his discussion of syntactically relevant nominal and verbal inflectional classes.

tions, i.e. both 'object' words, from a European perspective lexically identified as 'nouns', and 'action words', identified from this perspective as 'verbs', must be equally acceptable as syntactic predicates and as (heads of) syntactic arguments. According to the third criterion, this must be the case for all 'nouns' and all 'verbs'. The second criterion requires that the semantic difference between the same form in different syntactic positions, i.e. as a predicate and as an argument, must be fully attributable to the function of that position. According to the investigations of Evans and Osada, Mundari, like other languages of the Munda family, does not fulfill either of these criteria. Their resulting "verdict" is "that Munda clearly distinguishes nouns from verbs, though (like English, Chinese and many other languages) it has widespread zero conversion" (2005: 384). In addition they state that

> though it is clear that in many languages there is a "weak" noun-verb distinction, we do not believe there exist – as yet – attested cases of languages lacking a noun-verb distinction altogether, according to the highest standards of description and argumentation. (*ibid.*)

Peterson's (2005) reaction to Evans & Osada is mostly based on Kharia, another Munda language. His main points are that all the lexical morphemes in this language are 'precategorial' and that the meaning relationship between their nominal and verbal uses in syntactic structures is productive and predictable in that if a meaning of the nominal use is 'X', then the meaning of its verbal counterpart is 'turn (something) into X' or 'become X'. Restrictions are said to be only semantic. A brief look at Mundari leads him to the conclusion that the situation in this language is just as it is in Kharia. In a subsequent paper (2007), Peterson goes into more detail and finds his view on Kharia confirmed.

Hengeveld & Rijkhoff (2005) first point out various flaws in Evans & Osada's discussion of Mundari and then defend the view that this language, like others, is flexible, meaning that (1) there is no lexical determination of syntactic properties, and (2) the meanings of lexical forms are vague. Concerning the latter aspect, they claim:

> Both the verbal and nominal sense of a flexible lexeme are contained in its (vague) semantics and the context only highlights the meaning components that are already there, giving the flexible item its verbal or nominal flavour. (*ibid.*: 415)

I do not feel able to decide who is right and who is wrong in this controversy. I can only point out what the consequences are in each of the two cases. If

Evans & Osada are right, then nothing needs to be added to my conclusion drawn above: Approaches which describe lexical entries as the interface between the syntactic and semantic categories of words are more plausible than approaches which consider this interface to be either syntactic structures or linking rules. And this then holds cross-linguistically. If Peterson and Hengeveld & Rijkhoff (and others) are right, then different solutions are necessary for flexible and for 'rigid' languages like the Indo-European ones, because the latter, according to Hengeveld (1992) and Hengeveld & Rijkhoff (2005: 406 f.), are unlike Mundari and other languages and do lexically specify items for syntactic properties. This is a view shared by Himmelmann (2008), who classifies languages on the basis of whether they specify lexical as well as syntactic categories in the lexicon, claiming that Indo-European languages do but languages like Tagalog do not (cf. *ibid.*: 264). According to him, the latter languages specify syntactic categories only in the syntax. In this second case then, the conclusion above holds only for Indo-European languages and others that behave like them, whereas for Mundari, Tagalog and other languages it is more appropriate for syntactic structures or linking rules to provide the interface between the syntactic and semantic categories of words. It has to be noted though that in contrast to the RRG approach but like N-CxG, Hengeveld & Rijkhoff claim that no semantic distinction between lexical verbs and lexical nouns is justified. In the lexicon there is just one vague meaning shared by forms that can be used either verbally or nominally.

I leave it to future research to decide what the consequences to be drawn from this discussion must be. Nevertheless I will conclude with a personal comment and an open question. There is no doubt that words in languages like Mundari, Nootka, Tagalog and others are not lexically specified for the traditional parts of speech such as noun, verb, adjective, etc. and the syntactic properties associated with these. But I find it hard to imagine that they are not lexically specified for any syntactic properties, including contextual or distributional ones[25], for example, that a word can be used in positions not available for one and the same word in Indo-European languages. If they are not, how then do speakers of these

---

[25] As I have pointed out in various publications, it is often the case that parts of speech are confused with syntactic categories (cf. e.g. Rauh 2010, esp. chaps. 1, 2, 9.2 and 10). Parts of speech have certain syntactic consequences but they are not syntactic categories. In this context it should be noted that Hengeveld's categorization of language types, which is included in the discussion above, is based on his identification of parts of speech, not of syntactic categories.

languages know how to use a form appropriately in order to construct well-formed sentences?

References

Aronoff, M. 1994. *Morphology by itself. Stems and inflectional classes.* Cambridge, MA: The MIT Press.

Baeskow, H. 2002. *Abgeleitete Personenbezeichnungen im Deutschen und Englischen. Kontrastive Wortbildungsanalysen im Rahmen des Minimalistischen Programms und unter Berücksichtigung sprachhistorischer Aspekte.* Berlin: Mouton de Gruyter.

Barner, D. & A. Bale. 2002. No nouns, no verbs: psycholinguistic arguments in favor of lexical underspecification. *Lingua* 112: 771–791.

Bhat, D. N. S. 2000. Word classes and sentential function. In P. M. Vogel & B. Comrie (eds.), *Approaches to the typology of word classes*, 47–64. Berlin: Mouton de Gruyter.

Boas, H. C. 2008. Determining the structure of lexical entries and grammatical constructions in construction grammar. *Annual Review of Cognitive Linguistics* 6: 113–144.

Borer, H. 2003. Exo-skeletal vs. endo-skeletal explanations. In J. Moore & M. Polinsky (eds.), *The nature of explanation in linguistic theory*, 31–67. Chicago: CSLI Publications.

Borer, H. 2005a. *Structuring sense. In name only.* Oxford: Oxford University Press.

Borer, H. 2005b. *Structuring sense. The normal course of events.* Oxford: Oxford University Press.

Chomsky, N. 1965. *Aspects of the theory of syntax.* Cambridge, MA: The MIT Press.

Chomsky, N. 1981. *Lectures on government and binding.* Dordrecht: Foris Publications.

Chomsky, N., & H. Lasnik. 1993. Principles and parameters theory. In J. Jacobs, A. von Stechow, W. Sternfeld & T. Vennemann (eds.), *Syntax: an international handbook of contemporary research*, 506–569. Berlin: Mouton de Gruyter.

Clark, E. V. & H. Clark. 1979. When nouns surface as verbs. *Language* 55: 767–811.

Don, J. 2004. Categories in the lexicon. *Linguistics* 42: 931–956.

Dowty, D. R. 1979. *Word meaning and Montague Grammar. The semantics of verbs and times in generative semantics and in Montague's PTQ.* Dordrecht: Reidel.

Evans, N. 2000. Kinship verbs. In P. M. Vogel & B. Comrie (eds.), *Approaches to the typology of word classes*, 103–172. Berlin: Mouton de Gruyter.

Evans, N. & T. Osada. 2005. Mundari: the myth of a language without word classes. *Linguistic Typology* 9: 351–390.

Fillmore, C. J. 1999. Inversion and constructional inheritance. In G. Webelhuth, J.-P. Koenig & A. Kathol (eds.), *Lexical and constructional aspects of linguistic explanation*, 113–128. Stanford: CSLI Publications.

Fillmore, C. J. & P. Kay. 1993. Construction Grammar Coursebook. Ms. University of California, Berkeley.

Foley, W. A. & R. D. Van Valin, Jr. 1984. *Functional syntax and universal grammar.* Cambridge: Cambridge University Press.

Gil, D. 1995. Parts of speech in Tagalog. In M. Alves (ed.), *Papers from the Third Annual Meeting of the Southeast Asian Linguistics Society*, 67–90. Tempe, Arizona.

Goldberg, A. 1995. *Constructions. A construction grammar approach to argument structure.* Chicago: University of Chicago Press.

Goldberg, A. 2006. *Constructions at work.* Oxford: Oxford University Press.

Halle, M. 1973. Prolegoma to a theory of word-formation. *Linguistic Inquiry* 4: 3–16.

Hengeveld, K. 1992. Parts of Speech. In M. Fortescue, P. Harder & L. Kristoffersen (eds.), *Layered structure and reference in a functional perspective: papers from the Functional Grammar Conference in Copenhagen 1990*, 29–55. Amsterdam & Philadelphia: John Benjamins Publishing Company.

Hengeveld, K. & J. Rijkhoff. 2005. Mundari as a flexible language. *Linguistic Typology* 9: 406–431.

Higginbotham, J. 1985. On semantics. *Linguistic Inquiry* 16: 547–593.

Himmelmann, N. P. 2008. Lexical categories and voice in Tagalog. In S. Musgrave & P. Austin (eds.), *Voice and grammatical relations in Austronesian languages*, 247–293. Stanford: CSLI Publications.

Jackendoff, R. S. 1973. The base rules for prepositional phrases. In S. Anderson & P. Kiparsky (eds.), *A Festschrift for Morris Halle*, 345–356. New York: Holt, Rinehart and Winston.

Jackendoff, R. S. 1977. *X'-syntax: a study of phrase structure.* Cambridge, MA: The MIT Press.

References

Karius, I. 1985. *Die Ableitung der denominalen Verben mit Null-Suffigierung im Englischen*. Tübingen: Niemeyer.

Katz, J. & J. Fodor. 1963. The structure of a semantic theory. *Language* 39: 170–210.

Kay, J. 2002. An informal sketch of a formal architecture for construction grammar. *Grammars* 5: 1–19.

Kay, P. & C. J. Fillmore. 1999. Grammatical constructions and linguistic generalizations: the what's X doing Y? construction. *Language* 75: 1–33.

Kuhn, J. 2007. Interfaces in constraint-based theories of grammar. In G. Ramchand & C. Reiss (eds.), *The Oxford handbook of linguistic interfaces*, 613–650. Oxford: Oxford University Press.

Levine, R. D. & W. D. Meurers. 2006. Head-driven phrase structure grammar: linguistic approach, formal foundations, and computational realization. In K. Brown (ed.), *The encyclopedia of language and linguistics*, second edition, 237–252. Oxford: Elsevier Science Publisher B.V.

Mosel, U. & E. Hovdhaugen. 1992. *Samoan reference grammar*. Oslo: Scandinavian University Press.

Müller, S. 2010. *Grammatiktheorie*. Tübingen: Stauffenburg.

Peterson, J. 2005. There's a grain of truth in every "Myth", or, why the discussion of lexical classes in Mundari isn't quite over yet'. *Linguistic Typology* 9: 391–441.

Peterson, J. 2007. Languages without nouns and verbs? An alternative to lexical classes in Kharia. In C. P. Masica (ed.), *Old and new perspectives on South Asian languages: grammar and semantics. Papers growing out of the Fifth International Conference on South Asian Linguistics* (ICOSAL-5), 274–303.

Plag, I. 2003. *Word-formation in English*. Cambridge: Cambridge University Press.

Pollard, C. & I. A. Sag. 1987. *Information-based syntax and semantics. Vol. 1: fundamentals*. Stanford: CSLI Publications.

Pollard, C. & I. A. Sag. 1994. *Head-driven phrase structure grammar*. Chicago: University of Chicago Press.

Pustejovsky, J. 1991a. The generative lexicon. *Computational Linguistics* 17: 409–441.

Pustejovsky, J. 1991b. The syntax of event structure. *Cognition* 41: 47–81.

Pustejovsky, J. 1995. *The generative lexicon*. Cambridge, MA: The MIT Press.

Rauh, G. 1997. Englische Präpositionen zwischen lexikalischen und funktionalen Kategorien. In E. Löbel & G. Rauh (eds.), *Lexikalische Kategorien und Merk-*

male, 125–167. Tübingen: Max Niemeyer Verlag.

Rauh, G. 1999. Adverb oder Präposition? Von der Notwendigkeit einer Abgrenzung von Wortarten und grammatischen Kategorien und der Gefahr einer terminologischen Falle. In E. Eggers, J. Becker, J. Udolph & D. Weber (eds.), *Florilegium Linguisticum. Festschrift für Wolfgang P. Schmid zum 70. Geburtstag*, 367–392. Frankfurt/M: Lang.

Rauh, G. 2000a. Don't Call it "X"! or: why X does not represent grammatical categories. In H. Janßen (ed.), *Verbal Projections*, 1–21. Tübingen: Niemeyer.

Rauh, G. 2000b. Wi(e)der die Wortarten! Zum Problem linguistischer Kategorisierung. *Linguistische Berichte* 184: 485–507.

Rauh, G. 2002a. Prepositions, features and projections. In H. Cuyckens & G. Radden (eds.), *Perspectives on prepositions*, 3–23. Tübingen: Niemeyer.

Rauh, G. 2002b. Word classes as prototypical categories. In S. Scholz, M. Klages, E. Hantson & U. Römer (eds.), *Context and cognition. Papers in honour of Wolf-Dietrich bald's 60th birthday*, 259–270. München: Langenscheidt-Longman GmbH.

Rauh, G. 2010. *Syntactic categories. Their identification and description in linguistic theories.* Oxford: Oxford University Press.

Sag, I. A., T. Wasow & E. M. Bender. 2003. *Syntactic theory. A formal introduction*, second edition. Stanford: CSLI Publications.

Schachter, P. 1985. Parts of speech systems. In T. Shopen (ed.), *Language typology and syntactic description*, 3–61. Cambridge: Cambridge University Press.

Swadesh, M. 1939. Nootka internal syntax. *International Journal of American Linguistics* 9: 77–102.

Van Valin, R. D., Jr. 1993. A synopsis of role and reference grammar. In R. D. Van Valin, Jr. (ed.), *Advances in role and reference grammar*, 1–164. Amsterdam and Philadelphia: John Benjamins Publishing Company.

Van Valin, R. D., Jr. 2001. *An introduction to syntax.* Cambridge: Cambridge University Press.

Van Valin, R. D., Jr. 2005. *Exploring the syntax-semantics interface.* Cambridge: Cambridge University Press.

Van Valin, R. D., Jr. 2008. RPs and the nature of lexical and syntactic categories in role and reference grammar. In R. D. Van Valin, Jr. (ed.), *Investigations of the syntax-semantics-pragmatics interface*, 161–178. Amsterdam and Philadelphia: John Benjamins Publishing Company.

References

Van Valin, R. D., Jr. 2010. Role and reference grammar as a framework for linguistic analysis. In B. Heine and H. Narrog (eds.), *The Oxford handbook of linguistic analysis*, 703–738. Oxford: Oxford University Press.

Van Valin, R. D., Jr. 2013. Lexical representation, co-composition, and linking syntax and semantics. In J. Pustejovsky et al. (eds.), *Advances in Generative Lexicon theory*, 67–107. Dordrecht: Kluwer.

Van Valin, R.D., Jr. & W. A. Foley. 1980. Role and reference grammar. In E. A. Moravcsik & J. R. Wirth (eds.), *Syntax and semantics Vol. XIII: current approaches to syntax*, 329–352. New York: Academic Press.

Van Valin, R. D., Jr. & R. LaPolla. 1997. *Syntax. Structure, meaning, and function*. Cambridge: Cambridge University Press.

Vendler, Z. 1957 (1967). *Linguistics in philosophy*. Ithaca: Cornell University Press.

Vogel, P. M. & B. Comrie (eds.) 2000. *Approaches to the typology of word classes*. Berlin: Mouton de Gruyter.

Zwarts, J. 1992. *X'-syntax – X'-semantics. On the interpretation of functional and lexical heads*. Utrecht: OTS Dissertation Series.

Author

Gisa Rauh
University of Wuppertal
rauh@uni-wuppertal.de

Why Verb Meaning Matters to Syntax

Eunkyung Yi & Jean-Pierre Koenig[1]

1 Introduction

Since Gruber (1965) and particularly Fillmore (1968), it is known that we can predict a lot of the syntax of verbs from their meaning. To quote Green (1974) or thirty years later Koenig and Davis (2006):

'Syntactic properties of lexical items depend crucially and in regular ways on the meaning of those lexical items' (Green 1974)
'It is widely accepted that the semantic content of a lexical entry determines to a large extent its syntactic subcategorization' (Koenig & Davis 2006)

There are at least two ways in which this relation between verb meaning and the syntactic contexts in which verbs can occur manifests itself. First, the syntactic pattern can carry meaning. For example, the English ditransitive construction with which this paper is concerned is often claimed to be associated with a transfer of possession meaning (see Pinker 1989, Goldberg 1993 among others, although see Van Valin & La Polla 1997 for a dissenting view). Some researchers associate the meaning directly with the syntactic pattern itself (see Goldberg 1995, and Ramchand 2008 for a very different tack on the association of a transfer of possession meaning with the pattern). Others associate the meaning with the output of a rule mapping a set of lexical entries onto another set of lexical entries (Pinker 1989 is a representative example of such a view). Either way, a question that arises is what kinds of verb meaning components are cross-linguistically relevant for syntactic purposes (see Pinker 1989, Grimshaw 1993, Koenig et al.

---

[1] Both authors contributed equally to the paper. Order of mention is random. We thank members of the Psycholinguistics laboratory at the University at Buffalo for help with the experiments reported in the paper, and in particular Gail Mauner; we thank Doug Roland for help with the corpus studies.

2015). But, another aspect of this association between verb meaning and syntactic frames, the one we concentrate on in this paper, is that verbs that tend to have similar meanings tend to occur in similar syntactic frames. Consider the three following syntactic frames and some of the verbs that can occur in these frames.

(1) a. John gave his son a toy.
    b. *give, offer, hand, lend, promise, tell, grant...*
(2) a. John loaded the truck with hay.
    b. *load, spray, smear, cram, engrave, mark...*
(3) a. John kept his son from entering the room.
    b. *keep, prevent, bar, prohibit, discourage, deter...*

Intuitively, the verbs in each of these syntactic frames have something in common semantically, at least more so than verbs across the syntactic frames exemplified in (1)–(3). Thus, *give* seems more similar to *promise* than to *load*; *spray* seems more similar to *smear* than to *keep*, and so forth. Not all verbs that can occur in a particular syntactic frame are equally similar to each other, though. For example, *load* is certainly not as similar, intuitively, to *smear* than *spray* is. But, overall, most verbs that occur in most syntactic frames seem to denote kinds of situations that are similar to each other, possibly through some kind of metaphorical similarity, as Goldberg (1995) claims. As Levin (1993: 11) puts it:

> 'Studies of diathesis alternations show that verbs in English and other languages fall into classes on the basis of shared components of meaning.'

The question that occupies us in this paper is why this is the case. What accounts for the fact that verbs that occur in the ditransitive construction are semantically similar to each other? In other words, why is it the case that verbs that occur in the ditransitive construction share some meaning features rather than constitute a grab bag of verbs as dissimilar from each other as any randomly chosen set of verbs with three arguments? We will call *semantic clustering* the fact that verbs that occur in the same syntactic frames are typically semantically similar to each other. Semantic clustering "makes sense" at an intuitive level. There are in the order of fifty or so distinct syntactic frames in English and, according to surveys our lab conducted, college-educated speakers know around 4,000 verbs and about 12,000 verb meanings. Since there are many more verbs (and even more verb meanings) than syntactic frames, there must be a way of grouping verbs that occur in each syntactic frame. Grouping verbs on the basis of their shared meaning features seems eminently "reasonable." Our goal in this paper is to go beyond the intuition that "it makes sense" and identify some mechanisms that may *cause* semantic clustering and provide initial empirical support for these mechanisms.

Note that, although grouping based on similarity of the kinds of situation that verbs denote (henceforth, situation-type) is "reasonable," it is not impossible for the group of verbs that occur in a syntactic frame to have little to do semantically with each other. Consider the set of verbs that allow indefinite proto-patient arguments to be unexpressed in (4).

(4) a. John baked all day.
  b. *bake, drink, dust, fish, read, sing, sow, wash, write...*

Verbs that allow indefinite proto-patient omission do not seem to form a natural class of situation-types. Rather, what seems to determine the omission of the proto-patient is, to grossly oversimplify, its predictability given the verb (Resnik 1996). Although predictability of the proto-patient is still a semantic property, the grouping of verbs that allow object omission is not based on similarity in situation-types. The existence of patterns like proto-patient omission suggests that semantic clustering is not an a priori necessity and requires an explanation.

The answer we provide is that semantic clustering is due to *priming*, i. e., the fact that exposure to certain stimuli influences our response to subsequent (similar) stimuli. In the case at hand, the relevant kind of stimuli is exposure to the association between a verb meaning and the syntactic frame the verb occurs in. We suggest that two different priming mechanisms can lead to semantic clustering. Both mechanisms operate concurrently and we will not be able to determine how they interact in this paper. For our purposes, it will suffice to show that each mechanism seems to be at play in language production and may provide a partial account of semantic clustering.

We draw our inspiration for the first priming mechanism from an observation made by Goldberg and her colleagues (Goldberg et al. 2004). They observe that for many syntactic frames, one verb occurs in them with disproportionly high frequency. Focusing on the ditransitive frame exemplified in (1a) above, they note that *give* occurs first and the most in child directed speech. They further suggest and provide experimental evidence that the skewed distribution of verbs in the ditransitive frame helps children learn the construction. That *give* accounts for most of the tokens of the ditransitive frame is confirmed by Bresnan et al.'s (2007) corpus study. We found that, in their corpus, more than 80 % of the ditransitive frame tokens have *give* as their main verb. In our own study of the entire British National Corpus, which we discuss below, *give* accounts for 59 % of the ditransitive frame tokens. We call verbs such as *give* that account for the lion's share of the tokens of a syntactic frame a (global) *semantic anchor*.

2 The global semantic anchor hypothesis

Our first hypothesis, which we call *the global semantic anchor hypothesis*, is that when a verb accounts for such a large proportion of tokens of a syntactic frame, it can serve as an anchor and lead speakers to use the same syntactic frame when describing similar situation-types. The logic of our hypothesis is as follows. When thinking of a message that consists of the description of a situation, a particular situation-type concept is activated. Other concepts that share features with that situation-type concept are also activated. In some cases, one of the concepts sharing features with the situation-type concept about to be expressed is named by the *semantic anchor*. Since the lemma for the semantic anchor is strongly associated with a particular syntactic frame, the semantic anchor's syntactic frame will be strongly activated. As a result, the chances of that frame being chosen to verbalize the situation description will increase (see Reitter et al. 2011). Over time, this increase in activation of that frame for verbs that share features with the semantic anchor will result in those verbs being more likely to occur in the same syntactic frame as the semantic anchor.

If the global semantic anchor hypothesis is correct, verbs that are more similar to the ditransitive semantic anchor, *give*, ought to occur more in the ditransitive frame. Put differently, the more semantically similar a verb is to a global semantic anchor, the more similar it ought to be syntactically, i. e., we predict a correlation between the degree of semantic similarity between a verb and the global semantic anchor and the degree to which a verb occurs in the anchor's preferred syntactic frame. We tested the global semantic anchor hypothesis in two corpus studies.

The first corpus study looked at the ditransitive frame and its alternate prepositional object frame illustrated in (5a) and (5b), respectively; the second corpus study looked at the material object frame and its alternate locatum object frame illustrated in (6a) and (6b), respectively.

(5) a. John gave his boy a toy.
　　b. John gave a toy to his boy.

(6) a. John loaded grocery bags into the car.
　　b. John loaded the car with grocery bags.

Both studies used the same methodology. We first computed degree of semantic similarity and frequency of occurrence in a syntactic frame (ditransitive, prepositional object, material object, and locatum object frames). We then examined if there was, as predicted, a correlation between the two measures. We measured semantic similarity between verbs and semantic anchors, using Latent Semantic Analysis (hereafter LSA, Landauer et al. 1998) a computational technique that approximates the semantic similarity between two words (two texts, more generally) by measuring how similar the contexts of occurrence of these two words are. (The contexts of occurrence are the texts in which both words occur or the texts in which words that co-occur with both words being compared occur.) We measured syntactic similarity between verbs and semantic anchors by computing how biased verbs are to occur in the anchor's preferred syntactic frame in the British National Corpus. Since our hypothesis pertains to whether semantic similarity affects the *choice* of syntactic frame in sentence production, we only consider verbs that alternate between the ditransitive and prepositional object frames or material object and locatum object frames.

2.1 The ditransitive alternation

In the case of the ditransitive frame, we computed the LSA semantic similarity cosine between *give* and the 108 alternating verbs mentioned in Levin (1993) that occur in the British National Corpus (hereafter BNC). To measure semantic similarity between *give* and each of 108 other alternating verbs, we used the one-to-many application utility available on-line at http://lsa.colorado.edu.[2] We

---

[2] LSA applications take word forms as input. Thus, word forms that are least ambiguous grammatically constitute a better choice for similarity estimation. For the verb lemma *give*, we chose as input word the past tense form *gave* as it is the only form that is invariably used as a main verb. Choosing only the past form of a verb, however, may not always be the best option. For example, the present and past tense forms of the verb *read* are the same and are identical to the noun form, e. g., *a good*

measured syntactic similarity to *give* by computing the proportion of times each verb occurs in the ditransitive frame (that is, we divided the number of times a verb occurred in the ditransitive frame in the BNC by the number of times it occurred in either the ditransitive or prepositional object frames). Our prediction is that, as semantic similarity to *give* increases, so will the proportion of times a verb occurs in the ditransitive frame. We performed a partial correlation analysis between LSA similarity to *give* and proportion of occurrence in the ditransitive in the BNC, to partial out the effect of frequency, since more frequent pairs of words occur in more texts and therefore will tend to be measured as more semantically similar by the LSA. We did find a correlation, as predicted, between semantic similarity to *give* and proportion of occurrence in the ditransitive frame ($r = .427$; $p < .001$). The global semantic anchor hypothesis is thus supported by this first corpus study.

One potential concern with the result of our study is that the correlation we found may be epiphenomenal as it may reduce to the other factors Bresnan et al. (2007) have found to influence the choice of the ditransitive frame (e. g., whether or not the theme and recipient arguments are pronouns). To determine whether semantic similarity to *give* influences the choice of the ditransitive frame *independently* of the factors Bresnan and her colleagues identified, we conducted a logistic regression on Bresnan et al.'s corpus.[3] Their collection of sentences was from the Switchboard and the Wall Street Journal corpus and only included 38 verbs (rather than the 108 verbs our study included) and 2,360 sentences (rather than the 63,495 sentences our study included). When we included 'Verb Similarity to *give*' as an additional factor, we found it to be a significant predictor of the use of the ditransitive frame even when Bresnan et al.'s predictors were included in the model. We also conducted a separate logistic regression analysis on our full set of 108 alternating verbs and 63,495 sentences. Because it was impractical to hand-code that many sentences for all the factors mentioned in Bresnan et al.'s study, we restricted our analysis to pronominality of the theme and recipient ar-

---

read. We therefore took multiple verb forms as input for verbs that were compared to *gave*: the base form, the third person singular present form, and the past tense form, e. g., *offer, offers* and *offered*.

[3] Their collection is publicly available for download at the publisher's website of *Quantitative methods in linguistics* by Keith Johnson (2008), Blackwell. Some variables mentioned in their 2007 paper (*person, number, structural parallelism* and *concreteness of theme*) are omitted in the publicly available data set.

guments, which can be easily automatically coded for and are the best predictors of the choice of the ditransitive or prepositional object frames. Semantic similarity to *give* was still a predictor of ditransitive use when these additional factors were included. In brief, our original finding that semantic similarity to *give* correlates with proportion of the ditransitive frame does not reduce to other factors known to affect the choice of syntactic frame.

2.2 The locative alternation

Our second corpus study used the same methodology as our first study but concentrated on the locative alternation illustrated in (4). We investigated 45 verbs that participate in that alternation. Frequency of occurrence in the material object frame and semantic similarity to anchor verbs were measured as in the first study. We chose as semantic anchors *rub* for the material object frame as it is the most frequent verb in the frame. But finding a good anchor for the frame is more difficult in this case than it was for the ditransitive frame, as no verb accounts for a large portion of the material object frame. So, whereas *give* accounts for 59 % of *all* ditransitive tokens, *rub* only accounts for 13 % of the material object tokens. It is perhaps not surprising, then, that we did not find a correlation between semantic similarity to *rub* and proportion of occurrence in the material object frame.

The results of our two corpus studies are at odds. Our ditransitive study shows that, as predicted by the global semantic anchor hypothesis, similarity to a verb strongly associated with a syntactic frame increases the likelihood of occurrence in the anchor preferred syntactic frame. These results suggest that shared semantic features affect choice of syntactic frame and contribute to semantic clustering. The locative alternation, though, serves as a cautionary tale. Global semantic anchors like *give* might be rare. The material object frame does not seem to have a good anchor (as we pointed out, *rub* does not account for the lion's share of tokens of their preferred frame). So not all constructions where verbs seem to semantically cluster might have a distribution as skewed as the ditransitive frame.

Semantic anchors like *give* have a global clustering effect: Most of the verbs that participate in the ditransitive frame cluster around it, at least the verbs that entail caused change of possession (see Rappaport & Levin 2008 and Yi, Koenig & Roland 2014 for details). But verbs can play a more local role in semantic clustering, by which we mean that verbs that can occur in a syntactic frame might clump into small semantic clusters without any single verb anchoring the entire syntactic frame, as *give* does for the ditransitive construction (a point already made in Pinker 1989). That clustering might be more local for some frames is suggested by the material and locatum object frames. Consider the following three groups of verbs that participate in the locative alternation:

- **Group 1:** *mark, engrave, etch ...* (A mark or a symbol is created on the surface of some object.)
- **Group 2:** *brush, powder, rub, spray ...* (Some material is added on the surface of some object.)
- **Group 3:** *load, stock, pile ...* (Something is moved and put in another place.)

Intuitively, semantic similarity within each of these three groups is high, but semantic similarity across groups is low. LSA similarity measures confirm this intuition. Whereas the average LSA semantic similarity between verbs within the three groups was .23, .28, and .28, respectively, semantic similarity across groups was only between .13 and .15. So, even though there might not be any good global anchor for the material or locatum object frames, there might be several good anchors that could lead to semantic clustering, although each anchor would lead to clustering into narrower classes.

We would like to suggest that priming could be at play here, as it was in the clustering effect of global semantic anchors like *give*, but that the effect of priming takes a different form. In the case of global semantic anchors, it is the strong association between *give* and the ditransitive frame that helps verbs that share semantic features with *give* activate more strongly the ditransitive frame even in the absence of any contextual occurrence of *give*.

In the case of *local* clustering, it is the more frequent co-occurrence of verbs with similar meanings than verbs with dissimilar meanings that lead to the clustering. More specifically, we suggest that it is the fact that verbs with similar meanings are more likely to co-occur in the same texts (e.g., paragraphs) that helps semantic clustering. That verbs with more similar meanings tend to cooccur in the same texts more than verbs with less similar meanings is at the root of the relative success of computational techniques for measuring semantic similarity, be it LSA or the Hyperspace Analogue to Language (HAL, Lund et al. 1995).

The assumption on which these techniques rest, as we mentioned earlier, is that words with similar meanings tend to co-occur more or to co-occur with more words that tend to co-occur. We also know from much work in sentence processing that the use of a syntactic frame increases the likelihood of the same frame being reused in the not so distant future (see Bock 1986, and Jaeger & Snider 2008 for corpus evidence of syntactic priming). What we are suggesting is that shared semantic features between verbs increases the likelihood of reusing a syntactic frame and that this increased likelihood can also lead to semantic clustering. We call *local semantic anchor hypothesis* the hypothesis that semantic clustering may also be the result of (1) the tendency of verbs with similar meanings to co-occur more and (2) the increased likelihood of the re-use of a syntactic frame when verbs are semantically similar.

3 The local semantic anchor hypothesis

To test the local semantic anchor hypothesis, we conducted two pairs of syntactic priming experiments. The goal of these experiments was to determine whether the use of a verb in a syntactic frame primes the reuse of that frame more when a subsequent verb is more similar in meaning than when the subsequent verb is less similar in meaning. The first pair of experiments examined the priming of the ditransitive vs. prepositional object frames, whereas the second pair of experiments examined the priming of the locatum vs. material object frames. All experiments used a sentence reading and recall paradigm (Griffin & Weinstein-Tull 2003, Potter & Lombardi 1998). In this paradigm, participants read a pair of sentences and complete aloud partial sentence prompts. Prompts appear in reverse order of presentation of the sentences they read. Thus, they might read in succession the sentences in (7) and then, successively complete aloud sentences (8a) and (8b).

(7) a. The producer promised a large part to the actress
    b. The CEO guaranteed all employees a Christmas bonus

(8) a. The CEO guaranteed _____
    b. The producer promised _____

The logic of this read-and-recall paradigm is as follows. The syntactic frame of sentences that have just been produced can prime participants to produce subsequent sentences that exhibit the same syntactic frame. So, the frame in the just produced sentence (8a) might prime participants to use the same frame when completing aloud (8b), i.e., it might lead participants to shift the frame of the sentence they read from the prepositional object frame to the ditransitive frame. Priming is thus measured by a shift from the syntactic frame used in the sentence a participant has read to the syntactic frame of the sentence the participant produces in recall. (There could also be a shift from the sentence frame they read last, e.g., (7b), to the frame they produce next, e.g., (8a). But, this shift is less likely, as the memory trace of the sentence that was just read is stronger and in all four experiments such shifts were inconsistently significant. For this reason and because of space considerations, we do not discuss these shifts further in this paper.)

(9) presents an example stimulus set for Experiment 1.

(9) *Reading Phase*:
    a. The producer **promised** a large part to the actress
    b. [One of the three prime conditions]
        High semantic similarity condition:
            The CEO **guaranteed** all employees a Christmas bonus
        Low semantic similarity condition:
            The ball boy **bounced** the player a new ball
        Control condition:
            Organic food **is increasing** in popularity recently
   Recall Phase:
    b. [One of the three prime conditions presented in reading]
        The CEO **guaranteed**/The ball boy **bounced**/Organic food **is increasing**
        _____
    a. The producer **promised** _____

For each stimulus set, participants first read two sentences presented word by word (200ms per word) on the middle of the screen (so-called Rapid Serial Visual Presentation). The first sentence was a prepositional object sentence (9a). The second (9b) was either a ditransitive sentence whose verb was highly semantically similar or not very semantically similar to the verb in the first sentence or a control sentence (most of the times, an intransitive sentence). Participants then attempted to accurately recall, when prompted, the sentences they read in reverse order, i. e., the second sentence they read first, and the first sentence they read second. The sentence they recalled first served as a prime to the second sentence. First recalled sentences fell into three groups, (i) sentences whose verbs were highly similar semantically to the verb in the sentence they would have to recall next (*guaranteed* and *promised* in (9)); (ii) sentences whose verbs were not very similar semantically to the verb in the sentence they would have to recall next (*bounced* and *promised* in (9)), but whose verbs were alternating verbs; (iii) sentences whose verbs were not alternating verbs, mostly intransitive verbs. If the local semantic anchor hypothesis is correct, priming should increase when the two verbs are highly similar semantically as compared to when they are not very semantically similar. Priming was measured as increase in shifts from the prepositional object frame of the sentence that was read to the ditransitive frame of the first recalled sentence when compared to the baseline percentage of shifts provided by the control (mostly intransitive) sentences.

Table 1: Example stimulus sets for Experiments 1 and 2

	Experiment 1	**Expriment 2**
Reading Phase	The producer **promised** a large part to the actress (Prepositional Object frame (PO) frame)	The producer **promised** the actress a large part (Ditransitive or Double Object (DO) frame)
	The CEO **guaranteed** all employees a Christmas bonus (DO; high semantic similarity)	The CEO **guaranteed** a Christmas bonus to all employees (PO; high semantic similarity)
	The ball boy **bounced** the player a new ball (DO; Low semantic similarity)	The ball boy **bounced** a new ball to the player (PO; Low semantic similarity)
	Organic food **is increasing** in popularity recently (Intransitive control)	Organic food **is increasing** in popularity recently (Intransitive control)
Recall Phase	The CEO **guaranteed** _____/ The ball boy **bounced** _____/ Organic food **is increasing** _____ The producer **promised**_____	The CEO **guaranteed** _____/ The ball boy **bounced** _____/ Organic food **is increasing** _____ The producer **promised**_____

The logic of Experiments 2–4 is the same as that of Experiment 1. Tables 1–2 include example stimulus sets for all four experiments.

Materials for all experiments were normed for naturalness and, most importantly, for semantic similarity. For each experiment, we computed the LSA sim-

Table 2: Example stimulus sets for Experiments 3 and 4

	Experiment 3	Expriment 4
Reading Phase	The kid **smeared** mom's lipstick on her face (material object (MO) frame)	The kid **smeared** her face with mom's lipstick (locatum object (LO) frame)
	The New Yorker **spread** a toasted bagel with cream cheese (LO; high semantic similarity)	The New Yorker **spread** cream cheese on a toasted bagel (MO; high semantic similarity)
	The freight driver **loaded** the huge truck with lots of boxes (LO; low semantic similarity)	The freight driver **loaded** lots of boxes on the huge truck (MO; low semantic similarity)
	The congressman **decided** to run for the next election (Intransitive control)	The congressman **decided** to run for the next election (Intransitive control)
Recall Phase	The New Yorker **spread** _____ / The freight driver **loaded** _____ / Organic food **is increasing** _____ The kid **smeared** _____	The New Yorker **spread** _____ / The freight driver **loaded** _____ / Organic food **is increasing** _____ The kid **smeared** _____

ilarity of various pairs of verbs and we also had participants in a norming study evaluate the semantic similarity of the verbs on a Likert scale from 1 (least similar) to 7 (most similar). We used verb pairs where LSA measures and human judgments matched. We chose verbs that were either highly semantically similar or not very semantically similar to our target verbs (the second verb used in the recall phase in Tables 1–2). Table 3 provides mean similarity scores for all four experiments.

Table 3: Mean similarity scores for high and low semantic similarity pairs for the ditransitive (Experiments 1–2) and locative (Experiments 3–4) alternations

	Dative	Locative
HIGH similarity pairs	5.55	4.96
LOW similarity pairs	1.81	1.67

Our overall prediction was that verbs in the first recalled sentence would lead to stronger priming when the prime and target verbs are more semantically similar than when they are less semantically similar. To test this prediction, we compared the effect of both high and low semantic similarity primes to control primes. More specifically, priming was assessed by comparing shifts from the reading phase frame to the first recalled sentence frame in the experimental conditions (i. e., ditransitive frame (Experiment 1), prepositional object frame (Experiment 2), locatum object frame (Experiment 3), material object frame (Experiment 4)) vs. an intransitive control condition. Sixty University at Buffalo undergraduate students participated in each experiment. In Experiments 1, 3, and 4, we found, as predicted, significant priming when the prime verb was highly similar semantically to the target verb, compared to control primes, but not when the prime verb was not semantically similar to the target verb as Tables 4 and 5 show. In Experiment 1, participants were more likely to shift from the prepositional object frame to the ditransitive frame after producing a ditransitive sentence that contained a highly semantically similar verb than after producing a (mostly intransitive) control prime. But, they showed no such tendency after producing a ditransitive sentence that contained a semantically dissimilar verb. In Experiment 3, participants were only more likely to shift from the material object frame to the locatum object frame when recalling the first sentence they read after producing a locatum object sentence that contained a highly semantically similar verb. Finally, in experiment 4, participants were only more likely to shift from the locatum object frame to the material object frame when recalling the first sentence they read after producing a material sentence that contained a highly semantically similar verb.

Table 4: Percentages of increase in shifts from baseline (control condition) in Experiments 1–4

Experiment	Target shift	Low similarity condition	High similarity condition
Exp 1	PO to DO	2.3	4.5
Exp 2	DO to PO	20.5	19.5
Exp 3	MO to LO	2.4	5.2
Exp 4	LO to MO	4.4	11.4

Table 5: Results of the mixed effect logistic regression analyses for Experiments 1–4

Experiment	Condition	Coefficient Estimate	Std error	p value
Exp 1	Low vs. Ctrl	0.89	0.69	0.2
	High vs. Ctrl	1.24	0.61	.04*
Exp 2	Low vs. Ctrl	0.46	0.2	.02*
	High vs. Ctrl	0.55	0.2	.007*
Exp 3	Low vs. Ctrl	0.48	0.45	0.29
	High vs. Ctrl	0.89	0.44	.04*
Exp 4	Low vs. Ctrl	0.4	0.29	0.17
	High vs. Ctrl	0.79	0.29	.007*

Experiment 2 did not conform to our predictions in that both highly semantically similar and semantically dissimilar prime verbs lead to significantly more shifts from the ditransitive frame of the reading phase to the prepositional object frame in the recall phase as compared to control primes. We surmise that the different pattern of results in Experiment 2 is due to the fact that the shift in this experiment was to an overwhelmingly preferred prepositional object frame. Recall that in the case of Experiment 2, shifts were from the dis-preferred ditransitive frame in the reading phase to the preferred prepositional object frame in the recall phase. As is well known, the prepositional object frame is strongly preferred among alternating verbs, including the verbs we used in our materials. Furthermore, ditransitive frame sentences most often include a pronominal recipient, which our materials did not include. The combined effect of these two preferences is that for the verbs used in Experiment 2, over 95 % of the time, when the recipient is not encoded as a pronoun, the prepositional object frame is used. This explains that *in the control condition* shifts to the ditransitive frame in Experiment 1 occurred about 3 % of the time, but shifts to the prepositional object frame in the control condition in Experiment 2 occurred over 40 % of the time. It seems that when a syntactic frame is as overwhelmingly preferred as the prepositional object frame for full lexical NP recipients, syntactic priming occurs regardless of semantic similarity. More precisely, the increase in syntactic frame shifts due to semantic similarity is small when compared to the effect of syntactic preferences (about 2 % vs. about 20 %, see Table 4). A likely consequence is that any potential effect of semantic similarity is dwarfed by the effect of such a strong syntactic preference.

Overall, the results of our four experiments suggest that semantic similarity increases priming of syntactic frames: Speakers are more likely to incorrectly recall the frame they read when they just produced a sentence with an interfering alternative frame whose verb was highly semantically similar. The mechanism that we suggested may underlie local semantic clustering thus receives experimental support. Interestingly, we found effects of semantic similarity on priming, and support for the local semantic anchor hypothesis, for both the locative alternation as well as for the dative alternation. This is important, since, as we saw earlier, our corpus studies did not support the global semantic anchor hypothesis for the locative alternation. We suggested that global semantic anchors as strong as *give* for the ditransitive construction might be quite rare and that, since semantic clustering is rather general and obtains across many syntactic frames, some other mechanism must be at play. We suggested that two other possibly overlapping mechanisms might account for semantic clustering for alternations without a global semantic anchor. The first is a more circumscribed version of the semantic anchor hypothesis: Within narrower classes, there may be semantic anchors (maybe within classes akin to Pinker's narrow classes). Unfortunately, the small numbers of verbs in the locative alternation's narrow classes prevent us from testing this hypothesis. But a second possibility is that clustering might be the result of pairwise similarities, in that pairs of verbs that are semantically similar might share their relative propensity to occur in the same syntactic frame(s). Such clustering might lead to the intuition researchers have had that verbs that occur in a syntactic frame share semantic features. It is this second possibility our experiments tested and found support for.

4 General discussion

Most of our research, as linguists, focuses on determining what grammars are like. In the case of the effect of the meaning of verbs on the syntactic frames in which they can occur, that has meant figuring out how much of the syntax of verbs can be predicted from their meaning and what aspect of the meaning of verbs tends to be relevant for predicting their syntax. In this paper, we asked a question linguists ultimately strive for, an explanation for why grammars are the way they are, here why verbs with similar meanings tend to occur in similar syntactic frames. We suggested two mechanisms might provide a partial answer to this question.

The first, which we call *global semantic anchoring*, is operative when a verb accounts for much of the tokens of a frame, such as *give* for the ditransitive frame. Goldberg et al. (2004) suggest that syntactic frames like the ditransitive construction, are associated with "primary scenes" and that verbs like *give* are simply names of these "primary scenes," thus explaining their frequent occurrence in the frame. We hypothesized that these "primary scenes" verbs semantically anchor the syntactic frame, so that other verbs' occurrence in the syntactic frame will correlate with their semantic similarity to the anchor. The mechanism underlying this global anchoring, we suggest, works as follows. When thinking of a message and an event description for a planned utterance, speakers activate verbs that share semantic features with that event description. The more semantically similar two verbs are, the more the activation of one verb will activate the other verb. When a global semantic anchor is among the semantically similar verbs that are also activated, the activation of the global anchor's preferred syntactic frame is relatively high, because the anchor verb is strongly associated with that frame. As a result of this increase in activation of the anchor's preferred frame, speakers are more likely to choose that frame when producing their intended event description.

We provided evidence for the effect on syntactic frame selection of global semantic anchors like *give* through a corpus study. We showed that there was a correlation between a verb's semantic similarity to *give* (as measured by Latent Semantic Analysis) and the choice of the ditransitive frame rather than the prepositional object frame in the British National Corpus. We further showed that the influence of a verb's semantic similarity to *give* does not reduce to other factors known to affect the choice of the ditransitive frame (Bresnan et al. 2007). A comparable study of the locative alternation, however, suggests that what we call *global semantic anchors* like *give* for the ditransitive frame might not be that common and thus cannot constitute the only mechanism underlying semantic clustering. Indeed, we did not find a correlation between putative semantic anchors and the material object frame. There are several possible reasons that we suggested might explain the absence of a global semantic anchor for this frame. First, no verb accounts for so many of the tokens of the frame in the BNC (e. g., *rub*, the verb that occurs the most in the material object frame accounts for only 13 % of the tokens of this frame in the BNC). So, it is not clear that there is a strong anchor for this frame. Second, the material object frame includes verbs that are quite distant semantically. As less semantic features are shared between verbs, the activation of the concept associated with any verb selected by the speaker will activate less the concept associated with the anchor.

As we mentioned, Pinker (1989) noted that not all verbs that participate in a syntactic frame form a coherent semantic class and he distinguished between narrow and broad classes of alternating verbs. Only narrow classes constitute natural semantic classes. What this suggests is that while semantic priming and global semantic anchors can play a role in explaining semantic clustering, this cannot be the entire story. We suggested that a similar, but more local mechanism might play a role in explaining semantic clustering. We hypothesized that a verb that is just heard in a particular syntactic frame will prime semantically similar verbs to occur in the same syntactic frame. That the occurrence of a syntactic frame will prime the subsequent reuse of that frame is of course something that has been well established since Bock's seminal work. But, for that well-established observation to help explain semantic clustering, we must assume that verbs that share semantic features tend to be more likely to occur in the same stretch of discourse than verbs that are semantically further apart. And of course, this is what computational techniques that measure semantic similarity assume. So, the relative success of LSA or HAL suggests that there is something to the idea that semantically similar verbs will occur in the vicinity of each other.

The second part of our paper showed that *local semantic anchors* can indeed play a role in online sentence production. We hypothesized that semantic similarity would increase syntactic priming so that verbs would prime other verbs to occur in the same syntactic frame more than verbs that are not semantically similar. We conducted four syntactic priming experiments that tested the local semantic anchoring hypothesis. Two of these experiments involved the ditransitive/prepositional object frames and two involved the locatum object/material object frames. Each experiment tested the hypothesis that semantic similarity increases priming in the form of increasing shifts from alternating structure A in reading to alternating structure B in recall after speakers have just produced a sentence using structure B that contained a semantically similar verb. Three of the four experiments we conducted conformed to our predictions. Semantically similar prime verbs lead to more shifts to the alternating structure in recall than verbs that were semantically dissimilar. But in Experiment 2, the use of the prepositional object frame in recall did not vary as a function of the semantic similarity of the verb in the prime and target sentences. We surmised that the reason for the irrelevance of semantic similarity in this case lies with the fact that the prepositional object frame is overwhelmingly preferred when recipients are expressed as non-pronominal NPs (over 95 % in the BNC for the verbs included in our experiments). Priming of such a preferred structure is so strong that the relatively small effect of semantic similarity becomes invisible.

Overall, then, we found empirical support for both of the mechanisms that together or separately might begin to provide an explanation for semantic clustering. Global and local semantic anchors might be an important part of what gives rise to semantic clustering. Several issues remain to be explored, however. First, it is yet unclear what role global anchors play. The role of *give* for the ditransitive frame might be the exception, rather than the norm. Much ink has been shed on that frame in theories of linking lexical semantics to syntactic frames from Fillmore and Green on. The ditransitive frame, alongside passives, has also received most of the attention in the psycholinguistic study of syntactic priming. But a cursory look at other syntactic frames, including the locatum object/material object frames, suggests generalizing from the ditransitive to the bulk of syntactic frames might be unwarranted.

Second, criteria for selecting potential global semantic anchors must be refined. In this paper, we selected anchors on the basis of the proportions of tokens of the syntactic frame in the BNC they accounted for: Semantic anchors were simply the verbs that accounted for the largest number of tokens of the syntactic frame in the BNC. But other criteria or additional criteria might be needed. For example, we would expect anchors for a particular syntactic frame to occur significantly more often in that frame than in the alternative frame(s). Otherwise, how could they anchor that frame? In such circumstances what is more important? Is there a combination of the two criteria that is optimal? (See Yi et al. 2014 for a proposal.)

Third, what counts as a distinct syntactic frame is not always clear. Here again, the ditransitive construction might be quite unique. Aside from rather infrequent causatives (e. g., *Her victory made her the most sought after athlete*), the sequence of two post-verbal NPs in English is criterial of the ditransitive construction. But the post-verbal sequence NP+PP can be ambiguous between what *could be* considered several distinct syntactic frames (e. g., *John threw the ball into the basket* and *John loaded the suitcases into the car*).

Fourth, if local semantic anchors play an important role in semantic clustering, it would suggest that syntactic frames are a collection of related frames, each targeting a small, semantically coherent cluster of verbs, not unlike Pinker's (1989) narrow classes. If distinct semantic anchors might account for each small semantic clustering, what accounts for the collection of small semantic clusters? Take the small clusters of verbs like *load* and *engrave* that participate in both the material object and locatum object frames. Both semantic clusters are quite coherent semantically and members of each cluster alternate between the locatum object and the material object frames. If semantic anchoring accounts for membership in each small semantic cluster, what accounts for the fact that both clusters alternate between the same two syntactic frames (assuming, for now, that this is the case)? Obviously, we cannot provide an answer to these questions in this short, rather speculative paper. What we hope to have shown is that semantic anchors and "priming" in a broad sense might explain this recurring fact of the syntax of basic clauses: Verbs that participate in the same or a similar set of syntactic frames look alike semantically.

References

Bock, J. K. 1986. Syntactic persistence in language production. *Cognitive Psychology* 18: 355–387.

Bresnan, J., A. Cueni, T. Nikitina & R. H. Baayen. 2007. Predicting the dative alternation. In G. Boume, I. Kraemer & J. Zwarts (eds.), *Cognitive foundations of interpretation*, 69–94. Amsterdam: Royal Netherlands Academy of Science.

Fillmore, C. 1968. The case for case. In E. Bach & R. Harms (eds.), *Universals in linguistic theory*, 1–87. New York: Holt, Rinehart and Winston.

Goldberg, A. E. 1993. Another look at some learnability paradoxes. In E. V. Clark (ed.), *Proceedings of the twenty-fifth annual child language research forum*, 60–75. Stanford, CA: CSLI Publications.

Goldberg, A. E. 1995. *Constructions: A construction grammar approach to argument structure*. Chicago: Universtiy of Chicago Press.

Goldberg, A. E., D. M. Casenhiser & N. Sethuraman. 2004. Learning argument structure generalizations. *Cognitive Linguistics* 15: 289–316.

Green, G. 1974. *Semantics and syntactic regularity*. Bloomington: Indiana University Press.

Griffin, Z. M. & J. Weinstein-Tull. 2003. Conceptual structure modulates structural priming in the production of complex sentences. *Journal of Memory and Language* 49: 537–555.

Grimshaw, J. 1993. *Semantic structure and semantic content in lexical representation*. Department of Linguistics, Rutgers University.

Gruber, G. 1965. *Studies in lexical relations*. MIT dissertation.

Jaeger, F. & N. Snider. 2008. Implicit learning and syntactic persistence: surprisal and cumulativity. *Proceedings of the 30th Meeting of the Cognitive Science Society*, 1061–1066.

Koenig, J.-P. & A. R. Davis. 2006. The KEY to lexical semantics representations. *Journal of Linguistics* 42: 71–108.

Koenig, J.-P., D. Roland, H. Yun & G. Mauner. 2015. Which event properties matter for which cognitive task? In R. de Almeida & L. Manouilidou (eds.), *Cognitive* science perspectives on verb representation and processing, 213–234. Dordrecht: Springer.

Landauer, T. K., P. W. Foltz & D. Laham. 1998. An introduction to latent semantic analysis. *Discourse Processes* 25: 259–284.

Levin, B. 1993. *English verb classes and alternations.* Chicago: Universtiy of Chicago Press.

Lund, K., C. Burgess & R. A. Atchley. 1995. Semantic and associative priming in a high-dimensional semantic space. *Proceedings of the 17th Annual Conference of the Cognitive Science Society*, 660–665. Mahwah, NJ: Lawrence Erlbaum Associates.

Potter, M. & L. Lombardi. 1998. Syntactic priming in immediate recall of sentences. *Journal of Memory and Language* 38: 265–282.

Pinker, S. 1989. *Learnability and cognition: the acquisition of argument structure.* Cambridge, MA: MIT Press.

Rappaport, M. & B. Levin. 2008. The English dative alternation: the case for verb sensitivity. *Journal of Linguistics* 44: 129–167.

Ramchand, G. 2008. *Verb meaning and the lexicon: a first phase syntax.* Cambridge: Cambridge University Press.

Reitter, D., F. Keller & J. D. Moore. 2011. A computational cognitive model of syntactic priming. *Cognitive Science* 35: 587–637.

Resnik, P. 1996. Selectional constraints: an information-theoretic model and its computational realization. *Cognition* 61: 127–159.

Van Valin, R. D., Jr. & R. J. LaPolla. 1997. *Syntax: form, meaning and function.* Cambridge: Cambridge University Press.

Yi, E., J.-P. Koenig & D. Ronald. 2014. The role of frequency-driven association between verb and syntactic frame on syntactic frame selection. Manuscript submitted for publication.

Authors

Eunkyung Yi & Jean-Pierre Koenig
University at Buffalo
eyi@buffalo.edu, jpkoenig@buffalo.edu

Representing Constructional Schemata in the FunGramKB Grammaticon[1]

Ricardo Mairal & Carlos Periñán-Pascual

Recent research into FunGramKB has focused on the development of a proof-of-concept prototype, ARTEMIS, which intends to automatically provide a semantic representation of a text under the format of a *conceptual logical structure* by viewing the RRG linking algorithm from a conceptual perspective. However, little has been said about the format of the Grammaticon, the place where constructional schemata are claimed to reside within FunGramKB. With this in mind, the aim of this chapter is to discuss the format of constructional schemata in ARTEMIS. ARTEMIS's explanatory scope is not confined to argument constructions, as has been the case in RRG so far and most construction grammar approaches, but takes a step forward to account for those meaning dimensions that have a long tradition in pragmatics and discourse analysis, that is, the non-propositional dimension of meaning. In so doing, ARTEMIS resorts to the Lexical Constructional Model, a comprehensive model of meaning construction. The primary aim of this chapter is to discuss the format of these four level schemata and their representation in a natural language engineering project like ARTEMIS.

1 Introduction

FunGramKB Suite is an online knowledge-engineering environment for the semi-automatic construction of a multipurpose lexico-conceptual knowledge base for natural language processing (NLP) systems, i. e. FunGramKB (Periñán-Pascual & Arcas 2004, 2007, 2010, Periñán-Pascual & Mairal 2009, 2010a, Mairal & Periñán-Pascual 2009). On the one hand, FunGramKB is multipurpose in the sense that it is both multifunctional and multilingual. In other words, FunGramKB has been

---
[1] Financial support for this research has been provided by the DGI, Spanish Ministry of Education and Science, grant FFI2011-29798-C02-01.

designed to be reused in various NLP tasks (e. g. information retrieval and extraction, machine translation, dialogue-based systems, etc.) and with several natural languages. The English and Spanish lexica are fully supported in the current version of FunGramKB, although we also work with other languages, i. e. German, French, Italian, Bulgarian and Catalan. On the other hand, the knowledge base is lexico-conceptual, because it comprises three general levels of information: lexical, grammatical and conceptual.[2] Recent research into FunGramKB Suite has resulted in the development of ARTEMIS (Automatically Representing TExt Meaning via an Interlingua-based System), a proof-of-concept computer application which is able to automatically provide a semantic representation of a text under the format of a *conceptual logical structure* (CLS) (Periñán-Pascual 2013b, Periñán-Pascual & Arcas 2014). This research is based on previous work, which has explored the methodological repercussions of viewing the Role and Reference Grammar (hereafter, RRG) linking algorithm from a conceptual perspective. A brief description of some of the most relevant working proposals, together with some of the most representative references, is outlined below.

a) The RRG linking algorithm is claimed to have a conceptual grounding such that there exists a specific knowledge base, i. e. FunGramKB, which interfaces with the different linguistic modules of the RRG linking algorithm. Figure 1 illustrates this cognitive turn:

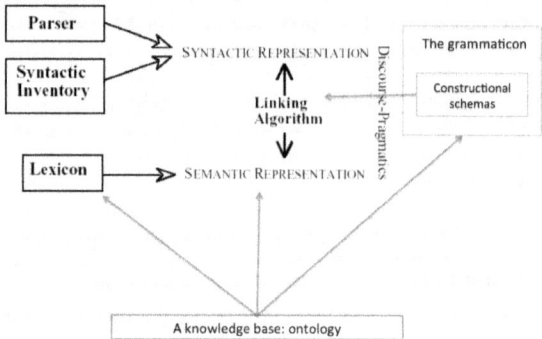

Figure 1: The RRG architecture within a conceptual framework.

---

[2] For further information about this previous background work, we refer the reader to the following websites where some of the most relevant literature can be downloaded: www.fungramkb.com and www.lexicom.es

The resulting semantic representations have a cognitive status, concurring with the assumption that primes in RRG standard *logical structures* are thought to be ontologically driven. However, nothing is said about the internal structure of the ontology that supports the cognitive nature of these primes. This is why this proposal comes to fill in an existing gap in the RRG apparatus.

b) From the preceding discussion, it follows that standard RRG lexical representations, i. e. *logical structures,* are now conceived in terms of *conceptual logical structures* (CLS) (cf. Mairal, Periñán-Pascual & Pérez 2012, Mairal 2012, Periñán-Pascual & Arcas 2014) for a detailed explanation of the format of this new type of lexical representation). This implies that primes are substituted for conceptual units that are part of the FunGramKB Ontology. Each conceptual unit, in turn, has its own distinguishing properties, i. e. a *thematic frame* and a *meaning postulate*[3], so that the resulting representation provides access to knowledge which goes beyond the grammatically relevant aspects of meaning. For example, a predicate like 'marchitar' (*wither*) in Spanish is linked to the terminal[4] conceptual unit $WITHER_00 in the Ontology. In terms of RRG, this is a one-place predicate which designates an accomplishment:

(1) BECOME **withered**' (x)

Hence, this representation only captures those aspects that are grammatically relevant, while nothing is said about those features that go beyond syntax. If conceptual units from an ontology are used instead of lexical units, then the resulting representation will have access to the information provided by the thematic frame and meaning postulate of the conceptual unit to which the predicate in the lexicon is linked to. In the case that concerns us here, as noted above, in the FunGramKB Spanish Lexicon the predicate 'marchitar' is linked to the terminal conceptual unit $WITHER_00, which includes a thematic frame (2a) with two arguments, the second of which is restricted by a number of selectional preferences. Moreover, this conceptual unit is provided with a meaning definition (2b) such that

---

[3] For a detailed description of the technicalities of these two notions, *thematic frames* and *meaning postulates*, we refer the reader to Periñán-Pascual & Arcas (2010), Periñán-Pascual & Mairal (2010a) and Mairal (2012).

[4] FunGramKB, unlike some other existing ontological engineering projects, follow a four-level classification of concepts: metaconcepts, basic concepts, terminal concepts and subconcepts, each occupying a different place in the conceptual hierarchy and represented by a different notational system (cf. Periñán-Pascual & Arcas 2010, Periñán-Pascual & Mairal 2010a, 2011).

someone dries something (usually a plant, flower or leaf) and as a result this entity becomes small and weak and begins to die. On the whole, an ontological framework provides an enriched version of standard logical structure (see Van Valin & Mairal (in press) for further elaboration of this issue)[5]:

(2) $WITHER_00
    a. (x1)Theme (x2: +PLANT_00 ˆ +FLOWER_00 ˆ +LEAF_00) Referent
    b. +(e1: +DRY_00 (x1) Theme (x2) Referent (f1: (e2: +BECOME_00 (x2)Theme (x3: +SMALL_00 & +WEAK_00) Attribute)) Result (f2: (e3: ing +DIE_00 (x2) Theme)Result

Entity1 dries entity2, typically a plant, flower or leaf, and consequently entity2 becomes small and weak and starts to die.

c) The final output is a fully specified semantic representation that is built around the notion of *aktionsart* and consists of conceptual units and operators (as those distinguished in Van Valin & LaPolla 1997, Van Valin 2005)[6], all of which offer a very comprehensive picture of a natural language user's linguistic knowledge of an input text (see Periñán-Pascual & Mairal 2009, 2012):

(3) a. Ron destroyed the building
    b. $<_{IF}DEC <_{TNS}PAST <_{ASP}PERF <_{CONSTR-L1}KER2 <[_{AKT}ACC\ [+DESTROY\_00\ (\%RON\_00\text{-Theme}, \$BUILDING\_00\text{-Referent})]]>>>>$

Hence, a semantic representation expressed in terms of a CLS is now connected up to a knowledge base from where it is possible to retrieve world knowledge information via a reasoning engine. By using artificial intelligence techniques, e. g. graph-based algorithms, our semantic knowledge as expressed in a CLS can be further enriched by information coming from different modules of the knowledge base (i. e. the Ontology, the Cognicon and the Onomasticon)[7].

---

[5] Note that the properties of conceptual units are expressed in COREL (Conceptual Representational Language). COREL-formatted schemata, which can be computationally considered as a combination of conceptual graphs and frames, are modelled through propositional representations consisting of logically-connected predications. We refer the reader to Periñán-Pascual & Arcas (2004) and Periñán-Pascual & Mairal (2010a) for a full description of its technicalities.

[6] As noted in (3b), there are two operators, AKT and CONSTR-L1, which are not part of Van Valin's (2005) inventory. These will be discussed later in Section 4.1.

[7] The cognitive level in FunGramKB, as extensively discussed elsewhere (cf. Periñán-Pascual & Arcas 2007, Periñán-Pascual 2012, 2013), consists of three modules: the Ontology where semantic knowledge is stored in terms of a hierarchy of concepts; (ii) the Cognicon where procedural knowledge is

d) In Figure 1, we note that a specific place has been allocated for constructional schemata given their prominent role in the lexical-grammatical interface[8]. However, in our view these constructional schemata have still a very linguistic descriptive flavor, which makes it a bit difficult to make use of when one is confronted with a natural language processing application. In connection with this, we believe that constructional schemata can be enriched if these are based on a conceptual framework. In this regard, there are two specific aspects that are worth mentioning: (i) the first one is concerned with the format of the constructional schemata; a more formalized scheme than the present RRG constructional schemata is needed; (ii) the second has to do with the fact that the semantics of standard RRG constructional templates can be enhanced via information coming from the Ontology (cf. Van Valin & Mairal in press, Periñán-Pascual 2013b, Mairal, 2012).

In essence, this previous work, which underlines the methodological advantages of driving RRG into a conceptually-oriented paradigm, has been influential in the first stages of the development of ARTEMIS. Notwithstanding, we still noted that an NLP application which aims to provide a semantic representation of an input text automatically cannot be silent about non-propositional aspects of meaning, since these are highly influential in meaning construction. As stated in the RRG literature, semantic interpretations only deal with the propositional dimension of meaning, that is, with 'who did what to whom', whereas nothing is said about the non-propositional dimension of meaning. For example, the following *wh*-questions not only seek information about a particular item in a given state of affairs but also all of them seem to suggest that the situation the speaker is asking is wrong, that is, the speaker is expressing his concern about the propositional content[9]:

---

coded in terms of a number of different scripts; (iii) the Onomasticon, where episodic knowledge is described. For a preliminary introduction on how a CLS can be enriched by using artificial intelligence techniques, we refer the reader to Periñán-Pascual and Mairal (2009, 2010b, 2012) which provided some insights in the area of machine translation and cross-linguistic information retrieval.

[8] See Van Valin (2005, 2013), Van Valin and Mairal (in press), Nolan (2011) and Diedrichsen (2011) for recent discussions on the role of constructions within RRG.

[9] Following the recommendation of an anonymous reviewer, it is fair to note that not all *Wh*-questions explain disapproval, but English abounds with examples of constructions based on *Wh*-questions that do express disapproval or at least some type of (usually negative) emotional reaction on the part of the speaker:

(1) Who do you think you are to talk to me like that?
(2) Where (on earth) have you put my glasses?

(4) a. Who has been messing up with the bulletin board?
b. Where have you been all night?
c. What is the child doing with the carving knife in the kitchen?
d. When was that order issued?

The semantic representations of these instances should be able to capture this non-propositional dimension of meaning, that is, to search for a type of representational mechanism that allows making explicit whatever is implicit. In connection with this, a lot of relevant work has been done within the Lexical Constructional Model (LCM), a comprehensive model of meaning construction that organizes constructional schemata around four levels of analysis: level-1 or argumental constructions, level-2 or implicative constructions, level-3 or illocutionary constructions and level-4 or discourse constructions (cf. Ruiz de Mendoza & Mairal 2008, Mairal & Ruiz de Mendoza 2009, Ruiz de Mendoza 2013), among others; see also Butler (2009, 2013) for an assessment of the LCM). As shown below, the LCM provides the analytical tools to deal with those aspects of meaning that go beyond grammar and have a long tradition in pragmatics and discourse studies.

In what follows, the primary aim of this chapter is to focus on how constructional schemata are actually dealt with within ARTEMIS. After a brief presentation of the computational architecture of ARTEMIS in Section 2, Section 3 contex-

---

(3) Why should JÓHN do that? (with stress prominence on "John")
(4) What is the child doing RÍGHT now? (with stress prominence on "right")
(5) When will she finally ARRÍVE? (with stress prominence of "arrive")
(6) Who's been messing with my laptop?
(7) What've you been doing (in the kitchen)?
(8) Who WÍLL then? (with added stress prominence on "will")
(9) What the heck are you talking about?
(10) Whenever is she going go learn?

These sentences make use of various linguistic resources to signal the speaker's emotional reaction:
a) Prosodic marking
b) Hedges like "ever", "the heck", "on earth"
c) Specialized constructional forms, like "What's X Doing Y?" and "Who's been V-ing Y?", "(non subject Wh-'s X been V-ing Y

Such marking points to level-2 or implicational meaning rather than argument-structure meaning, which corresponds to level 1. The presence of explicit linguistic marking (whether prosodic or grammatical) of the speaker's attitude points to a stable form-meaning association, i. e. to a constructional configuration, which goes beyond level 1.

tualizes the Grammaticon, the linguistic module that stores the inventory of constructional schemata in FunGramKB. Section 4 focuses on the representation and processing of both argument (Level-1 constructions) and idiomatic constructions (Level-2, 3 and 4 constructions), while Section 5 is concerned with the syntactic representation of this typology within the framework of the layered structure of the clause. Finally, Section 6 includes a few concluding remarks and future prospects.

2 ARTEMIS and FunGramKB: a preliminary discussion

It is not the aim of this section to spell out the exact details of the whole architectures of ARTEMIS and FunGramKB, but simply to draw your attention to the fact that these two NLP resources are intended to represent the semantics of an input text by using RRG. This is a major step that should not go unnoticed, since in the emergent field of cross-linguistic information retrieval most projects are based on probabilistic, context-free grammars and follow stochastic approaches. In turn, our proposal is one of the first systems which, given an input text, employs a robust knowledge base to generate a full-fledged CLS to be used in NLP applications requiring language comprehension capabilities. Figure 2 is a simplified illustration of the architecture of FunGramKB, the source from where the ARTEMIS parser extracts all the information for the automatic construction of a semantic representation of an input text.

FunGramKB comprises three major knowledge levels (i. e. lexical, grammatical and conceptual), consisting of several independent but interrelated modules:

- a. Lexical level:
- a.1. The Lexicon stores morphosyntactic and collocational information about lexical units. The FunGramKB lexical model is not a literal implementation of the RRG lexicon, although some of the major linguistic assumptions of RRG are still preserved.
- a.2. The Morphicon helps our system to handle cases of inflectional morphology.
- b. Grammatical level:

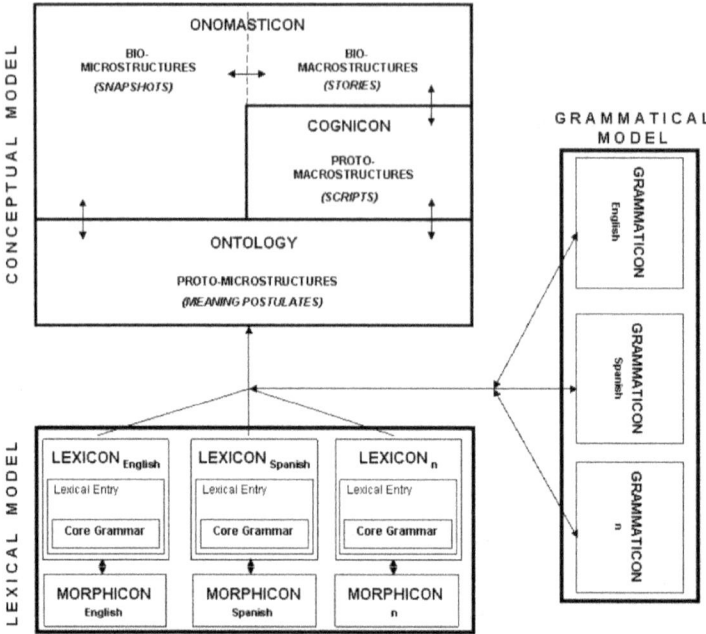

Figure 2: The FunGramKB architecture (reproduced from Periñán-Pascual and Mairal, 2012: 335).

b.1. The Grammaticon stores the constructional schemata which help RRG to construct the syntax-semantics linking algorithm. More particularly, the Grammaticon is composed of several Constructicon modules that are inspired in the four levels of the LCM, i. e. argumental, implicational, illocutionary and discursive.

c. Conceptual level:

c.1. The Ontology is presented as a hierarchical catalogue of the concepts that a person has in mind, so here is where semantic knowledge is stored in the form of meaning postulates. The Ontology consists of a general-purpose module (i. e. Core Ontology) and several domain-specific terminological modules (i. e. Satellite Ontologies).

c.2. The Cognicon stores procedural knowledge by means of scripts, i.e. schemata in which a sequence of stereotypical actions is organised on the basis of temporal continuity.

c.3. The Onomasticon stores information about instances of entities and events, such as Bill Gates or 9/11. This module stores two different types of schemata (i.e. snapshots and stories), since instances can be portrayed synchronically or diachronically.

In this part, we will just highlight those theoretical issues which are directly related to the central aim of this paper, that is, the Grammaticon and the computational treatment of constructional schemata. However, it is unavoidable to make at least a cursory reference to the Lexicon given the interaction between the two components.[10] In the FunGramKB Lexicon, each lexical entry includes the following information (cf. Mairal & Periñán-Pascual 2009):

- Basic: headword, index, and language.
- Morphosyntax: graphical variant, abbreviation, phrase constituents, category, number, gender, countability, degree, adjectival position, verb paradigm and constraints, and pronominalization.
- Core grammar: aktionsart, lexical template (variables, macrorole assignment and thematic frame mapping) and constructions.
- Miscellaneous: dialect, style, domain, example and translation.

In the case of verbal predicates, the most important lexical component is the core grammar, which contains those attributes whose values allow the system to build the basic CLS of verbs automatically. Figure 3 is a representation of these attributes for the predicate 'break'.

At this stage of the paper, what is noteworthy is the fact that a lexical entry contains pointers to the whole repertoire of constructions a given verb can occur in. In addition to the constructions derived from the Grammaticon, every verb in the Lexicon is provided with one and only one kernel Construction, which is built on the basis of the knowledge in the core grammar, primarily the aktionsart and the lexical template (i.e. variables, thematic frame mapping and macrorole

---

[10] In close connection with this statement, we do think that both projectionist and constructivist approaches are correct since both constructions and lexical entries are essential for constructing the propositional dimension of meaning. As a matter of fact, we postulate a complementary relationship between the two since it is often the case that it is impossible to account for the semantic representation of an input text without recurring to the Grammaticon and the information contained therein.

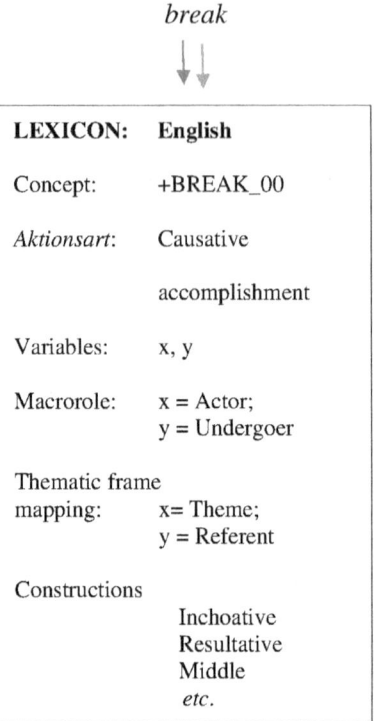

Figure 3: Simplified representation of 'break'.

assignment). Depending on the number of variables in the lexical template, the verb will typically occur in a Kernel-1, Kernel-2 or Kernel-3 Construction. For instance, the system can directly derive the Kernel-2 Construction from the core grammar of *break*:

(5) [John broke the window]$_{Kernel-2}$

So, every lexical entry in the Lexicon has one basic kernel structure together with pointers to the rest of constructions, which will be stored in the Grammaticon. The Grammaticon, which is directly linked to the Lexicon in terms of what has been termed the lexical-grammatical interface, stores the inventory of constructional schemata to which words in the Lexicon are linked. As a matter of fact, a given construction can be licensed in a particular language if and only if there is at least one entry in the Lexicon which contains a pointer to that construction. In the case of *break*, this predicate can occur with a resultative construction since there is a pointer in the Lexicon that shows this connection:

(6) [[John broke the window]$_{\text{Kernel-2}}$ into pieces]$_{\text{Transitive-Resultative}}$

The FunGramKB Grammaticon, unlike the RRG constructional schemata, stores both argumental and non-argumental (or idiomatic) constructional schemata, although it is fair to say that the computational implementation of idiomatic constructions is still preliminary.

In sum, the linguistic level in FunGramKB includes a Lexicon, which is connected to the Ontology, and a Grammaticon. From this architecture, Periñán-Pascual (2013b) and Periñán-Pascual & Arcas (2014) began to elaborate ARTEMIS, where the Ontology, the Lexicon and the Grammaticon are the sources of information for the elaboration of the grammar rules through the FunGramKB Grammar Development Environment. Here is a general representation of the architecture of ARTEMIS:

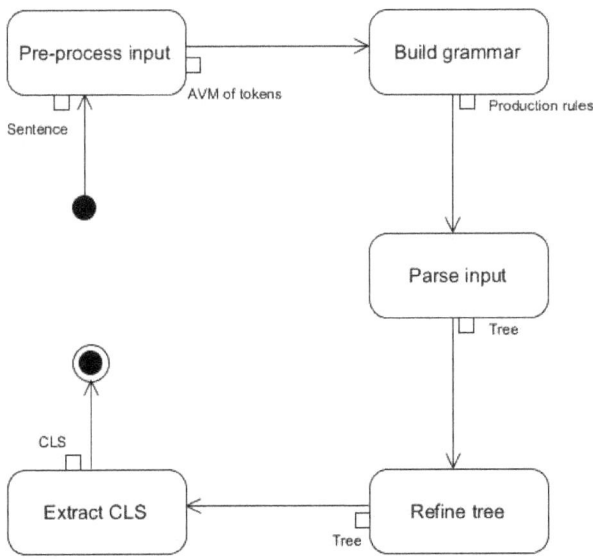

Figure 4: The architecture of ARTEMIS (Periñán-Pascual & Arcas, 2014).

For the purposes of this paper, we focus on the 'Build grammar' task, which implies three types of feature-based production rules, i. e. lexical, constructional and syntactic. These rules automatically generate a parse tree, from which a fully-specified semantic representation is constructed, that is, the CLS acting as a sort of interlingua. While syntactic rules are concerned with the construction of the layered structure of the clause (LSC), constructional and lexical rules specify the properties of constructional schemata and lexical entries respectively. Unlike syntactic rules, both constructional and lexical rules are generated automatically, so we can affirm that a significant amount of grammar rules is dynamically built through ARTEMIS. More particularly, constructional rules are generated with the aid of the Lexicon and the Grammaticon (i. e. the core grammar of the verb together with all its constructional schemata), and lexical rules mainly require the Lexicon and the Ontology.

Continuing with the Grammar Builder module, this is inspired in the paradigm of constraint-based grammars, or also called unification grammars. Each grammatical unit is described in terms of an attribute value matrix (AVM), which includes a number of features that can be eventually merged by means of unification. Hence, phrase structure rules are not longer used but rather parsing will be guided by a number of satisfaction constraints, which are responsible for determining structural preference and semantic plausibility. Both lexical entries and constructional schemata are described in terms of AVMs, each including a number of descriptors and constraints (cf. below). Figure 5 is an example of the representation of the lexical entry for the predicate 'pound'.

Rather than going into the formal expression of these rules — see Periñán-Pascual & Arcas (2014) for a detailed description, we would like to concentrate on the Grammaticon and the representation of constructional schemata, both argumental and idiomatic, which provide the material for the automatic generation of constructional rules. Additionally, we should comment on how the RRG LSC is actually enhanced.

3 The FunGramKB Grammaticon

The FunGramKB Grammaticon stores an inventory of constructional schemata, both argumental and non-argumental, which are language specific. We maintain that constructional schemata play a fundamental role in propositional meaning constructions, since it is very often the case that it is impossible to account for the semantic structure of an input text by looking only at its argument structure

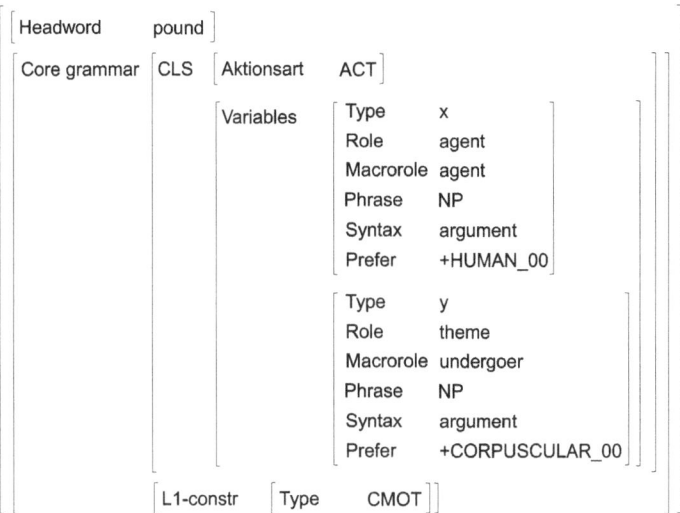

Figure 5: AVM of the lexical entry for the predicate *pound*.

in the Lexicon. This overrides any further debate on whether a theory should be projectionist or constructivist since we maintain that both perspectives are correct (cf. Mairal & Gonzálvez 2010, Periñán-Pascual 2013b, and footnote 10 above). The Lexicon and the Grammaticon are fully interconnected in such a way that every lexical entry in the Lexicon should have pointers to all those constructions in which this predicate participates. So, we vindicate the explanatory potential of both lexical entries and constructions.

Constructional schemata within ARTEMIS are conceived as machine-tractable representations of constructions. It is important to emphasize the fact that constructional schemata have a semantic load, i.e. they are meaning-bearing devices, regardless of whether their semantics is coded in the CLS or in the COREL scheme[11]. Unlike RRG, and we would venture to claim most construction-based models, FunGramKB, following work within the LCM, works with a four-level typology of schemata, thus aspiring to provide an explanatory scheme for both the propositional and the non-propositional dimension of meaning. Following the work of Ruiz de Mendoza & Mairal (2008) and Mairal & Ruiz de Mendoza

---

[11] As discussed later in sections 4.1. and 4.2., each constructional schema consists of two types of descriptors, a CLS, a syntactically-oriented notational formalism which serves to build a bridge between the linguistic realization of an input text and the conceptual realm, and the COREL scheme, which is a language-independent conceptual representation of the semantics of the text.

(2009), here is a brief summary of the description of the four levels of analysis, which are thought to account for the way meaning constructions processes take place at all descriptive levels, including those meaning dimensions that have a long tradition in pragmatics and discourse:

- Level-1, or argumental level, is concerned with the type of argument constructions distinguished in standard constructional grammar approaches (e.g. Goldberg 1995, 2006), although ARTEMIS differs substantially from these approaches. For example, the ditransitive, the resultative or the caused motion construction belong to this level-1 Constructicon.
- Level-2, or implicational level, accounts for the way meaning can be obtained on the basis of a combination of degrees of pragmatically guided and linguistically guided situation-based low-level inferencing. The former has been termed implicature while the latter - the linguistically guided inferencing - has been called presupposition[12]. Recall the instances above: the What is X doing Y construction (e.g. *What is the child doing in the kitchen?*, cf. Kay & Fillmore 1999), which suggests that the situation the speaker is asking about is wrong; Don't you X me!, (e.g. *Don't you honey me!*), which is used to indicate annoyance at the addressee unawareness that (s)he has done something wrong; Who's Been VP Y? (e.g. *Who's been messing up the*

---

[12] The best way to understand presuppositions is to think of them as covert assertions that naturally follow from the constructional properties of an utterance. For example, if someone says "I'm sorry that your cat died", we are certain that the speaker thinks that the hearer's cat has died on the basis of the constructional properties of "Be Sorry That X". Some scholars have argued that "be sorry" is a factive predicate, but we should bear in mind that there are uses of "(be) sorry" that do not convey any clear presupposition that something is or has been the case:

- She will never be sorry about anything.
- Better safe than sorry.
- How could I be sorry?

The predicate "(be) sorry" has to be part of the right constructional configuration to become a factive predicate:

- I am sorry that you didn't pass your exam [the speaker thinks the hearer didn't pass the exam]
- I am sorry to be so harsh [the speaker thinks he's being harsh]
- She is sorry about the incident [the speaker thinks that there was an incident]
- You will be sorry that you retire [the speaker thinks the hearer is going to retire]

These examples suggest that "(be) sorry" develops factive predicate properties if it has a specific (rather than a generic) complement, which is a constructional issue.

bulletin board?) which carries the meaning implication that someone has done something that irritates and bothers the speaker. [13]
- Level-3, or illocutionary level, deals with the inferential and constructional mechanisms involved in the derivation of speech act meaning. The semantic component is made up of high-level situational cognitive models usually corresponding to traditional speech act categories (e. g. requesting, offering or apologizing) (cf. Ruiz de Mendoza & Baicchi 2007). Consider the following examples: You shall have X (e. g. *You shall have a bicycle*), which is used to make promises; Would you mind if I X? (e. g. *Would you mind if I sat next to you?*), which is used to ask for permission; I won't X (e. g. *I won't give up*), which involves a refusal.
- Level-4, or discourse level which deals with cohesion and coherence phenomena from the point of view of the activity of discourse constructions based on high-level non-situational cognitive models like reason-result, cause-effect, condition-consequence. For example, X let alone Y (Fillmore, Kay & O'Connor 1988) (e. g. *I won't eat that garbage, let alone pay for it*), which is used to refer to two unlikely states of affairs where the second one is less likely to be the case than the first; Just because X doesn't mean Y: *Just because we don't talk doesn't mean I don't think about you*) (cf. Bender & Kathol 2001), which sets up an evidence conclusion relationship according to which Y does not necessarily follow from X[14].

While Level-1 deals with the propositional dimension of meaning, levels 2, 3 and 4 provide the analytical tools to account for the non-propositional dimension of meaning[15]. In relation to the format, both argumental and idiomatic constructions are expressed in terms of AVMs, which are used to express the descriptors

---

[13] Then, presupposition arises from level 1. Implicature from level 2. Implicature is an inferred assumption that follows from the application of a reasoning schema of the premise-conclusion kind and it is context-dependent. Presupposition is a context-independent covert assumption that is derived from the properties of a construction as a necessary implication of what is said. For this reason, it remains constant under negation ("I [don't] regret stepping on your toe" presupposes that the speaker thinks that he stepped on the hearer's toe), although it is cancellable by making explicit further information: "I don't regret stepping on your toe because I didn't step on your toe".

[14] All the examples plus the accompanying comments have been taken from Mairal & Ruiz de Mendoza (2009) and Ruiz de Mendoza (2013).

[15] Following Ruiz de Mendoza (2013), idiomatic constructions in the LCM are classified according to the following two parameters: (i) their degree of fixity, i. e. whether they are fully fixed or they contain some variable elements; (ii) their meaning function, which is essential to determine the level of description that they belong to, that is, whether they belong to levels 2, 3 or 4.

and their corresponding constraints, where the latter license compositionality with other constructs or constructions by means of unification.

4 The representation of constructional schemata

While the initial phase of the FunGramKB Grammaticon has been devoted to the analysis and representation of argument constructions, in the last few months the second phase of the project has focused on the representation of idiomatic constructions (Levels 2, 3 and 4). This has been indeed a major challenge given the complexity of providing a machine tractable framework to codify the pervasive nature of non-propositional meaning. While Section 4.1 summarizes previous work on argument constructional schemata, Sections 4.2 and 5 offer a first approximation to the inventory of idiomatic constructions.

4.1 Argument (Level-1) constructional schemata

Argument constructions have been the first focus of the FunGramKB Grammaticon. As a matter of fact, Periñán-Pascual (2013b) and Periñán-Pascual & Arcas (2014) evaluate ARTEMIS within the framework of various constructional schemata, i.e. the caused motion and the resultative. Moreover, Van Valin & Mairal (in press) compare the RRG formalism and the FunGramKB formalism and contend that both are compatible to the extent that FunGramKB schemata can enrich the insufficient semantic description of RRG schemata. All in all, ARTEMIS, which retrieves information from the Grammaticon to generate the construction rules that form part of the Grammatical Development Environment, seems to function fairly well within a conceptual framework like that provided in FunGramKB.

Summarizing a bit, argument constructions, like lexical entries in the Lexicon, are represented in FunGramKB by means of AVMs. Let us use the format of the intransitive resultative construction for illustration purposes. The FunGramKB Grammaticon provides the interface shown in Figure 6. This interface is divided into two blocks of information:

a) The CLS which includes the following items:

    a. Type of aktionsart: accomplishment.
    b. Number and type of variables: y and w.

Representing Constructional Schemata in the FunGramKB Grammaticon

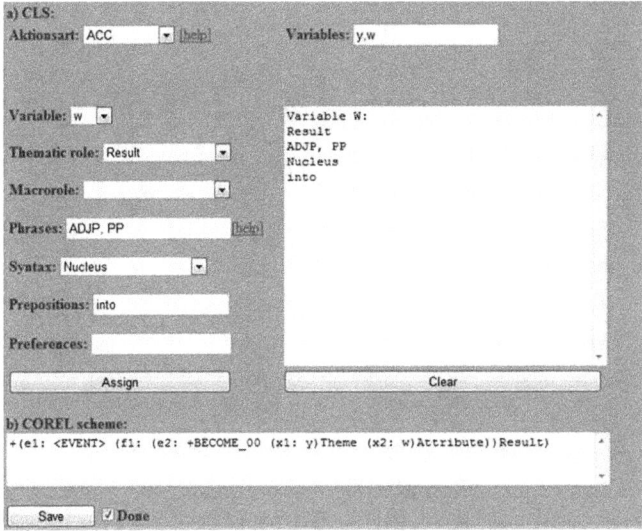

Figure 6: Interface of the English intransitive resultative construction.

c. For each new variable, that is, for that variable that is contributed by the construction, the following information should also be provided:

- Thematic role.
- Macrorole status, if any.
- Phrases: morphosyntactic realization.
- Syntax: the status of this new constituent in the LSC, i. e. argument or a nucleus.
- Preposition, if any.
- Selectional preferences, if any.

b) The COREL scheme includes a language-independent semantic description: in this case, there is an event and as a result the *y* participant comes to get a new state.

Note that in the representation in Figure 6, the *y* variable is inherited from the information in the Lexicon, so there is no need to specify this information again. In contrast, the *w* is the argument that is contributed by the resultative construction. Therefore, the different properties of this variable are spelled out. The following AVM includes the information of the FunGramKB editor:

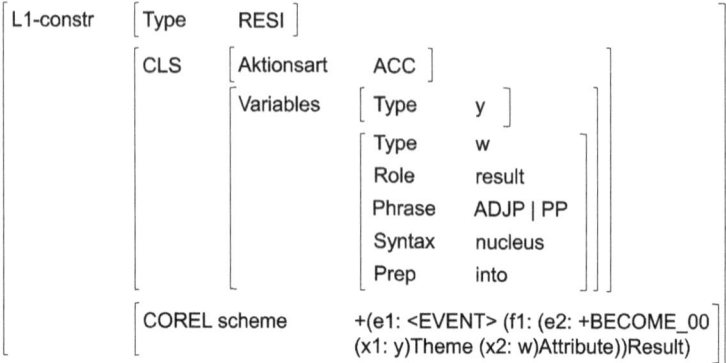

Figure 7: AVM of the English intransitive resultative construction.

From this information FunGramKB is able to automatically generate the following CLS as in (7c) for an input text such as (7a):

(7) a. The milk froze black in the basement.
   b. <_IF DEC <_TNS PAST < be-in' (basement, [[do' (milk, [freeze' (milk)])] CAUSE [BECOME **black'** (milk)])>>>
   c. (<_IF DECL <_Tense past <_CONSTR-L1 RESI <_CONSTR-L1 INCH <_AKT ACC [+FREEZE_00 (+MILK_00-Referent, +BLACK_00-Result)] (+BASEMENT_00-Location) >>>>>

What is noteworthy is the fact that two of the operators in (7c), AKT and Constr-L1, are not part of the RRG inventory. Why are they used? What is the motivation behind this proposal? Following Periñán-Pascual (2013a: 219):

> (...) the RRG decompositional system turns out to be excessively noisy from a computational view, since the semantic burden of the sentence is not actually carried by the CLS but by its corresponding COREL scheme.

The RRG logical structure in (7b) includes a number of operators, i. e. CAUSE and BECOME, which can be ignored without any loss of information providing that we explicitly state the aktionsart together with the argument pattern headed by the event. Therefore, the CLS in (7c) can be deprived of the RRG skeleton, resulting in a full-fledged formalism which can be effectively employed by computer applications. Moreover, a constructional operator is incorporated (i. e. CONSTR-

L1),[16] which plays a prominent role in the syntax-semantics linkage, as will be discussed in Section 5.

4.2 Idiomatic constructions: the non-propositional dimension of meaning

Idiomatic constructions are a cover term that includes those constructions ranging from implicational to discourse constructions. Unlike argument constructions (i.e. Level-1), idiomatic constructions consist of fixed and variable elements that can be parametrized in different degrees. Let us consider the following schemata:

Level-2: What is X doing Y?
Double Be
Level-3: I won't X
I shall X
I wonder if you could X
Level-4: Just because X doesn't mean Y
X on condition that Y
(*You can have the day off tomorrow* on condition that *you work on Saturday*)

In the case of idiomatic constructions, we shall distinguish two types of units: (i) fixed (or non-parametrizable) elements and (ii) parametrizable (or variable) elements. In our application of this distinction to Fillmore and Kay's treatment of *What's X Doing Y?*, the lexical unit *doing* would be distinguished as a non-parametrizable element, while the X and Y elements are highly parametrizable, since they admit a large amount of variability. A similar example is the so-called *Double Be* (or *copula doubling*) construction (e.g. *The thing is, is that he didn't tell the truth*). McConwell (1988), Tuggy (1996), and Massam (1999) have studied the details of this construction, which serves to call the hearer's attention to a given situation while asserting its truthfulness or relevance. It usually takes the configuration *X is, is Y*, where X, which is marked by a high tone, is the topic and Y, which takes a low tone, is the focus. While Y is a relatively unconstrained element (it can be realized by any that-clause), there is a fairly limited range of

---

[16] Indeed, every argumental construction is embodied in a constructional operator whose scope is the core.

options for X, normally *the thing, the problem, the question, what I mean*, and *what happens*. The same applies to the level-3 constructions, where the *I won't* element is fixed while the X is subject to parametrization. Finally, discourse constructions are subject to the same pattern: in the case of X on condition that Y, X and Y can represent any clause while the element – *on condition that* – is fixed (see Ruiz de Mendoza & Mairal 2008 for an extensive discussion of fixed and variable elements in the different types of constructions).

Unlike argument constructions, idiomatic constructions only serve to embed some constructional operator into the CLS; in other words, they do not alter the CLS of the text but only extend their COREL scheme. As shown in the following interfaces, only the COREL scheme is relevant, while the box containing the different realizations serves for ARTEMIS to identify through pattern matching the type of constructional type. Here is the interface of the illocutionary construction *Requesting*, an example of Level-3:

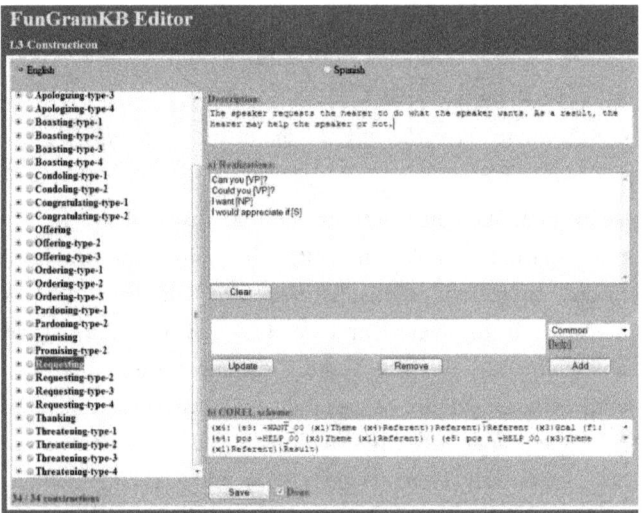

Figure 8: Interface of the Level-3 construction *Requesting*.

Unlike argument (or Level-1) constructions, Level-2, Level-3 and Level-4 constructions do not include a CLS. Only the possible realizations are indicated in terms of fixed and variable elements, usually signaled by means of X, Y and Z. These variables will be filled in by items in the Lexicon or by a Level-1 construction (cf. below). Idiomatic constructions add a non-propositional dimension of meaning, something which is represented in terms of a COREL scheme, that is, a semantic description of this dimension of meaning:

(8) +(e1: +REQUEST_01 (x1: <SPEAKER>)Theme (x2: (e2: +DO_00 (x3: <HEARER>)Theme (x4: (e3: +WANT_00 (x1)Theme (x4)Referent)) Referent)) Referent (x3)Goal (f1: (e4: pos +HELP_00 (x3)Theme (x1)Referent) | (e5: pos n +HELP_00 (x3)Theme (x1)Referent))Result)

The speaker requests the hearer to do what the speaker wants. As a result, the hearer may help the speaker or not.

The different realizations that are included in the box 'Realizations' carry this semantic load written in COREL (see footnote 5), which can be translated in natural language as follows: a speaker says something to a hearer with the purpose that the hearer gives something to the speaker because the speaker needs whatever is requested. A similar example of a Level-3 construction is that which includes those constructions which express the illocutionary act of 'promising'. As noted in Figure 9, the format will be the same: first, the different possible realizations are included and second a semantic description in terms of COREL is provided. In this case, the speaker says something (x2) to a hearer and whatever the speaker says refers to something that the speaker will do in the future.

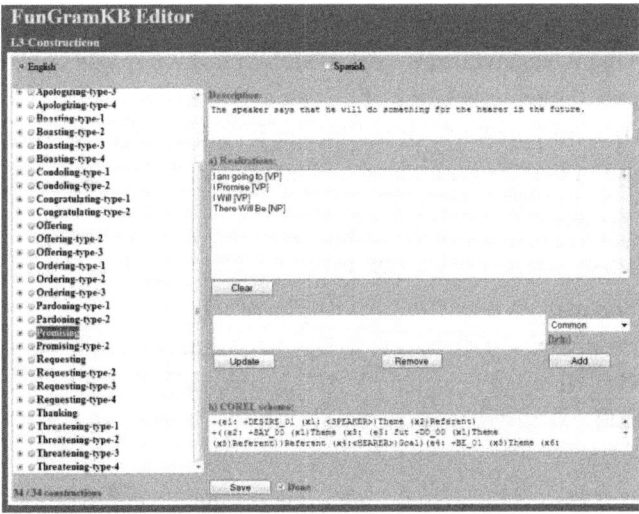

Figure 9: Interface of the Level-3 construction *Promising*.

Finally, we shall like to include the analysis of the *What is X doing Y construction?* given that this is a good example to show that it is possible to arrive at a fine-grained semantic analysis via the COREL scheme. Here are a few examples:

(9) a. What's the child doing?
   b. What's the child doing in the kitchen?
   c. What's the child doing in the kitchen with the carving knife?

As discussed in Mairal and Ruiz de Mendoza (2009) and noted above, this construction and its variants (e. g. *Who's –ing X?*) seem to convey the idea that there is something wrong about the situation described; this value readily cues for a complaint reading. However, what is noteworthy at this state is the fact that the variable element Y is subject to different degrees of elaboration, that is, this can range from a simple prepositional phrase (e. g. *in the kitchen* as in 9a) to two prepositional phrases (9b) or even more (e. g. *what is the child doing in the kitchen with a carving knife hitting the new tiles on the wall?*). Interestingly enough, this arrangement is not accidental but semantically motivated by the fact that the greater the elaboration of the Y element, the greater the idea that something is wrong, and consequently, the complaint interpretation becomes greater. It seems that the speaker, in being able to supply so much information about the propositional content, already knows the answer to his/her question. Undoubtedly, this implicated meaning seems to be crucial for a comprehensive semantic representation of this input text and therefore any NLP application should be sensitive to it. If we compare the representation of this input text in terms of a standard logical structure (10b), this proves itself insufficient to capture this implicated meaning, while this is not the case with the representation in (10c):

(10) a. What's Tom doing in the kitchen with the carving knife?
   b. <IF INT <TNS PRES <ASP PROGR <be-in' (kitchen, [[do' (Tom, [do' (Tom, what) ∧ **use'** (Tom, carving knife])]]
   c. +(e1: pro pres +DO_00 (x1: %TOM_00) Theme (x2: ?) Referent (f1: +KITCHEN_00) Location (f2: $CARVING_KNIFE_00) Instrument) +(e2: +FEEL_00 (x1: e1) Agent (x2: <SPEAKER>) Theme (x3: +ANGRY_00) Attribute)
   The speaker wants to know what Tom is doing in the kitchen with the carving knife; Tom's action makes the speaker feel angry as well.

When the utterance matches the syntactic pattern *What is NP doing Y?* or any of its related variants, then the FunGramKB Grammaticon will extend the COREL schema, as can be seen in (10c), since this Level-2 *Call for Redressive Action* construction contributes with the following meaning:

(11) +(e1: +FEEL_00 (x1: <EVENT>) Agent (x2: <SPEAKER>) Theme (x3: +ANGRY_00)Attribute)
The event makes the speaker feel angry.

Here, the conceptual metavariable <SPEAKER> should be replaced by an instance from the Onomasticon representing the speaker involved in the utterance, e. g. %TOM_00, %MARY_00, etc., and the metavariable <EVENT> stands for the eventive causer that makes the speaker feel angry about this state of affairs.

5 Revisiting the parser

At this stage, we have seen that a CLS is sensitive to the four-level distinctions in the Grammaticon. As a matter of fact, as discussed in Section 4.1, a CLS includes two new operators, AKT and CONSTR-L1. Let us retake the CLS for the input text *the milk froze black in the basement*:

(12) ($<_{IF}$ DECL $<_{Tense}$ past $<_{CONSTR-L1}$ RESI $<_{CONSTR-L1}$ INCH $<_{AKT}$ ACC [+FREEZE_00 (+MILK_00-Referent, +BLACK_00-Result)] (+BASEMENT_00-Location) $>>>>>$

In this case, the lexical entry for *freeze* in the Lexicon includes a structure with two arguments that designate a causative accomplishment (e. g. *Peter froze the milk*), i. e. a Kernel-2 structure[17]. However, this predicate now occurs in the context of an inchoative construction and a resultative construction. So, it seems as if these two constructions are modeling the output lexical entry for *freeze*. In other words, ARTEMIS will have to go to the Grammaticon and retrieve that informa-

---

[17] As noted in Periñán-Pascual & Arcas (2014), kernel constructions are the only type of constructions which are not formalised in the Grammaticon, but they are modeled within the lexical entry of the verb: Kernel-1, Kernel-2 and Kernel-3 are distinguished depending on the number of arguments of the verb in the Lexicon. On the contrary, the L1-constructions, e. g. the inchoative and the resultative, come from the Grammaticon. Moreover, note as a methodological decision we understand that the causative use is regarded as basic although we are aware that this should be backed up with some empirical data, something which is out of the scope of this paper.

tion which is needed to generate the correct representation. This means that the AVM for the inchoative construction will unify with the lexical entry, the output of which will then unify with the AVM for the resultative construction[18]. Hence, ARTEMIS needs a label to identify each of these constructs that are functional in the semantic representation of an input text. Moreover, we could affirm that the very same notion of constructional meaning seems to be a universal distinction regardless of the fact that the constructional inventory is language specific. If this is so, and in line with Van Valin's (2005: 3) corollary that *"a theory of clause structure should capture all of the universal features of clauses"*, the construction as a universal category should be part of the LSC. Therefore, the clause is configured now as one or more argumental constructions (L1-CONSTRUCTION) which are recursively arranged:

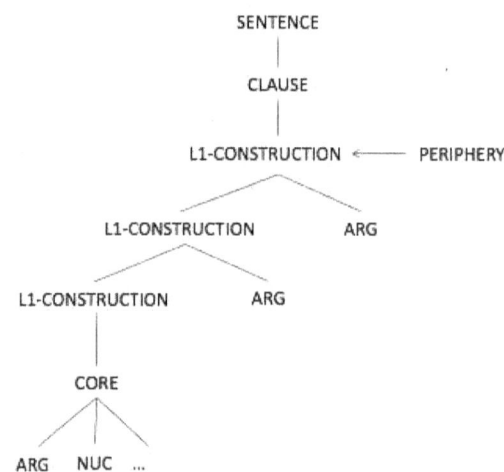

Figure 10: A new look at the LSC (Periñán-Pascual, 2013b).

The innermost construction introduces the core, which can be modeled by other L1-constructions adding a new argument. Unlike idiomatic constructions, Level-1 constructions can occur more than once within the same clause. For example, the inchoative, the resultative and the caused motion constructions are present in the following instance:

---

[18] This process of unification is similar to that of coercion as stated in most construction grammar approaches (cf. Michaelis 2003): constructional meaning (i.e. a constructional AVM) always wins over lexical meaning (i.e. a lexical AVM).

Representing Constructional Schemata in the FunGramKB Grammaticon

(13) a. John kicked the ball flat out of the stadium.
b. [[[John kicked the ball]$_{Kernel-2}$ flat]$_{Transitive-Resultative}$ out of the stadium]$_{Caused-Motion}$

So, the lexical entry for *kick* is a Kernel-2 structure, which is further modeled by the presence of two argument (Level-1) constructions that are retrieved from the Grammaticon.

However, ARTEMIS is also sensitive to non-propositional meaning as encoded in Level-2, Level-3 and Level-4 constructional schemata. In much the same way as was the case for Level-1 argument constructions, the LSC also contains these new distinctions. Recall that in the case of idiomatic constructions, each constructional node (i. e. L2, L3 and L4) consists of a fixed and a variable element, which is subject to parametrization: the fixed element will be represented under a node provisionally termed CLM (Constructional Level Marker), while the variable elements will be broken down into the predicate and its potential arguments under the clause node. Here is the enhanced representation of the LSC:

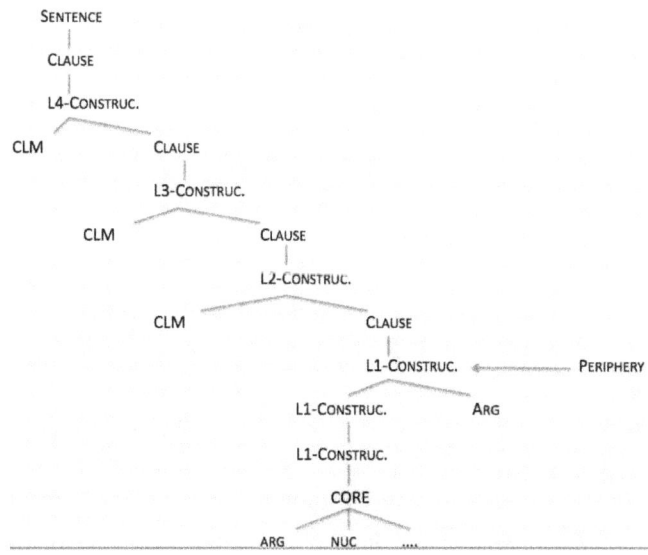

Figure 11: Enhanced model of LSC (refined tree).

This new format of the LSC identifies that constructional schema which is most salient, most prominent, whether be these a Level-2, Level-3 or Level-4. Once identified, the process will go to Level-1 and/or to the Lexicon to saturate those elements which are not fixed. For example, let us consider the following instances, whose LSC representations are presented in Figures 12 and 13:

(14) a. I wonder if you could get a copy:
   [Level-3 Constructicon → Lexicon]
   b. I won't eat that garbage let alone pay for it:
   [Level-4 Constructicon → Level-3 Constructicon → Lexicon]

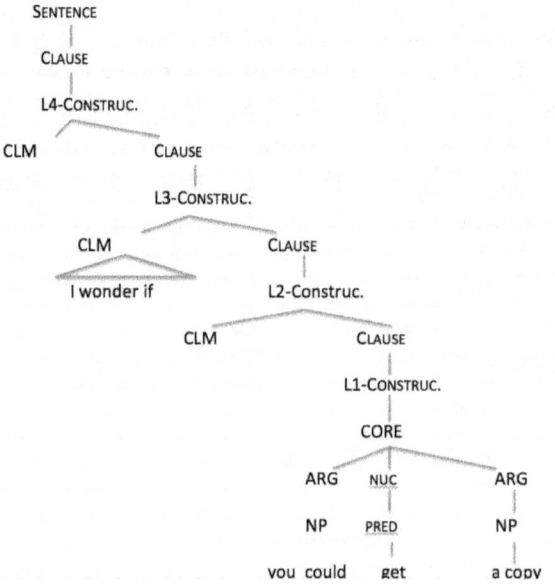

Figure 12: Enhanced LSC of 'I wonder if you could get a copy'.

In (14a), ARTEMIS identifies, through pattern matching, an instance of a Level-3 constructional schema (i. e. *I wonder if you could X*), from which the engine will employ information from the Lexicon to saturate the rest of the elements. In (14b), ARTEMIS, using the same pattern matching technique, will identify an instance of a Level-4 construction (i. e. *X let alone Y*), from which the processor will go to each of the two clauses; in the first case, *I won't eat that garbage*, ARTEMIS will find the realization *I won't X* in the Level-3 Grammaticon, while the remaining part will be saturated in the Lexicon.

Representing Constructional Schemata in the FunGramKB Grammaticon

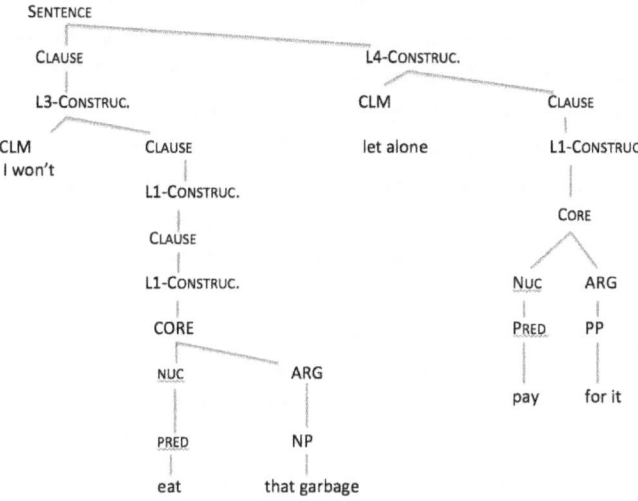

Figure 13: Enhanced LSC of 'I won't eat that garbage let alone pay for it'.

This type of processing imposes a number of restrictions:

a) Idiomatic constructions (Level-2, Level-3 and Level-4) have their own unique features which are not shared by other level constructions: a given lexical item cannot be shared by other idiomatic constructions in the same sentence. For example, a lexical item cannot activate both a Level-2 construction and a Level-3 construction in the same sentence.
b) Every sentence must have at least an argumental construction, that is, ARTEMIS will always visit Level-1. In other words, there must be at least one instantiation of a Level-1 construction.
c) There can be only one instantiation of the same non-propositional constructional level, i.e. if there is a level-2 instantiation, there cannot be another instantiation of the same level. The same applied to Levels 3 and 4. However, as noted above, this is not the case with Level-1, where more than one instantiation of different argumental constructions can occur within the same text.

Finally, let us consider the following instance and its representation within the framework of the new format of the LSC:

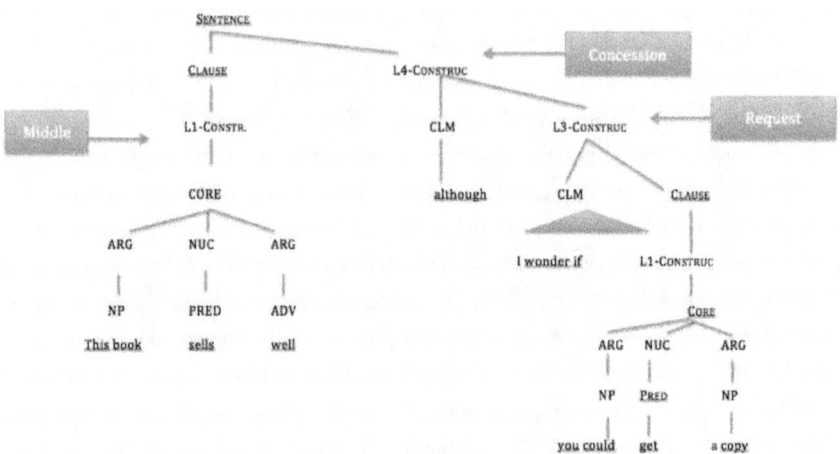

Figure 14: Enhanced LSC of 'This book sells well although I wonder if you could get a copy'.

Firstly, ARTEMIS identifies that this is an instance of a Level-4 construction, given that there is a realization with the format *X although Y*. From there, the processor analyzes each of the two clauses: in the first case, there are no idiomatic constructions but just the presence of a Level-1 construction, i. e. the middle. This is part of the Level-1 Grammaticon and thus it is saturated there with the help of the Lexicon. As for the second clause, the processor finds an exact match with the Level-3 constructional schema *I wonder if you could X*, which is a realization of the illocutionary construction Requesting. The fixed element goes under the node CLM, while the rest is saturated in the Lexicon as a kernel structure. This is an incomplete representation since nodes in the parse tree are represented by means of feature structures and not purely syntactic features.

6 Conclusions

This paper is concerned with the representation of constructional schemata within the framework of ARTEMIS, one of the first systems which employs a robust knowledge base (FunGramKB) to generate a full-fledged semantic representation of an input text. We show that any computer application designed with the aim of understanding the meaning of a text cannot be silent about the non-proposional dimension of meaning, a facet RRG does not include as part of the theory. In this regard, this paper discusses the way both argument and idiomatic constructions are formalized and represented within the Grammar Development Environment in ARTEMIS. The research done in the LCM is used for the description and identification of idiomatic constructions, L2, L3 and L4 constructions. Both lexical entries and constructional schemata are represented in terms of AVMs, describing features which can be merged through the unification operation, the output of which is a CLS. Moreover, we discuss the repercussions of these four-level constructional schemata in the parser, that is, in the LSC. A constructional node marking the different constructional levels is part of the enhanced LSC. Unlike argument constructions, idiomatic constructions consist of a fixed element (CLM) and a variable element. Finally, a preliminary discussion is offered in terms of how the parser actually functions. This is an issue, which is related to the psychological adequacy of the model, an aspect that needs further work in the future.

References

Bender, E. & A. Kathol. 2001. Constructional effects of just because ... doesn't mean ... . In *BLS* 27: 13–25. Berkeley: University of California.

Butler, Ch. S. 2009. The lexical constructional model: genesis, strengths and challenges. In Ch. S. Butler & J. M. Arista (eds.), *Deconstructing constructions*, 117–151. Amsterdam: John Benjamins.

Butler, Ch. S. 2013. Constructions in the lexical constructional model. In B. Nolan & E. Diedrichsen (eds.), *Linking constructions into functional linguistics: The role of constructions in grammar*, 271–294. Amsterdam: John Benjamins.

Diedrichsen, E. 2011. The theoretical importance of constructional schemas in RRG. In W. Nakamura (ed.), *New perspectives in role and reference grammar*, 168–197. Newcastle upon Tyne: Cambridge Scholars Publishing.

Fillmore, Ch. J., P. Kay & M. C. O'Connor. 1988. Regularity and idiomaticity in grammatical constructions: The case of let alone. *Language* 64: 501–538.

Goldberg, A. E. 1995. *A construction grammar approach to argument structure.* Chicago: University of Chicago Press.

Goldberg, A. E. 2006. *Constructions at work: The nature of generalization in language.* New York: Oxford University Press.

Kay, P. & Ch. J. Fillmore. 1999. Grammatical constructions and linguistic generalizations: The 'What's X doing Y' construction. *Language* 75, 1–33.

Mairal, R. 2012. La arquitectura de una base de conocimiento léxico conceptual: implicaciones lingüísticas. In M. Giammatteo, L. Ferrari & H. Albano (eds.), *Léxico y Sintaxis. Volumen temático de la serie editada po la Sociedad Argentina de Lingüística*, 183–210. Editorial FFyL, UNCuyo: Mendoza.

Mairal, R. & F. Gonzálvez. 2010. Verbos y construcciones en el espacio cognitivo-funcional del siglo XXI. In J. F. Val Álvaro & M. C. Horno Chéliz (eds.), *La gramática del sentido: Léxico y sintaxis en la encrucijada*, 123–152. Zaragoza: Prensas Universitarias de Zaragoza.

Mairal, R. & C. Periñán-Pascual. 2009. The anatomy of the lexicon component within the framework of a conceptual knowledge base. *Revista Española de Lingüística Aplicada* 22: 217–244.

Mairal, R., C. Periñán-Pascual & M. B. Pérez Cabello de Alba. 2012. La representación léxica. Hacia un enfoque ontológico. In R. Mairal, L. Guerrero & C. González (eds.), *El funcionalismo en la teoría lingüística. La Gramática del Papel y la Referencia. Introducción, avances y aplicaciones*, 85–102. Madrid: Akal.

Mairal, R. & J. F. Ruiz de Mendoza. 2009. Levels of description and explanation in meaning construction. In Ch. S. Butler & J. Martín Arista (eds.), *Deconstructing constructions*, 153–198. Amsterdam: John Benjamins.

Massam, D. 1999. Thing is constructions: The thing is, is what's the right analysis? *English Language and Linguistics* 3: 335–352.

McConvell, P. 1988. To be or double be: Current change in the English copula. *Australian Journal of Linguistics* 8: 287–305.

Michaelis, L. A. 2003. Word meaning, sentence meaning, and syntactic meaning. In H. Cuykens, R. Dirven & J. R. Taylor (eds.), *Cognitive approaches to lexical semantics*, 93–122. Berlin-New York: Mouton de Gruyter.

Nolan, B. 2011. Meaning construction and grammatical inflection in the layered structure of the Irish word: An RRG account of morphological constructions. In W. Nakamura (ed.), *New perspectives in role and reference grammar*, 64–101. Newcastle upon Tyne: Cambridge Scholars Publishing.

Periñán-Pascual, C. 2012. The situated common-sense knowledge in FunGramKB. *Review of Cognitive Linguistics* 10 (1): 184–214.

Periñán-Pascual, C. 2013a. A knowledge-engineering approach to the cognitive categorization of lexical meaning. *VIAL: Vigo International Journal of Applied Linguistics* 10: 85–104.

References

Periñán-Pascual, C. 2013b. Towards a model of constructional meaning for natural language understanding. In B. Nolan & E. Diedrichsen (eds.), *Linking constructions into functional linguistics: The role of constructions in a functional grammar*, 205–230. Amsterdam: John Benjamins.

Periñán-Pascual, C. & F. Arcas. 2004. Meaning postulates in a lexico-conceptual knowledge base. In *15th International Workshop on Databases and Expert Systems Applications*, 38–42. Los Alamitos: IEEE.

Periñán-Pascual, C. & F. Arcas. 2007. Cognitive modules of an NLP knowledge base for language understanding. *Procesamiento del Lenguaje Natural* 39: 197–204.

Periñán-Pascual, C. & F. Arcas. 2010. Ontological commitments in FunGramKB. *Procesamiento del Lenguaje Natural* 44: 27–34.

Periñán-Pascual, C. & F. Arcas. 2014. The implementation of the FunGramKB CLS Constructor in ARTEMIS. In B. Nolan & C. Periñán-Pascual (eds.), *Language processing and grammars: The role of functionally oriented computational models*, 165–196. Amsterdam: John Benjamins.

Periñán-Pascual, C. & R. Mairal. 2009. Bringing role and reference grammar to natural language understanding. *Procesamiento del Lenguaje Natural* 43: 265–273.

Periñán-Pascual, C. & R. Mairal. 2010a. La Gramática de COREL: un lenguaje de representación conceptual. *Onomazein* 21: 11–45.

Periñán-Pascual, C. & R. Mairal. 2010b. Enhancing UniArab with FunGramKB. *Procesamiento del Lenguaje Natural* 44: 19–26.

Periñán-Pascual, C. & R. Mairal. 2011. The coherent methodology in FunGramKB. *Onomazein* 24: 13–33.

Periñán-Pascual, C. & R. Mairal. 2012. La dimensión computacional de la Gramática del Papel y la Referencia: la estructura lógica conceptual y su aplicación en el procesamiento del lenguaje natural. In R. Mairal, L. Guerrero & C. González (eds.), *El funcionalismo en la teoría lingüística. La Gramática del Papel y la Referencia. Introducción, avances y aplicaciones*, 333–348. Madrid: Akal.

Ruiz de Mendoza, F. J. 2013. Meaning construction, meaning interpretation and formal expression in the lexical constructional model. In B. Nolan & E. Diedrichsen (eds.), *Linking constructions into functional linguistics: The role of constructions in a functional grammar*, 231–270. Amsterdam: John Benjamins.

Ruiz de Mendoza, F. J. & A. Baicchi. 2007. Illocutionary constructions: cognitive motivation and linguistic realization. In I. Kecskes & L. Horn (eds.), *Explorations in pragmatics: linguistic, cognitive, and intercultural aspects*, 95–128. Berlin-New York: Mouton de Gruyter.

Ruiz de Mendoza, F. J. & R. Mairal. 2008. Levels of description and constraining factors in meaning construction: an introduction to the Lexical Constructional Model. *Folia Linguistica* 42 (2): 355–400.

Tuggy, D. 1996. The thing is is that people talk that way. The question is is why? In E. H. Casad (ed.), *Cognitive linguistics in the Redwoods: The expansion of a new paradigm in linguistics*, 713–752. Berlin-New York: Mouton de Gruyter.

Van Valin, R. D., Jr. 2005. *Exploring the syntax-semantics interface*. Cambridge: Cambridge University Press.

Van Valin, R. D., Jr. 2013. Lexical representation, co-composition, and linking syntax and semantics. In J. Pustejovsky, P. Bouillon, H. Isahara, K. Kanzaki, & C. Lee (eds.), *Advances in Generative Lexicon theory*, 67–107. Dordrecht: Springer.

Van Valin, R, D., Jr. & R. J. LaPolla. 1997. *Syntax: structure, meaning and function*. Cambridge: Cambridge University Press.

Van Valin, R., D., Jr. & R. Mairal. in press. Interfacing the lexicon and an ontology in a linking algorithm. In M. Ángeles Gómez, F. Ruiz de Mendoza & F. Gonzálvez-García (eds.), *Form and function in language: functional, cognitive and applied perspectives. Essays in honour of Christopher S. Butler*. Amsterdam: John Benjamins.

Authors

Ricardo Mairal
UNED
rmairal@flog.uned.es

Carlos Periñán-Pascual
Universidad Politécnica de Valencia
jopepas3@upv.es

Multilingualism, Multilectalism and Register Variation in Linguistic Theory – Extending the Diasystematic Approach[1]

John Peterson

> Although perhaps half of the world's population actively uses two or more languages in their daily lives, most formal linguistic theories are modeled on monolingual speakers of a single, invariant linguistic register. The present study attempts to rectify this by proposing a model of multilingual speech within the framework of Role and Reference Grammar (RRG). This model makes use of the "diasystematic" approach developed in Höder (2012) within a Construction Grammar framework, in which some "constructions" – ranging from lexical entries to abstract sentence patterns – are language-specific while others are unspecified for language, and extends this notion to include register variation, so that grammatical structures of all types are either specified or unspecified for both REGISTER and LANGUAGE. This allows us to capture the complex and multifarious interrelations between register variation and multilingualism, but also allows us to account for the many different types of multilingual speech.

1 Introduction

A large percentage of the world's population – more than half by some estimates – actively uses two or more languages in their daily lives, e. g., speaking

---

[1] I wish to thank Utz Maas, Steffen Höder and an anonymous reviewer for their comments on earlier versions of this paper as well as the participants of the second Kiel RRG Workshop and the RRG conference in Freiburg, although I alone am responsible for any oversights and errors which the present study may contain.

one language (the "Low" form, in Ferguson's 1959 terms) at home or with close friends and another in official or formal settings (the "High" form). Similar comments hold for speakers of "dialects" (Low), who are "multilectal" to the extent that they are also fluent in the standard language (High), which they use e. g. in more formal situations. A considerable amount of research shows that all of a multilingual speaker's languages are simultaneously "activated" whenever s/he speaks, even in cases where forms from only one language are encountered (e. g., Bialystok 2001: 114, Grosjean 1989). In multilingual speech this is even more apparent, as the speaker here makes use of elements from two or more languages within one and the same utterance or from one utterance to the next.

Despite these facts, most formal linguistic theories are either explicitly or at least implicitly modelled on monolingual language use, forcing us to view bilinguals as "two monolinguals in one person" (cf. Grosjean 1989), despite all evidence to the contrary.[2] In fact, as many researchers point out (e. g., Gardner-Chloros 2009: 112–113), even most theoretical accounts of bilingual speech assume that the speaker is speaking EITHER one language OR the other at any one moment, again despite considerable evidence to the contrary.

These problems are not restricted to bilingualism, however, since variation is also found in monolinguals, who regularly switch from one register to another in their daily routines, i.e., these speakers may be considered "multilectal" in this respect. Although this is often viewed as merely a matter of the appropriate choice of a particular lexeme or pronunciation, it can also involve other areas of grammar. Consider for example the Standard English sentence (1) with its more informal variant (2).

(1) *She and I were going to go.*

(2) *Me 'n' her were gonna go.*

In addition to any differences in pronunciation, alluded to here by spelling differences, it is clear that any rule to derive the appropriate form of the subject will have to be different for the two register variants, i.e. *she and I* in their so-called "nominative" forms vs. *me 'n' her* in their so-called "accusative" forms.

---

[2] Following convention, in the following I will consistently speak of "bilinguals", although the following comments all hold as well for multilinguals who speak three or more languages.

Although the colloquial form in (2) is considered substandard or even wrong by many speakers, it is nevertheless common in spontaneous informal speech and must therefore be accounted for in any full description of English. One possibility would be to make two separate descriptions, one for each of the two varieties, since in this case the two forms are generally not interchangeable: Where one is appropriate, the other typically is not. However, this is not a viable option, since a distinction between "informal" and "formal" – or perhaps "written" and "spoken" – is far too simplistic to account for the full range of register variation found in English (or any other language).

In my study, I will make use of the diasystematic approach developed in Höder (2012) within a Construction Grammar framework, in which some "constructions" – ranging from lexical entries to abstract sentence patterns – are language-specific while others are unspecified for language. I will extend this notion to include register variation, so that grammatical structures of all types are either specified or unspecified for both REGISTER and LANGUAGE, working within the framework of Role and Reference Grammar (RRG). As the bilingual's languages fulfill many of the same functions as the monolingual's intralingual register variation, these two phenomena clearly interact with one another, yet as each of the bilingual's languages may also show a certain amount of intralingual register variation, register variation and choice of language must be viewed as separate phenomena.

Role and Reference Grammar or "RRG", the language theory which we will use in this study, is a typologically informed, monostratal theory of language. It has been chosen here for its flexibility and for the fact that it consciously avoids assuming "universal" categories for human language whose universality is questionable, e. g., grammatical relations such as "subject" and "object" or lexical classes such as "noun", "adjective" and "verb",[3] while at the same time providing a theoretical framework which can adequately account for the diversity found in human language. Furthermore, as noted in Van Valin (2005: 2), "RRG seeks to be more than a descriptive framework for the analysis of languages; it also strives to provide an explanatory framework for the analysis of language acquisition

---

[3] For example, RRG can easily deal with languages such as Maltese (Neo-Arabic), in which grammatical relations such as "subject" and "object" are quite problematic (Peterson 2009), or languages such as Kharia (Munda, Austro-Asiatic), for which we have no evidence for the presence of nouns, verbs and adjectives (and considerable evidence against their presence) (Peterson 2011, 2013).

and language processing." As we are ultimately interested here in a descriptively adequate account of the processes involved in bilingual speech as well as their acquisition by the bilingual learner, RRG would seem to be the natural choice for a theoretical account of this phenomenon as it allows us to capture all of these aspects in a unified manner.

Finally, the model developed here allows us to account for the many different types of bilingual speech, including those which contain a genuine "switch" from one language to another but also interference phenomena.

This study is structured as follows.[4] Section 2 presents an overview of some of the different types of bilingual speech. As the present study cannot provide an exhaustive treatment of bilingual speech in general, this section provides a brief overview of what is traditionally referred to as "code-switching" or "code-mixing" as well as a very brief introduction to interference phenomena. Following this, section 3 presents an overview of the theoretical approach to (mono- and bilingual) speech assumed in the present study, which assumes the basic tenets of Role and Reference Grammar but which also draws heavily on the models proposed in Matras (2009) and Höder (2012), reinterpreting their discussions within the framework of RRG. In section 4 we then illustrate this model by applying it to a selection of the examples presented in section 2 for different language pairs, illustrating how structures from the two languages involved intertwine to form new structures. Section 5 then extends this analysis to intralingual variation. Here we will see that the same methods which apply to bilingual speech can also productively be applied to register variation. Finally, section 6 provides a summary of the present study and a brief outlook for future work.

2 Multilingual speech

The present section provides a brief overview of some of the different types of bilingual speech. We will restrict ourselves here to two very general headings: 1. code-switching / code-mixing, and 2. "interference" in its broadest sense. As any attempt at exhaustiveness would greatly exceed the scope of the present study,

---

[4] As an introduction to RRG is beyond the scope of the present study, every attempt has been made here to avoid theory-internal details and to keep the discussion as intuitive as possible, so that readers who are unfamiliar with RRG should nevertheless have few problems in following the discussion.

the following discussion must necessarily remain schematic and cannot deal with many important issues in any detail, such as e. g. the distinction between loanwords and code-switching.[5]

2.1 Functional bilingualism: code-switching / code-mixing[6]

The terms "code-switching" and "code-mixing" – both as one word (with or without a hyphen) or as two words – are used differently by different researchers to refer to more-or-less different phenomena, such as whether or not the "switch" from one linguistic variety to another occurs inter- or intrasententially, or according to any number of other defining characteristics. The two terms will be used here interchangeably to refer to the more-or-less *ad hoc* use of elements from two linguistic varieties in one conversation, whether inter- or intrasententially.

The restriction to the more-or-less *ad hoc* use of elements from two linguistic varieties in the definition above refers to the fact that we exclude loanwords from this definition of code-switching / code-mixing. Although it is generally assumed that code-switching and borrowing are two distinct processes, it has proven enormously difficult, if not impossible, to maintain this distinction in practice. One solution, followed by Myers-Scotton (1993: 16), is to limit the occurrences of a particular linguistic form (i. e., a lexeme or word) to occurring in a maximum number of different conversations, in this case to fewer than three. As convenient as this may be, as Myers-Scotton herself acknowledges, this is a rather arbitrary choice. For these and other reasons, most other researchers have chosen alternative solutions to this issue, such as the composite "codeswitching-borrowing continuum" by Matras (2009), which acknowledges a number of relevant characteristics, such as "bilinguality", "composition", "functionality", etc. (cf. Matras 2009: 110–114 for further details). In the present discussion, we tacitly assume a continuum of this type but will not deal with this issue further here, for reasons of space.

---

[5] There is a large number of excellent introductory works which deal with language contact in detail; two of the most recent works in this direction are Matras (2009) and Winford (2003).

[6] While we will not assume here that bilingual speakers are necessarily conscious of the fact that they are using elements from two linguistic varieties in the same utterance (although this may be the case), we will assume that code-switching generally fulfills a function in discourse, e. g., highlighting information. In this sense, code-switching is much like intonation, which is "functional" as it conveys information, although the speaker him-/herself need not be aware of this fact.

According to Muysken (2000), there are three basic types of code-mixing from a structural perspective: 1. *insertion*, 2. *alternation* and 3. *congruent lexicalization*.[7] These are illustrated in the following.

1. Insertion – As its name implies, this type of code-switching involves the "**insertion** of material (lexical items or entire constituents) from one language into a structure from the other language." (Muysken 2000: 3, emphasis in original) The following two examples from student presentations, both containing German-Russian switches, provide an example of this type of code-switching (German lexemes and words are given in their written form here, Russian elements have been transliterated).

Russian-German:

(3) <u>koška</u> ha-t abgenommen!
    cat   PERF.AUX-3SG lose.weight.PTCP
    '<u>The cat</u> has lost weight!'[8]

In (3) the so-called matrix or "main" language is arguably German and the embedded language (underlined here) is Russian.[9] Arguments for viewing German as the matrix language include the typical V2-position of the finite auxiliary verb, *hat* 'has', and the sentence-final position of the perfect participle form of the lexical predicate, *abgenommen* 'lost weight', which together form the so-called "perfect" in German. Furthermore, the very fact that the auxiliary, a grammatical morpheme, is in German strengthens the assumption that German is the matrix language here. In this analysis, the Russian word *koška* 'cat' is inserted into this structure in the pre-verbal slot referred to in German linguistics as the *Vorfeld* 'prefield', which is mandatory in declarative V2-sentences and which allows for only one element.

---

[7] In Muysken (2013: 713) a fourth type of code-switching is mentioned, "backflagging", in which "the principal or matrix language in the code-switched discourse is not the original community language, but the language some speakers have shifted towards as an L2, and this L2 is marked with flagging elements from the original community language" which speakers use "to signal their traditional ethnic identity even though they themselves may have shifted to a dominant non-ethnic language." However, as this does not represent a separate structural type, we will not deal with it further here.

[8] Example courtesy of Valeria Biller.

[9] Cf. however the discussion in section 4 below, where it will be argued that the underlying sentence structure in (3) (= example (10) in section 4) could be either Russian or German.

However, even assuming that German here is unambiguously the matrix language, the example is perhaps not as simple as it appears to be at first sight: The Russian expression *koška* in (3) is, structurally speaking, not just the insertion of a single noun (*koška*) into an otherwise German sentence but rather the entire noun phrase *koška*; as Russian does not have obligatory determiners such as definite articles, a Russian NP can consist of a simple N, as in (3), whereas German, like English, generally requires NPs in the singular to contain an obligatory determiner such as the definite article. In (3) this would be the feminine, singular, nominative form of the definite article, *die*, as the noun *Katze* 'cat' is feminine in German and is here the subject of the clause, which appears in the nominative in German. As (3) does not contain such a determiner, we conclude that the entire NP is Russian, not just the N.

A slightly more complex example is presented in (4).

Russian-German:

(4) *Ja* *putz-a-l-a* *heute* v *Büro*.
    1SG clean-STV-PST-F.SG today in office
    'I cleaned today in the office.'[10]

In one analysis, the matrix language here is Russian and the underlined elements are all insertions from German. The first insertion, *putz-* 'clean (v)', is at the lexical level, while the predicate is otherwise Russian and is marked for Russian inflectional and derivational categories (past tense, feminine, singular and stem vowel). The next two insertions are more reminiscent of the structure in (3): *heute* 'today' is here not only a lexeme and word, it is an entire adverbial phrase and with that an insertion at the syntactic level; *Büro* 'office', on the other hand, is slightly different – here we have the Russian preposition *v* 'in', which requires an NP as its complement, so that *Büro* here is a full NP, not just an N. As in (3) this is best considered a Russian-language NP, as a German NP here would require the appropriate article; as this NP does not have a determiner, it is a Russian NP consisting of the German-language N *Büro*.

2. Alternation – In this type of code-switching, longer stretches from one language alternate with those from another language linearly. The following presents a simple example, in which the English-Spanish bilingual speaker begins an ut-

---

[10] Example courtesy of Xenia Dulghir.

terance in English and then switches into Spanish, then English, then Spanish, but each switch contains extended monolingual stretches.

English-Spanish:

(5) Why make Carol sent-ar-se   atras   pa'que   everybody has to move pa'que
              sit-INF-REFL behind PURP   PURP

   se   salga?
   REFL go.out.SUBJ.3SG
   'Why make Carol sit in the back so everybody has to move for her to get out?'

(Poplack 1981: 589; my gloss)

3. Finally, Muysken assumes a third type of bilingual speech which he refers to as "congruent lexicalization". This is particularly relevant in cases of highly similar language structures, such as with dialects or linguistic varieties which have been in close contact with one another for a long time, so that they share a large number of structures which may then be congruently lexicalized "from different lexical inventories into a shared grammatical structure." (Muysken 2000: 3). (6) presents an example of this type of switching.

Dutch-West Frisian

(6) En de partij dy't hy derby   blaasde,   (Frisian)
    En de partij die hij erbij   blies   (Dutch)
    and the part   that he thereby blew

    is net [**foar** herhaling vatbaar].   (Frisian)
    is niet **voor** herhaling vatbaar.   (Dutch)
    is not for   repetition handable
    'And the song he sang then is not fit to be repeated.'

(Wolf 1995: 12, cited in Muysken 2000: 6)

Muysken (2000: 6) writes: "Here, Frisian *foar* 'for' is sufficiently similar to Dutch *voor* 'for' to be an ambiguous switchpoint; Dutch *herhaling vatbaar* is not a constituent, but two words that form an idiom together with *voor*."

These three types should be viewed as ideal types, so that code-switching between a particular language pair may be (and often is) best viewed as more-or-less insertional, more-or-less alternating and / or more-or-less of the congruent lexicalization type, depending on a number of factors, both structural and other (cf.

the discussion in Muysken 2000), and membership to one or more types is not always entirely unambiguous.[11]

The inclusion of the preceding discussion of these three types here is simply to point out that code-switching strategies can and do vary considerably and can affect various linguistic levels, from phonology (although this is seldom encountered in the literature on code-switching) to the lexicon and morphosyntax. As such, any attempt to account for code-switching between any two languages must be able to account for all three types:

- Insertion and alternation appear to be the two most difficult to account for theoretically: With insertion, we have two grammars which combine directly within one and the same clause (or at least sentence), with some structures deriving from one language, some from another, but a number of constructions containing intertwined elements from both languages.
- In alternation, we at least tendentially have longer stretches of monolingual speech in one language followed by longer stretches in the other language. Nonetheless, here as well we can find examples in which two grammars combine to form a single clause; cf. e.g. (5), where the predicate of the first clause is *make sentarse*, with elements from English and Spanish.
- With congruent lexicalization, on the other hand, the two languages involved have essentially the same structure (at least within the unit under consideration) so that it is often not possible nor desirable to decide which language which structures derive from, other than perhaps at the lexical level. Nevertheless, any model for bilingual speech must also provide an adequate account of this form of code-mixing, and as we will argue in the following sections, the approach taken here will be to consider these structures neither one language nor the other but rather structures which are unspecified for language.

With respect to function, there is a considerable amount of literature dealing with the many "metaphorical" functions (Gumperz 1982) which have been attributed to code-switching / code-mixing, and no attempt will be made here to give an exhaustive account of these, as the present study is primarily concerned with structural issues. For an overview of literature on this topic, the reader is

---

[11] This claim is strengthened by the fact that Muysken (2013: 713) views (5) as typical for congruent lexicalization, whereas I view it as a typical example of alternation. In fact, arguments can be made for both analyses.

referred to works such as Gardner-Chloros (2009), Gumperz (1982) and Winford (2003).

One of these "metaphorical" functions which has often been overlooked but which seems to be one of the major motivations behind code-switching is information structure: As Kaschubat (2004: 117–119) argues in her study of Russian-German code-switching, ca. 90 % of all cases of insertional code-switching in her corpus involving a single switched item occurred within the "rhematic" part of the sentence or, in RRG terms, within the actual focus domain, while virtually all of the remaining 10 % are cases in which the German unit, within an otherwise Russian sentence, refers to an argument which has already been activated in the discourse. With that, this highlighting function of code-switching is clearly one of the primary functions of code-switching, and as we shall see in section 4, this is also easily captured within the framework of RRG.

2.2 Non-functional switches: "interference" and "slips of the tongue"

Generally speaking, there are two types of contact phenomena which can be considered non-functional in the sense that they do not fulfill any of the "metaphorical" functions discussed above in section 2.1. In the one type, we find utterances which contain at least some non-lexical structures from more than one language (e. g., word order), whereas the second type consists of lexical material stemming from the contextually "wrong" language. For ease of presentation, we discuss the two together in the following under the term "interference" and do not differentiate further between them.

We begin our discussion here with example (7), taken from Matras (2009: 73; gloss has been added here) and deriving from a seven-year-old German-English bilingual whose dominant language is English.

German (non-standard), influenced by English

(7) er   ist   gröss-er   denn   mir
    3SG.M.NOM COP.NPST.3SG big-COMPAR 'than' 1SG.DAT
    'he is taller/bigger than me'

As Matras notes, the non-standard use of *denn mir* in (7) in all likelihood derives from its similarity to the English form *than me*, whereas the standard German form would be *als* 'than' (in comparison) and *ich* '1SG.NOM': *denn* has most likely been selected due to its phonological similarity to English *than* as well as to a number of vague semantic similarities[12] and the use of the dative form *mir* instead of the standard form *ich* (nominative) also derives in all probability from its phonological similarity to the oblique form of the English pronoun *me* (Matras 2009: 73–74).

Although interference has traditionally been viewed negatively, e. g., in studies dealing with L2 teaching, where interference (or "transfer") phenomena are viewed as mistakes stemming from L1, as Matras (2009: 74) argues, interference can be viewed more neutrally as a creative process in which a speaker makes full use of his or her entire linguistic repertoire in a context in which elements from just one subset, i. e., from the appropriate "language", would be expected.

The "transfer" of an abstract construction from one language to another can be due to any number of reasons, including the lack of proficiency in the "importing" language or the fact that the constructions in both languages are structurally quite similar, as in (7). However, even ignoring the cases in which this transfer is indeed due to the lack of proficiency in one of the two languages, such unintentional switches are nevertheless still quite common and are often due to influence from what Matras (2009) refers to as the *pragmatically dominant language*, which he defines as "the language that the speaker associates most closely at the moment of interaction with the routine implementation of communicative tasks that are similar to the ongoing task" (Matras 2009: 98). That is, the simple fact that the speaker has been speaking one language for some time and then switches to another language can be enough to trigger the presence of linguistic structure from the "wrong" or contextually inappropriate repertoire. This particularly affects what Matras (2009) refers to as the "monitoring-and-directing apparatus" and affects above all routine-like language activities such as semi-lexical speech-act markers (e. g., tags, affirmative signals, etc.) as well as connectivity and interaction operators (coordinating and subordinating conjunctions, sequential markers, fillers), among others (cf. e. g. Matras 2009: 98–99).

Cf. the following example, adapted from Maas (2008: 469), in which we find an extrasentential German interjection (underlined) at the beginning of an otherwise Finnish sentence:

---

[12] As Matras (2009: 73–74) notes, *denn* can in fact be used in formal and literary constructions as a marker of comparison, although he rightly notes that this seven-year-old is unlikely to be familiar with this construciton.

German-Finnish

(8) <u>Ach</u>   on-k[o]   su-ll   kiire?
    INTERJ COP.PRS.3SG-Q 2SG-ADESS (< *sinu-lla*) haste
    'Oh, you're in a hurry?'

Although such "transferred" elements tend to be identifiable as language-specific elements, the monitoring-and-directing function which they fulfill appears to require considerable attention, so that these elements can "slip through" the context filter unnoticed. The case with abstract structures is somewhat different – although these structures can also belong to one repertoire or the other, their respective membership is not as apparent as with lexical material, which tends to flag an utterance as belonging to a particular language in a way that the use of an abstract construction does not. Hence, the fact that the speaker is "mixing languages" may even go entirely unnoticed by the speaker him- or herself as well as by his or her interlocutor(s).

The following presents an example of such a structural "borrowing": Jarząbkowska (2012) contrasts Polish as it is spoken in Germany with that spoken in Poland. In her study, Jarząbkowska shows among other things that speakers of Polish in Germany overtly mention the subject NP altogether about twice as often as Polish speakers in Poland, although this varies considerably according to topic and genre. For example, two speakers of Polish living in Germany used four times as many personal pronouns in describing a picture of a market place as did a comparable speaker of Polish living in Poland (cf. Jarząbkowska 2012: 56).

This can be explained as follows: (Standard) Polish is a so-called "pro-drop" language in which the subject is marked on the verb and need not be overtly expressed by means of an independent NP; when an overt subject NP is present, this unit is typically focused. German, on the other hand, is not a "pro-drop" language, and with few exceptions (e. g., subject ellipsis in topic chains) all subjects must be mentioned overtly, despite the presence of subject marking on the verb. Consider now example (9).

German-influenced Polish

(9) *Jak pierwsz-y   raz   by-ł-a-m   na urlopi-e, ...*
    as   first-NOM.SG.M once.NOM.SG.M COP-PST-F-1SG on vacation-LOC.SG.M

   gdzie ja   by-ł-a-m?   To   ja   by-ł-a-m   sam-a, ...
   where 1SG.NOM COP-PST-F-1SG then 1SG.NOM COP-PST-F-1SG alone-NOM.SG.F
   'When I was on vacation for the first time, ... where was I? I was alone then
   ...'   [Dan II: 4_50–4_51][13]

At issue is the fact that the subject pronoun in the last clause, the underlined *ja* '1SG.NOM', is overtly present in (9), although it is generally only found with focus in the speech of native speakers living in Poland (cf. e. g. Bartnicka et al. 2004: 280–281, 499–501, Bielec 1998: 14–148). Although the presence of the 1st person, singular pronoun *ja* in (9) may not qualify as "incorrect", for most speakers of Polish its use in (9) is nonetheless not typical, and its presence here is most likely due to the influence of German in the daily lives of these speakers.[14]

In a situation in which two or more languages are used in daily speech, it is likely that the structures of these languages will gradually converge to some extent, potentially resulting in convergence areas (Weinreich 1958: 379).[15] There is now abundant research showing that such convergence areas can be found in all parts of the world.[16] Given enough time and a high level of bilingualism (among other factors), the processes outlined above can lead to considerable convergence, so that even non-related languages which were once typologically very different can come to resemble one another quite closely.

In the following section, we present an overview of the model of (bilingual) speech which we assume here, which essentially follows that in Matras (2009).

---

[13] This example is taken from a corpus compiled by Jarząbkowska and myself and financed by the University of Kiel, whose support I gratefully acknowledge here.

[14] Similarly, cf. Johanson (2008: 73) on overmarking with respect to anaphora.

[15] Although the term *Sprachbund* or "language league" is undoubtedly more common, I follow Weinreich (1958: 379) in using the term "convergence area" to refer to such areas, as it is questionable whether languages can form any meaningful kind of "league" (or what this term could actually mean) and since what is at issue is to what extent the languages of a particular region have converged over the course of time.

[16] One example from my own research is Jharkhand in central-eastern India, in which languages of the Munda and Indo-Aryan families have come to share a number of traits due to their prolonged contact. Cf. Peterson (2010) for details.

We will then adapt the diasystematic approach to bilingual speech, developed in Höder (2012) within the framework of Construction Grammar, to an RRG format and illustrate this with a number of examples in section 4.

3 The diasystematic approach

In recent years, research into bilingual speech has increasingly been turning away from viewing languages as "discrete, identifiable and internally consistent wholes" (Gardner-Chloros 2009: 9) and towards viewing them as more permeable complex systems of rules, patterns, and / or constructions (cf. also e.g. Muysken 2000: 250–278).[17] As such, many rules can be viewed as common to both languages, while other rules will of course be unique to one language or the other. These rules, both the language-specific as well as the unspecified ones, can refer to any structural level, such as clausal word order or prosody, or overt structures such as lexical morphemes (including their meanings), interjections and much more. This view is perhaps best summarized by the following quote, from Matras (2009: 4):

> My principal assumption [...] is that bilingual (or multilingual) speakers have a complex repertoire of linguistic structures at their disposal. This repertoire is not organised in the form of 'languages' or 'language systems'; the latter is a metalinguistic construct and a label which speakers learn to apply to their patterns of linguistic behaviour as part of a process of linguistic socialisation. Rather, elements of the repertoire (word-forms, phonological rules, constructions, and so on) gradually become associated, through a process of linguistic socialisation, with a range of social activities, including factors such as sets of interlocutors, topics, and institutional settings. Mature multilingual speakers face a constant challenge to maintain control over their complex repertoire of forms and structures and to select those forms that are context-appropriate.

It is essentially this view which we also assume here, although we will freely speak of "languages" to refer to the patterns of linguistic behavior referred to in the quote above which speakers view as different linguistic systems (including "dialects").[18] That is, we follow other researchers in assuming that neither of the bilingual's languages is ever "turned off" simply because s/he at any one

---
[17] Although it is not always clear whether a description in terms of rules, patterns or constructions is most appropriate, in the following I will simply speak of "rules" for ease of discussion.

[18] We will, however, not speculate further here as to when bilingual speakers come to realize that they speak two separate "languages".

particular moment is making exclusive use of forms which belong to only one of the two repertoires (i. e., "languages"). That is, the bilingual has at any given moment the option of using linguistic structures (in the broadest sense) from either repertoire for any number of reasons, such as the "metaphorical" uses referred to in section 2.1.

In line with this view, it appears that linguistic structures – regardless of which language they belong to – are presumably first learned as general structures which are unmarked for context: "From the very beginning of the language acquisition process, the child-speaker learns that some linguistic items are 'universal', that is, they can be employed irrespective of setting or interlocutor. This principle of the existence of unique referents within the repertoire continues to accompany the bilingual speaker even in later states. Even the more mature communicator entertains the notion that certain items are exempt from the need to select among repertoire subsets." (Matras 2009: 39)

This is a gradual process in which the multilingual speaker presumably assumes that all structures are generally employable until evidence is encountered that a particular structure is restricted to one language or the other:

> As the repertoire expands, so does the realisation that the use of word-forms (and later of constructions) is subject to situational and contextual constraints. Until such realisation is achieved, communication is a trial-and-error, experimental activity. The child tries to balance the benefits from exploiting the full repertoire for maximum effectiveness of expression against the need to maintain communicative harmony by complying with constraints on the appropriateness of the selection of word-forms and constructions. It is through this kind of prolonged process of linguistic socialisation that the repertoire is gradually shaped into subsets, or 'languages'. (Matras 2009: 68)

Figure 1, from Matras (2009: 5), summarizes this view of bilingualism schematically. In this model, the bilingual has a number of context-bound forms at his or her disposal. Like all speakers, the bilingual speaker wishes to be as fully expressive as possible, but unlike the monolingual speaker, s/he can choose from a number of constructions from different languages, some of which s/he may consider better suited for a particular purpose than others. However, bilingual speakers are not entirely free to choose from their full linguistic repertoire – successful communication crucially depends upon the interlocutor's ability to understand a particular linguistic structure. Hence, the interplay between the context-bound selection of forms and the full exploitation of the resources at one's disposal is regulated by the need to maximally reduce the number of communicatory hurdles in successful communication.

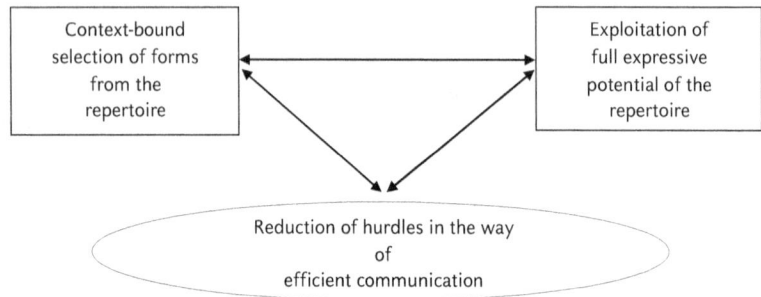

Figure 1: The interplay of factors in communication in language contact situations (Matras 2009: 5)

In such a model not only are both languages necessarily "switched on" during communication, it must also be assumed that the speaker (and in the case of effective multilingual communication also the interloctur(s)) at all times have direct access to all levels of linguistic structure and the corresponding meanings from both or all repertoires, from prosody and segmental phonology, the lexicon, morphosyntax, information structure and also "monitoring-and-directing" structures such as tag questions, etc. But equally importantly, this model adequately takes into account the context-bound nature of linguistic structures, whether from different languages, dialects or registers, as the difference between "languages" and "dialects" is one of degree (cf. Matras 2009: 99). We will return to this point in section 5.

In a recent study on bilingualism within a Constructive Grammar approach, Höder (2012) develops what he refers to as the "Diasystematic Construction Grammar (DCxG)" model to account for bilingual structures, especially within closely related languages and dialects. This model, which has much in common with the basic assumptions on bilingualism outlined above, is based on the notion of "diasystem" developed by Weinreich (1954) to account for structures which are shared between two linguistic varieties.

As Höder (2012: 245) notes, the basic process in establishing a diasystem is that of "interlingual identification" (Weinreich 1953: 7–8), in which components in two different linguistic systems are essentially viewed as equivalent due to perceived similarities.[19] However, it must be emphasized that the determination of such "equivalents" is not entirely a straightforward matter, as what is at issue are not so much verifiable equivalents but rather equivalents which the speakers themselves view as such (cf. Höder: 2012: 245). This complex system of perceived differences and similarities between the two (or more) linguistic systems plays a central role in organizing the speech of multilinguals, and the more closely related two varieties are (from a purely structural perspective), the more highly developed their diasystematicity will be.

> Diasystematic links and dia-elements constitute a network through which two language systems used within a multilingual speaker group are interconnected. The degree to which two varieties in contact participate in the common diasystem depends, of course, on their typological similarity: closely related and typologically similar languages can more easily develop a high degree of diasystematicity – i.e. the common intersection of their systems is larger – than more distant languages, which retain a larger proportion of idiosyncrasies in their systems... (Höder 2012: 246)

As already noted, this extension of Weinreich's notion of diasystematicity fits in well with the model of multilingualism outlined above from Matras (2009), hence Höder's (2012) model can serve as our point of departure for a theoretical approach to bilingual speech within RRG. The model we assume here is summarized in Figure 2, where two languages, L1 and L2, both possess a number of structures which are unique to these two languages, although a number of structures are also shared by both. As just noted, the number of common linguistic structures will depend upon the typological similarity of the two (or more) languages involved.

"Structures" here refers to elements from all levels of grammar, both concrete forms and abstract rules and patterns. This thus includes, among others, morphs and morphemes (grammatical and contentive), logical structures from the lexicon, syntactic templates, potential and actual focus domains, case-assigning rules, constructional schemas[20] (or parts thereof), etc.

---

[19] Although Weinreich was primarily concerned with the relationships between dialects in his writings, the notion of interlingual identification, like that of diasystem, can easily be extended to other types of linguistic varieties.

[20] Constructional schemas in RRG bring together various areas of the grammar involved in a particular construction, including syntax, morphology, semantics and pragmatics. For reasons of space, we will only refer to these very generally in the following discussion. Cf. Van Valin (2005: 131–135) for further discussion.

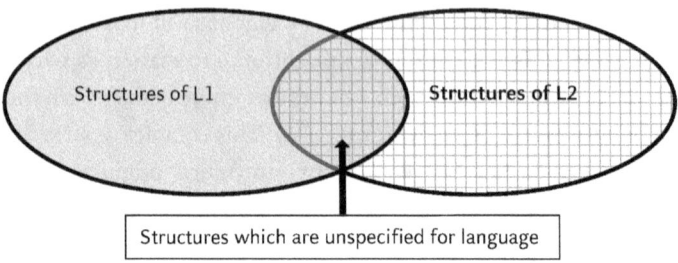

Figure 2: A schematic representation of bilingual linguistic structures

As RRG essentially views "languages" as networks of structures from the areas just mentioned, as well as rules for linking one level with another (e. g. semantics and syntax), the theory is well equipped to handle bilingual speech as this is understood here – both languages are viewed as networks of context-bound structures, to both of which the speaker and interlocutor have access and from both of which the speaker may freely combine structures to the extent that these are viewed as "interlingual equivalents" by speakers. This in turn can only be ascertained by a detailed analysis of the data, not by any pre-conceived notion of equivalence. Thus, the only real novelty to RRG proposed here is that these two networks are not viewed as completely discrete but rather as "permeable" or "penetrable", as they allow the inclusion of structures from other repertoires, to the extent that these are felt by speakers to "fit".

In the following section, this approach will be outlined in more detail and illustrated by applying it to a number of the examples from section 2. In section 5, we will then expand this model to include intralingual register differences.

4 Applying the model

In the view of language assumed here, not only are both languages activated during bilingual speech, we have also argued that these languages are not to be viewed as discrete systems but rather as repertoires of linguistic structures bound together by convention, and that the bilingual in the course of his or her socialization learns to view these networks of structures as different languages. This essentially means that, in a formal language theory such as RRG, all information – including the form of a lexeme, its logical structure (i. e., "definition"), the language's syntactic inventory, information structure, etc. – can be indexed for the respective sub-repertoire to which it belongs, and that some structures will be unique to L1, others to L2, while others will be unspecified, as they are common to both L1 and L2. Furthermore, the individual structures of both repertoires may be combined with elements from the other repertoire to the extent that speakers view them as equivalent.

In this section, we illustrate this model by applying the principles from section 3 to a number of the examples of bilingual speech from section 2, concentrating on cases in which the two languages intertwine within the sentence or clause, such as insertional code-switching and interference. Let us begin with example (3), repeated here as (10).

Russian-German:

(10) <u>koška</u> ha-t   abgenommen!
     cat   PERF.AUX-3SG lose.weight.PTCP
     'The cat has lost weight!'

At first glance, this would appear to be a simple case of insertion, in which a Russian referential phrase or "RP" (RP_{RUS}, realized here by an NP_{RUS}), koška, has been inserted into a German core ($CORE_{GER}$). In this interpretation, the structure RP_{RUS} has been "interlingually identified" or equated with an RP_{GER}. We will abbreviate interlingual identification here through the sign "≡", so that the interlingual identification of a Russian and German RP can be abbreviated as $RP_{RUS≡GER}$. This is illustrated in (11).[21]

(11)

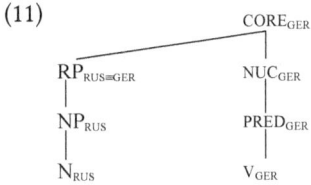

However, the overall structure of the core in (11) could also be Russian, since Russian also possesses a syntactic template for a CORE consisting of an RP followed by NUC in an intransitive CORE in sentence-focus structures (Rodionova 2001: 13–14; 25; 47), as in (10), which is an example of sentence focus. Hence, considering this

---

[21] I follow Ruhnau (2011) here in not assuming the presence of an obligatory precore slot (PrCS) in German.

particular structure to be either Russian or German is at best an arbitrary decision. As such, we consider it better to view it as neither Russian nor German but rather simply as a core structure underspecified for language for the German-Russian bilingual: Although the clause-initial NP is Russian and the overt form of the predicate and the operators are from German (although the categories expressed by the operators are found in both Russian and German), the overall syntactic structure of the CORE, i. e., the syntactic template, is unspecified for language. We can illustrate this in a simplified manner as in (12), where elements which do not have a subscript are considered to be common to both languages.

(12)

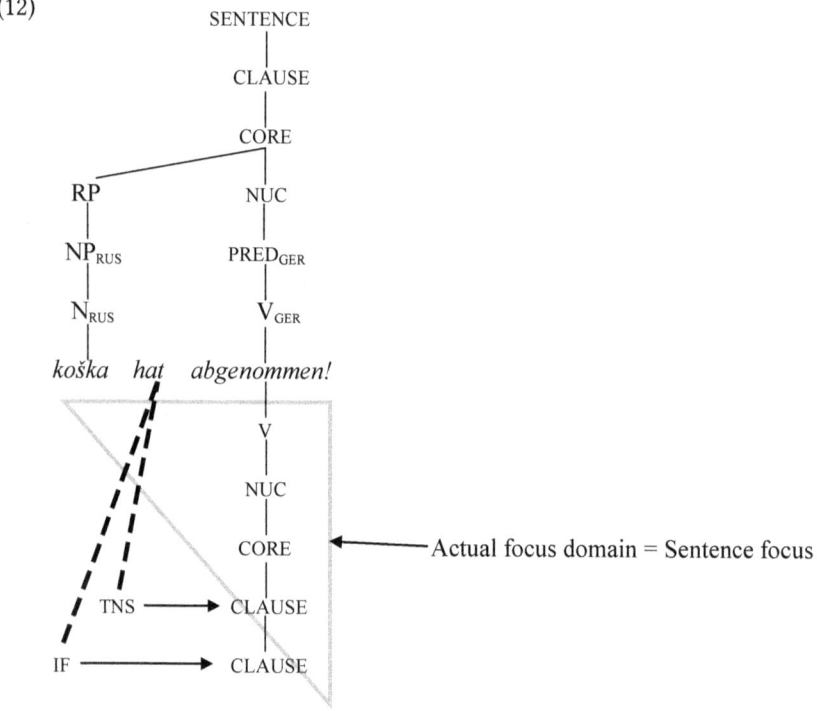

Logical Structure: ⟨$_{\mathrm{IF}}$DEC ⟨$_{\mathrm{TNS}}$ PST ⟨do' (koška$_{\mathrm{RUS}}$ [lose.weight' (koška$_{\mathrm{RUS}}$)])⟩ $_{\mathrm{GER}}$⟩⟩

The lack of an index in (12) does not have the same meaning as interlingual identification denoted by the sign "≡": Although much work must still be done here, intuitively at least there is a difference between those structures belonging to the area of overlap in Figure 2 (usually at an abstract level, such as word order or identity of the operators) which are **structurally identical** in both linguistic systems, such as SENTENCE, CLAUSE, CORE, RP and NUC in (12) (as well as the two operators indicated there), and those structures which differ from one another in both languages, from a strictly structural-linguistic perspective, but which are (more-or-less spontaneously)[22] **equated by the bilingual speaker during discourse**, i. e., which have been interlingually identified. Although it may prove to be unfeasible to maintain this distinction in the long-run, it seems advisable at least for now to maintain this distinction wherever possible.

It should be stressed here that elements from both systems can be "inserted" into both systems at all levels of grammatical description. This includes both Johanson's (2008: 64) "selective copying", where "only individual selected properties – material, semantic, combinational and frequential properties" are "copied" (in his terminology) from one language into another, as well as "global copying", in which elements are copied "as a whole, including their material shape (substance) and properties of meaning, combinability and frequency." Furthermore, speakers can freely alternate within one and the same utterance / sentence between the two repertoires; cf. once again (4), where the speaker switches back and forth between German and Russian three times. Thus (4) is structurally similar to (10) – the main difference is that most overt material in (4) stems from Russian, as opposed to (10), where most overt material stems from German.

Thus, the present approach does not force us to decide arbitrarily which language a particular structure belongs to when its surface structure is ambiguous, as with the units SENTENCE, CLAUSE, CORE, RP and NUC in (12). As the research on code-switching abounds in ambiguous structures, an approach such as the present one is to be preferred over one which requires all structures to exclusively derive either from one language or the other.[23] At the same time, it allows us to index structures which unambiguously belong to a particular language as well as those which have been interlingually identified as equivalent. Through this descriptive precision, the present modified version of RRG can eventually help us come to a better understanding of the processes involved in bilingual

---

[22] Note that Höder (2012: 245) emphasizes the conventionalized nature of such interlingual identifications more than I do, although he also recognizes that "interlingual equivalence is to some degree arbitrary and always reflects a creative act of a multilingual community", whereas I do not differentiate in principle between spontaneous and conventionalized equivalents nor any intervening degrees thereof. This issue requires further discussion, which is however beyond the scope of the present study.

[23] Compare this, e. g., with the often quite complex attempt to determine the identity of the matrix language in Myers-Scotton (1993: 66–74; 2002: 59–69).

speech, such as identifying the structural properties[24] which can trigger interlingual identification or "switches" from one repertoire to another.

Note that the approach taken here, along with its Construction Grammar precursor (Höder, 2012), essentially reverses the usual approach to the question of what linguistic units may or may not be "switched"; in stark contrast to many other theoretical approaches which aim to determine *a priori* which structures may derive from which language in which language pair, the present model is decidedly descriptive in its approach. This is not to say that this approach will not eventually be capable of predicting which elements may or may not be "switched" in a particular language pair, however, for the moment we are primarily interested in a descriptively adequate theoretical account of actual cases of bilingual speech, which the present model provides.

The present approach is not restricted to code-switching but may be applied to any bilingual language activity, including interference of the type found in (8), repeated here as (13) (from Maas 2008: 469).

German-Finnish

(13) <u>Ach</u>   on-k[o]   su-ll   kiire?
     INTERJ COP.PRS.3SG-Q 2SG-ADESS(<*sinu-lla*) haste
     'Oh, you're in a hurry?'

(13) provides an especially simple example of bilingual interference: We have a SENTENCE structure, unmarked for language (for this speaker), consisting of a left-detached position (LDP) containing a German interjection, *ach*, and preceding a monolingual Finnish CLAUSE. Whatever may have motivated this interference (cf., e.g., the discussion of the monitoring-and-directing apparatus in section 2), the approach taken here allows us to capture the structural facts easily without forcing a prefabricated analysis on the data. Similar comments hold for (7), repeated here as (14) (adapted from Matras 2009: 73).

---

[24] As Gardner-Chloros (2009: 7–9) points out, code-switching can and should be studied in a holistic manner. Due to the nature of this study however, we concentrate here on structural and lexical properties of bilingual speech, although the present approach should eventually also prove capable of dealing with other aspects of bilingual speech as well.

German (non-standard), influenced by English

(14) er   ist   größ-er   denn   mir
     3SG.M.NOM COP.NPST.3SG tall-COMPAR   'than' 1SG.DAT
     'he is taller/bigger than me'

English and German share a similar structure for marking comparatives, namely (in the written language) ADJECTIVE-er + MARKER + STANDARD, i. e., an adjective marked (in regular cases) by the suffix *-er* followed by a marker – English *than*, German *als* – which precedes the standard of comparison, which appears in the oblique (or "accusative") case with pronouns in colloquial English, whereas in German this appears in the same case as the unit with which it is being compared; in the case of (14) this would be the nominative singular form *ich*. Thus, while the realization of the individual morphemes is different, the overall structure is the same for the two languages.

In (14) we find this general overall structure realized by morphs from German. However, the example is not Standard German – the form *denn* is indeed a German word, but one which is not normally used in this construction. As noted in section 2 (following the argumentation in Matras 2009: 73–74), *denn* in (14) is a case of interference presumably motivated by the fact that its form is similar to the English form *than*. Similarly, *mir* is a German word but its use here is not standard – the Standard German form would be *ich*. The use of *mir* in (14) is motivated by the fact that it sounds similar to English *me*, which may not be "correct" English (in a prescriptive sense, where *I* would be required) but which is certainly standard colloquial English.

Summarizing, the German forms *denn* and *mir* in (14) are in effect "not German" but rather English, but the speaker here has identified the two German words which are closest, phonologically speaking, to English *than me*, i. e., *denn mir*, as being equivalent with their English counterparts, presumably in an attempt to realize the entire utterance in German. Thus in (14) we have in effect the lexical entries for English *than* and *me* but realized by their closest German counterparts, phonologically speaking. In other words, the **morphemes** are English but the actual **morphs** are German, as the German morphs have been identified with the English morphs, which are bound to the English morphemes. This is reminiscent of "relexification", in which the overt form of a lexical entry derives from one language while the logical structure of this entry (i. e., its "definition") derives from another, which is easily accounted for in the present model.[25]

The present model also adequately captures cases of interference between two languages such as "borrowings" at the syntactic level. Consider example (9), repeated here as (15).

German-influenced Polish

(15) *Jak pierwsz-y raz by-ł-a-m na urlopi-e, ...*
  as first-NOM.SG.M once.NOM.SG.M COP-PST-1SG-F on vacation-LOC.SG.M

  gdzie ja by-ł-a-m? To ja by-ł-a-m sam-a,
  where 1SG.NOM COP-PST-1SG-F then 1SG.NOM COP-PST-F-1SG alone-NOM.SG.F
  'When I was on vacation for the first time, ... where was I? I was alone then ...'
  [Dan II: 4_50–4_51]

As was noted above, (15) is interesting as the overt subject pronoun in the last clause, *ja* '1SG.NOM', is used here, although an overt subject is generally only found in standard monolingual speech when it is in focus. As the subject pronoun is not focused in (15) – rather, *sama* 'alone' is focused – its presence is presumably due to contact with German, as (15) stems from a speaker of Polish living in Germany. For ease of presentation, in the following discussion of this example we focus our attention only on the structure of the last CLAUSE.

Assuming that the subject pronoun is only overt when focused, this yields the two possible structures for (standard, monolingual) Polish in (16) and (17) which are relevant for the structure in (15). In (16) we find the subject expressed directly on the predicate itself, whereas in (17) it is expressed by a separate pronoun, provided that this pronoun is the "actual focus domain".[26]

---

[25] For a brief overview of relexification and its role in contact linguistics, cf. the entries for "relexification" in the index in Winford (2003: 409).

[26] This is in line with the discussion in Van Valin (2005: 18–19) for Latin, Polish and Croatian. As Polish is predominantly dependent marking, with RPs marked for case, when the "subject RP" is present, it is considered the subject of the clause. When however the "subject RP" is omitted, the subject marking on the verb itself is viewed as the subject of the core. The presence of the actual focus domain in (17) is to indicate that this structure is only licensed when the RP is (part of) the actual focus domain. While a constructional schema would arguably be a better means of representing this information, for ease of presentation we will not introduce the use of constructional schemas here, as the representation in (17) is most likely intuitively easier to understand without prior knowledge of RRG.

(16)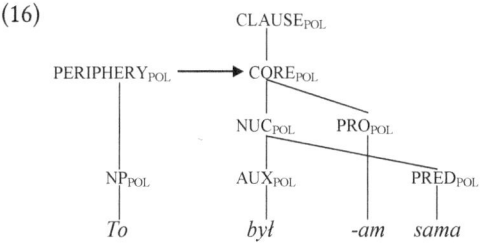

(17)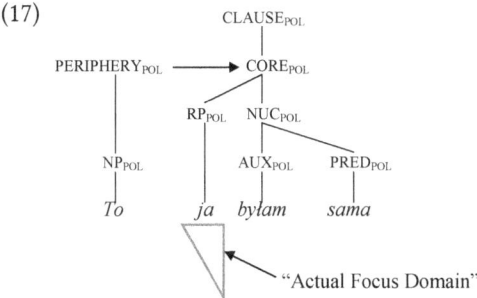

In German, on the other hand, the subject RP must always be overtly mentioned, even when its marking on the predicate is unambiguous. This is illustrated by the syntactic template in (18) for the German equivalent (slightly simplified).

(18)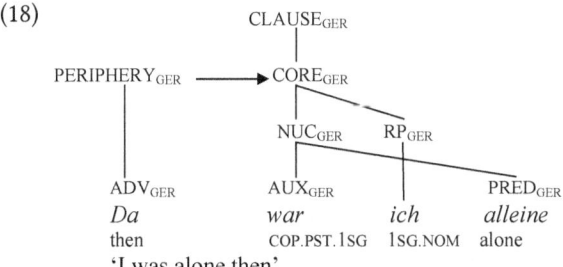

'I was alone then'

The Polish template in (17) with an overt subject pronoun is only licensed when the pronoun is in the actual focus domain, which however is not the case in (15). On the other hand, the German structure in (18) would seem to account for this, but note that word order with respect to finite verbs is quite rigid in German, so that the structure in (18), which requires an overt subject RP, is still not adequate to account for (15), although it is arguably the German requirement that subject RPs be explicit which is motivating the presence of *ja* in (15), although the order of the elements is decidedly Polish. Hence, the resulting core structure is at the same time neither Polish nor German, but yet it is both: Here, the speaker has interlingually identified two possible structures with one another, neither of which would be prescriptively acceptable in either language in the present context. The result is a structure which is otherwise restricted in standard Polish to focused subjects, but this restriction has been relaxed here due to German influence. This is illustrated in (19), where the sign "⋈",[27] "natural join", has been borrowed from relational algebra (with a somewhat different meaning here) to indicate a structure which has been interlingually identified in both languages but which is not found in exactly this form and function in either of the two languages involved.

(19)

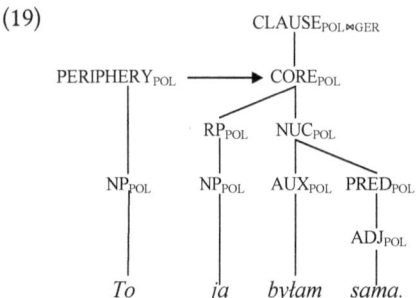

Natural join, or "⋈", presently has no theoretical value and is simply a convenient means of denoting a unit in the syntactic structure whose interlingual structure cannot easily be shown by syntactic trees alone. For example, in order to fully describe (19) we would need a constructional schema for pronominalization which would essentially be unspecified for German or Polish, and the Polish constraint requiring that this element be in focus would be replaced by the value "unspecified" for the corresponding pragmatic criterium in the German constructional schema.

According to the data in Jarząbkowska (2012), many Polish speakers in Germany regularly use the combined German⋈Polish structure in (19) when speaking Polish. As such, we are no longer dealing with "interference" with these speakers except from a historical perspective, but rather with a new variety of

---

[27] I am grateful to Julia Beck for suggesting the use of this sign to indicate this function.

Polish in which the presence of the subject RP is not restricted to focus. Interlingual identifications such as these are undoubtedly the driving force behind the evolution of convergence areas, discussed in section 2.

5 Extending the diasystematic approach – register-variation

As noted in section 1, structural variation is by no means restricted to bilinguals: Just as code-switching is typical of the spontaneous, informal speech of bilinguals, monolinguals also regularly make use of different structures according to register. Consider the following two examples from English:

(20) *She and I were going to go.*

(21) *Me 'n' her were gonna go.*

Although only sentence (20) is correct in terms of prescriptive Standard American English and structures such as that in (21) are avoided by many speakers, (21) is nonetheless perfectly well-formed for many speakers in a number of contexts, e. g., a spontaneous, relaxed, face-to-face conversation between close friends. If we were to write a descriptive grammar of American English, excluding (to the extent possible) all prescriptive tendencies, it is clear that we would have to include a grammatical rule to account for the different forms of the subject in both of these utterances, not just that in (20).[28]

The form of the subject in (20) can easily be determined by rule (4.25a) for the nominative from Van Valin (2005: 108), given here as (22a).

(22) Case assignment rules for accusative constructions:
    a. Assign nominative case to the highest ranking macrorole argument (in terms of [the privileged syntactic argument selection hierarchy: arg. of DO > 1st arg. of **do'** > 1st arg. of **pred'** (x, y) > 2nd arg. of **pred'**]).[29]
    b. Assign accusative case to the other macrorole argument.

---

[28] In the following, for the sake of presentation we will only deal with the different forms of the subject of these two sentences, ignoring all other differences between them, such as the phonologcal difference e. g. between [ænd] vs. [ɛn]/[n̩] for <and> or [gowɪŋtʰu] vs. [gʌnnʌ] for <going to>, indicated in examples (20) and (21) by differences in spelling.

[29] The privileged syntactic argument selection hierarchy which has been inserted here is from Van Valin (2005: 100).

However, (22) will not predict the form found in (21), although (21) is in a very real sense the same language as (20). Here, a rule differentiating between subject RP's consisting of simple vs. conjoined pronominal forms is required. RP's consisting of a single pronominal will then appear in the "nominative", such as *I was gonna go*, in contrast to RP's consisting of two units, at least one of which is a pronominal, as in *Me 'n' her* in (21) or *Me 'n' Sean* in *Me 'n' Sean used to live next door to each other*, which appear in the oblique or "accusative" case.

The rule to derive the structure in (21) will of course only apply in certain contexts or registers, which we at first glance might wish to term "informal", in contrast to rule (22) above, which might be said to apply in more "formal" contexts. Viewed in this manner, we are primarily dealing here with two distinct – but closely related – varieties of English, both with their own grammar and lexicon, and one solution to the apparent contradiction in subject-formation rules for English and other such differences might be to write two different grammars, one of "formal English" and one of "informal English", or perhaps "written English" and "spoken English", respectively.

This is, however, not a viable option since such a simple binary distinction (informal / formal or written / spoken) is far too simplistic to account for the full range of register variation found in English (or any other language). For example, there are many "informal" situations where the prescriptive rule might nevertheless be expected, e. g., a meeting at work among colleagues who for the most part know each other quite well but perhaps are still interested in maintaining an image of "correctness", or children who use the non-prescriptive construction with their friends but whose parents do not approve of its use, so that the children try to use the prescriptive construction at home with their parents, etc. Needless to say, it is not possible – nor desirable – to construct a separate grammar for each context.

Similar examples can easily be found in other languages. For example, the discussion in Sharbau (2011) strongly suggests that, while more formal registers of Russian obligatorily make use of a precore slot at least for constituent questions (*wh*-questions), this is not the case with less formal, spoken Russian, where the interrogative may also appear core-internally. Here again we have different "grammars" for different versions of the "same language".

Weinreich (1954) speaks of "standardized" and "non-standardized" or "folk" languages. For example, with respect to the question of "dialect", he notes that, while it is easy to distinguish between standardized languages, where "it is part of the process of standardization itself to affirm the identity of a language", this is not as true of non-standardized languages (to which we can add non-prescriptive and other register-dependent forms), where "it is NOT a part of the experience of its speakers, and is much more difficult to supply." (Weinreich, 1954: 396, emphasis in original) In fact, as he argues, it is not even possible to divide the "continuum of folk language" on the basis of purely structural criteria, as the criteria will not always point to the same division, so that some criteria and bundles of criteria will necessarily be (arbitrarily) taken as the primary division.[30]

There are two aspects here which must be dealt with separately – the **structures involved** and the **contexts in which they (may) occur**. With respect to the **contexts in which the various structures (may) occur**, there are a large number of factors which may contribute to the choice of one structure over another. For example, Biber (1988: 30–33) lists eight major components of the speech situation, most of which have a number of sub-components. These are given in Table 1 (adapted from Biber 1988: 30–31). Although Table 1 presents a quite detailed list of factors which contribute to the identification of a "context", this list is not likely to be exhaustive.

With respect to **structure**, it is clear that some structures are more complex than others, e. g. subordinated structures as opposed to adjoined structures, informationally dense structures (e. g., NPs with attributive adjectives and relative clauses) as opposed to structures consisting of one contentive or "lexical" morpheme, etc. In a number of recent studies, Maas (e. g. 2006, 2008, 2010) refers to these two structural extremes by the terms "orate" and "literate", which should not be confused with "spoken" and "written" – e. g., it is possible to have literate structures in spoken language (e. g., a formal speech) and orate structures in written language (e. g., chat-rooms).

In recent years, typologists have made considerable progress in the field of register-based, language-internal variation, and it has become increasingly apparent that many of the descriptive devices used for literate structures cannot simply be applied to orate structures, especially highly orate structures found e. g. in spontaneous, relaxed face-to-face conversations.[31] Above all, the traditional no-

---

[30] "It is evident that no unambiguous concept of dialect could emerge even from this optimistic methodology any more than a society can be exhaustively and uniquely divided into 'groups'." (Weinreich 1954: 397)

[31] For reasons of space, it is not possible to provide a detailed discussion of the many advances which have been made in the field of language structure and register variation in recent years. For an

I.	Participant roles and characteristics	
	A.	Communicative roles of participants
		1. addressor(s)
		2. addressee(s)
		3. audience
	B.	Personal characteristics
		1. stable: personality, interests, beliefs, etc.
		2. temporary: mood, emotions, etc.
	C.	Group characteristics
		1. social class, ethnic group, gender, age, occupation, education, etc.
II.	Relations among participants	
	A.	Social role relations: relative social power, status, etc.
	B.	Person relations: like, respect, etc.
	C.	Extent of shared knowledge
		1. cultural world knowledge
		2. specific personal knowledge
	D.	'Plurality' of participants
III.	Setting	
	A.	Physical context
	B.	Temporal context
	C.	Superordinate activity type
	D.	Extent to which space and time are shared by participants
IV.	Topic	
V.	Purpose	
	A.	Conventional goals
	B.	Personal goals
VI.	Social evaluation	
	A.	Evaluation of the communicative event
		1. values shared by whole culture
		2. values held by sub-cultures or individuals
	B.	Speaker's attitudes towards content
		1. feelings, judgements, attitudinal 'stance'
		2. key: tone or manner of speech
		3. degree of commitment towards the content, epistemological 'stance'
VII.	Relations of participants to the text	
VIII.	Channel	
	A.	Primary channel: speech, writing, drums, signs, etc.
	B.	Number of sub-channels available

Table 1: Components of the speech situation (Biber 1988: 30–31)

tion of "sentence" has been called into question, as many (if not in fact most) utterances in informal, spontaneous speech are not grammatically well-formed sentences in the traditional sense of a predicate and its arguments and optional adjuncts (cf. e. g. Miller & Weinert 1998). Rather, spoken language is increasingly described in terms of "intonation units",[32] where the individual intonation units in spontaneous, informal speech tend to be short units consisting maximally of one new concept (Chafe 1994), which tends to be restricted to S or P function (or, in RRG terms, A*I*, U*I*, U*T*) (cf. Du Bois 1987, 2003), although there is considerable cross-linguistic variation with respect to whether or not arguments are overtly mentioned at all (cf., e. g., Bickel 2003). These intonation units are also often referred to structurally as "information chunks" to highlight their "non-sentential" structure. This methodology is increasingly leading to new insights in a number of areas, such as Tao's important study of the structures found in spoken Chinese (Tao 1996) as well as the importance of register variation in field research (cf. e. g. Foley 2003).

In line with most research on bilingualism from the past decades, it was argued in the previous sections that the linguistic repertoire of bilingual individuals is best viewed not as two separate "languages" but rather as context-sensitive competing forms and combinatory rules for these forms which only gradually come to be viewed as two distinct languages during the course of the bilingual's socialization. In view of the comments made above with respect to orate and literate structures, I argue that "multilectalism" can best be viewed in a similar fashion by assuming that the (mono- or multilingual) individual has a number of linguistic structures such as forms, syntactic templates and rules at his or her disposal, some of which are unmarked for context while others are only appropriate in certain contexts. For most speakers of a particular "language", the vast majority of linguistic structures will be unmarked for context, although in many diglossic situations, such as those found in much of South Asia,[33] there may be a considerably higher number of context-specific lexical items, rules and syntactic templates.

---

overview, cf. e. g. (in alphabetical order) Biber (1988, 1995), Chafe (1994) and Maas (2006, 2008, 2010).

[32] Or "IUs", not to be confused with the "information units" (IUs) of RRG!

[33] For an overview of diglossia in South Asia, cf. the discussion of diglossia in Shapiro & Schiffman (1981: 164–173).

It thus seems best to employ the same general indexing strategy to indicate contextually restricted forms, syntactic templates, etc., as was used in the previous section to mark these for distinct languages. The main difference is that a much larger portion of linguistic structures will tend not to be indexed here, as many if not most structures in a particular language will not be restricted to a particular context. Although much work is necessary for a fully adequate system of indexing, I would suggest for the time-being that structures whose use is restricted by context be indexed for those contexts for which they are appropriate, whereas contextually unmarked structures are not indexed for context.

With respect to the particular criteria, I would suggest using a subset of the criteria given above in Table 1, listing only those criteria which are deemed relevant; (23) provides an example of some of the indices which could be used. While determining the most suitable criteria will require much further research, as a first approximation we can assume this small list of variables, where each criterion could have a number of potential values. (23) makes no claims to exhaustivity with respect to the various categories, with respect to their potential values, nor does it lay any claim to universality.

(23) <ADDRESSEE> with any of a number of possible values for the following subclasses:
 <PERCEIVED POWER-RELATION; AGE-RELATION; GENDER; (DIS)LIKE;
 ±SHARED GROUP STATUS; ±FAMILIAR; EDUCATION LEVEL, ... >
 <TOPIC> (potentially infinite number of values)
 <PURPOSE> (potentially infinite number of values)
 <ATTITUDINAL STANCE OF SPEAKER>
 <EXPECTED ATTITUDINAL STANCE OF INTERLOCUTOR>
 <CHANNEL> (e. g., written, spoken, ...)

For example, with the prescriptive and colloquial forms of composite subjects discussed above for examples (20) and (21), a possible indexation of the prescriptive form for a young speaker who has observed that the prescriptive construction is to be used with teachers and parents – or perhaps with older persons in general – could have the form <ADDRESSEE: OLDER> to indicate that this rule is used with older addressees in general. On the other hand, an upwardly striving member of the middle class could have a very different view of the prescriptively correct con-

Multilingualism, Multilectalism and Register Variation in Linguistic Theory

struction in (20), e. g. either as the unmarked construction or perhaps as a marked construction to be used with addressees of a particular type, e. g. <ADDRESSEE: EDUCATED; +SHARED GROUP STATUS>. Again, we stress that the determination of the most appropriate criteria and their possible values awaits further study, although it would seem that the present approach provides a good basis for dealing with language-internal and -external variation by means of the same basic approach, while also allowing us to account for speaker-specific variation.[34]

6 Summary and outlook

Although a large portion of the world's population – over half by some estimates – is multilingual, most formal linguistic theories are either explicitly or at least implicitly modelled on monolingual language use, forcing us to view bilinguals as "two monolinguals in one person" (cf. Grosjean 1989), despite all evidence to the contrary. Even most theoretical accounts of bilingual speech assume that the speaker is speaking either one language or the other at any one moment, and few make any explicit mention of register. We have tried to rectify this situation here by developing a theoretical model of mono- and bilingual language variation which is compatible with the general tenets of Role and Reference Grammar (RRG), a typologically informed, monostratic linguistic theory which strives to make as few assumptions as possible with respect to "universal" structures, assuming only those which are necessary for the description of all languages.

The underlying idea in this model is that "languages" are not discrete systems which are stored separately in the brain. Rather, following Matras (2009), languages are viewed here as patterns of context-bound structures which are associated with a range of social activities (e. g., interlocutors, topics, etc.) and which bilingual speakers in the course of their linguistic socialisation learn to view as distinct "languages". Indeed, the very fact that bilingual speakers can and regularly do employ structures from different languages in the course of their daily routines forces us to recognize the fact that linguistic structures from both languages are simultaneously accessed and combined to form bilingual utterances,

---

[34] In fact, as Balthasar Bickel (personal communication) suggests, even this model is overly simplistic, as multiple factors are at work in any situation, so that we are dealing with statistical probability here, not with absolute predictability. In this case, the individual criteria can be combined with one another and can be weighted differently for individual speakers and situations, which can then serve as the basis for further analysis. Clearly, much work remains to be done in this area.

thus the view of languages as discrete systems cannot be upheld and must be replaced by a more dynamic model.

Following Höder's (2012) recent approach to bilingual speech within a Construction Grammar framework, the present study makes use of Weinreich's (1954) notion of "diasystem" to account for related structures in different languages and dialects, a notion which relies heavily on Weinreich's (1953: 7–8) notion of "interlingual identification", in which components from two different linguistic systems are viewed as equivalent due to perceived similarities: Although interlingual equivalents from two different linguistic systems will, by definition, share a number of common characteristics, their identification is not a straightforward matter but rather a question of what the speakers themselves view as equivalent (cf. Höder 2012: 245), which can only be determined through the analysis of real-language data.

As RRG essentially views languages as networks of structures for various levels of description and rules for linking one level with another (e. g. semantics and syntax), it is especially well-equipped to handle bilingual speech as this is understood here: Both languages are viewed as networks of context-bound structures, to both of which the bilingual speaker and interlocutor have access and from both of which the speaker may freely combine structures, to the extent that s/he views these as interlingual equivalents. These structures may be indexed as belonging to one language or the other, but they may also be unspecified for language, as they belong to both linguistic repertoires. Thus, the only real innovation to mainstream RRG being proposed here is that these two networks are not viewed as entirely discrete systems but rather as "permeable" or "penetrable", as they allow the inclusion of structures from other repertoires, to the extent that these are felt by speakers to "fit". To my knowledge, this violates none of the basic principles of RRG and can easily be incorporated into the theory in its present form.

This view of language has the additional benefit that it not only allows us to describe bilingual speech, it can also be extended to include dialectal variation as well as register variation within a particular language, e. g. the different forms of the subject in sentences such as *She and I were going to go* vs. *Me 'n' her were gonna go*. Just as linguistic structures can be indexed for "language", structures within one of these languages can also be indexed as being (preferentially)[35] re-

---

[35] Cf. note 34.

stricted to specific discourse constellations. E. g., the sentence *She and I were going to go* could be indexed by some speakers (e. g., young children) as restricted to discourse situations involving older speakers, and *Me 'n' her were gonna go* would then be unmarked, while for other speakers (e. g., upper middle class adults) the first construction would be unmarked while the second would be indexed as preferentially informal, etc. As code-switching with bilinguals is similar in many ways to register variation with monolinguals (and bilinguals as well!), this allows us a uniform approach to two different but related phenomena.

As research into the area of register variation is increasingly showing, spontaneous informal speech, to which bilingual utterances generally belong, cannot always be accounted for by the categories of traditional grammatical description, above all by categories such as the "sentence" as this has traditionally been understood – i. e., a predicate with its arguments and perhaps also one or more adjuncts. Although we of course do find sentential structures in spontaneous spoken language, we also regularly find structures, often referred to as "information chunks", which are perfectly acceptable in the context in which they are uttered but which cannot be accounted for in terms of a grammatically acceptable "sentence", at least not as this term is traditionally understood, such as *What?! Me?! Drink beer?! Never!* None of these is a "sentence" in the traditional interpretation of this term, although all four utterances are perfectly acceptable in a number of (informal) situations, and any recording of naturally occurring, spontaneous spoken language will yield many further, similarly "ungrammatical" examples from a prescriptive perspective.

Not only do utterances such as these not disrupt the flow of discourse, they tend to not be viewed as "incorrect" or to even be noticed during the discourse itself. As such, a descriptively adequate grammatical theory must find a way of accounting for utterances such as these, in addition to the typical sentential structures found in most formal linguistic studies, which even today still show a strong predilection for sentences which have either been invented by the researcher or at least edited somewhat to make them "grammatical". There are probably few other formal grammatical theories which are as well equipped as RRG to undertake this challenge, and it is hoped here that the present model will prove to be at least a small first step in this direction.

Abbreviations used

1, 2, 3 – first / second / third persons	INTERJ – interjection	PURP – purposive
ADESS – adessive	LOC - locative	Q – interrogative marker
AUX – auxiliary verb	M – masculine	PTCP – participle
COMPAR – comparative	NEG – negative	REFL – reflexive
COP – copula	NOM - nominative	SG – singular
DAT – dative	NPST – nonpast	STV – stem vowel
F – feminine	PERF – perfect	SUBJ – subjunctive
INF – infinitive	PRS – present	
	PST – past	

References

Bartnicka, B., B. Hansen, W. Klemm, V. Lehmann & H. Satkiewicz. 2004. *Grammatik des Polnischen*. München: Sagner.

Bialystok, E. 2001. *Bilingualism in development. Language, literacy and cognition.* Cambridge: Cambridge University Press.

Biber, D. 1988. *Variation across speech and writing*. Cambridge: Cambridge University Press.

Biber, D. 1995. *Dimensions of register variation*. Cambridge: Cambridge University Press.

Bickel, B. 2003. Referential density in discourse and syntactic typology. *Language* 79: 708–736.

Bielec, D. 1998. *Polish. An essential grammar.* London / New York: Routledge.

Chafe, W. 1994. *Discourse, consciousness, and time. The flow and displacement of conscious experience in speaking and writing.* Chicago: Chicago University Press.

Du Bois, J. W. 1987. The discourse basis of ergativity. *Language* 63: 805–855.

Du Bois, J. W. 2003. Discourse and grammar. In M. Tomasello (ed.), *The new psychology of language. Cognitive and functional approaches to language structure*, 47–87. Mahwah, NJ / London: Erlbaum.

Ferguson, C. A. 1959. Diglossia. *Word* 15: 325–340.

Foley, W. A. 2003. Genre, register, and language documentation in literate and preliterate communities. In P. K. Austin (ed.), *Language documentation and description 1*, 85–98. London: School of Oriental und African Languages.

References

Gardner-Chloros, P. 2009. *Codeswitching*. Cambridge: Cambridge University Press.

Grosjean, F. 1989. Neurolinguists beware! The bilingual is not two monolinguals in one person. *Brain and Language* 36: 3–15.

Gumperz, J. 1982. *Discourse strategies*. Cambridge: Cambridge University Press.

Höder, S. 2012. Multilingual constructions: a diasystematic approach to common structures. In K. Braunmüller & C. Gabriel (eds.), *Multilingual individuals and multilingual societies*, 241–257. Amsterdam / Philadelphia: Benjamins.

Jarząbkowska, P. E. 2012. Pronomina in der polnischen Sprache polnischer Migranten in Deutschland. Christian-Albrechts-Universität zu Kiel, Master's thesis.

Johanson, L. 2008. Remodeling grammar. Copying, conventionalization, grammaticalization. In P. Siemund & N. Kintana (eds.), *Language contact and contact languages*, 61–80. Amsterdam: Benjamins.

Kaschubat, S. 2004. Code-Switching in der Sprache der russisch-deutschen Migranten in Deutschland. University of Osnabrück, Master's thesis.

Maas, U. 2006. Der Übergang von Oralität zu Skribalität in soziolinguistischer Perspektive. In U. Ammon et al. (eds.), *Soziolinguistik. Ein internationales Handbuch, Vol. 3/3*, 2147–2170. Berlin: de Gruyter.

Maas, U. 2008. *Sprache und Sprachen in der Migrationsgesellschaft*. Osnabrück: V&R Unipress, Universitätsverlag Osnabrück.

Maas, U. 2010. Literat und orat. Grundbegriffe der Analyse geschriebener und gesprochener Sprache. *Grazer Linguistische Studien* 73: 21–150.

Matras, Y. 2009. *Language contact*. Cambridge: Cambridge University Press.

Miller, J. & R. Weinert. 1998. *Spontaneous spoken language. Syntax and discourse*. Oxford: Oxford University Press.

Muysken, P. 2000. *Bilingual speech. A typology of code-mixing*. Cambridge: Cambridge University Press.

Muysken, P. 2013. Language contact outcomes as the result of bilingual optimization strategies. *Bilingualism: Language and Cognition* 16(4): 709–730.

Myers-Scotton, C. 1993. *Duelling languages: Grammatical structure in codeswitching*. Oxford: Clarendon Press.

Myers-Scotton, Carol. 2002. *Contact linguistics: Bilingual encounters and grammatical outcomes*. Oxford: Oxford University Press.

Peterson, J. 2009. "Pseudo-Verbs" – an analysis of non-verbal (co-)predication in Maltese. In B. Comrie, R. Fabri, M. Mifsud, T. Stolz & M. Vanhove (eds.),

Introducing Maltese linguistics. Proceedings of the 1st international conference on Maltese linguistics, 181–204. Amsterdam / Philadelphia: John Benjamins.

Peterson, J. 2010. Language contact in Jharkhand: Linguistic convergence between Munda and Indo-Aryan in eastern-central India. *Himalayan Linguistics* 9(2): 56–86.

Peterson, J. 2011. Aspects of Kharia grammar – A Role and Reference Grammar (RRG) approach. In R. Singh & Gh. Sharma (eds.), *Annual Review of South Asian Languages and Linguistics, 2011*, 81–124. Berlin / New York: Mouton de Gruyter.

Peterson, J. 2013. Parts of Speech in Kharia – A formal account. In J. Rijkhoff & E. van Lier (eds.), *Flexible word classes. Typological studies of underspecified parts of speech*, 131–168. Oxford: Oxford University Press.

Poplack, S. 1981. Sometimes I'll start a sentence in Spanish Y TERMINO EN ESPAÑOL: Toward a typology of code-switching. *Linguistics* 18: 581–618.

Rodionova, E. 2001. Word order and information structure in Russian syntax. University of North Dakota, Master's thesis.
Available online: http://arts-sciences.und.edu/summer-institute-of-linguistics/theses/_files/docs/2001-rodionova-elena.pdf

Ruhnau, A. 2011. Interpretation of the topological field model of the German clause in Role and Reference Grammar. Heinrich-Heine Universität Düsseldorf, Master's thesis.
Available online: http://linguistics.buffalo.edu/people/faculty/vanvalin/rrg/Arne%20Ruhnau%20-%20Masterthesis%20%28revised%29.pdf, accessed February 2, 2013.

Shapiro, M. C. & H. F. Schiffman. 1981. *Language and society in South Asia*. Delhi / Varanasi / Patna: Motilal Banarsidass.

Sharbau, I. 2011. Question formation in English and Russian: A Role and Reference Grammar analysis. Universität Osnabrück, Master's thesis.

Tao, H. 1996. *Units in Mandarin conversation: Prosody, discourse, and grammar*. Amsterdam / Philadelphia: Benjamins.

Van Valin, R. D., Jr. 2005. *Exploring the syntax-semantics interface*. Cambridge: Cambridge University Press.

Weinreich, U. 1953. *Languages in contact: Findings and problems*. The Hague: Mouton.

Weinreich, U. 1954. Is a structural dialectology possible? *Word* 10: 388–400.

References

Weinreich, U. 1958. On the compatibility of genetic relationship and convergent development. *Word* 14: 374–379.
Winford, D. 2003. *An introduction to contact linguistics.* Malden, MA: Blackwell.
Wolf, H. 1995. Fries-Nederlandse Code-wisseling. University of Utrecht, seminar paper.

Author

John Peterson
Department of General Linguistics
University of Kiel
jpeterson@linguistik.uni-kiel.de

RRG and the Exploration of Syntactically Based Relativistic Effects

Caleb Everett

In the last two decades there has been a florescence of experimental research demonstrating that crosslinguistic disparities foster differences in nonlinguistic thought across human populations. The linguistic influences on thought that have been uncovered are associated with a number of cognitive phenomena including spatial orientation, quantity recognition, color perception, gender discrimination, and others (Everett 2013). While the extent of such 'relativistic' effects remains a matter of some debate, their existence is now generally incontrovertible. Significantly, most of the effects in question relate to crosslinguistic semantic variation instantiated lexically and/or morphologically. One question that remains largely unexplored in such research is whether syntactic crosslinguistic disparities yield differences in the way speakers construe associated entities and relationships in nonlinguistic contexts. For instance, as McGregor (2009) notes, it is unclear whether speakers of syntactically ergative languages differentiate nonlinguistic concepts (e. g. agency in perceived events) in a more 'ergative' manner than speakers of non-ergative languages. In this chapter I suggest that the framework of Role and Reference Grammar (Van Valin 2005, 2009 *inter alia*) could be fruitfully utilized in the exploration of potential syntactic effects on nonlinguistic thought. The strong typological grounding of RRG and its characteristic lack of presuppositions about putatively universal syntactic phenomena such as subject-hood (along with its associated rejection of opaque movement rules and null elements in syntax) make it an ideal approach for distinguishing some of the core ways in which syntactic dissimilarities across languages might create disparities in nonlinguistic thought. I conclude that RRG-specific claims about the way languages differ syntactically, for instance by relying on actor-based PSA's or undergoer-based PSA's, reveal interesting ways in which researchers might empirically explore the influence of syntactic variation on nonlinguistic cognition.

1 Introduction

Researchers in a variety of disciplines have long been fascinated with the following question: Are humans' thought processes influenced by their native language? Put differently, is there evidence for cross-cultural disparities in cognition that owe themselves in some fundamental manner to the languages of the cultures in question? The search for answers to such interrelated questions, i.e. investigation into the topic of 'linguistic relativity', has long stood at the nexus of anthropology, linguistics, and psychology. While the linguistic relativity hypothesis remains closely associated with the work of Edward Sapir and, most significantly, Benjamin Whorf, related ideas have been promulgated over the course of centuries by numerous researchers and philosophers (see Lucy 1992). Nevertheless, the work of Whorf in particular brought the notion to the forefront of discussions on human language and cognition. Subsequent to Whorf's, work, however, the influence of the core ideas of linguistic relativity receded, in large measure due to the rising tide of universalist, innatist theories of human language. In turn, however, linguistics has begun to pay more serious attention to the profound extant linguistic diversity, and the influence of universalist approaches to language and human cognition have now begun to recede. (See e.g. the discussion in Evans & Levinson 2009.)

In the contemporary intellectual climate, in which many linguists consider the understanding of fundamental linguistic diversity to be a *sine qua non* of their research programs, and in which linguists increasingly rely on experimental and quantitative methods standard to other branches of the social sciences, there has been an associated resurgence of work on linguistic relativity. Unlike the work of Whorf and many others, this more recent work relies on nonlinguistic experiments, conducted across groups of speakers of different languages. In many cases these experiments are, crucially, informed by detailed ethnographic and linguistic studies.

The florescence of experimental research on linguistic relativity was germinated by the contributions of many scholars (including Whorf), but clearly grew out of the work of contemporary researchers such as John Lucy and Stephen Levinson. In the last two decades, and most visibly in the last few years, there have been dozens of studies published on the topic, many in highly visible journals. This research has uncovered evidence for linguistic effects on thought processes associated with numerous cognitive domains, including spatial orientation, color perception, gender discrimination, and quantity recognition, *inter alia*. For a comprehensive survey of this recent research, I refer the reader to Everett (2013a).

Despite the variety of cognitive domains addressed by the current crop of research on this topic, it is restricted somewhat in terms of the kinds of linguistic phenomena it addresses. Put simply, the vast majority of the work on this topic examines the role of crosslinguistic variation associated with lexical and morphological variables. Many studies examine, for instance, different recurring metaphors that are instantiated at the phrasal level in given languages, but the studies do not specifically address the potential role of syntactic variation in fostering cognitive differences across populations. This is perhaps not surprising, since it is unclear what sorts of hypotheses one might generate vis-à-vis any association between syntax and nonlinguistic thought. In contrast, the clear semantic implications of many lexical and morphological differences between languages yield clear testable predictions regarding nonlinguistic cognitive processes. For instance, in Everett (2013b) I note that the members of two populations without access to lexical or morphological means of denoting numerical concepts struggle with the mere differentiation of exact quantities greater than three. This conclusion is based on experimental work carried out by several researchers (including myself) among the populations in question, and such claims are not based simply on linguistic facts. Nevertheless, one can see how the linguistic facts in this case could generate a testable hypothesis: Speakers of the two groups in question do not have particular lexical and morphological categories (cardinal numerals and number inflection, respectively) common to most languages. The testable hypothesis is readily discernible because of the clear association between these grammatical categories and semantic categories. Such an association is not typically available in the case of syntactic phenomena. Nevertheless, I would like to suggest that the existence of syntactically motivated relativistic effects could be explored. While I remain agnostic with respect to their existence, that existence cannot be ruled out without careful nonlinguistic experimentation conducted with speakers of languages that vary significantly according to some syntactic parameter.

(After all, a number of the recently uncovered relativistic effects were once ruled out—most notably in the case of linguistic effects on the discrimination of colors.) In order to generate adequate testable hypotheses regarding this matter, however, it would be useful to have a guiding framework. I would like to suggest that Role and Reference Grammar could serve as such a framework, for the reasons that will crystallize in the subsequent discussion. In short: RRG serves as an ideal approach towards framing such research since it relies heavily on meaning, always heeding the interaction of semantic and syntactic variation. In addition, RRG is typologically well grounded, and so it can be used to generate hypotheses regarding the major typological disparities evident in crosslinguistic syntactic data.

2 Some related research

As I note in Everett (2013a), there is at least some research that addresses relativistic effects that relate to syntactic phenomena, even if the research does not directly address the role of syntactic variation in fostering relativistic effects. In a recent pilot study (Everett 2014), I examined the potential effects of a semantic transitivity/intransitivity distinction on speakers' nonlinguistic construal of actions. This study was undertaken in part to begin exploring the possibility of the influence of ergative linguistic phenomena on nonlinguistic thought. (The possibility of such an influence was presented by McGregor (2009).)[1] It is worth recapitulating some of the basic findings of the pilot study, since its results demonstrate a) that it is not unreasonable to think that fundamental syntactic variation may yield some disparities in nonlinguistic thought, and b) how RRG can prove useful in attempting to uncover such disparities. The latter point is particularly relevant, of course, in a book honoring Van Valin's sizable contributions to the typologically oriented study of grammar.

Some background information is in order. Karitiâna is a Tupí language spoken by about 330 individuals in southern Amazonia. The language has been described by several linguists, beginning with David Landin (Landin 1984). In my own research on the language, I have focused on some of its more typologically remarkable features, most notably the pattern of random-like nasal variation that

---

[1] It is worth mentioning that some of Van's earlier major contributions to the field addressed ergativity. (See Van Valin 1977, 1981).

has not been described for any other language (See Everett 2011). With respect to morphosyntax, I have suggested that one of the fundamental principles in Karitiâna grammar, which has numerous effects on a variety of morphological and syntactic parameters, is the distinction between semantically intransitive and semantically transitive verbs. As noted in Everett (2006, 2010), verbs in the language are rigidly categorized into one of these two categories. Semantically intransitive verbs describe events in which only one participant is involved. Semantically transitive verbs describe events in which at least two participants are involved.

Like other languages such as Dyirbal and Latin (Dixon 1994), the language relies pervasively on a division between *semantic* intransitivity and transitivity. Crucially, though, this division is reified both morphologically and syntactically. Morphologically, semantically intransitive and transitive verbs are inflected differentially in declarative clauses, as we see in Table 1. Verbs of the former type may be prefixed with an *i-* affix, while verbs of the latter type may not. In fact, semantically transitive verbs may only be inflected with an *i-* prefix if they are embedded in negative or interrogative clauses (see discussion in Everett 2010).

Intransitive Verb	Translation	Transitive Verb	Translation
in i-taktaktaŋa-t	'I swam'	in naka-mi-t	'I hit X'
in i-sombak	'I looked around'	in naka-kip	'I cut X'
in i-hadna-t	'I breathed'	in naka-i-t	'I ate X'
in i-seŋa-t	'I crouched'	in naka-ma-t	'I made X'
in i-mbik	'I sat'	in naka-mhip	'I cooked X'
in i-pikina-t	'I ran'	in naka-hira-t	'I smelled X'
in i-tarika-t	'I walked'	in naka-hit	'I gave X'
in i-tat	'I went'	in naka-pit	'I took X'
in i-kisep	'I jumped'	in naka-pidn	'I kicked X'

Table 1: Examples of the semantic intransitivity/transitivity distinction in Karitiâna.

In addition to such morphological ramifications, this crucial semantic distinction surfaces syntactically. For instance, only semantically transitive verbs may be followed by a noun phrase that is not marked with an oblique marker, as we see in (1) and (2).

(1) *in i-mbik   bikipa
    iN i-mbik   bikipa-ti
    1S INT-sit chair-OBL
    'I sat in the chair.'

(2) *in naka-pɨdn bikipa-ti
    ɨN   naka-pɨdn bikipa
    'I kicked the chair.'

For a discussion of the other ways in which the distinction in question surfaces, see Everett (2010). As noted in that article and in Everett (2006), the theoretical framework of RRG readily accounts for such phenomena, since it places crucial emphasis on the part that macroroles play in structuring morphosyntax. From the perspective of RRG, all Karitiâna verbs are categorized as being semantically multivalent or semantically monovalent. In the case of verbs of the former type, their argument structure houses one, but no more than one, macrorole. In contrast, for verbs of the latter type, their argument structure hosts two or more macroroles. Put differently, such verbs require an 'actor' *and* an 'undergoer' (see e. g. Van Valin 2005).

The question addressed in the aforementioned pilot study was whether the deep division in Karitiâna between verbs requiring one macrorole and verbs requiring two macroroles impacts speakers' perceptions of nonlinguistic events. Put differently, the study explored whether Karitiâna speakers were more inclined to discriminate perceived events in accordance with semantic transitivity, when contrasted to speakers of a language like English, in which verbs are not rigidly categorized according to this parameter. In English, after all, verbs are generally fairly flexible and typically may occur in syntactically intransitive or transitive contexts. (In contrast, the transitivity distinction in Karitiâna is a rigid one, reflected in large measure syntactically as evident in (1) and (2) and in other features of the language not detailed here.) While the results of the study are not dispositive, they suggest that syntactically reified semantic phenomena may in fact impact nonlinguistic performance on relevant cognitive tasks.

Twenty-eight English speakers participated in the task. Fifteen Karitiâna speakers also participated. The latter were tested in the city of Porto Velho. The subjects were presented with a triad-based discrimination task, a type that has proven useful in other studies on relativistic effects (e. g. Lucy & Gaskins 2001). The task consisted of fifteen separate stimuli triads, which were interspersed with distracter triads so as to prevent subjects from discerning the purpose of the study. Each triad was presented on the screen of a MacBook Pro. The triads consisted of three simultaneously presented abstract videos, two of which were presented

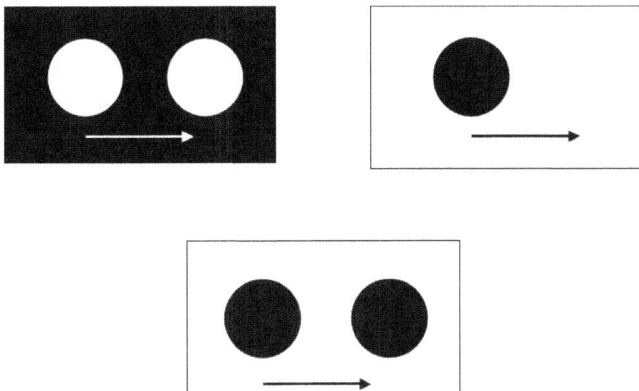

Figure 1: One of the fifteen triads employed in Everett (2014), in which discrimination could be based on a 'transitivity-oriented' choice or a color-oriented choice. Arrows represent direction of movement of a circle in the actual video.

on the top of the screen while a third was centered at the bottom of the screen, equidistant from the other two videos. Each video depicted the movement of abstract figures, inspired by the billiard-ball model of action framing, as utilized by Langacker (1987). One of the top videos consisted of the interaction/movement of two abstract figures (akin to abstract 'macroroles'), while the other top video depicted the movement of only one abstract figure (one 'macrorole'). The bottom video, referred to as the 'pivot', also depicted the interaction of two abstract figures. In this sense, it was visibly similar to the top video schematically depicting the interaction of two 'macroroles'. In every triad, however, the bottom event was also similar to the other top video according to another readily discernible factor. For example, in many cases the two videos depicted actions involving figures of the same color. As we see in Figure 1, for example, the pivot video and the top-right video depict events involving black circles. In contrast, the pivot video and the top-left video both depict events involving two figures.

Subjects were asked to group two members of the triads, at the expense of another, by selecting the event at the top of the screen that they construed to be most similar to the bottom event. The heuristic conjecture at play was that Karitiâna speakers might be more likely to exhibit 'transitivity-oriented' discrimination, i. e. be more likely to group events based on the number of figures in the abstract videos, rather than according to some other factor such as the color of the figures. For instance, in the case of Figure 1, the relativistic account would

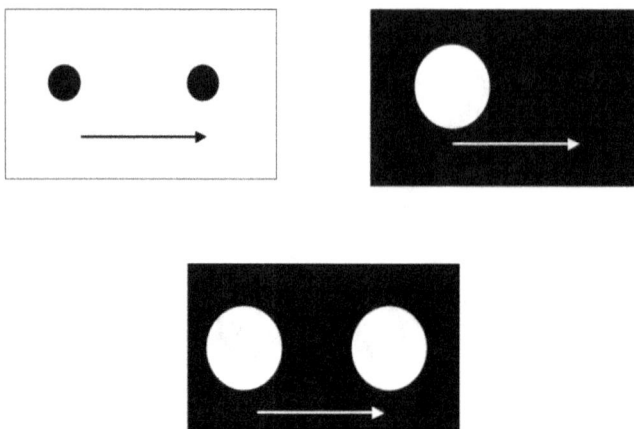

Figure 2: Another of the fifteen triads employed, in which discrimination could be based on a 'transitivity-oriented' choice or a size/color-oriented choice. Once again, arrows represent direction of movement of a circle in the actual video.

seem to predict that Karitiâna speakers would be more likely to group the bottom action with the top-left action, rather than the top-right one. The former discrimination strategy would rely on the number of participants in the perceived event, much as Karitiâna grammar relies so heavily on the distinction between one or more macroroles in verbal categorization. The latter discrimination would rely on similarity of color, a categorization strategy that has no analog in Karitiâna grammar. In the case of Figure 2, the relativistic account would once again predict that Karitiâna speakers would more frequently group the bottom action with the top-left one (when compared with English speakers), since that grouping relies on 'transitivity orientation'. The alternate grouping in this case is favored by two categorization strategies: reliance on the identical color of the figures and reliance on the identical size of the figures. (It should be noted that the order of transitivity-based choices were counterbalanced across stimuli, so that some occurred in the top-left portion of the screen and an equal number occurred in the top-right portion of the screen.)

While we will not consider the results of the pilot study in great detail, they did generally support the relativistic hypothesis. Karitiâna speakers were significantly more likely than English speakers to utilize 'transitivity-orientation' in their action groupings.

In the case of the English-speaking respondents, 107 out of 420 responses (28 participants x 15 stimuli videos) were consistent with the transitivity-oriented discrimination pattern. In the case of the Karitiâna-speaking respondents, 103 out of 270 responses (18 participants x 15 stimuli videos) were consistent with the transitivity-oriented discrimination pattern. This difference was significant (p=0.0006, χ^2(with Yates correction)=11.874). Since the distribution of these responses are not entirely independent data points, more nuanced approaches to the data analysis are required, as suggested in Everett (2014). Nevertheless, the χ^2 results are indicative of the pattern that surfaced. English speakers selected the transitivity-oriented grouping approximately 25 % of the time, while Karitiâna speakers did so 38 % of the time. This disparity was not simply due to outliers among either population, as we see in Figure 3.

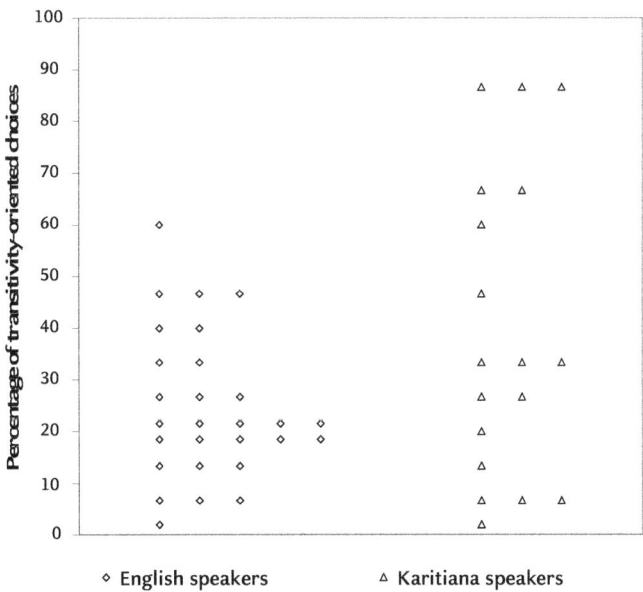

Figure 3: Plot of all individuals' response rates. Identical response rates within a group are staggered along the x-axis.

As we see in the figure, Karitiâna speakers' proclivity for transitivity-orientation in event discrimination varied significantly. In contrast, English speakers were more tightly clustered around the 20 % range. As I discuss in Everett (2014), however, monolingual Karitiâna speakers were particularly likely to use transitivity-orientation as a basis for event discrimination, when contrasted to English speakers and more bilingual Karitiâna speakers. This finding lends greater support to the notion that the results are due to crosslinguistic variation rather than some other sort of cross-cultural variation.

In short, the findings in Everett (2014) suggest that a basic semantic division crucial to the grammar of the language, namely its reliance on a deep division between verbs with one macrorole or more than one macrorole in their logical structure, does appear to impact the performance of speakers of that language on nonlinguistic cognitive tasks. At the least, the results were consistent with such a claim. It is worth stressing that the deep semantic division in question is instantiated in numerous ways in the morphology and syntax of the language in question. Given that such a pervasive, syntactically reified grammatical distinction appears to impact nonlinguistic cognition (at least according to the results of the pilot study), it does not seem altogether unreasonable to believe that pervasive syntactic patterns could influence nonlinguistic thought. In the light of the study just discussed, not to mention the dozens of other recent studies on linguistic relativity, I believe that such an influence should at least be explored.

3 The potential role of RRG

In Role and Reference Grammar, the syntactic representation of a clause and the semantic representation of that clause are directly mapped onto each other, and the mapping in question results from discourse-pragmatic factors, principally related to information structure. These discourse-pragmatic factors can of course vary from language to language, and this variance yields fundamental differences in the form of languages (see e.g. Van Valin 2005). The direct mapping between syntax and semantics characteristic of RRG makes it useful in the study of relativistic effects, since syntactic form is not presumed to be the result of abstract derivations that are inaccessible. As the reader is likely aware, many generatively influenced approaches to syntax treat it in a modular fashion, and syntax is often practically treated as being dissociated from real online performance and interactive discourse-pragmatic factors. This dissociation precludes the usage of such approaches in generating testable predictions regarding the putative influence of syntactic form on nonlinguistic thought. To reiterate, I am not claiming that the syntactic form of a given language does impact its speakers' nonlinguistic cognition. I am simply suggesting that this unexplored possibility merits inquiry, and that RRG serves as a useful framework for such inquiry. This is so for two primary reasons. The first is that which I have already mentioned, namely that RRG actually allows for the direct mapping between a language's syntactic form and its speakers' conceptualizations of events, actors, and the like. The second reason is that RRG provides a toolkit of basic syntactic components that exist in the world's languages, but are deployed differentially by the grammars of different languages. These syntactic components include the NUCLEUS, the CORE, the PERIPHERY and other associated ones such as the precore slot and the PSA, or Privileged Syntactic Argument. I refer the reader to one of Van Valin's introductions to RRG for a description of these crucial components.

For our present purposes, I would like to evaluate the manner in which one of the crucial syntactic components of RRG, the PSA, might be used in the exploration of syntactic effects on thought. Much as RRG's emphasis on macroroles proved useful in the discussion of the event conceptualization study in the preceding section, its reliance on the notion of a PSA could prove useful in examining the effect of fundamental crosslinguistic disparities of syntax on speakers' conceptualizations of the roles of arguments within events.

RRG's precise formulation of the PSA is offered at various places in the literature (see e.g. Van Valin 2005), so I will not re-present a detailed account here. Bearing in mind the aforementioned point that there are two macroroles, actor and undergoer, I would like to focus on the following heuristic description of PSA's:

> For a language like English... in an active voice clause with a transitive verb, the actor is the PSA, whereas for a language like Dyirbal, in an active voice clause with a transitive verb the undergoer is the PSA... These are the default choices; it is possible for an undergoer to serve as PSA in a passive construction in an accusative language like English or German, and it is likewise possible for an actor to serve as PSA in an antipassive construction in syntactically ergative languages like Dyirbal and Sama (Van Valin 2009: 17).

Note that these are the "default" choices for PSA's, and Van Valin notes in the same passage that some languages allow non-macroroles to serve as the PSA.

The nature of a language's PSA will of course have multifarious morphosyntactic effects on its grammatical relations. For instance, in those languages in which the PSA is typically the actor macrorole, we would expect there to be a variety of ways in which a nominative-accusative pattern should surface. With respect to syntax we would expect, for example, the actor argument of a transitive clause to function as the controller of a clause, governing coreferential deletion. Conversely, in those languages in which which the PSA is typically the undergoer, we would expect clear evidence of an absolutive-ergative alignment. We would expect, for instance, that the undergoer of a transitive clause would function as the controller of a clause, governing coreferential deletion.

English is of course a well-known case of a language in which the PSA is generally the actor of a transitive clause. As a result, the controller/pivot relationship indexes the actor, as in (3) and (4).

(3) Lebron James$_i$ embarrassed Kobe$_j$ and then ___$_{i/*j}$ dunked.

(4) Messi$_i$ nutmegged Ronaldo$_j$ and then ___ $_{i/*j}$ scored.

In contrast, in languages in which the PSA is typically the undergoer (which, admittedly, are much fewer in number), the controller/pivot relationship indexes that macrorole. If English were such a language, the deleted argument in (3) would refer to Kobe and the deleted argument in (4) would refer to Ronaldo. Dyirbal is an oft-cited case in which the controller-pivot relationship does in fact operate in this manner.

(5) ŋuma$_j$ yabu-ŋgu$_i$ bura-n ___$_{j/*i}$ banaga-n^{y}u
    father.ABSOLUTIVE mother-ERGATIVE see-NONFUTURE return-NONFUTURE
    'Mother saw father and he returned.' (Farrell 2005: 51)

These sorts of examples are familiar to most linguists. Here is the crucial question in the context of the current discussion: Does the crosslinguistic syntactic variation described vis-à-vis PSA's and associated controller-pivot phenomena impact speakers' construal of entities in nonlinguistic contexts? Admittedly, many would be skeptical of such an influence and its existence likely strikes some as counterintuitive. Intuition can often mislead in such cases, however, and many of the relativistic effects described in my recent survey of research on this topic (Everett 2013a) are counter-intuitive to some but supported by robust empirical findings acquired through careful experimentation. (Here I am not referring to findings such as those from the pilot study described in the preceding section, but to better established findings associated with color perception, the construal of time, and numerical cognition, *inter alia*.) So we should consider how the matter could be approached empirically.

What sort of predictions might follow from the PSA-status discrepancy between languages like English and Dyirbal, assuming for the sake of argument that syntactic factors impact nonlinguistic construal? Given that the PSA governs coreference, we might expect that the referents represented by PSA's might have some sort of heightened topical salience in the minds of speakers. That is, since speakers are predisposed to recurrently refer to syntactically privileged arguments, the referents denoted by such arguments might be kept foregrounded by the speakers even in nonlinguistic contexts, since they are more likely than other referents to subsequently be indexed by clausal arguments. For instance, suppose a speaker of a language such as English witnesses the situation described by (4), though s/he does not utter anything in response to that perceived stimulus. We might expect that the referent construed as initiating the action (Messi), who would more than likely be encoded as the PSA should the clause in (4) be verbalized, might be more likely to be foregrounded in some manner. That is, given the likelihood that such a referent might come to have a central referential role in potential utterances, and given that such agentive referents have tended to have a central referential role in past utterances of the perceiver in question, the person witnessing the action may be predisposed (however slightly) to mentally track the player initiating the soccer maneuver in question.

Now suppose that a different person witnesses the same event, and that their native language is one like Dyirbal, in which the PSA is typically the undergoer of a transitive declarative clause. Even assuming that this person does not describe the event in question, we might expect the second referent in the perceived event (i.e. not the one initiating the action) to have relatively high salience for them, when contrasted to its salience for speakers of a language in which the PSA is typically the actor of a transitive declarative clause. After all, should such a witness choose to subsequently verbalize the event in question, s/he would likely need to refer multiple times to the person undergoing the soccer maneuver in question.

Note that this tentative hypothesis does not imply gross disparities in the way such actions are perceived by speakers of languages with such fundamentally disparate syntax. We might, for instance, expect the salience of agentive referents to be very high across all human observers in such nonlinguistic contexts.

Nevertheless, the relative salience of agentive and patientive referents might vary somewhat across speakers of such languages. Recall that, for the pilot study described in section 2, both English and Karitiâna speakers tended to group events according to factors such as the color of objects in the events. So there were clear similarities between the populations' construal patterns. Nevertheless, the Karitiâna speakers evinced a greater tendency to utilize transitivity-oriented discrimination strategies.

How would we test the conjecture just offered? That is, how might we explore whether in fact speakers of languages with actor-based PSA's perceive stimuli in some differential manner, when contrasted with speakers of languages with undergoer-based PSA's? There are a number of factors that must be accounted for methodologically in such experimental work, not all of which I will address here (see Everett 2013a for a more detailed discussion of the methodological obstacles to relativistic research). Among other factors, we would need to ensure that the subjects participating in the experiment are native speakers of languages of the two basic syntactic types described above. For instance, we might contrast speakers of English and Dyirbal. Ideally, of course, we would conduct experiments among speakers of numerous languages that can be categorized into one of the two basic syntactic types mentioned. Utilizing speakers of many languages helps to reduce the influence of confounding cultural variables such as differences in literacy rates.

In order to uncover disparities in the nonlinguistic cognitive processes of two groups (or at least explore the possibility of such disparities), one needs to generate a series of experimental stimuli to be used in an entirely nonlinguistic task. Let me offer a sample stimulus that could potentially be used as a starting point for a pilot study examining the influence of PSA status on the nonlinguistic construal of perceived referents. In Figure 4 we see a basic static depiction of an event that could be presented via video on a computer screen, in a remote field setting or in a laboratory. The figure represents the movement of a large figure towards a smaller one. As the video progresses, the larger (more actor-like) figure alters the shape of the smaller one (more undergoer-like). The video might be described in English as follows: "The large dark circle squished the small gray one."

In one potential experiment, speakers of languages with different PSA types would be presented with the video stimulus depicted in Figure 4. The envisioned experiment would test the salience of the referents in the abstract video by forcing

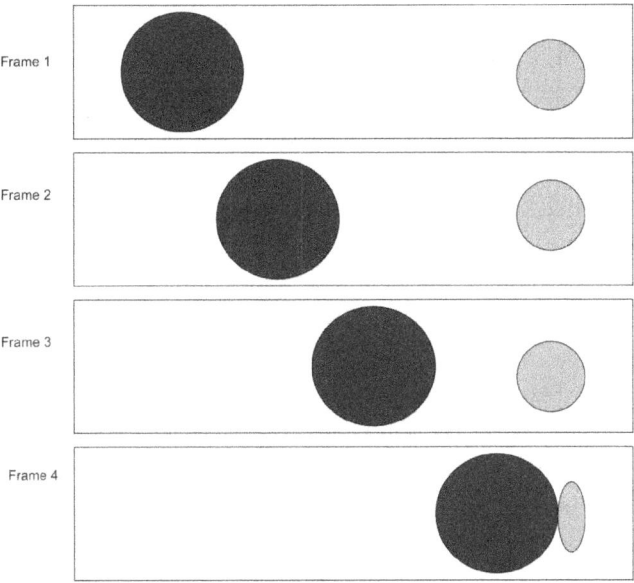

Figure 4: One potential stimulus for a task testing the salience of referents in a transitive event.

speakers to recall details of the referent initiating the action and the referent undergoing the action. For instance, in the task utilizing the stimulus depicted in Figure 4, participants might view the relevant video, unaware that they would subsequently be asked to recall details regarding the two referents in question. They might be presented with filler videos prior to or following (or both prior to and following) the stimulus video. Then, at some point they would be asked to recall the details of the event depicted in Figure 4. For instance, they might be asked to select the agentive referent (the large dark circle) from a number of depicted objects, all of which might be similar to the agentive referent but only one of which would be identical. Similarly, they might be asked to select the patientive referent from a number of depicted objects, all of which would be similar to the patientive referent but only one of which would be exactly the same. In this manner, the relative topical salience of the two kinds of referents might be tested across the two linguistic populations. Crucially, the entire task would be nonlinguistic.

Obviously, numerous stimuli of the sort depicted in Figure 4 would have to be generated, and numerous participants would be required for each language group represented in the experiment. Ideally, a third group of participants might be recruited. This group would be bilingual, speaking both a language with an actor-oriented PSA and an undergoer-oriented PSA. Via this sort of systematic exploration of this topic, we might uncover cross-population disparities that are consistent with a relativistic interpretation. For example, suppose that speakers of a language like Dyirbal were relatively adept at recalling details regarding the undergoer-type referents, while speakers of a language like English were relatively adept at recalling the features of actor-type ones. Furthermore, suppose that participants that spoke both kinds of languages exhibited a sort of mixed performance, vis-à-vis referent recall. A distribution of recall strategies of this sort would hint at syntactic effects on nonlinguistic cognition. Such results would not necessarily be conclusive, and a number of external variables would need to be ruled out. Nevertheless, we can get a sense of how such an experiment might be carried out in order to test the role of PSA status in nonlinguistic thought. (Interestingly, similar methods have been sucessfully employed, with videos of real [non-abstract] events, in a recent related study (Fausey & Boroditsky 2011).)

4 Discussion and conclusion

In the last several decades there has been an explosion of research on linguistic relativity. Much of this work has suggested fairly conclusively that linguistic disparities help generate nonlinguistic differences in cognitive processes across human populations. The work in question is generally based on morphological and lexical differences between languages (see Everett 2013a), and no studies have exclusively explored the potential effects of syntactic disparities on nonlinguistic thought. In this chapter I have summarized evidence from a recent pilot study suggesting that morphosyntactic differences between Karitiâna and English speakers appear to impact their nonlinguistic construal of events. Relying on RRG, I demonstrated how the morphosynctactic differences in question are the result of the centrality, in Karitiâna grammar, of the number of macroroles housed by each verb. In other words, I suggested that RRG serves as a useful framework for describing the crosslinguistic disparities that appear to yield nonlinguistic disparities in event construal.

In a similar vein, I suggested that RRG's straightforward approach to syntax, according to which syntax is mapped directly on semantic form and not mediated by some modular algorithm, offers a useful framework for future investigations of the role of syntax on nonlinguistic cognition. In particular, I have suggested that the basic distinctions between PSA types presented in RRG allow for the straightforward generation of testable hypotheses on the influences of syntax on nonlinguistic thought. This does not imply, of course, that such influences will in fact surface in future experimental work of the sort hinted at above. I am simply suggesting that the typologically well-informed approach of RRG offers a useful point of departure for future explorations of the type described here.

References

Dixon, R. 1994. *Ergativity*. Cambridge: Cambridge University Press.

Evans, N. & S. Levinson. 2009. The myth of language universals. Language diversity and its importance for cognitive science. *Behavioral and Brain Sciences* 32: 429–492.

Everett, C. 2014. Evidence for relativistic effects in the construal of transitive events. *Selected papers from UK-CLA Meetings, Vol II*: 84–101.

Everett, C. 2013a. *Linguistic relativity: Evidence across languages and cognitive domains*. Berlin: De Gruyter Mouton.

Everett, C. 2013b. Independent cross-cultural data reveal linguistic effects on basic numerical cognition. *Language and Cognition* 5: 99–104.

Everett, C. 2011. Variable velic movement in Karitiâna. *International Journal of American Linguistics* 77: 33–58.

Everett, C. 2010. Negation and the untransitive category in Karitiâna. *Proceedings of the Berkeley Linguistics Society* 35: 379–390.

Everett, C. 2006. *Patterns in Karitiâna: Articulation, perception, and grammar*. Rice University dissertation.

Farrell, P. 2005. *Grammatical relations*. Oxford: Oxford University Press.

Fausey, C., & L. Boroditsky. 2011. Who dunnit? Cross-linguistic differences in eye-witness memory. *Psychonomic Bulletin & Review* 13: 275–280.

Landin. D. 1984. An outline of the syntactic structure of Karitiana sentence. In B. Dooley (ed.), *Estudos Sobre Línguas Tupí do Brasil*, 219–254. Brasilia: SIL.

Langacker, R. 1987. *Foundations of cognitive grammar*. Palo Alto: Stanford University Press.

Lucy, J. 1992. *Language diversity and thought.* Cambridge: Cambridge University Press

Lucy, J. & S. Gaskins. 2001. Grammatical categories and the development of classification preferences: A comparative approach. In M. Bowerman & S. Levinson (eds.), *Language acquisition and conceptual development,* 257–283. Cambridge: CUP.

McGregor, W. 2009. Typology of ergativity. *Language and Linguistics Compass* 3: 480–508.

Van Valin, R. D., Jr. 2009. An overview of Role and Reference Grammar. Available online: http://linguistics.buffalo.edu/people/faculty/vanvalin/rrg/RRG_overview.pdf.

Van Valin, R. D., Jr. 2005. *Exploring the syntax-semantics interface.* Cambridge: Cambridge University Press.

Van Valin, R. D., Jr. 1981. Grammatical relations in ergative languages. *Studies in Language* 5: 361–394.

Van Valin, R. D., Jr. 1977. Ergativity and the universality of subjects. *Proceedings of the Chicago Linguistic Society* 13: 689–706.

Author

Caleb Everett
Department of Anthropology
University of Miami
caleb@miami.edu

Case Studies of the Syntax-Semantics Interface

Head-Marking and Agreement: Evidence from Yucatec Maya[1]

Jürgen Bohnemeyer, Lindsay K. Butler & T. Florian Jaeger

1 Introduction

This chapter revisits one of the foundational analyses of Role and Reference Grammar (RRG; cf. Foley & Van Valin 1984, Van Valin & LaPolla 1997, Van Valin 1993, 2005, *inter alia*), according to which in head-marking polysynthetic languages such as Lakhota, the pronominal markers morphophonologically bound to a syntactic head saturate its valency requirements (Van Valin 1977, 1985, 2013). Given the architecture of the Layered Structure of the Clause (LSC), this entails that syntactically optional reference phrases (RPs) coindexed with clause-mate bound pronominal argument markers (henceforth, 'cross-reference markers') cannot be core constituents, since cores are by definition constituted by heads (nuclei) and their syntactic arguments. The most recent proposal within RRG places RPs in 'Extra-Core Slots'. These positions are immediate daughters of the clause, but their presence in it is licensed by the occurrence of cross-reference markers on a nucleus (Van Valin 2013).

---

[1] Robert D. Van Valin, Jr., pointed out to us the fit between our data and Bresnan & Mchombo's proposal. We are grateful for his advice, as well as for that of Kay Bock and Lorena Pool Balam. We would like to thank Randi Tucker for help with the manuscript, and of course the editors for inviting us to contribute and for their patience with us. The material presented in Section 5 is based upon work supported by the National Science Foundation under Grant No. BCS-0848353 and BCS-0848298 *Collaborative Research: Studying Language Production in the Field* (PIs TFJ and JB). Additional support came from a Dissertation Improvement Grant from SBSRI, University of Arizona to LKB and the Wilmot Award to TFJ. None of the scholars and institutions mentioned bear any responsibility for the content presented here or the form in which it is presented.

Jens Fleischhauer, Anja Latrouite & Rainer Osswald (eds.). 2016.
Explorations of the Syntax-Semantics Interface. Düsseldorf: dup.

We present two sources of evidence from Yucatec Maya that point to the need for a modification of the above analysis. First, distributional evidence suggests that cross-referenced RPs are not, in fact, immediate daughters of the clause in Yucatec. Specifically, in core cosubordination, in which two cores form a higher core, sharing an operator projection and a periphery, RPs cross-referenced on the first verb may appear between the two verbs. Since Yucatec otherwise lacks discontinuous syntactic projections, this makes direct dominance by the clause implausible.

Secondly, Yucatec is a language with optional number marking on both nouns and verbs. We discuss data from two production experiments on the production of plural marking in Yucatec (first reported in Butler, Jaeger & Bohnemeyer 2014). In the clear majority of responses, participants marked the cardinality of the set of individuals involved in the stimulus actions on either both the verb and the cross-referenced RP or on neither. We argue that this finding supports an analysis according to which the cross-reference markers fill the syntactic argument positions of the verb in case they are not accompanied by clause-mate RPs, but express agreement with cross-referenced clause-mate RPs when the latter are present. In the second case it is the RPs that saturate the valency of the verb. A similar analysis was proposed by Bresnan & Mchombo (1987) for the so-called subject markers of Cicheŵa. This is consistent with the distributional evidence pointing to the cross-referenced RPs being core constituents.

The remainder of the chapter is organized as follows: Section 2 introduces relevant background on the grammar of Yucatec. Section 3 summarizes the analysis of head-marking advanced in Van Valin (1977, 1985, 2013) in the broader context of the literature on the topic. The following sections present the distributional evidence for cross-referenced RPs not being immediate daughters of the clause (Section 4) and the production evidence for agreement (Section 5). Section 6 offers a discussion of the findings and concludes.

2 Head-marking in Yucatec

2.1 The language and its speakers

Yucatec is the largest member of the Yucatecan branch of the Mayan language family. It is spoken across the Yucatan peninsula in the Mexican states of Campeche, Quintana Roo, and Yucatán and in the Orange Walk and Corozal districts of Belize. Mexican census data from 2005 puts the number of speakers age 5 or older at 759,000 (PHLI 2009). The Ethnologue places an additional 6,000 speakers in Belize as of 2006 (Lewis 2009).

2.2 Cross-reference marking

Yucatec is an exclusively head-marking language – there is no nominal case marking of any kind. Like most Mayan languages, Yucatec has two paradigms of morphologically bound pronominal argument or 'cross-reference' markers (following Bloomfield 1933: 191–194). Mayanists have become accustomed to labeling these paradigms 'Set A' and 'Set B'. The arbitrariness of these labels reflects the polyfunctionality of the two sets and the complex and highly variable nature of the argument marking splits found across the Mayan language family. Table 1 summarizes the distribution and functions of the paradigms in Yucatec:

Environment	Set A	Set B
Transitive verbs (active voice)	A(ctor)	U(ndergoer)
Intransitive verbs; transitive verbs in non-active voice	S (incompletive 'status')	S (completive, subjunctive, extrafocal 'status')
Other lexical categories	Possessor of nominals	S of non-verbal predicates

Table 1: Distribution and functions of the two paradigms of Yucatec cross-reference markers

For illustration, (1) shows two possessed nominal predicates, each carrying the 1SG Set-A marker cross-referencing the possessor and the 2SG Set-B marker cross-referencing the theme.

(1) *Síih **in**=ìiho-**ech**,   **in**=pàal-**ech**,   ko'x!*
    yes **A1SG**=son-**B2SG** **A1SG**=child-**B2SG** EXHORT
    'You ARE my son alright, you ARE my child; let's go!' (Lehmann 1991)

The next example shows the same two cross-reference markers realizing the two arguments of a transitive verb:

(2) *T-**inw**=il-ah-**ech**   te=ha'ts+kab+k'ìin=a'.*
    PRV-**A1SG**=see-CMP-**B2SG** PREP:DEF=divide:PASS+Earth+sun=D1
    'I saw you this morning.'

Lastly, (3)–(4) feature the same transitive matrix verb *il* 'see' of (2) and a second verb, the unaccusative *lúub* 'fall'. The argument of the second verb is realized by a 2SG cross-reference marker in both cases. In (3), the intransitive verb appears in incompletive status, and consequently, the S-argument is realized by the 2SG Set-A clitic *a=*. This sentence instantiates a direct (i. e., event) perception construction. In contrast, in (4), the intransitive verb appears in completive status and the argument is consequently realized by the 2SG Set-B suffix. In this case, the perception verb is used as a transferred expression of a cognitive inference.

(3) T-inw=il-ah   *a=lúub-ul.*
PRV-A1SG=see-CMP(B3SG) **A2**=fall-INC
'I saw you fall(ing).'

(4) T-inw=il-ah   déekeh h-lúub-**ech.**
PRV-A1SG=see-CMP(B3SG) COMP LPRV-fall-**B2SG**
'I saw that you fell.'

We treat the cross-reference markers as (nearly) direct expressions of semantic macro-roles rather than of grammatical relations, following Bohnemeyer (2004, 2009a). Following established practice in RRG, we use 'A(ctor)' for the thematically highest-ranked, most agent-like argument of active-voice transitive verb forms, 'U(ndergoer)' for the lower-ranked argument, and 'S' for the single argument of intransitive verbs and the theme of non-verbal predicates. (There are arguably no syntactically ditransitive clauses in Yucatec; recipients of transfer events are expressed by oblique arguments.) The evidence against the cross-reference markers expressing grammatical relations can be summarized as follows:

- Intransitive verbs show a split marking pattern – there is thus no uniformly marked subject (Bohnemeyer 2004 and references within; see below);
- Intra-clausal linking is subject to alignment/obviation constraints, which prevent actors from being uniformly linked to a designated argument – the subject – in active voice (Bohnemeyer 2009a);
- Inter-clausal linking is governed by construction-specific rules, which do not submit to an overall characterization in terms of a uniform grammatical 'pivot' – the subject – on which they operate (Bohnemeyer 2009a).

Table 1 and examples (2)–(4) suggest a typologically unusual argument marking split in verbal cores: the S-argument of intransitive cores is realized by Set-A in 'incompletive status', but by Set-B in 'completive', 'subjunctive', and 'extrafocal status'. Status is a functional category of the Mayan verb that conflates viewpoint aspect and mood. Incompletive status can be treated as unmarked for both. Historically, it seems to have originated as a nominalization and still functions as such in certain contexts (Bohnemeyer 2002: 157–159, 216–228). Completive status expresses perfective aspect and realis/indicative mood, while subjunctive status can be considered in first approximation an aspectually neutral irrealis mood (Bohnemeyer 2012). 'Extra-focal' status expresses perfective aspect in certain focus constructions. The Yucatec argument marking split fits with viewpoint-aspect-based splits in other languages – for example, Indo-Iranian languages such as Hindi – in that it associates an "ergative-absolutive" (S=U) pattern with perfective aspect and a "nominative-accusative" (S=A) pattern with non-perfective aspect. What makes it typologically rare is that the split occurs in intransitive rather than in transitive clauses (see Bohnemeyer 2004, Krämer & Wunderlich 1999, and reference therein for discussion).

Table 2 lists the cells of the two cross-reference paradigms. The Set-B markers are suffixes; the Set-A markers clitics. They either procliticize to the head (in which case they end in the glides *y/w* if the head starts with a vowel) or form a portmanteau with a preceding host; the second process appears to be restricted to a few fixed combinations.

Number	Person	Set A	Set B
SG	1	*in(w)=*	*-en*
	2	*a(w)=*	*-ech*
	3	*u(y)=*	*-Ø (/-ih)*[2]
PL	1	*(a)k-…(o'n)*	*-o'n*
	1 INCL	*(a)k=…-o'ne'x*	*-o'ne'x*
	2	*a(w)= …-e'x*	*-e'x*
	3	*u(y)= …-o'b*	*-o'b*

Table 2: The morphological forms of the two paradigms of cross-reference markers

---

[2] The 3SG (3rd-person singular) Set-B suffix is zero-marked across the Mayan language family. However, in Yucatec, the string /ih/ appears in this cell – and exclusively in this cell – on intransitive verbs of all classes, basic or derived (but exclusively on intransitive verbs). It is restricted to completive status and absolute clause-final position, i. e., when not followed by another morpheme or word belonging to the same clause. This string /ih/ can be analyzed as an innovated 3SG Set-B suffix that is restricted to clause-final position, intransitive verbs, and completive status. Alternatively, it can be treated as part of a completive status suffix the complete form of which varies across verb classes. The second analysis, however, requires a rule that deletes a particular segment of a

As the table shows, the Set-B plural suffixes are also "grafted" onto Set-A-marked forms to express their plural cells. Even though these combinations do not appear to be compositional, the same strategy is also used to express the inclusive forms of the 1PL cell.

2.3 Clause structure

The Layered-Structure-of-the-Clause (LCS) theory of RRG states that, whereas verb phrases are language-specific constructions, clauses universally contain a so-called 'core', constituted in its turn by the expression of a semantic predicate – the 'nucleus' – in combination with its syntactic arguments. A 'verbal core' is thus a kind of subject-internal verb phrase. In addition, each layer – the nucleus, the core, and the clause – has its own 'periphery', which accommodates modifiers specific to that layer. (More recent versions of RRG generalize LCS-like structures across lexical categories, postulating, in addition to verbal cores, nominal cores, adjectival cores, and so on.)

Nuclei, cores, and clauses can be complex, constituted by 'junctures' of units. There are three 'nexus' types that account for the relations between the units: subordination, whereby a unit is embedded as a an argument or modifier of another; coordination, whereby two otherwise independent units enter into a symmetrical combination; and cosubordination, a symmetrical combination between two nuclei, cores, or clauses that to some extent together behave like a single nucleus, core, or clause in that they have a shared operator projection and periphery and often also share arguments (cf. Van Valin 2005: 6–30, Bohnemeyer & Van Valin ms., and Section 4).

Examples (3)–(4) above illustrate the contrast between verbal projections that carry a preverbal aspect marker, such as perfective *h-* in *déekeh h-lúub-ech* 'that you fell' in (4), and those that lack such a marker, such as the corresponding projection of *lúub* 'fall' in (3). We treat the presence of the preverbal aspect marker as expressing finiteness, following Bohnemeyer (2009b). It is no accident that the finite projection in (4) occurs with a (syntactically optional) complementizer, whereas the non-finite one in (3) does not and in fact excludes it.

---

particular morpheme – and only this segment of this morpheme – in a certain position. These two analyses seem to be about equally problematic.

We assume that (4) instantiates clausal subordination, whereas (3) is a core cosubordination. Verbal cores constitute (matrix or subordinate) clauses by combining with exactly one member of a paradigm of 15 preverbal markers that express notions of viewpoint aspect, modality, and temporal 'remoteness' or distance from a reference time. Bohnemeyer (1998) coined the somewhat misleading term 'aspect-mood marker' for this preverbal slot. The term is misleading because mood, as opposed to modality, is not actually expressed in this position, but exclusively by the status suffixes on the verb. However, the preverbal marker in fact determines the status category the verb is inflected for. By hypothesis, the reason why no expressions of deictic or anaphoric tense – other than those 'remoteness' or 'metrical tense' markers – appear in the preverbal slot, even though this position appears to be tied to finiteness, is that Yucatec is a tenseless language (Bohnemeyer 1998, 2002, 2009a). In the matrix clauses of (2)–(6), the preverbal aspect-mood slot is filled by the perfective aspect marker *t-*. In the complement clause in (4), it is filled by the allomorph *h-* of the same marker, which is restricted to intransitive verbs. The examples in (7) below feature the remote future marker *bíin* in the preverbal slot.

Stative predicates such as those in (1), however, neither inflect for status nor do they combine with the preverbal aspect-mood markers. Moreover, they do not occur in embedded verbal cores. This is illustrated by the examples in (5). The desiderative matrix predicate subcategorizes for a core juncture. The second core cannot be projected by the nominal predicates *xch'úupo'b* 'they are women' and *xibo'b* 'they are men' unless inchoative verbs are first derived from these nouns, as in (5b).[3]

(5) a. **Bíin u=ts'íib+óol-t   x-ch'úup-o'b xib-o'b,*
   REM.FUT A3=write+soul-APP(B3SG) F-female-B3PL male-PL

   *bíin u=ts'íib+óol-t   xib-o'b   x-ch'úup-o'b.
   REM.FUT A3=write+soul-APP(B3SG) male-B3PL F-female-PL

   Intended: 'The men shall wish to be women, the women shall wish to be men.'

---

[3] Note that the Set-A marker of the embedded cores in (5b) is omitted due to control by the matrix predicate. See Bohnemeyer (2009a) for a sketch of the grammar of control constructions in Yucatec.

b. *Bíin   u=ts'íib+óol-t   x-ch'úup-tal   xib-o'b,*
   REM.FUT A3=write+soul-APP(B3SG) F-female-PROC.INC male-PL
   bíin   u=ts'íib+óol-t   xib-tal   x-ch'úup-o'b.
   REM.FUT A3=write+soul-APP(B3SG) male-PROC.INC F-female-PL
   'The men shall wish to become women, the women shall wish to become men.' (Vapnarsky 1995: 89)[4]

The same holds for all types of stative predicates: the propositions 'I want to be tall/dead' cannot be expressed in a single sentence in Yucatec; only 'I want to *become* tall/dead' can.

With the exception of the morphologically bound perfective and imperfective markers (the former of which is illustrated in (2)–(4)), the preverbal aspect-mood markers can be shown to constitute stative predicates themselves. Thus, the mutually exclusive distribution of verbal cores and stative predicates partially explains why projections that carry preverbal aspect-mood markers are clauses rather than verbal cores. This generalization however in fact extends to projections formed with the morphologically bound perfective and imperfective markers as well – these too never occur in environments such as in (3) and (5), and we thus treat them as clauses rather than as verbal cores. Clauses can be embedded as relative clauses, but arguably not as complements in Yucatec. Finite complements such as that in (4) are, at least by hypothesis, adjoined rather than embedded.[5]

The morphological and distributional differences between clauses and verbal cores are important to the argumentation we present in Section 4, where we attempt to show that cross-referenced RPs can be core constituents in Yucatec.

---

[4] This is a prophecy attributed by the narrator to spiritual leaders of the Cruzo'b Maya in the 19th century. The term Cruzo'b was coined by Villa Rojas (1945) to designate a religious-military movement in the center of what is now the Mexican state of Quintana Roo, which erected an indigenous theocratic state in the midst of a guerilla war against the Mexican army in the second half of the 19th century.

[5] That clauses can in fact be embedded in Yucatec is assumed without argument in Norcliffe (2009). The main argument against this view comes from the observation that, whenever the expression of a proposition or state of affairs cross-referenced on a Yucatec predicate is 'finite', i.e., has its own preverbal aspect-mood marker, and thus has the structural properties of a Yucatec clause, it is always possible to have a member of the paradigm of clause-final indexical particles (mentioned below) intervening between the predicate and the clause. Since these particles mark the left edge of their clause, this suggests that the second clause is not a constituent of the first. In contrast, these particles do not intervene in core junctures. Cf. Bohnemeyer (2002: 90–98).

The examples (1)–(4) illustrate two further properties that are of some consequence in the following. First, Yucatec is a verb-initial language, a trait shared throughout the Mayan language family. In transitive clauses with two clause-mate cross-referenced RPs, both follow the verb, with the RP referring to the actor in final position, as illustrated in (6a):

(6) a. *T-u=nes-ah*   *hun-túul*   *pàal*
     PRV-A3=gnaw-CMP(B3SG) one-CL.AN child
     le=xoh=o'
     DEF=cockroach=D2
     'The cockroach bit a child' [elicited]

    b. *T-u=nes-ah*
     PRV-A3=gnaw-CMP(B3SG)
     'It bit it' [constructed]

Example (6b) illustrates the optionality of the RPs. In spontaneous connected discourse, clauses with multiple RPs are dispreferred (Skopeteas & Verhoeven 2009). Instead, the RP with the most topical referent tends to be left-dislocated, as in (7):

(7) *Le=xoh=o',*   *t-u=nes-ah*   *hun-túul*   *pàal*
    DEF=cockroach=D2 PRV-A3=gnaw-CMP(B3SG) one-CL.AN child
    'The cockroach, it bit a child'

For topical agent referents, this pattern is so pervasive that it has led some authors to analyze AVU (or Subject-Verb-Object, depending on the syntactic framework) as the basic constituent order in Yucatec clauses (Durbin and Ojeda 1978, Gutiérrez Bravo & Monforte y Madera 2008, ms.). However, a variety of sources of evidence point to the conclusion that the initial RP in (7) is in fact left-dislocated (cf. Bohnemeyer 2009a, Skopeteas & Verhoeven 2009):

- The position in question hosts the clitic indexical particles =*a'* (D1), =*o'* (D2, illustrated in (7)), and =*e'* (D3/TOP) on its left edge. These particles do not occur clause-internally.
- The position is also routinely separated from the rest of the clause by an intonation break.

- Expressions that occur in this position are not restricted to RPs and not necessarily cross-referenced on the verb. They may instead be adverbials designating the time or place about which the following clause makes an assertion or asks a question, etc., or RPs that stand in a variety of semantic relations to the arguments of the clause.
- The preference for a sentence-initial RP does not extend to intransitive clauses.
- The position in question does not admit non-topical elements. For instance, indefinite RPs only occur in this position in generic sentences and in sentences that do not contain a definite RP (e. g., in the very first sentence of a story).

We tentatively conclude that the position in question is the type of position identified in more recent versions of RRG (starting with Van Valin 1993) as the Left-Detached Position (LDP).

2.4 Configurationality

A question that has attracted considerable attention in the literature on cross-reference marking is that of its relation to polysynthesis and configurationality. Jelinek's (1984) Pronominal Argument Hypothesis entails a direct causal link between cross-reference marking and non-configurationality: the non-configurational properties of languages such as Warlpiri – in particular, the syntactic optionality of RPs; their pragmatically determined position in linear order; their potential discontinuity; the occurrence of ergative argument marking splits between RPs and pronouns; and the absence of a VP node – are treated as a direct consequence of the adjoined syntactic status of RPs. Building on Jelinek's proposal, Baker (1991, 1996) argues that cross-reference marking, along with noun incorporation, is a hallmark of polysynthesis. However, Simpson (1991) and Austin & Bresnan (1996), building on Hale (1983), present evidence from Warlpiri and other Australian languages that casts doubt both on the detached position of cross-referenced RPs (see Section 3) and on the typological co-distribution of the relevant properties. These authors argue that a framework such as Lexical Functional Grammar (LFG), which treats constituent structure, argument structure, and functional structure – the latter encoding grammatical relations and functional relations in terms of feature structures – as independent of one another, affords a superior treatment of cross-reference marking. RRG, the theory we assume for the purposes of this chapter, likewise offers treatments of constituency and functional categories in terms of independent representations. Syntactic aspects of argument structure are treated in RRG as encoded in the LSC, which does not map isomorphically into a traditional immediate-constituency representation, phrase structure grammar, or X-bar syntax. However, RRG parts company with LFG in that it treats grammatical relations as language-specific.

At first blush, Yucatec may appear to be a fairly configurational language. While RPs are syntactically optional (see (5)) and frequently appear in adjoined positions such as the LDP in (6), they are never discontinuous,[6] and constituent order within the clause is relatively rigid (but see Skopeteas & Verhoeven 2005). However, on closer inspection, the thematic relation a referent is assigned depends exclusively on the cross-reference marker that refers to it, not on the position of an RP in the clause. This can be seen from the fact that in a transitive clause with two 3rd-person arguments, the actor must outrank the undergoer on a topicality hierarchy if both arguments are to be realized by a combination of a cross-reference marker and a clause-internal RP. Aside from topicality, the ranking of the two argument referents is also sensitive to definiteness, humanness, and animacy.[7] In (5) above, it is possible for a non-human actor to act on a human undergoer because the former is definite while the latter is indefinite. If this distribution is reversed, as in (8a), the intended interpretation can no longer be obtained. Native speakers confronted with such examples tend to express puzzlement and hilarity, explaining that the sentence can only mean that the child bit the spider. However, (8a) is not how the proposition 'The child bit a tarantula' would be expressed in spontaneous discourse – (8b) would be used for that instead.

---

[6] RP constituents may trigger the selection of a clause-final indexical particle. For example, the definite article *le* in (8)–(9) triggers the distal/anaphoric particle =*o'* in clause-final position. The combination of the article and the particle serves as the Yucatec equivalent of a distal/anaphoric demonstrative. To express the meaning conveyed by the proximal demonstrative *this* in English, *le* combines with the clause-final particle =*a'* instead. However, triggering of the clause-final particles is not restricted to RP constituents. Triggers also include certain adverbs, preverbal aspect-mood markers, and negation. And irrespective of the position of the trigger, the particles occur exclusively on the right edge of the core clause and on that of the LDP. Hence, an analysis of these particles as discontinuous RP constituents is not parsimonious.

[7] In addition, a clause-internal RP referring to the actor of the clause cannot be possessed by a clause-internal RP referring to the undergoer. The agent-focus construction in (10) below was elicited as a consultant's repair of a stimulus utterance that was in violation of this constraint. A similar constraint has been described for other Mayan languages (e. g., Aissen 1999 for Tsotsil).

(8) a. ??*T-u=chi'-ah*   *le=pàal*   *hun-túul*   *x-chìiwol=o'*
PRV-A3=mouth-CMP(B3SG) DEF=child one-CL.AN F=tarantula=D2
'The child bit a tarantula'
#'A tarantula bit the child'

b. *T-u=chi'-ah*   *hun-túul*   *x-chìiwol*   *le=pàal=o'*
PRV-A3=mouth-CMP(B3SG) one-CL.AN F=tarantula DEF=child=D2
'The child bit a tarantula'

Meanwhile, the proposition 'A tarantula bit the child' simply cannot be expressed in an active transitive clause. Under predicate or sentence focus, either the actor RP is left-dislocated, as in (9a), or the verb is passivized, as in (9b).

(9) a. *Hun-túul*   *x-chìiwol=e'*,
one-CL.AN F-tarantula=TOP
t-u=chi'-ah   *le=pàal=o'*
PRV-A3=mouth-CMP(B3SG) DEF=child=D2
'A tarantula, it bit the child'

b. *H-chi'-b*   *le=pàal*
PRV-mouth-PASS.CMP(B3SG) DEF=child
tumèen hun-túul   *x-chìiwol=o'*
CAUSE one-CL.AN F-tarantula=D2
'The child was bitten by a tarantula'

A third option is the so-called 'agent focus construction' (Norcliffe 2009 and references therein). This construction is illustrated in (10). It involves an RP coreferential with the actor argument of the transitive verb in a focus position, which occurs between the LDP and the verb,[8] deletion of the Set-A marker, special and defective aspect-mood and status paradigms, and, with habitual, generic, and future time reference, a special irrealis subordinator (cf. Bohnemeyer 2002: 116–129).

---

[8] It has been a matter of some controversy whether this focus position is clause-internal – in which case it would likely instantiate the 'pre-core slot' position distinguished in Van Valin (1993, 2005) and Van Valin & LaPolla (1997) – or whether all Yucatec focus constructions are biclausal, a kind of clefts in the broadest possible sense. The former position has been taken by Lehmann (2003), Gutiérrez Bravo & Monforte (2009), and Skopeteas & Verhoeven (2009, ms.), whereas the latter is advocated in Bricker (1979), Bohnemeyer (2002), Tonhauser (2003, 2007, ms.), and most recently in Vapnarsky (2013).

(10) *Pedro=e'   uy=atan   p'at-eh*
    Pedro=TOP A3=wife(B3SG) abandon-SUBJ(B3SG)
    'Pedro, his wife (was the one who) left him'

Bohnemeyer (2009a) argues that the obviation/alignment constraints serve to regulate the coindexing between cross-reference markers and RPs. This suggests that, whether or not the Yucatec clause is considered configurational, its syntactic arguments are not realized by RPs alone. In the presence of cross-referenced RPs, the syntactic arguments of the clause might be the cross-reference markers alone or the combination of cross-reference markers and RPs, depending on the nature of the relation between cross-reference markers and cross-referenced RPs. This relation is the proper topic of this chapter. In the absence of cross-referenced RPs, the cross-reference markers are sufficient to realize the arguments.

In line with the set of facts just delineated, there is no evidence of a (subject-external) verb phrase node in Yucatec syntax. There are, for example, no VP anaphora (as in *Sally wrote a paper on head-marking, and so did Floyd*), VP ellipsis (as in *Sally is writing a paper on head-marking and Floyd is too*), or VP fronting constructions (as in *What Sally did was write/writing a paper on head-marking*) in this language. The following examples illustrate predicate focus constructions, the closest Yucatec equivalent to VP fronting. It is not possible for a focalized verb in this construction to retain an undergoer argument. In both instances, the focalized root-transitive verb is detransitivized, in (11) through antipassivization and in (12) through noun incorporation.[9]

(11) *Hàats'   t-in=mèet-ah   ti'   hit.*
    beat\ATP PRV-A1SG=make-CMP(B3SG) PREP hit
    'Batting was what I did (lit. hitting was what I did to hits).'

(12) *Hats'(-ah)+hit k-in=mèet-ik*
    beat(-ATP)+hit IMPF-A1SG=make-INC(B3SG)
    'Batting (lit. hit-hitting) is what I do.'

The only verbal projection of Yucatec that can be argued to dominate a U-argument, but no A-argument, is the agent-focus verb form illustrated in (10) above.

---

[9] The concept of batting (baseball is a popular sport across the Mexican Yucatan) is expressed by the idiom *hats' hit* composed out of the Yucatec verb 'hit' and the performance object (Dowty 1979) *hit* borrowed from English.

This, however, is an odd candidate for a traditional VP, since it is restricted to transitive verbs and involves a co-constituent that necessarily has narrow focus and special aspect-mood and status patterns distinct from those of verbs under predicate or sentence focus.

As for split argument marking, Yucatec does indeed exhibit such a system, as illustrated above. But the split is based on status (semantically, on mood and viewpoint aspect), not on a nominal-pronominal contrast. To summarize, Yucatec shows those traits of non-configurationality that are robustly associated with cross-reference marking (or head-marking in a narrow sense of the term; see Section 3): RPs are syntactically optional; their referents receive semantic roles via their coindexing with cross-reference markers, not via their linear position in the clause; and there is no evidence of a subject-external VP node. But the language lacks other proposed non-configurational features such as discontinuity of RPs and a nominal-pronominal argument marking split.

3 Head-marking in Role and Reference Grammar

In this section, we discuss basic properties of cross-reference or head-marking and their current treatment in RRG and elsewhere in the literature. Where appropriate, we illustrate the relevant properties cited in the literature with Yucatec examples, in the process extending the discussion of cross-reference marking in Yucatec started in the previous section.

Nichols (1986) introduces the term 'head-marking' with a broader meaning than that adopted in Van Valin (1985) and the subsequent RRG literature. In Nichols' usage, any head-dependent relation can be morphologically encoded on the dependent, the head, both, or neither, where 'encoded' covers any morphological reflex of the relation. Head-marking in this broad sense thus includes subject-verb agreement in English and the 'construct state' form of nouns that occur with dependents in Semitic languages. In contrast, Van Valin narrows the term to a rough equivalent of what Bloomfield (1933: 191–194) called 'cross-reference' and Milewski (1950) a 'concentric' construction: a head carrying one or more bound morphemes which refer to the individuals that fill the head's semantic argument positions and which in the absence of clause-mate coreferential noun phrases or 'reference phrases' (RPs) act as pronouns. Depending on the language and construction, such RPs may optionally co-occur with the cross-reference markers (see the Yucatec examples in Section 2).

The traditional view of cross-reference markers (Humboldt 1836: 531, Boas 1911: 30, Bloomfield 1933: 191–194, Milewski 1950: 174, Nichols 1986: 107) can be summarized as follows:

- The head in combination with the cross-reference markers alone, in the absence of cross-referenced RPs, is syntactically complete and semantically readily interpretable, expressing the application of a semantic predicate to anaphoric arguments represented by the cross-reference markers. Therefore, the cross-reference markers *are* the syntactic arguments of the head.
- If there are cross-referenced RPs, they and the cross-reference markers cannot both realize the arguments – at least not separately. Since both are traditionally assumed to be referring expressions, are coindexed, and cannot stand in an anaphoric relation if they are constituents of the same clause (cf., e. g., Principle B of Chomsky's (1981) Binding Theory), they are treated as standing in an appositive relation instead. However, as Lehmann (1985: 92) points out, it is difficult to understand this appositive relation in its ordinary syntactic sense, since that would require the cross-reference markers to form higher RPs in combination with the cross-referenced RPs.

Jelinek (1984) analyzes the cross-referenced RPs as adjoined to the clause in Warlpiri (Ngarrkic, Pama-Nyungang; Northern Territories, Australia) and the Coast Salish languages Lummi and Klallam of British Columbia (see Pensalfini 2004 for a recent adaption based on Minimalism and Distributed Morphology). Simpson (1991) and Austin & Bresnan (1996) point out one important obstacle for this analysis: if the RPs are detached, they should be able to anaphorically bind the cross-reference markers. But if the cross-reference markers are morphologically bound pronouns even in the presence of cross-referenced RPs, then they should be strictly definite, in the sense that they should only be able to pick up previously introduced discourse referents. The cross-reference markers of Warlpiri and other pronominal argument languages, however, occur with both definite and indefinite cross-referenced RPs, and cross-reference markers are used in combination with indefinite RPs to introduce new discourse referents. The same is true in Yucatec, as illustrated in (6)–(8) above.

Diesing & Jelinek (1995) develop an account of the semantics of cross-reference markers that treats them as ordinary pronouns in isolation and in combination with definite cross-referenced RPs, but as denoting variables in combination with indefinite cross-referenced RPs. These variables become the argument predicated over by the coindexed RP and are subsequently bound by existential closure. As Austin & Bresnan (1996) point out, the same range of interpretations can be obtained under an alternative 'PRO-drop'-style account of cross-reference marking such as that proposed by Bresnan & Mchombo (1987) for the subject markers of the Bantu language Chicheŵa of Malawi, Zambia, and Mozambique. Chicheŵa verbs cross-reference both subjects and objects. The object cross-reference markers are optional and in complementary distribution with object RPs, whereas the subject markers are obligatory and co-occur with syntactically optional RPs. Bresnan & Mchombo analyze the object markers as incorporated pronouns, the presence of which excludes that of a clause-mate cross-referenced RP. In the presence of an object marker, a cross-referenced RP, if present, is relegated to a detached ('topic') position adjoined at the sentence level. The authors term the relation between the object marker and the detached RP 'anaphoric agreement'. In contrast, they argue the subject markers to be ambiguous between anaphoric and grammatical agreement: in the absence of a clause-internal subject RP, they function as incorporated pronouns, like the object markers; but in the presence of a clause-internal subject RP, they express grammatical agreement. This is the same distribution shown by the verb agreement morphology of Romance languages and many languages of the Balkan *sprachbund* (e. g., Jaeger & Gerassimova 2002 on Bulgarian). Perlmutter 1971 coined the term 'PRO-drop' for this phenomenon.

Van Valin (2013) points out two additional problems with applying Jelinek's analysis cross-linguistically: in Lakhota (Siouan; Great Planes), detached material tends to be separated from the matrix clause by intonation breaks, whereas RPs inside the intonation contour of the main clause are perfectly inconspicuous. The same is true in Yucatec: whereas the left-dislocated RPs on the left edge of the sentence in (7), (9a), and (10) above are separated from the following material by both a pause and a discontinuity in the pitch contour, neither property applies to the post-verbal RPs in (5)–(9).[10]

---

[10] The focus position in (10) is likewise intonationally integrated with the following material. There is also a 'right-detached position' expressing an 'anti-topic' in the sense of Lambrecht (1994) on the right edge of the sentence that is intonationally isolated from the rest.

Moreover, detached material is not expected to appear in embedded clauses, and cross-referenced RPs do occur in this environment in Lakhota. This argument likewise applies to Yucatec as well, as the relative clauses in (13)–(14) illustrate:

(13) *K'àas   le=máak*
 bad(B3SG) DEF=person
 [t-a=ts'a'-ah   le=ta'kin   ti']=o'
 PRV-A2=put-CMP(B3SG) DEF=money PREP(B3SG)=D2
 'The person you gave the money to is bad'

(14) *Káa=h-òok*
 CON=PRV-enter(B3SG)
 le=x-ch'úup   [chak   u=nòok']=o', (...)
 DEF=F-female red(B3SG) A3=garment=D2
 'And (then) the woman in the red dress (lit. the woman her dress is red) entered, (...)'

Since the relative clauses occur on the right edge of the matrix clause, it might be argued that they are themselves adjoined to the clause. However, the placement of the clause-final deictic particle excludes this possible analysis in (14), as this particle is triggered by the definite article of the RP modified by the relative clause. Nor can this entire higher RP be detached in (14) – if it were, the verb would carry the suffix -*ih*, which can be analyzed as either an allomorph of the – normally zero-marked – 3SG Set-B cross-reference marker or a segment of a completive status marker (see footnote 2).

Van Valin (1985) develops an analysis of the cross-referenced RPs as clause-internal adjuncts in the early version of the LCS model of RRG proposed in Foley & Van Valin (1984).[11] This early model assumes a single periphery, which in combination with the core constitutes a clause. A key assumption of the RRG analysis – then and now – is that the cross-reference markers, and not the cross-referenced RPs, are the true syntactic arguments of the head. This entails that the cross-referenced RPs cannot be core constituents, since the core is constituted *by definition* by the predicate nucleus and its syntactic arguments. Van Valin (1985) concludes that the cross-referenced RPs, when occurring clause-internally, must occupy the (clausal) periphery, much like adjuncts.

---

[11] Although published later, Van Valin's account predates Jelinek's, being a restatement of Van Valin (1977) in the framework first sketched in Van Valin & Foley (1980).

This adjunct analysis faces several complications, as discussed in Van Valin (2013). Unlike true adjuncts in Lakhota, cross-referenced RPs may not be headed by adpositions. And true adjuncts in turn are not cross-referenced on the verb, nor does the verb subcategorize for them. Both of these problems are in fact addressed in Van Valin (1985): The cross-referenced RPs are analyzed as 'reference-restricting modifiers' of the cross-reference markers. This would explain why they do not behave like adjuncts. And the subcategorization facts are explained with reference to a 'Coherence Condition' (Van Valin 1985: 380) adopted from Bresnan (1982) and an additional 'Agreement Condition', which requires the RPs to be semantically compatible with the cross-reference markers in the relevant semantic features person, number, and animacy, following up on the idea that it is the cross-referenced RPs that agree with the head, rather than the other way around, first proposed in Van Valin (1977).

However, while it is thus in fact possible to solve the problems resulting from the adjunct analysis, the proposed solutions remain somewhat stipulative. The fundamental fact remains that cross-referenced RPs are not adjuncts and thus do not really belong in the periphery. In search of alternatives, Van Valin (2013) explores the syntactic positions newly added to the model in Van Valin (1993) and the subsequent literature (e.g., Shimojo 1995): in particular, the left- (LDP) and right-detached positions (RDP) and the pre-core (PrCS) and post-core slot (PoCS). As already mentioned, the LDP and RDP cannot account for the properties of the post-verbal RPs in (5)–(9), since the former, but not the latter, are separated from the verb and the main clause by intonation breaks and the placement of the clause-final clitic particles. Moreover, as illustrated above, cross-referenced RPs are freely permissible in subordinate clauses, which the LDP and RDP are not. This second source of evidence also discourages an association with the PrCS and PoCS, both of which express marked information perspectives, in particular (though not restricted to) focus.

Van Valin (2013) therefore proposes a new type of position to accommodate the cross-referenced RPs in Lakhota and other head-marking languages: the 'extra-core slot' (ECS). Like the PrCS and PoCS, ECSs are immediate daughters of the clause. However, they differ from the PrCS and PoCS in the following properties:

- ECSs are not associated with marked information perspective.
- ECSs are licensed by the cross-reference markers on the nucleus. Therefore, ECSs occur exclusively in head-marking constructions, are restricted to

cross-referenced RPs (whereas the PrCS and PoCS can accommodate other syntactic categories), and a clause has exactly as many ECSs as its nucleus or nuclei carry cross-reference markers (whereas every clause has exactly one PrCS and PoCS).

In the next section, we present evidence discouraging the analysis of the cross-referenced RPs as immediately dominated by the clause in Yucatec. This is followed by a section reviewing evidence from two production experiments on plural marking in Yucatec. The results of these studies are best explained assuming that, in the presence of a cross-referenced RP, the number component of the cross-reference marker does in fact express agreement with the RP. Together, these facts encourage a PRO-drop-style analysis of the Yucatec cross-reference markers following the model of Bresnan & Mchombo's analysis of the subject markers of Chichewa.

4 The case for core-internal RPs

Core cosubordinations are constituted by two cores forming a superordinate core through sharing an operator projection and periphery and typically (possibly necessarily; cf. Bohnemeyer & Van Valin ms.) also an argument in a control- (or 'equi-NP-deletion') or matrix-coding-like (i. e., 'raising'-like) structure. An example is the event perception construction in (3) above, repeated in (15) for convenience:

(15) *T-inw=il-ah*   *a=lúub-ul.*
     PRV-A1SG=see-CMP(B3SG) **A2**=fall-INC
     'I saw you fall(ing).

The crucial property of Yucatec core cosubordinations for our purposes is the ability for an RP cross-referenced on the nucleus of the first core to be realized between the two verbs, as illustrated in (19)–(21) below. The first author tested these examples with six native speakers, all of whom accepted all of them. The examples instantiate event perception (17), causative light verb (18), and 'motion-cum-purpose'[12] (19) constructions.

---

[12] Motion-cum-purpose constructions combine a 'path' verb (Talmy 2000) with a second verbal projection that describes an eventuality intended and/or expected to occur at the goal of the path (cf.

How do we know that these constructions are core cosubordinations? Before we attempt to answer this question, let us introduce a terminological convention. Non-RRG syntacticians might call the first verbal projection in these examples the 'matrix' and the second 'embedded'. However, RRG distinguishes three different 'nexus' relations between verbs (or, more generally, nuclei) or their projections (or, more generally, the projections of nuclei) – subordination, coordination, and cosubordination. Only one of these – subordination – is defined as involving embedding of one nucleus, core, or clause into another in an argument or adjunct position. At first blush, one might think that that is exactly what is going on in (19)–(21): in all cases, the first verb semantically opens up an argument position filled by the projection of the second verb. However, on closer inspection, this second projection turns out not to be a *syntactic* argument of the first verb in any of the examples. The first verb is in all cases a transitive verb with a human actor argument. If the second projection were the undergoer argument of these transitive verbs, it ought to be possible to passivize the verb and turn the second projection into the S-argument of the passivized verb. This is, however, not possible in any of these cases. We will therefore use the terms 'licensing' verb/core for the first verb and the core it projects, respectively, and 'licensed' verb/core for the second verb and its core (cf. also Bohnemeyer & Van Valin ms.).

The second verbal projection in these examples is quite clearly a core, given the absence of the preverbal aspect-mood marker (cf. Section 2). Assuming subordinative nexus is out of the question and the other two nexus types, coordination and cosubordination, are symmetrical (nucleus-nucleus, core-core, clause-clause), this leaves us with two competing analyses: core coordination and core cosubordination. Definitionally, these are distinguished by the two cores in the latter, but not the former, forming a single superordinate constituent with all the trappings of a core in the LSC – that is, by sharing an operator projection and a periphery. Argument sharing – control and matrix coding (or 'raising') – occurs with both coordinative and cosubordinative nexus, although by hypothesis, the latter, but not the former, *necessarily* involves argument sharing (and most commonly apparently control; cf. Bohnemeyer & Van Valin ms.). There is a variety of diagnostics for periphery sharing. One of them is the ability to have separate temporal modifiers in the two cores: a shared periphery excludes this ability. Ex-

---

Aissen 1987 for Tsotsil and Zavala Maldonado 1993 for an overview including other members of the Mayan language family).

clusion of distinct temporal modifiers is illustrated in (16) for the event perception construction, in (17) for the causative light verb construction, and in (18) for the motion-cum-purpose construction. In each case, it is acceptable to use a single time adverbial denoting an interval in which both sub-events fall.[13]

(16) *Las sèeyse', t-inw=il-ah*
six.o'clock PRV-A1SG=see-CMP(B3SG)
u=hàan-t-ik   le=bak'   le=pèek' (#las syèeteh)=o'.
A3=eat-APP-INC(B3SG) DEF=bone DEF=dog seven.o'clock=D2
'At six, I saw the dog eat(ing) the bone (#at seven).'

(17) *Juanita=e'   byèernes-ak=e'   t-u=mèet-ah*
Juanita=TOP Friday-CAL=TOP PRFV-A3=make-CMP(B3SG)
u=mìis-t-ik   u=nah-il   Pedro (#sàabado)
A3=broom-APP-INC(B3SG) A3=house-REL Pedro Saturday
'Juanita, last Friday, she made Pedro sweep her/his house (#on Saturday)'

(18) *Juanita=e'   byèernes-ak=e'   h-bin*
Juanita=TOP Friday-CAL=TOP PRV-go(B3SG)
uy=il   Pedro (#sàabado)
A3=see(B3SG) Pedro Saturday
'Juanita, last Friday, she went to see Pedro (#on Saturday)'

Contemporaneity is a necessary feature of event perception (called 'direct perception' in the RRG literature), so all the inadmissibility of adverbials denoting non-overlapping time intervals in (16) tells us is that we are indeed dealing with event perception. The causative and motion-cum-purpose examples in (17) and (18) are more revealing in this respect, as there is no obvious semantic factor excluding distinct time adverbials here.[14]

---

[13] Lorena Pool Balam (p.c.) points out that, whereas (16) is uninterpretable, (17)–(18) sound merely awkward. However, a group of seven speakers tested by the first author in 2002 rejected (17).

[14] We include the event perception example in (16) because the event perception construction, like the other two construction types, allows core-medial RPs. And it should go without saying that just because the semantics of this construction severely limits the possibility for temporal modification does not mean that it should not be treated as a core cosubordination. After all, it is the semantic properties of the complex events described by a particular nexus type that condition the use of that nexus type.

Under the assumption of cosubordinative nexus, the possible positioning of an RP cross-referenced on the licensing verb between the two verbs is at odds with the assumption that the cross-referenced RPs are immediate daughters of the clause. In (19a), the RP *le pèek'* 'the dog' refers to the undergoer of the perception verb and to the actor of the ingestion verb. These two semantic arguments are 'shared' in a control (i. e., 'equi') construction. Control is realized in Yucatec by cross-referencing both the controller and the target argument (put differently, by cross-referencing the controlled argument on both the 'licensing' and the 'licensed' nucleus), but allowing at most one cross-referenced RP (cf. Bohnemeyer 2009a). In (19a), this RP appears between the two verbs. Given general properties of Yucatec clause structure (see Section 2), this RP cannot be a constituent of the second core or even adjoined to the second core. It can, however, be a constituent of the first core or be adjoined to it. But if the ECS is directly dominated by the clause, the superordinate core formed by the two constituent cores would have to be discontinuous in order to accommodate the RP. Given the absence of discontinuous syntactic projections in Yucatec, this analysis lacks parsimony.

(19) a. *T-inw=il-ah   le=pèek'*
       PRV-A1SG=see-CMP(B3SG) DEF=dog
       u=hàan-t-ik   le=bak'=o'
       A3=eat-APP-INC(B3SG) DEF=bone=D2
       'I saw the dog eat(ing) the bone.'
    b. *T-inw=il-ah   u=hàan-t-ik*
       PRV-A1SG=CMP(B3SG) A3=eat-APP-INC(B3SG)
       le=bak'   le=pèek'=o'
       DEF=bone DEF=dog=D2
       'I saw the dog eat(ing) the bone.'

As (19b) illustrates, it is also possible for the cross-referenced RP to be realized after the second verb, and most speakers in fact prefer this position to the one in (19a).[15] Intonation and the placement of clause-final deictic particles once again suggest that the position of the right-most RP in (19b) is not the RDP. We

---

[15] Note that the speakers were asked to rank the different realizations *after* they had already established that all of them were grammatical. Thus, the preference for the sentence-final realization in a forced-choice ranking task is interesting, but it is unclear what it reflects. The same point applies to the following examples, all of which produced similar rankings.

assume that the right-most RP in (19b) is either a constituent of the higher core or adjoined to it. Meanwhile, the possibility of a cross-referenced RP to occur between the verbs in (19a) discourages the analysis of the cross-referenced RP as an immediate daughter of the clause.

The examples in (20) instantiate the causative light verb construction with *mèet* 'make'. The actor of the licensing verb is the causer, while the undergoer of the licensing verb controls the actor of the licensed verb, which is the causee. In (20a-b), both verbs are transitive active-voice forms. In (20a), the RP *Pedro* occurs between the two verbs and can be interpreted as referring to either the causer or the causee. Our consultant seemed to find both interpretations about equally salient. In contrast, in (20b), with *Pedro* in final position, this RP is apparently more likely to be understood to refer to the causee. In (20c), where the licensed core is passivized and *Pedro* is flagged by the oblique-actor preposition *tuméen*, it can of course refer exclusively to the causee. When asked to rank these examples, most consultants indicated a preference for (20c) over (20b) and for (20b) over (20a). Nonetheless, all judged (20a) to be wellformed, suggesting that *Pedro* is not immediately dominated by the clause.[16]

(20) a. *Le=òok'ol=o' t-u=mèet-ah Pedro*
   DEF=steal=D2 PRV-A3=make-CMP(B3SG) Pedro
   u=ch'a'-ik le=ta'kin=o'
   A3=take-INC(B3SG) DEF=money=D2
   'The thief, (s)he made Pedro take the money'
   or 'The Thief, Pedro made him/her take the money'

b. *Le=òok'ol=o' t-u=mèet-ah u=ch'a'-ik*
   DEF=steal=D2 PRV-A3=make-CMP(B3SG) A3=take-INC(B3SG)
   le=ta'kin Pedro=o'
   DEF=money Pedro=D2
   'The thief, (s)he made Pedro take the money'
   (or 'The Thief, Pedro made him/her take the money')

---

[16] An anonymous reviewer wonders whether the participants' preference for (20a) and (20b) over (20c) does not invalidate the analysis we are arguing for. However, the key fact here is that all consultants judged the structures with the medial RPs to be wellformed. That they also preferred the sentence-final strategy when asked to make a forced choice is interesting, but it is unclear what this ranking reflects.

c. *Le=òok'ol=o'   t-u=mèet-ah   u=ch'a'-b-al*
   DEF=steal=D2 PRV-A3=make-CMP(B3SG) A3=take-PASS-INC
   le=ta'kin   tuméen Pedro=o'
   DEF=money CAUSE Pedro=D2
   'The thief, (s)he made Pedro take the money (lit. made the money be taken by Pedro)'

Lastly, in the motion-cum-purpose constructions in (21), the RP *le pàal* 'the child' refers to the undergoer of the licensing verb and the actor of the licensed verb. The two verbs again 'share' this argument via control. The alternative final realization of the RP is again possible as well. In this case, both orders are considered equally good.

(21) a. *Pablo=e'   t-u=túuxt-ah   le=pàal*
       Pablo=TO PPRV-A3=send-CMP(B3SG) DEF=child
       u=ch'a'   le=ta'kin=o'
       A3=take(SUBJ)(B3SG) DEF=money=D2
       'Pablo, he sent the child to take the money'

   b. *Pablo=e'   t-u=túuxt-ah   u=ch'a'*
       Pablo=TOP PRV-A3=send-CMP(B3SG) A3=take(SUBJ)(B3SG)
       le=ta'kin   le=pàal=o'
       DEF=money DEF=child=D2
       'Pablo, he sent the child to take the money'

Given the absence of discontinuous syntactic projections in Yucatec, the cross-referenced RP on the right edge of the first core is unlikely to be immediately dominated by the clause in these examples, since it would be interrupting the higher core formed by the two cosubordinate cores, as illustrated in Figure 1 for (21a).

There are two conceivable alternative analyses of the cross-referenced RP that would be consistent with its position on the right edge of the first core. First, the cross-referenced RP might be adjoined to the first core. To our knowledge, the existence of core-layer adjunction has never been argued for before, but such an analysis would seem consistent with the observable facts. Or secondly, the cross-referenced RP is in fact a constituent of the first core. In this case, it has

Head-Marking and Agreement: Evidence from Yucatec Maya

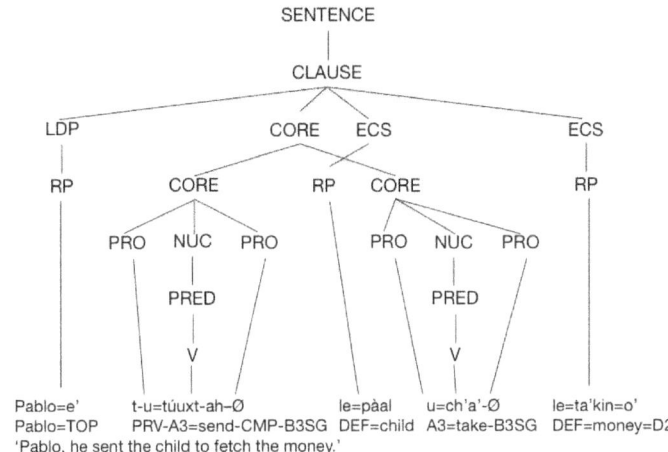

Figure 1: An analysis of (21a) in the style of Van Valin (2013)

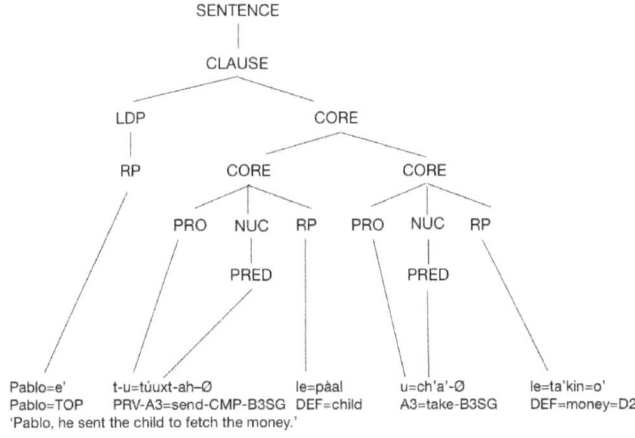

Figure 2: A pro-drop analysis of (21a)

to be an argument of the first verb by definition, which means the coindexed cross-reference marker can only express agreement, in line with an ambiguous, PRO-drop-style analysis along the lines of Bresnan & Mchombo (1987). In the next section, we present evidence from two production experiments supporting the latter analysis. This analysis is represented in Figure 2.

5 The case for syntactic agreement

5.1 Introduction

Both nouns and verbs inflect for number in Yucatec. On the verb, semantic plurality of an argument can be expressed by selection of the plural cells of the cross-reference markers (cf. Table 2 in Section 2). RPs with nominal heads can express plurality of the referent through the noun suffix -o'b, which is homophonous with the B3PL pronoun. The ambiguous analysis of cross-reference marking in Yucatec predicts that cross-referenced RPs and their coindexed cross-reference markers coincide in the inflectional category expressed on Yucatec nouns, which is number. Any core-external (i.e., non-argument) analysis of the cross-referenced RPs makes the same prediction in connection with the Agreement Condition of Van Valin (1985) (see Section 3). However, there is a difference, which results from the serendipitous fact that plural marking is optional on 3rd-person arguments in Yucatec, in the sense that the 3SG cells of the cross-reference paradigms (shown in Table 2 above) and RPs which lack the plural suffix are also compatible with plural interpretations, as illustrated in (22):

(22) a. *Táan u=k'àay   le=x-ch'úupal=o'*
    PROG A3=sing\ATP DEF=F-female:child=D2
    'The girl(s) is/are singing'

   b. *Táan u=k'àay-o'b   le=x-ch'úupal=o'*
    PROG A3=sing\ATP-**3PL** DEF=F-female:child=D2
    'The girls are singing'

   c. *Táan u=k'àay   le=x-ch'úupal-o'b=o'*
    PROG A3=sing\ATP DEF=F-female:child-**PL**=D2
    'The girls are singing'

   d. *Táan u=k'àay-o'b   le=x-ch'úupal-o'b=o'*
    PROG A3=sing\ATP-**3PL** DEF=F-female:child-**PL**=D2
    'The girls are singing'

The unmarked forms in (22a) are compatible with both singular and plural interpretations – they are semantically transnumeral. In contrast, if the verb (22b), the RP (22c), or both (22d) are plural-marked, a plural interpretation is entailed (cf. Butler 2012, Butler et al. 2014).

Crucially, the Agreement Condition of Van Valin (1985) merely requires cross-reference markers and cross-referenced RPs to be semantically compatible in terms of the expressed features. This constraint is met in all four examples in (22). In contrast, under the ambiguous analysis, the cross-reference marker expresses *syntactic* agreement with the cross-referenced RP. We take this to mean that the same feature must be morphologically specified in both positions. This constraint is met in (22a) and (22d), but not in (22b)–(22c).

The fact that native speakers accept all four configurations in (22) as syntactically wellformed and consistent with the interpretations indicated by the translations represents *prima facie* evidence against the ambiguous analysis. However, very little is known about number agreement in languages with optional plural marking outside Wiltschko (2008) and Butler (2012). It is conceivable that the distribution of plural markers across nouns and verbs is less categorical in such a language. If so, corpus and production studies are what is called for to adjudicate between the two competing analyses.

In Butler et al. (2014), we reported two production experiments. During the first, Yucatec native speakers translated stimulus utterances from the contact language Spanish; during the second, they described stimulus pictures. In both cases, the stimuli featured various actions, some involving a single individual (the 'One' condition), some two individuals (the 'Two' condition), and some many (seven in the picture stimuli; the 'Many' condition).

The distinction between the Two and Many conditions is relevant because Yucatec has numeral classifiers. Yucatec numerals prefix to these classifiers. However, these autochthonous Yucatec numerals are used only for numbers in the subitizing range (up to three, sometimes four; cf. (23)). Higher numbers are expressed with Spanish loans, which do not combine with the classifiers, as in (24). Classifiers in turn are sometimes assumed to be in complementary distribution with respect to plural markers, because they are argued to overlap in their semantics (cf. Borer 2005 and references therein). Hence the contrast in (23)–(24):

(23) *kan-túul máak*
four-**CL.AN** person
'four people'

(24) *sìinko máak-o'b*
five person-**PL**
'five people' (constructed)

We thus included the Two condition specifically in the hopes that it might afford us a dissociation between plural reference and plural marking.

Next we provide a brief description of the methodology (for more detail, we refer to Butler et al. 2014).

5.2 Method summary

Table 3 exemplifies the stimuli we used for the translation task, along with some possible Yucatec responses. There were a total of 30 intransitive stimulus sentences and 32 fillers, consisting of transitive sentences and sentences with adjectival predicates.

Cond.	Spanish stimulus	Possible Yucatec response
One	El muchacho está jugando DEF boy be.at:3SG play:GER 'The boy is playing'	Táan u=bàaxal le=xibpal=o' PROG A3=play DEF=male:child=D2 'The boy is playing'
Two	Dos muchachos están jugando two boy:PL be.at:3PL play:GER 'Two boys are playing'	Táan u=bàaxal(-o'b) ka'-túul xibpal(-o'b) PROG A3=play(-PL) two-CL.AN male:child(-PL) 'Two boys are playing'
Many	Los muchachos están jugando DEF.PL boy:PL be.at:3PL play.GER 'The boys are playing'	Táan u=bàaxal(-o'b) le=xibpal(-o'b)=o' PROG A3=play(-PL) DEF=male:child(-PL)=D2 'The boys are playing'

Table 3: Some stimuli in the translation experiment and possible Yucatec responses

The stimuli were created with a speech synthesizer. Participants would listen to them over a headset and then record their responses. They would hear each sentence at least once, but had the option of listening to two repetitions.

Figure 3 shows some of the stimulus pictures we used for the picture description task. There were 24 items, all featuring single-participant actions, and 48 fillers showing two-participant actions, the latter varied in terms of the number of entities involved as undergoers. Participants would view the pictures on a computer screen and then record single-sentence responses.

The experiments were conducted by the second author at the Universidad del Oriente in Valladolid, Yucatan, Mexico. Thirty speakers (mostly college-aged) participated in the translation study and 37 speakers aged 19–26 in the picture description task. The participants were given oral instructions from the experimenter and written instructions on screen in Spanish and then completed four practice trials before the experimental trials began.

Head-Marking and Agreement: Evidence from Yucatec Maya

Figure 3: Examples of stimulus pictures in the One (left), Two (center), and Many (right) conditions

Responses were transcribed and coded by the second author with the assistance of two native speakers. Only intransitive Yucatec responses that represent the content of the stimuli items broadly correctly and feature a verb, an RP, and a numeral are included in the analyses presented below. Responses with Spanish words are included in case the words in question carry Yucatec morphology where appropriate. These criteria netted 704 of the 900 critical responses to the translation task (78.2 %) and 556 out of 648 critical responses to the picture description task (86 %) for inclusion in the analysis.

5.3 Result summary

The graphs in Figures 4 shows the proportion of plural marking on the noun only, on the verb only, on both, and on neither for the two tasks.

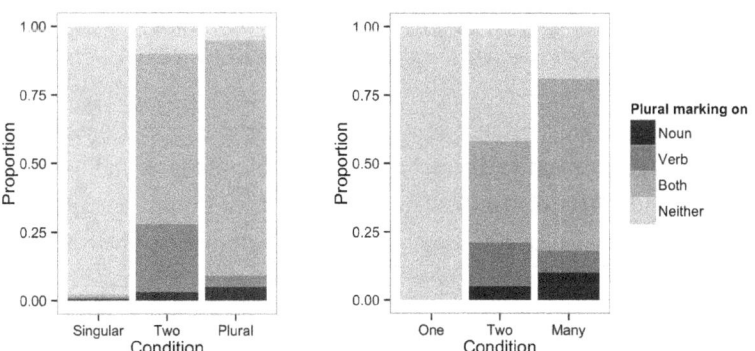

Figure 4: Proportion of plural marking on the noun, verb, both, and neither by condition (left: translation task; right: picture description task)

The results confirm, first of all, that plural marking is indeed optional in Yucatec, as a sizeable percentage of responses to the picture description task in the semantically plural Two and Many conditions did not feature any plural marking.

The difference between the two tasks is significant and likely the result of crosslinguistic priming, which we do not discuss further here (but see Butler et al. 2014). Despite the overall difference in the rate of plural marking between the two experiments, participants in both experiments exhibited qualitatively similar (though not identical) patterns of plural marking for the three conditions.

As predicted, the rate of nominal plural marking in the Two condition fell between those in the One and Many conditions. Nominal plural marking was more frequent in the Two condition than in the One condition (translation: $\chi^2(1) = 212.6$, $p< .0001$; picture description: $\chi^2(1) = 101.5$, $p< .0001$), but less frequent than in the Many condition (translation: $\chi^2(1) = 44.1$, $p< .0001$; picture description: $\chi^2(1) = 33.5$, $p< .0001$). Verbal plural marking was likewise more frequent in the Two than in the One condition (translation: $\chi^2(1) = 340.0$, $p< .0001$; picture description: $\chi^2(1) = 139.7$, $p< .0001$). However, a significant difference in verbal plural marking between the Two and Many conditions emerged only in the picture description experiment (translation: $\chi^2(1) = 1.0$, $p> .3$; picture description: $\chi^2(1) = 11.0$, $p< .0001$).

Crucially for present purposes, participants in both experiments preferred to mark plural on either both the noun and the verb or neither (translation: Spearman rank $R^2 = 0.58$, $p< .0001$; picture description: $R^2 = .54$, $p< .0001$). This finding is in line with the predictions of the PRO-drop/agreement hypothesis. In contrast, under the core-external analysis of the cross-referenced RPs, plural marking on both nouns and verbs is redundant and thus might be expected to be dispreferred on pragmatic grounds.

At the same time, the existence of a sizeable proportion of responses that featured plural marking on either the verb or the noun, but not both, indicates that if there is indeed an effect of morphosyntactic agreement in our data, it is at the very least not of a categorical nature. But this is to some extent the case even in *bona fide* cases of syntactic agreement, such as subject-verb agreement in English, where agreement *errors* are reported to occur in a frequency range not too far off from what the frequency of mismatches we found produced by Yucatec speakers (e. g., Bock & Eberhard 1993, Bock & Miller 1991, Hartsuiker, Schriefers, Bock & Kikstra 2003, Vigliocco, Butterworth & Semenza 1995).

Conspicuously, verbal plural marking unaccompanied by nominal plural marking was more common than the inverse: out of 362 responses to the translation task that featured plural marking on the noun, 343 (94.8 %) also contained plural marking on the verb. The proportion of cases with plural marking on the verb that also contained plural marking on the noun was smaller (83.7 %). The same asymmetry manifests itself in the responses to the picture description task, though to a somewhat lesser extent, 87.4 % vs. 80.4 %.

In both experiments, this asymmetry was mostly driven by responses to the Two condition. Responses to the Two condition of the translation experiment associated plural marking on the noun with covarying plural marking on the verb in 133 out of 140 cases (95.0 %). Plural marking on the verb occurred with plural marking on the noun in only 70.7 % of all cases. In the Two condition of the picture description task, the distribution was 88.3 % vs. 69.4 %. In contrast, the asymmetry did not manifest itself in the responses to the Many condition. For instance, in the translation study, nominal plural marking co-occurred with verbal plural marking 95 % of all times and verbal plural marking with nominal plural marking 95.4 % of times. For the picture descriptions study, the proportions are 86.9 % vs. 89 %.

One possible explanation of this asymmetry attributes it to left dislocations (cf. Section 2). Since the left-dislocated position (LDP) is outside the clause, it permits an anaphoric relationship between cross-reference markers and cross-referenced RPs. In this environment, cross-reference markers and cross-referenced RPs are merely required to be semantically compatible in terms of the features they express, rather than to express the same features ('anaphoric agreement' as defined by Bresnan & Mchombo 1987, as opposed to the 'grammatical agreement' inside the clause). And since it is the cross-reference markers that saturate the head's argument positions under anaphoric agreement, the cross-reference markers might be expected to be more likely than the cross-referenced RPs to reflect the cardinality of the set of referents of the arguments. This hypothesis remains to be tested.[17] If borne out, it would entail that number agreement inside the clause approaches the kind of production frequencies known from languages in which it is obligatory and in which the absence of agreement is considered an error (see references to the literature on agreement production cited above).

---

[17] We have not (yet) coded the data for the syntactic position of the cross-referenced RP.

6 Conclusions

Van Valin's early (1977) insight that cross-reference markers saturate the syntactic argument positions of heads in head-marking languages and that such languages consequently lack traditional subject-external VPs is one of the foundational ideas of RRG. Ramifications of this idea can be found throughout the theory. It particularly influenced the notion of the verbal core, a cornerstone of the Layered Structure of the Clause model, and the treatment of predication and grammatical relations as independent of phrase structure.

Yet, the question of the relation between cross-reference markers and cross-referenced RPs has always remained somewhat of a challenge. To the extent that cross-referenced RPs occur outside the clause, this relation is straightforwardly anaphoric. In mainstream Generative Grammar, this situation is often assumed to be canonical in head-marking (e. g. Jelinek 1984, Baker 1991, 1996, Pensalfini 2004). But, as pointed out by Simpson (1991), Austin & Bresnan (1996), and Van Valin (2013), *inter alia*, this assumption is in many cases unwarranted: many languages clearly allow the co-occurrence of cross-reference markers with cross-referenced RPs inside the clause.

A number of alternative analyses have been proposed for the relation between cross-reference markers and cross-referenced clause-mate RPs. A traditional view that can be traced back as far as Humboldt (1836) is that the two stand in an appositive relation. But as Lehmann (1985) observes, this view seems to presuppose an understanding of apposition that so far nobody has been able to formally explicate.

Van Valin (1985) instead treats clause-mate cross-referenced RPs as restrictive modifiers of the cross-reference markers and as occupying the same position as clause-level adjuncts. However, the morphological and distributional properties of cross-referenced RPs are clearly distinct from those of *bona fide* adjuncts, rendering this analysis rather *ad hoc* within more recent versions of the LSC model. Van Valin (2013) instead suggests that cross-referenced RPs may be hosted in a previously unrecognized 'Extra-Core Slot' position, which does not belong to the clausal periphery, but is nonetheless directly dominated by the clause.

Lastly, a fourth option was prominently proposed by Bresnan & Mchombo (1987). On this proposal, there are two kinds of cross-reference markers. Those that exclude clause-mate cross-referenced RPs are incorporated pronominal arguments, whereas those that can co-occur with clause-mate cross-referenced RPs are ambiguous between incorporated pronominal arguments and agreement markers with the PRO-drop property of Latin and Roman subject agreement markers (Perlmutter 1971, Jaeger & Gerassimova 2002, *inter alia*), realizing the arguments of the head in the absence of a clause-mate cross-referenced RP, but expressing agreement with it in its presence.

In this paper, we have presented two sources of evidence that we think argue in favor of an ambiguous, PRO-drop-style analysis of cross-reference marking in Yucatec Maya, a purely head-marking language. First, the possibility of cross-referenced clause-mate RPs to occur between the two nuclei of a core cosubordination discourages the analysis of these RPs as direct daughters of the clause, given the general absence of discontinuous syntactic projections in the language. Secondly, the results of two production experiments suggest that speakers prefer to mark the number of an argument on both the head and cross-referenced RPs. We argue that, given that plural marking is optional in Yucatec, this distribution is more in line with a PRO-drop analysis than with a core-external analysis of the cross-referenced RPs.

Neither of the arguments we have advanced here is cut-and-dried. While the distributional evidence from core cosubordinations in Yucatec seems hard to reconcile with an analysis of the Extra-Core Slot (ECS) of Van Valin (2013) as an immediate daughter of the clause, the data is in fact consistent with an alternative treatment of the ECS as adjoined to the core. The relative merits of such a core-layer adjunction analysis over an ambiguous analysis would have to be carefully examined.

As for our production data, while it is suggestive of syntactic agreement, it does not show a categorical pattern. It may be that richer coding of the data and a more sophisticated analysis will in fact unearth something more approaching a categorical distribution. It is also conceivable that syntactic agreement in optionally marked functional categories never approaches a categorical distribution. This is unclear simply because the production of agreement in optionally marked categories has rarely ever been studied to date (one recent partial exception is Lorimor 2007 on Lebanese Arabic). Similarly, it is possible that the covariation between verbal and nominal plural marking we observed in our production data is not in fact the result of syntactic agreement, but is driven by other factors that are not yet well understood.

Thus, the debate over the relation between head-marking and agreement will continue, and it seems impossible to predict what theoretical innovations it may yet inspire. Meanwhile, beyond the question of the relation between head-marking and agreement, we hope that our study illustrates the potential for traditional syntactic analysis and the analysis of variation in experimental or corpus data to inform one another – including in research on indigenous languages in the field.

References

Aissen, J. 1987. *Tzotzil clause structure*. Dordrecht, Netherlands: Reidel Publishing.

Aissen, J. 1999. Agent focus and inverse in Tzotzil. *Language* 75: 451–485.

Austin, P. & J. Bresnan. 1996. Non-configurationality in Australian Aboriginal languages. *Natural Language and Linguistic Theory* 14: 215–268.

Baker, M. 1991. On some subject/object asymmetries in Mohawk. *Natural Language and Linguistic Theory* 9: 537–576.

Baker, M. 1996. *The polysynthesis parameter*. Oxford: Oxford University Press.

Bloomfield, L. 1933. *Language*. New York, NY: Henry Holt.

Boas, F. 1911. Linguistics and ethnology. In F. Boas (ed.), *Handbook of American Indian languages*, 59–73. Washington, DC: Smithsonian Institution.

Bock, J. K. & K. M. Eberhard. 1993. Meaning, sound and syntax in English number agreement. *Language and Cognitive Processes* 8: 57–99.

Bock, J. K. & C. A. Miller. 1991. Broken agreement. *Cognitive Psychology* 23(1): 45–93.

Bock, J. K. & K. M. Eberhard. 1993. Meaning, sound and syntax in English number agreement. *Language and Cognitive Processes* 8: 57–99.

Bohnemeyer, J. 1998. *Time relations in discourse: Evidence from Yukatek Maya*. Tilburg University dissertation.

Bohnemeyer, J. 2002. *The grammar of time reference in Yukatek Maya*. Munich: LINCOM.

Bohnemeyer, J. 2004. Split intransitivity, linking, and lexical representation: the case of Yukatek Maya. *Linguistics* 42(1): 67–107.

Bohnemeyer, J. 2009a. Linking without grammatical relations in Yucatec: Alignment, extraction, and control. In Y. Nishina, Y. M. Shin, S. Skopeteas, E. Verhoeven & J. Helmbrecht (eds.), *Issues in functional-typological linguistics and*

References

language theory: A Festschrift for Christian Lehmann on the occasion of his 60th birthday, 185–214. Berlin: Mouton de Gruyter.

Bohnemeyer, J. 2009b. Temporal anaphora in a tenseless language. In W. Klein & P. Li (eds.), *The expression of time in language*, 83–128. Berlin: Mouton de Gruyter.

Bohnemeyer, J. 2012. In the mood for status: Subjunctive and irrealis in Yucatec. Presented at *SULA 7: The semantics of under-represented languages in the Americas*. Cornell University.

Bohnemeyer, J. & R. D. Van Valin, Jr. The Macro-Event Property and the layered structure of the clause. Manuscript – University at Buffalo.

Borer, H. 2005. *In name only: Structuring sense*. Oxford: Oxford University Press.

Bresnan, J. 1982. Polyadicity. In J. Bresnan (ed.), *The mental representation of grammatical relations*, 149–172. Cambridge, MA: MIT Press.

Bresnan, J. & S. Mchombo. 1987. Topic, pronoun, and agreement in Chicheŵa. *Language* 63: 741–782.

Bricker, V. R. 1979. Wh-questions, relativization, and clefting in Yucatec Maya. In L. Martin (ed.), *Papers in Mayan linguistics 3*, 107–136. Columbia, MO: Lucas Brothers.

Butler, L. K. 2012. Crosslinguistic and experimental evidence for non-number plurals. *Linguistic Variation* 12(1): 27–56.

Butler, L. K., J. Bohnemeyer & T. F. Jaeger. 2014. Syntactic constraints and production preferences for optional plural marking in Yucatec Maya. In A. Machicao y Priemer, A. Nolda & A. Sioupi (eds.), *Zwischen Kern und Peripherie: Untersuchungen zu Randbereichen in Sprache und Grammatik* [Between core and periphery: Studies on peripheral phenomena in language and grammar], 181–208. Berlin: de Gruyter.

Chomsky, N. 1981. *Lectures on Government and Binding*. Dordrecht: Foris.

Diesing, M. & E. Jelinek. 1995. Distributing arguments. *Natural Language Semantics* 3(2): 123–176.

Dowty, D. R. 1979. *Word meaning and Montague Grammar: The semantics of verbs and times in Generative Semantics and Montague's PTQ*. Dordrecht: Reidel.

Durbin, M. & F. Ojeda. 1978. Basic word-order in Yucatec Maya. In N. C. England (ed.), *Papers in Mayan linguistics 2*, 69–77. Columbia: University of Missouri, Department of Anthropology.

Foley, W. & R. D. Van Valin, Jr. 1984. *Functional syntax and universal grammar*. Cambridge: Cambridge University Press.

Gutiérrez Bravo, R. & J. Monforte y Madera. 2008. On the nature of unmarked word order in Yucatec Maya. Presented at the 2008 Annual Meeting of the Society for the Study of the Indigenous Languages of the Americas, Chicago.

Gutiérrez Bravo, R. & J. Monforte y Madera. 2009. Focus, agent focus and relative clauses in Yucatec Maya. In H. Avelino, J. Coon & E. Norcliffe (eds.), *MIT working papers in linguistics 59* (New perspectives in Mayan linguistics), 83–96. Cambridge, MA: Massachusetts Institute of Technology.

Gutiérrez Bravo, R. & J. Monforte y Madera. La alternancia sujeto inicial/verbo inicial y la teoría de la optimidad (Subject-initial/verb-initial alternation and Optimality Theory). Manuscript – El Colegio de Mexico.

Hale, K. 1983. Warlpiri and the grammar of non-configurational languages. *Natural Language and Linguistic Theory* 1: 5–74.

Hartsuiker, R. J., H. J. Schriefers, K. Bock & G. M. Kikstra. 2003. Morphophonological influences on the construction of subject-verb agreement. *Memory & cognition* 31(8): 1316–1326.

Humboldt, W. von. 1836. *Über die Verschiedenheit des menschlichen Sprachbaues und ihren Einfluss aft die geistige Entwicklung des Menschengeschlects*. Berlin: Dümmler.

Jaeger, T. F. & V. Gerassimova. 2002. Bulgarian word order and the role of the direct object clitic in LFG. In M. Butt & T. H. King (eds.), *Proceedings of the LFG02 Conference*. Stanford: CSLI Publications.

Jelinek, E. 1984. Empty categories and non-configurational languages. *Natural Language and Linguistic Theory* 2: 39–76.

Krämer, M. & D. Wunderlich. 1999. Transitivity alternations in Yucatec, and the correlation between aspect and argument roles. *Linguistics* 37: 431–480.

Lambrecht, K. 1994. *Information structure and sentence form: Topic, focus, and the mental representations of discourse referents*. Cambridge: Cambridge University Press.

Lehmann, C. 1985. On grammatical relationality. *Folia Linguistica* 19: 67–109.

Lehmann, C. 1991. *El hijo prodigo – The prodigal son*. Story narrated by Gregorio Vivas and recorded and transcribed by Christian Lehmann with the help of Julio Ek May. Erfurt: Seminar für Sprachwissenschaft, Philosophische Fakultät, University of Erfurt.

References

Lehmann, C. 2003. *Possession in Yucatec Maya*, Second revised edition. ASSidUE Nr. 10, Erfurt: Seminar für Sprachwissenschaft der Universität.

Lewis, M. P. (ed.). 2009. *Ethnologue: Languages of the World*, Sixteenth edition. Dallas, TX: SIL International. Available online: http://www.ethnologue.com, accessed December 13th 2010.

Lorimor, H. 2007. *Conjunctions and grammatical agreement.* University of Illinois at Urbana-Champaign, dissertation.

Milewski, T. 1950. La structure de la phrase dans les langues indigenes de l'Amérique du Nord. In T. Milewski (ed.), *Études typologiques sur les langues indigenes de l' Amérique*, 7–101. Kraków, Poland : Polska Akademia Nauk.

Nichols, J. 1986. Head-marking and dependent-marking grammar. *Language* 62: 56–119.

Norcliffe, E. 2009. *Head-marking in usage and grammar: A study of variation and change in Yucatec Maya.* Stanford University dissertation.

Pensalfini, R. 2004. Towards a typology of non-configurationality. *Natural language and linguistic theory* 22: 359–408.

Perlmutter, D. 1971. *Deep and surface structure constraints in syntax.* New York: Holt Rinehart Winston.

PHLI. 2009. *Perfil sociodemográfico de la población que habla lengua indígena* [socio-demographic profile of the speakers of indigenous languages]. Aguascalientes: Instituto Nacional de Estadística y Geografía. Available online: http://www.inegi.org.mx/prod_serv/contenidos/espanol/bvinegi/productos/censos/poblacion/poblacion_indigena/leng_indi/PHLI.pdf, accessed June 23rd 2011.

Shimojo, M. 1995. *Focus structure and morphosyntax in Japanese:* wa *and* ga, *and word order flexibility.* University at Buffalo dissertation.

Simpson, J. 1991. *Warlpiri morpho-Syntax: A lexicalist approach.* Dordrecht: Kluwer.

Skopeteas, S. & E. Verhoeven. 2005. Postverbal argument order in Yucatec Maya. *Language typology & universals* 58(4): 347–373.

Skopeteas, S. & E. Verhoeven. 2009. Distinctness effects on VOS order: Evidence from Yucatec Maya. In H. Avelino, J. Coon & E. Norcliffe (eds.), *MIT working papers in linguistics 59* (New perspectives in Mayan linguistics), 135–152.

Skopeteas S. & E. Verhoeven. Licensing focus constructions in Yucatec Maya. Manuscript – Bielefeld University.

Talmy, L. 2000. *Toward a cognitive semantics. Volume I.* Cambridge, MA: MIT Press.

Tonhauser, J. 2003. F-constructions in Yucatec Maya. In J. Anderssen, P. Menéndez Benito & A. Werle, (eds.), *Proceedings of SULA 2*, 203–223. Amherst, MA: GLSA.

Tonhauser, J. 2007. Agent focus and voice in Yucatec Maya. *Proceedings of the 39th meeting of the Chicago Linguistic Society,* 540–558. Chicago: Chicago Linguistic Society.

Tonhauser, J. The syntax and semantics of Yucatec Mayan focus constructions. Manuscript – The Ohio State University.

Van Valin, R. D., Jr. 1977. *Aspects of Lakhota syntax.* University of California, Berkeley, dissertation.

Van Valin, R. D., Jr. 1985. Case marking and the structure of the Lakhota clause. In J. Nichols & T. Woodbury (eds.), *Grammar inside and outside the clause*, 363–413. Cambridge: Cambridge University Press.

Van Valin, R. D., Jr. (ed.). 1993. *Advances in role and reference grammar.* Amsterdam: Benjamins.

Van Valin, R. D., Jr. 2005. *Exploring the syntax-semantics interface.* Cambridge: Cambridge University Press.

Van Valin, R. D., Jr. 2013. Head-marking languages and linguistic theory. In B. Bickel, L. A. Grenoble, D. A. Peterson, & A. Timberlake (eds.), *Language typology and historical contingency: In honor of Johanna Nichols*, 91–123. Amsterdam: John Benjamins.

Van Valin, R. D., Jr. & W. Foley. 1980. Role and Reference Grammar. In E. A. Moravcsik & J. R. Wirth (eds.), *Current approaches to syntax. Syntax and semantics 13*, 329–352. New York: Academic Press.

Van Valin, R. D., Jr. & R. J. LaPolla. 1997. *Syntax.* Cambridge: Cambridge University Press.

Vapnarsky, V. 1995. Las voces de las profecías: Expresiones y visiones del futuro en maya yucateco [The voices of the prophesies: Expressions and visions of the future in Yucatec Maya]. *Trace* 28: 88–105.

Vapnarsky, V. 2013. Is Yucatec Maya an omnipredicative language? Predication, the copula and focus constructions. *STUF – Language Typology and Universals* 66(1): 40–86.

References

Vigliocco, G., Butterworth, B., & C. Semenza. 1995. Constructing subject-verb agreement in speech: The role of semantic and morphological factors. *Journal of Memory and Language* 43(2): 186–215.

Villa Rojas, A. 1945. *The Maya of East Central Quintana Roo, Mexico.* Washington: Carnegie Institution of Washington Publication 559.

Wiltschko, M. 2008. The syntax of non-inflectional plural marking. *Natural Language and Linguistic Theory* 26: 639–694.

Zavala Maldonado, R. 1993. *Clause integration with verbs of motion in Mayan languages.* University of Oregon, Master's thesis.

Authors

Jürgen Bohnemeyer (Corresponding author)
Department of Linguistics
University at Buffalo, The State University of New York
609 Baldy Hall
Buffalo, NY 14260
jb77@buffalo.edu

Lindsay K. Butler
Communication Sciences and Disorders, The Pennsylvania State University

T. Florian Jaeger
Department of Brain and Cognitive Sciences, University of Rochester

Degree Expressions at the Syntax-Semantics Interface

Jens Fleischhauer

1 Introduction

This paper aims at extending the Role and Reference Grammar (RRG) approach to adverbs set out in Van Valin & LaPolla (1997) and Van Valin (2005). Apart from the work by Nuyts (1993), Ortigosa (2003), Toratani (2007) and Mora-Bustos (2009), adverbs have received comparatively little attention in RRG. Degree adverbs have not been analyzed in RRG at all and have also been given comparatively less attention in other frameworks (for different analyses embedded in a generative tradition cf. Doetjes 1997, Vecchiato 1999). In this paper, I will primarily focus on adverbially used degree expressions, as exemplified by the English examples in (1). *A lot* is used to indicate the intensity of frightening in (a). Following Bolinger (1972), cases like in (a) are called '(verbal) degree gradation' (I adopt the terminology put forward in Löbner 2012). In (b) *a lot* is used to specify the temporal duration of the sleeping event, whereas in (c) it indicates the frequency of his going to the cinema. Examples (b) and (c) are subsumed under the label 'extent gradation.'

(1) a. The dog frightens the boy a lot.
    b. Last night, the boy slept a lot.
    c. He goes to the cinema a lot.

Although English makes use of a single adverb for extent and degree gradation, other languages like Polish use different adverbs for both subtypes of verb gradation. In Polish, the degree expression *bardzo* 'very' is used for degree gradation and it makes use of *dużo* 'much' for extent gradation.[1]

(2) a. *Ta   dziewczyna bardzo lubi   tego psa.*
    DEM girl   very   likes DEM dog
    'The girl likes the dog very much.'
  b. *On dużo spał.*
     he much slept
     'He slept a lot.'
  c. *Ona chodzi dużo do   kin-a.*
     she goes   much PREP cinema-GEN
     'She goes to the cinema a lot.'

English and Polish exemplify two different patterns in the distribution of adverbial degree expressions. In English, the same degree expression is used for extent and degree gradation and it can also be used as an adnominal quantity expression, as shown in (3).[2] Polish, on the other hand, uses two different degree expressions for both subtypes of verb gradation. The one used for extent gradation – *dużo* – is also used adnominally to specify a nominal quantity (4). *Bardzo*, the degree expression used for verbal degree gradation, does not have an adnominal use but rather also functions as an intensifier of adjectives in the positive form (5). In English, *a lot* cannot be used for grading adjectives, instead *very* has to be used (as indicated in the translation of example (5)).

(3) There is a lot of chocolate in the cake.

(4) a. *Ten mężczyzna ma dużo książek.*
    DEM man   has much books.GEN
    'The man has many books.'
  b. *W   jeziorze jest dużo wod-y.*
     PREP lake.LOC is   much water-GEN
     'There is much water in the sea.'

---

[1] List of abbreviations used in the paper: ABL 'ablative', ACC 'accusative', AOR 'aorist', AUX 'auxiliary', CAUS 'causative', COMP 'comparative', DAT 'dative', DEF 'definite', DEM 'demonstrative', DISTR 'distributive', E 'exclusive', GEN 'genitive', INCEP 'inceptive', IPFV 'imperfective', LOC 'locative', PERF 'perfective', PL 'plural', POSS 'possessive', PST 'past', PREP 'preposition', PROG 'progressive', REFL 'reflexive', REMPST 'remote past', SG 'singular'.

[2] I use the term 'adnominal quantity expression' to refer to the use of degree expressions in the nominal domain.

(5) *Ten chłopiec jest bardzo wysoki.*
   DEM boy   is very tall
   'The boy is very tall.'

The contrast indicated by the English and Polish examples leads to different questions. First, is there any particular reason why degree expressions used for extent gradation (English *a lot*, Polish *dużo*) are also used as adnominal quantity expressions and those restricted to degree gradation (Polish *bardzo* and English *very*) are not? Second, do languages like Polish display a difference between extent and degree gradation that, as such, does not exist in, for example, English? Or is it a universal distinction between extent and degree gradation, which in English is only masked by the use of the same adverbial expression for both?

In this paper, I will present answers to both questions. The central claim will be that languages like English display the same distinction between extent and degree gradation as languages such as Polish do. Essentially, the distinction between extent and degree gradation will be related to two different syntactic configurations in which adverbially used degree expressions show up. This results in the claim that degree expressions in English and similar languages are syntactically ambiguous, whereas Polish, for example, uses two distinct and syntactically unambiguous adverbial degree expressions. In RRG terms, I will propose that extent gradation is syntactically realized at the core layer, whereas degree gradation is expressed at the nucleus layer. This syntactic difference will also explain the cross-categorical distribution of degree expressions, namely why expressions used for extent gradation also function as adnominal quantity expressions. In this paper, I will focus on data from French and German, which display the same kind of difference exemplified by the English and Polish examples above. Section 2 will provide the relevant background on verb gradation. The cross-categorical distribution of degree expression will be discussed in section 3. Section 4 provides a discussion of the French degree adverb *beaucoup* 'a lot' and argues that it is syntactically ambiguous. The relevant background of adverbs in RRG is introduced in section 5. Section 6 presents the crucial data on which the syntactic analysis of adverbial degree expressions in section 7 is based. The data will consist of scope interactions between degree adverbs and (aspectual) operators. In section 8, I extend the syntactic analysis to adnominal uses of degree expressions and end with a conclusion in section 9.

2 Verb gradation

Gradation is usually considered to be a prototypical property of adjectives.[3] For adjectives, gradability is grammatically relevant since only gradable adjectives appear in degree constructions without coercion of their meaning. In languages that have degree morphology, such as English with its comparative *-er* or superlative *-est*, only gradable adjectives take these morphemes (6a). Although degree morphology is not universal, all languages that have gradable adjectives also have special degree constructions (Bhat & Pustet 2000) such as the equative (6b) or the combination of the adjective with a degree expression like English *very* (c).

(6) a. tall – taller – tallest; dead - #deader - #deadest
 b. He is as tall as his brother.
 c. He is very tall.

As argued quite early by Sapir (1944) and embedded in a broader discussion by Bolinger (1972), gradation is not restricted to adjectives, but a characteristic of all word classes. Even degree morphology is not restricted to adjectives and languages such as Jalonke (Mande) combine verbs with degree morphemes. The prefix *ma-* in Jalonke either functions as a distributive marker (7) expressing a multiplicity of actions or it is used as a degree expression with verbs as in (8).

Jalonke (Mande, Lüpke 2005: 309)
(7) *Nxo ma-giri xure-n' i.*
 1PL.E DISTR-cross stream-DEF at
 'We crossed the stream a lot.'

Jalonke (Mande, Lüpke 2005: 308)
(8) a. *bundaa ma-bundaa*
 'be wet' 'be a little wet'
 b. *fisa ma-fisa*
 'be better' 'be a little better'

In the case of adjectives, gradation affects the gradable property expressed by the adjective. Gradation has the effect of further specifying the degree of the property of the referent of the adjective by comparing it to some other degree (cf.

---

[3] Throughout this paper I use the terms 'gradation' and 'intensification' interchangeably.

Bierwisch 1989, Kennedy 1999 among others). The comparandum can either be explicitly represented, as in the comparative or equative construction, or it can be a context-dependent standard value as in (5c).[4] For *very* Kennedy & McNally (2005) assume that it introduces a context-dependent standard value, which is conceived as 'high' in the given context. (6c) then has the reading that among those who are tall his tallness is conceived of as (contextually) high, meaning he is not only tall but tall to a high degree.

Gradation as illustrated by the examples above and in the first section can intuitively be described as the specification of the degree of a property, which allows for variable instantiation. Formally, this is captured by the notion of 'scale,' meaning that gradable properties are analyzed as scalar predications. Scales are understood as linearly ordered degrees in a certain dimension and can be formally described by three parameters: a measurement dimension (Δ) such as WIDTH or PRICE, a set of values (D), for example, size or price values, and an ordering relation (R) that determines the linear order of the degrees (Kennedy & McNally 2005). Different analyses of gradable adjectives are proposed in the literature (cf. Kennedy 1999 for an overview of the discussion) and the currently most popular ones assume a degree-based analysis.[5] Gradable adjectives somehow encode a scale in their lexical semantics and gradation is related to a specification of a degree on that scale.

Gradation is more complex for verbs than it is for adjectives. There are at least two reasons for that higher complexity on the side of verbs. First, although all gradable adjectives are analyzed as expressing scalar predications, most verbs are not considered to express scalar predications. Rappaport Hovav (2008) and Rappaport Hovav & Levin (2010) argue that only verbs expressing a directed change in a single dimension are scalar. This leads to the claim that only lexical change of state verbs like *broaden, widen* or *grow* and a subset of verbs of directed motion such as *rise* and *enter* are scalar. Basically, all activity predicates like *bleed* or *hit* are considered as expressing nonscalar changes, whereby 'change' is understood in the sense of Dowty (1979) and is used to capture dynamicity.[6]

---

[4] Kennedy & McNally (2005) among others also assume that the positive form of adjectives expresses a comparison with a standard value.

[5] Note that there have also been nondegree based analyses of gradable adjectives – for example, Klein (1980).

[6] Beavers (2011) also argues for a latent scalar structure of verbs of impact like *hit*.

The German examples in (9) indicate that gradability is not restricted to scalar verbs in the narrow sense of Rappaport Hovav & Levin, but also activities such as *bluten* 'bleed' and states like *lieben* 'love' can be graded.[7] In (a), *sehr* specifies the quantity of emitted blood, whereas in (b) the degree expression is used to indicate the intensity of the boy's love. (c) shows an example of a degree gradation of a scalar verb in the narrow sense of Rappaport Hovav & Levin. In this case, *sehr* specifies the degree of change (see Hay et al. 1999 as well as Fleischhauer 2013, 2016 for the discussion of such cases).

(9) a. *Der Junge blutet sehr.*
 the boy bleeds very
 'The boy is bleeding a lot.'
 b. *Der Junge liebt seine Mutter sehr.*
 the boy loves his mother very
 'The boy loves his mother very much.'
 c. *Der Junge ist sehr gewachsen.*
 the boy is very grown
 'The boy has grown a lot.'

Up to now, there has been no clear notion of scalarity of verbs and Rappaport Hovav & Levin's distinction between scalar and nonscalar changes does not coincide with gradability. This shows that scales are independent of the notion of 'change' and that it is an open question whether gradability of verbs depends on some specific property (and is therefore predictable) or not (cf. Tsujimura 2001 for a discussion of gradability of verbs in Japanese).

The second argument for the higher complexity of verb gradation compared to adjectives is that, contrary to adjectives, verbs denote eventualities. Verb gradation can either be related to specifying the degree of a gradable property lexicalized by the verb (degree gradation as in (9)) or it can be related to a gradable property of the event (extent gradation as in (10)). German uses *sehr* 'very' for degree gradation and *viel* 'much' for extent gradation. In (10a) it is the frequency of raining events that is specified by *viel*, whereas it is the temporal duration of the sleeping event in (b).

---

[7] See Gamerschlag (2014) and Fleischhauer & Gamerschlag (2014) for the argumentation that stative verbs can be distinguished into scalar and nonscalar ones similarly to Rappaport Hovav & Levin's partitioning of dynamic verbs.

(10) a. *Letzten Sommer hat es viel geregnet.*
      last summer has it much rained
      'Last summer, it rained a lot.'
   b. *Letzte Nacht hat der Junge viel geschlafen.*
      last night has the boy much slept
      'The boy slept a lot last night.'

Extent gradation is restricted to eventive predications and hence not possible with attributively used adjectives. Predicatively used adjectives allow extent gradation as (11) indicates.

(11) *Der Junge ist viel krank.*
     the boy is much ill
     'The boy is ill a lot.'

As the data in (9) and (10) show, German uses different degree expressions for extent and degree gradation, just like Polish does. French, as shown in (12), is like English in using the same degree expression for extent and degree gradation. In (12a) *beaucoup* 'a lot' specifies the frequency of going to the cinema, whereas in (b) it is the degree of appreciation. The example in (c) is ambiguous in the sense that both a durative and frequentative interpretation of *beaucoup* are possible, which means that John either slept for a long time or that he slept often during some implicit period of time.

(12) a. *Jean va beaucoup au cinéma.*
        Jean goes a lot to.the cinema
        'Jean goes to the movies a lot.' (Doetjes 2007: 685)
     b. *Jean a beaucoup apprécié ses conseils.*
        Jean has a lot appreciated his advice
        'Jean appreciated his advice a lot.' (Abeille et al. 2004: 186)
     c. *Jean a beaucoup dormi.*
        Jean has a lot slept
        'John slept a lot.'

The frequency reading of extent gradation is nearly synonymous to corresponding sentences that contain frequency adverbs such as French *souvent* 'often' (13). Different authors, such as de Swart (1993) and Abeille et al. (2004), analyze frequency adverbs as quantifiers. *Beaucoup,* on the other hand, is not treated as a quantifier due to its use in degree contexts like (12b). Bosque & Masullo (1998) go even further and subsume Spanish examples like those in (14) under the label 'verbal quantification.'

(13) *Jean va souvent au cinéma.*
Jean goes often to.the cinema
'Jean goes to the movies a lot.'

(14) a. *Llovió muy poco.*
rained very little
'It rained very little.' (Bosque & Masullo 1998: 19)
b. *Dormir un poco.*
sleep a bit
'Sleep a little bit.' (Bosque & Masullo 1998: 26)
c. *Ir poco en tren.*
go little by train
'Go rarely by train.' (Bosque & Masullo 1998: 25)

Example (14a) corresponds to Bolinger's degree gradation, whereas those in (b) and (c) are instances of extent gradation. Bosque & Masullo assume that (*un*) *poco* 'a bit/little' functions as a quantifier in all cases in (14), but do not provide arguments for this view. This is probably an overgeneralization from the more well-studied case of adnominal quantification to less studied cases such as those in (14). In the next section, I discuss the cross-categorical distribution of degree expressions in more detail and turn to the question whether expressions such as *mucho, beaucoup* or *viel* are really quantifiers or not in section 8.

3 Cross-categorical distribution of degree expressions

In the last section, Bosque & Masullo's claim that gradation is a subtype of quantification was mentioned. A possible reason for this assumption, which I rejected, could be the cross-categorical distribution of degree/quantity expressions. The Spanish degree expressions *mucho* 'a lot' and (*un*) *poco* 'a bit/little' are used adverbially as well as adnominally.⁸ As already pointed out in the previous sections, French, but also Spanish and English, show a different cross-categorical distribution of degree expressions from the distribution found in German and Polish. I will distinguish three contexts in which degree expressions are used: they can be used as adverbial, adnominal or adadjectival degree expressions. Starting with the adnominal use, the examples in (15) and (16) show that French and German use *beaucoup* and *viel* respectively for specifying a quantity of mass as well as count nouns. German indirectly displays the mass/count distinction by the inflection of *viel*. In the case of plural count nouns, *viel* is also inflected for plurality (16b), whereas the plurality marking is absent if it modifies a mass noun (a). In French, *beaucoup* is neutral with regard to the mass/count distinction and does not show an overt reflex of it. English *a lot* is like French *beaucoup* and only *much* and *many* are sensitive to the mass/count dichotomy.

(15) a. *beaucoup de soup*
      a lot   of soup
      'much soup'
   b. *beaucoup de livres*
      a lot   of books
      'many books'

(16) a. *viel   Suppe*
      much soup
      'much soup'
   b. *viele   Bücher*
      much.PL books
      'many books'

The examples in (17) and (18) show the combination of degree expressions with the positive form of adjectives as well as comparatives in French and German. French uses *très* 'very' for the positive form but *beaucoup* for the comparative. In addition to this, in German different degree expressions are used for intensifying the positive and comparative form of adjectives. For the positive, German uses *sehr*, whereas it makes use of *viel* for the comparative. In both languages the

---

⁸ While Bosque & Masullo argue that degree is a subtype of quantity, Sapir (1944: 93) argues that "grading [...] precedes measurement and counting" and Gary (1979) takes degree and quantity as manifestations of the same category.

expression used for grading comparatives is the same one that is also used in adnominal contexts, whereas the positive requires a different intensifier.

(17) a. *Paul est très/*beaucoup grand.*
    Paul is very/much   tall
    'Paul is very tall.'
  b. *Paul est beaucoup/*très plus grand que Daniel.*
    Paul is a lot/very   more tall than Daniel
    'Paul is much taller than Daniel.'

(18) a. *Paul ist sehr/*viel groß.*
    Paul is very/*much tall
    'Paul is very tall.'
  b. *Paul ist viel/*sehr größer als Daniel.*
    Paul is much/*very taller than Daniel
    'Paul is much taller than Daniel.'

The adverbial context has already been discussed in the last section. The examples in (9) and (10) for German and in (12) for French revealed that German uses *sehr* for degree gradation and *viel* for extent gradation, whereas French uses *beaucoup* for both. French and German show a slightly different cross-categorical distribution of the degree expressions discussed in this section. In French, it is only the positive form of adjectives that requires a different intensifier. German marks both gradation of adjectives in the positive form as well as degree gradation of verbs similarly. Table 1 summarizes the distribution of degree expressions for French, English, Spanish, German, Bulgarian and Polish. In addition, data from two non-Indo-European languages are included in the table. Finnish (Finno-Ugric) has the same pattern that also shows up in French and Spanish, whereas Tatar (Turkic) is like German and Polish.[9] It is not always the case that languages use a different intensifier for adjectives in the positive than they use for the other degree contexts. Bulgarian, for example, makes use of *mnogo* 'very, a lot' in all the contexts distinguished in table 1.[10]

---

[9] The data from Tatar and Bulgarian are shown in the appendix. The data of the other languages have already been discussed throughout the paper, except Finnish. The Finnish data are taken from Karttunen (1975). For a broader cross-linguistic investigation of the distribution of degree expressions see Fleischhauer (2016).

[10] An anonymous reviewer mentioned that colloquial Serbian also uses *mnogo* in all the contexts mentioned above.

Degree Expressions at the Syntax-Semantics Interface

Language	adjectival domain		nominal domain		verbal domain	
	Positive	Comparative	Mass	Count	Extent	Degree
French	très	beaucoup	beaucoup	beaucoup	beaucoup	beaucoup
English	very	a lot	a lot	a lot	a lot	a lot
Spanish	muy	mucho	mucho	mucho	mucho	mucho
Finnish	hyvin	paljon	paljon	paljon	paljon	paljon
Bulgarian	mnogo	mnogo	mnogo	mnogo	mnogo	mnogo
German	sehr	viel	viel	viel	viel	sehr
Polish	bardzo	dużo	dużo	dużo	dużo	bardzo
Tatar	bik	küp	küp	küp	küp	bik

Table 1: Cross-categorical distribution of degree expressions.

Table 1 merely lists eight languages, which does not allow for any conclusive typological generalizations. Nevertheless, it shows that in these languages the expression used for verbal extent gradation is also always used as an adnominal quantity expression. And if a language has different expressions for extent and degree gradation, the expression used for degree gradation also applies to the positive form of adjectives. It has to be mentioned that languages usually have several synonymous degree expressions which can differ in their distribution, as is the case for English (*very*) *much* and *a lot*. Only the latter is used for extent gradation and used as an adnominal quantity expression. Hence the claims made in this section have to be substantiated by looking at a larger range of data and also by looking into more languages. But at the present stage, I have decided to concentrate on the most neutral degree expressions, meaning such expressions that do not convey emphatic content and have the broadest distribution. For German, these are *sehr* and *viel*, even if several hundred intensifiers can be listed for German (see Van Os 1989).

In section 8, I will argue that it is no accident that German, for example, uses *viel* rather than *sehr* for extent gradation. But first, I focus on the difference between verbal extent and degree gradation and thereby follow Doetjes (1997) in assuming that expressions like French *beaucoup* are not semantically ambiguous in terms of expressing a high degree and a high frequency. Assuming a uniform semantics for these expressions, I will rather show in the next section that *beaucoup* is syntactically ambiguous.

4 Syntactic ambiguity of *beaucoup*

The aim of this section is to show that the adverbially used French degree expression *beaucoup* is syntactically ambiguous. With 'syntactically ambiguous' I mean that an expression can be used in two clearly distinct syntactic configurations which are associated with two different semantic interpretations. Two arguments will be presented in support of this claim. First, it will be shown that adverbial *beaucoup* allows for multiple realizations in a single sentence. It can simultaneously be realized as a degree as well as an extent intensifier. Second, it will be shown that the syntactic position of *beaucoup* constrains its interpretation. Similar claims are made by Vecchiato (1999), who argues that differences in the syntactic distribution of degree and extent *beaucoup* as well as the multiple realization of *beaucoup* indicate an apparent syntactic ambiguity of the degree expression. Working in the cartographic enterprise of Cinque (1999), she claims that the data indicate that extent and degree *beaucoup* are related to two different functional projections in the clause. But in the end, she assumes the same functional projection for both uses without an indication of how the different readings of *beaucoup* arise. My analysis differs from hers in assuming that *beaucoup* is really and not only apparently syntactically ambiguous and that the difference between extent and degree gradation arises through two different syntactic configurations in which *beaucoup* can be used.

In (19) the multiple realization of *beaucoup* is shown. The degree adverb is realized twice in the sentence and this leads to a specification of the frequency of bleeding events as well as to the degree of bleeding. It is the quantity of blood emitted in the event that is specified in the degree interpretation of *beaucoup*. If each linguistic category can only be specified once, the example in (19) shows that extent and degree *beaucoup* are related to the expression of different linguistic categories. Taken alone this does not show that there is also a syntactic difference between both uses of *beaucoup*, but it suggests that degree and extent intensifiers belong to two different semantic classes of adverbs.

(19) Il   a   beaucoup saigné beaucoup de   nez.
     he has a lot   bled   a lot   from nose
     'He often bled out of his nose a lot.'

Degree Expressions at the Syntax-Semantics Interface

It can be more clearly shown which use of *beaucoup* in (19) contributes the frequency and which one contributes the degree interpretation. The examples in (20) help to identify the syntactic positions and how they are related to the interpretation of *beaucoup*. If *beaucoup* is placed between the auxiliary and the main verb (20a), it is ambiguous as to whether a degree or an extent interpretation is possible. But as the examples in (b) and (c) show there are two unambiguous positions for *beaucoup*. If *beaucoup* directly follows the main verb, it can only be interpreted as a degree intensifier. Following the undergoer argument *beaucoup* only allows for an extent interpretation. For (19) this means that the first occurrence of *beaucoup* has to specify the event's frequency, since the syntactic position of the second one only allows for the degree reading.

(20) a. *Il a   beaucoup admiré   cette chanteuse à l'opera.*
       he has a lot   admired this chanteuse at the opera
       'He has (often) admired this chanteuse (very much) at the opera.'
   b. *Il a   admiré   beaucoup cette chanteuse à l'opera*
       'He has admired this chanteuse very much at the opera.'
   c. *Il a   admiré   cette   chanteuse beaucoup à l'opera.*
       'He has often admired this chanteuse at the opera.'

The sentences in (21) indicate that the syntactic position of *beaucoup* really puts constraints on its interpretation. The main clause in the examples contains *beaucoup* in a position between the auxiliary and the main verb (a) and following the main verb in (b). In the subordinate sentence a degree specification is added, which introduces an inconsistent degree specification with that of *beaucoup*. *Un peu* 'a little bit' indicates a low degree, whereas *beaucoup* specifies a high degree. Example (b) is contradictory since it would simultaneously express that he emitted a large quantity of blood (main clause) but that the quantity of blood he emitted was small (subordinated clause). The sentence is contradictory since *beaucoup* allows only for a degree reading in the position after the participle. If *beaucoup* is placed between the auxiliary and the participle, no contradiction arises since it allows for a frequency reading. Sentence (21a) has the interpretation that he often bled, but only emitted a small quantity of blood.

(21) a. *Il a   beaucoup saigné du   nez, mais seulement un peu.*
       he has a lot   bled   of.the nose but only   a little bit
       'He often bled out of his nose, but only a little bit.'

b. #Il a saigné beaucoup du nez, mais seulement un peu.
   he has bled a lot of.the nose but only a little bit
   'He bled a lot out of his nose, but only a little bit.'

The data in this section have shown that the interpretation of *beaucoup* is constrained by the syntax. This leads to the claim that extent and degree gradation are related to two different syntactic configurations.[11] In the next section, I will present RRG's view on adverbs, before I come to my analysis of the syntax of adverbially used degree expressions in section 6.

5 Adverbs in RRG

Role and Reference Grammar assumes different structured representations for predicates, their arguments and adjuncts on the one hand and grammatical operators on the other. These representations are called 'constituent' and 'operator projection' respectively (Van Valin & LaPolla 1997, Van Valin 2005). Operators are expressions for grammatical categories such as tense and aspect. Both, the constituent and the operator structure, are built on the same semantically motivated layered structure of the clause. RRG distinguishes between nucleus, core and clause layers (leaving the sentence level aside). The nucleus contains only the predicate, irrespective of whether it is a verb or some other predicating element such as a predicatively used adjective. The core consists of the nucleus and the arguments of the predicate. The highest layer – clause – contains the core and some optional elements (cf. Van Valin 2005). Each layer has an optional periphery that contains adjuncts and adverbials. Figure 1 gives a schematic representation of the layered structure of the clause and the connection of the constituent and the operator projection. Both structures are a mirror image of each other and are connected through the predicate.

Adverbs are realized in the periphery of the constituent projection and can attach to each of the three layers of the clause. Unlike in other approaches, such as Cinque (1999), it is not assumed that adverbs have a fixed base position. Nevertheless, the positioning of adverbs is not totally unconstrained. If multiple adverbs are realized in a sentence, the layered structure of the clause constrains their

---

[11] The analysis presented in this paper differs from the one by Doetjes (1997) who assumes there is no syntactic difference between the extent and degree interpretation of *beaucoup*.

Degree Expressions at the Syntax-Semantics Interface

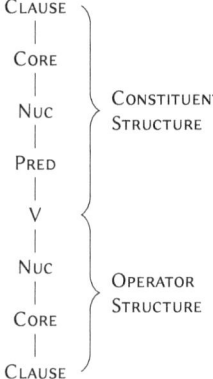

Figure 1: Schematic representation of constituent and operator projections in RRG (following Van Valin 2005: 12)

positioning. This means that the layered structure of the clause constraints the linear order of multiple adverbs. Nucleus adverbs are realized closer to the predicate than core adverbs, whereas core adverbs are again closer to the predicate than clausal ones (Van Valin 2005: 21). Also, a relationship between adverbs and operators is proposed. Adverbs are not operators, but "adverbs related to more outer operators occur outside of adverbs related to more inner operators" (Van Valin 2005: 20). Hence, the order of adverbs matches the order of operators to the extent that they semantically correspond to each other. Innermost operators are those specifying the nucleus, whereas the outermost ones are clausal operators. A list of operator types is shown in (22). Nuclear operators modify the action or event, whereas core operators are concerned with the relation between the nucleus and its arguments. Finally, clausal operators modify the whole clause.

(22) a. Nucleus operators: aspect, negation, directional
     b. Core operators: directionals, event quantification, modality, negation
     c. Clause operators: status, tense, evidentials, illocutionary force
        (Van Valin 2005: 12)

As mentioned above, adverbs and operators can semantically correspond to each other in expressing the same semantic category, such as aspect. Grammatical aspect can either be expressed by grammatical operators, like *-ing* in English, or such adverbs as *continuously*. As a first indication, one can assume that adverbs are realized at the same syntactic layer as their corresponding operators. The order of operators can therefore be roughly used as an indication of the syntax of corresponding adverbs. But this is not a perfect correspondence since tense is considered to be a sentence operator, whereas temporal adverbials are treated as core adverbs (Van Valin & LaPolla 1997: 162).

There is no discussion of degree operators in RRG (as example (8) from Jalonke showed, some languages have such operators in the verbal domain), but event quantification, which I consider similar to extent gradation, is discussed. Amele (Papua-New Guinea) has a distributive morpheme –*ad*– which indicates a multiplicity of actions. This can be seen by the example in (23a), in contrast to (b) which expresses a single action.

Amele (Papua-New Guinea; Roberts 1987, cited after Van Valin 2005: 11)
(23) a. *Age bel-ad-ein.*
    3PL go-DISTR-3PL.REMPST
    'They went in all directions.'
  b. *Age bel-ein.*
    3PL go-3PL.REMPST
    'They went.'

Van Valin argues that event quantification is a core layer operator. There are two arguments in support of this view: first, the distributive morpheme is closer to the stem than the tense operator. Tense is taken to be a clause operator and clausal operators occur outside of core operators. Athapaskan languages also show that nucleus operators are closer to the stem than distributive morphemes. In Slave, the inceptivity and perfectivity markers are realized to the right of the distributive morpheme *yá-* (19). Rice (2000) discusses the order of verbal affixes in Athapaskan languages and shows that the order of aspect and distributive marker shown in (24) also holds for other Athapaskan languages such as Koyukon, Athna and Deni'ina.

Slave (Athapaskan; Rice 1989: 678, Rice 2000: 52)
(24) *yá-d- i̜-ta*
    DISTR-INCEP-PERF-kick
    'It kicked many times.'

The data in (23) and (24) show that distributive morphemes have to follow nucleus operators such as aspect and that they precede clause operators as tense.

Degree Expressions at the Syntax-Semantics Interface

The second argument in favor of analyzing event quantification as an operation at the core layer is that the core is the minimal expression of an event (Van Valin 2005: 11). At the core, all semantically necessary components of an event – the event predicate and the event participants (Bohnemeyer & Van Valin 2013) – are realized. The nucleus is too small to be a syntactic expression of the event since it only contains the predicate but not the event participants. Also, operators that locate the event, either temporal or spatial ones, are core/clausal operators and therefore not present at the nucleus layer (Bohnemeyer & Van Valin 2013: 13). Therefore, operators that specify the quantity of an event are realized at the core layer or even higher up in the layered structure of the clause.

Based on Van Valin's analysis of event quantifiers as core operators, I predict that adverbial extent intensifiers should be core adverbs. In the next section I will provide the crucial data that show that this prediction is true. A similar prediction for adverbial degree intensifiers cannot be derived from the analysis of operators in RRG. However, the next section will show that degree intensifiers are nucleus adverbs and therefore differ syntactically from extent intensifiers.

Before I turn to the discussion of the crucial data, a short note on methodology is in order. Van Valin, following Jackendoff (1972), proposes that the relative order of adverbs reflects semantic scope relationships. Hence, analyzing the relative order of adverbs allows determining the syntax of adverbs.[12] A complicating factor is that information structure can affect the order of adverbs as shown by Maienborn (1996, 2001) for locative adverbials in German. The German examples in (25) show that no fixed order of the degree intensifier *sehr* and the directional adverbial *aus der Nase* 'out of the nose' can be established.[13] *Sehr* can either follow or precede the directional and no semantic difference exists between the sentences. Nevertheless, native speakers agree that the sentence in (a) is preferred, even if (b) is fully grammatical.

(25) a. *Er hat sehr aus der Nase geblutet.*
 he has very out the nose bled
 'He bled a lot out of his nose.'

---

[12] This kind of approach to the syntax of adverbs is also used in generative frameworks such as Cinque (1999).

[13] Van Valin (p.c.) mentions that *aus der Nase* is probably an argument adjunct rather than an adverbial. I leave this question open for future work since it does not affect the principals of the current analysis.

b. *Er hat aus der Nase sehr geblutet.*
   he has out the nose very bled
   'He bled a lot out of his nose.'

To determine the relative order of adverbs, it would be necessary to discuss information structure, which goes beyond the limits of the current paper. I will use a different strategy and base my analysis on scope relationships that exist between degree adverbs and aspectual operators.

6 Scope relationships

In this section, I will show that degree and extent intensifiers have different scope relationships with regard to grammatical aspect. It will be shown that extent intensifiers have scope over grammatical aspect, whereas grammatical aspect has scope over degree intensifiers. Scope can informally be defined as "a relational notion, where the interpretation of one expression depends on another one in a certain way" (de Swart 1998: 29). If extent intensifiers have scope over grammatical aspect, then the interpretation of aspect should be constrained or influenced by the intensifier. On the other hand, if aspect operators have scope over degree intensifiers, the interpretation of degree gradation should be affected by grammatical aspect.

Generally speaking, grammatical aspect is a distinction between a perfective and an imperfective description of a situation (cf. Comrie 1976). Under a perfective description, a situation is conceived as complete and without reference to its internal structure. Imperfective aspect, on the other hand, is more diverse and subsumes the progressive, continuous, and habitual subtypes. In all these cases, a situation is not (necessarily) described as complete but rather with reference to its internal structure. The continuous and progressive aspect describes a situation as ongoing, whereas habitual aspect indicates that a certain type of situation is characteristic for an extended interval.

French has a grammaticalized aspect distinction in the past tense between a perfective past (*passé composé*) and an imperfective past (*imparfait*). German does not have one, but provides different strategies for the expression of aspect. The German *Perfekt*, for example, substitutes for the perfective aspect in some contexts. But the *Perfekt* is also compatible with an imperfective state of affairs (cf.

Löbner 2002). Both French and German, also make use of a periphrastic progressive construction which can be combined with all tenses. In the French construction, the inflected auxiliary *être* 'to be' is combined with *en train de* 'in the process of' and the main verb is realized as an infinitive (26a). German uses a construction consisting of the inflected auxiliary *sein* (*to be*), a contracted form of the preposition *an* (*at*) and the definite article in dative case which is realized as *am* 'at.the' and the main verb as a nominalized infinitive (26b). This construction is called the 'rheinische Verlaufsform' and is often mentioned as being restricted to northern dialects. Ebert (2000), for example, shows that this construction is developing towards a grammaticalized progressive construction in colloquial German.

(26) a. *Nous sommes en train de rénover notre maison.*
we are PROG renovate our house
'We are renovating our house.'
b. *Wir sind unser Haus am Renovieren.*
we are our house at.the renovating
'We are renovating our house.'

Starting with German, the examples in (27) show the combination of the degree intensifier *sehr* with a verb in the perfective (a) and progressive aspect (b). The perfective sentence in (a) has the interpretation that the total amount of blood emitted in the course of the event is large. A paraphrasing of the sentence is 'the boy emitted a lot of blood.' For the progressive sentence in (b) the interpretation is different. *Sehr* does not specify the total amount of emitted blood, but the amount of blood emitted at a certain stage of the event. Since the progressive describes an ongoing event, no reference to the total amount of blood is possible. Also, both interpretations do not entail each other. If someone emitted a lot of blood during an event, he does not necessarily emit a lot of blood at each stage of the event. Rather he could only emit a bit of blood at each stage of the event which adds up to a large amount over the course of the whole event. Also, if one emits a lot of blood at a single stage of an event, it does not mean that the total quantity of blood has to be large as well. These are two related, but distinct interpretations of degree gradation that depend on the choice of grammatical aspect.

(27) a. *Der Junge hat sehr geblutet.*
the boy has very bled
'The boy bled a lot.'

b. *Der Junge war sehr am   Bluten.*
      the boy   was very at.the bleeding
      'The boy was bleeding a lot.'

The same effect of aspect on the interpretation of the degree use of *beaucoup* can be found in French (28). In (28a) we get the total quantity interpretation for the perfective verb and for the verb used in the progressive construction we get a specification of the quantity of blood emitted at a certain stage of the event. In contrast to the German example in (27a), the perfective sentence in (28a) also licenses an extent reading of the intensifier. *Beaucoup* does not give rise to an extent reading in the progressive sentence in (b).

(28) a. *Il a   beaucoup saigné.*
        he has a lot   bled
        'He bled a lot.'
     b. *Il est en train de saigner beaucoup.*
        he is PROG   to bleed a lot
        'He is bleeding a lot.'

German allows the combination of the adverbially used extent intensifier *viel* with verbs in the perfective (29a) as well as progressive aspect (b). In the case of the perfective verb *bluten* 'bleed' in (a) *viel* specifies the frequency of bleeding events. The sentence can be paraphrased as 'last week, the wound bled often.' Also, in combination with the progressive in (b) *viel* specifies the frequency of the event and the sentence can be paraphrased as 'the wound was bleeding often.' This frequency interpretation is incompatible with the meaning of the progressive, as describing a single, ongoing event. In the context of extent gradation, the progressive is shifted towards a habitual interpretation of the imperfective aspect. Comrie observes the same effect for English examples as in (30). *A lot* specifies the frequency of events denoted by the perfective verb in (a), but it has the same effect with the progressive verb in (b). Comrie (1976: 37) mentions that (30b) is an example of a habitual interpretation of the English progressive aspect. Even without *these days, a lot* would force a habitual interpretation of the progressive verb, which shows that it really is the extent intensifier that constrains the interpretation of grammatical aspect.

(29) a. *Letzte Woche hat die Wunde viel geblutet.*
    last week has the wound much bled
    'Last week, the wound bled a lot.'
  b. *Die Wunde war viel am Bluten.*
    the wound was much at.the bleeding
    'The wound was bleeding a lot.'

(30) a. We have gone to the opera a lot (these days).
  b. We're going to the opera a lot these days.
    (Comrie 1976: 37)

The German and English examples have shown that the interpretation of extent gradation does not change depending on the choice of grammatical aspect. Rather it is the other way round and progressive aspect is shifted towards a habitual reading by the extent intensifier. This is expected given the incompatible requirements of the frequency reading of extent gradation, which requires a multiplicity of events, and the progressive aspect, which describes a single and ongoing event. As aspect shifts in its interpretation, it is reasonable to conclude that extent intensifiers have scope over aspect. One open question is why French does not allow for an extent reading of *beaucoup* with verbs used in the periphrastic progressive constructions. Answering this question would go beyond the limits of this paper.

This section has shown that extent and degree intensifiers have different scope relationships with regard to grammatical aspect. Extent intensifiers have scope over grammatical aspect, whereas grammatical aspect has scope over degree intensifiers. In the next section, I will show what this reveals for a RRG analysis of the syntax of degree and extent intensifiers.

7 Syntax of verb gradation

The last section has shown that extent and degree intensifiers differ in scope relationships with regard to grammatical aspect. I assume that semantic scope relationships are also syntactically reflected. Since grammatical aspect is expressed by nucleus operators, degree gradation has to be located at the nucleus layer too. Degree intensifiers therefore have to be nucleus adverbs; otherwise aspect could not have scope over degree gradation. Extent intensifiers do not fall under the scope of aspect, which perfectly fits the assumption formulated in section 5 that extent gradation is expressed at the core layer. Based on this prediction, I assume that adverbially used extent intensifiers are core adverbs. It follows that degree and extent gradation are realized at two different syntactic layers. The difference between German *viel* and *sehr* is basically a syntactic one. Since adverbial *viel* is an extent intensifier, it is a core adverb, whereas the degree intensifier *sehr* is a nucleus adverb. Figure 2 shows the syntactic structure of the sentence *Er hat sehr geblutet* 'He bled a lot' on the left and *Er hat viel geblutet* 'He bled a lot' on the right. A note on the representation of the aspectual operator is required. As discussed above, the German *Perfekt* cannot be conceived as expressing perfective aspect. But since each sentence has an aspectual interpretation, I assume an aspectual operator, but it is not the *Perfekt* construction in German does functions as an expression of perfective aspect. Therefore aspect is not linked to a certain constituent in the constituent structure.

French adverbially used *beaucoup* is ambiguous between a degree and extent reading. Both readings are related to different syntactic configurations, as has been shown in section 4. Given the data discussed in the last section, it is reasonable to conclude that *beaucoup* in its extent use is realized at the core layer, whereas the degree interpretation of *beaucoup* arises if it is used as a nucleus adverb. Figure 3 shows the syntactic trees for verbal degree gradation (left) and extent gradation (right) in French. Syntactically, extent and degree gradation are realized in the same way in German and French, the only difference is that *beaucoup* is syntactically ambiguous between being a nucleus as well as core adverb, whereas the corresponding German degree expressions are not.

The syntactic difference between extent and degree gradation is semantically motivated. Degree gradation affects a gradable property lexicalized by the verb; therefore the intensifier directly applies to the verb. In case of *bluten* 'bleed', the gradable property is a volume scale, measuring the volume of the emitted substance. Extent gradation does not affect a gradable property of the verb but is an attribute of the event. Temporal duration and frequency are gradable properties of the event itself and not of the verb. Hence two different sources contribute the scales for verb gradation and the syntactic distinction discussed above is merely a reflection of this fact.

The distinction between extent and degree gradation can be reduced to a syntactic one and a uniform semantic analysis of adverbial degree expressions is possible. Adverbial intensifiers always specify a degree on a scale and only the

Degree Expressions at the Syntax-Semantics Interface

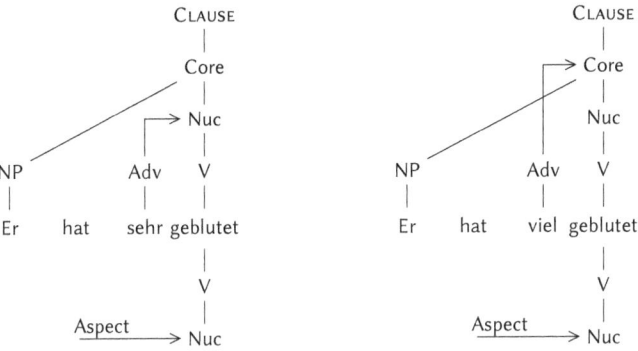

Figure 2: Syntactic structure of verbal degree gradation (left) and extent gradation (right) in German.[14]

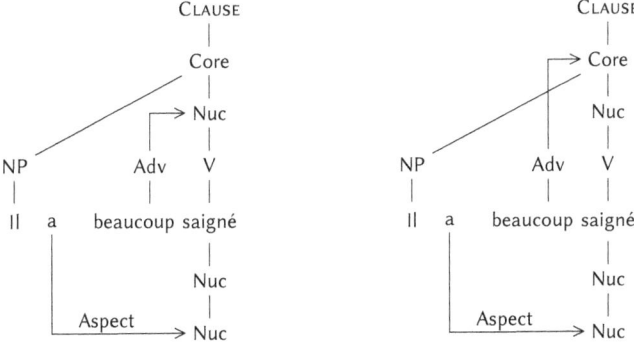

Figure 3: Syntactic structure of verbal degree gradation (left) and extent gradation (right) in French.

source of the scale determines whether it results in degree or extent gradation. Languages such as German, Polish or Tatar, which use different adverbs for extent and degree gradation, use different adverbs depending on the source of the scale. If the scale is contributed by the verb, a degree intensifier is used. But if the event contributes the scale, an extent intensifier is used for gradation. French, Spanish and also English do not overtly distinguish between adverbial degree and extent intensifiers, but rather have a syntactically ambiguous general degree expression. It is the syntactic configuration in which the degree expression is used that determines whether it results in degree or extent gradation.

---

[14] Van Valin (2008) argues that the nominal of 'NP' has to be replaced by the notion of a 'referential phrase' (RP). Since this does not affect my analysis, I stay with the more traditional term NP.

For indicating scope relationships, which are only implicit in the syntactic trees above, RRG makes use of lexical decomposition. The original intention of lexical decomposition in RRG is not to represent scope relationships but to determine the linking of the verb's arguments. Therefore the decompositional system, which is based on Dowty (1979), is used to capture the grammatically relevant components of verb meaning. RRG builds its lexical decomposition on Vendler's (1957) system of aktionsart classes, which I will not discuss in detail (for a full overview of the lexical decompositions assumed in RRG cf. Van Valin 2005). Van Valin assumes two basic types of predicates: states and activities. Activities are either one- or two-place predicates that are always marked by the operator **do'**. This is a two-place operator which takes the actor as its first argument and the predicate denoting the activity as its second one. The predicate decomposition for the verb *bluten* is shown in (31).

(31) *bluten* **do'**(x, **bleed'**(x))

Adverbs are represented in the predicate decompositional system as one-place predicates that modify logical structures or parts of logical structures. Operators, on the other hand, which do not receive a semantic interpretation in RRG, are merely indicated by angled brackets in the logical structures. In (32a) the (partial) logical structure for German extent gradation – *hat viel geblutet* 'has bled a lot' – is shown. **viel'** takes the activity predicate as well as the aspectual operator in its scope. In (b) the logical representation for degree gradation is indicated. **sehr'** only has the logical structure representing the activity predicate in its scope, whereas the aspectual operator precedes the adverb. The representations in (32) clearly allow the indication of the scope relationships, even if operators and adverbs are realized in two different projections.

(32) a. *hat viel geblutet*   **viel'** ($\langle_{ASP}$ PERF (**do'**(x, **bleed'**(x)))$\rangle$)
     b. *hat sehr geblutet*   ($\langle_{ASP}$ PERF (**sehr'**(**do'**(x, **bleed'**(x))))$\rangle$)

Although the representations in (32) can be used to indicate scope relationships, they are not sufficient to explain differences with respect to verb gradation which show up between verbs belonging to the same semantic class (in the sense of Levin 1993). First, verbs differ with regard to the scale they lexicalize. Compare *bluten*, which was discussed above, with another verb of emission like *dröhnen* 'drone'. *Dröhnen* is a verb of sound emission and example (33) has the interpretation that the intensity of the sound (meaning the loudness) is high. Both *dröhnen* and *bluten* are activity predicates and belong to the same semantic class; hence they do not differ with respect to lexical decomposition (34). Nevertheless, with respect to degree gradation both verbs differ in lexicalizing different types of scales. This difference between the verbs can only be captured by a deeper lexical decomposition, which further decomposes the constant elements (cf. Löbner 2012 for a similar claim).

(33) *Der Motor hat sehr gedröhnt.*
the engine has very droned
'The engine drones a lot.'

(34) a. *bluten* **do'**(x, **bleed'**(x))
b. *dröhnen* **do'**(x, **drone'**(x))

A second reason for a deeper lexical decomposition is that otherwise the interaction of grammatical aspect and degree gradation cannot be explained. Not all gradable verbs show an effect of grammatical aspect on degree gradation, only change of state verbs like *widen, grow* and *stabilize* and verbs of substance emission do (cf. Fleischhauer 2013, 2016). By considering the examples in (33) and (35) it can be shown that grammatical aspect does not affect degree gradation of verbs of sound emission. In the perfective example in (33) *sehr* specifies the sound intensity, the emitted sound is described as 'very loud.' The same interpretation obtains for the progressive sentence in (35). To explain why degree gradation interacts for some verbs with grammatical aspect and for others not requires a closer look at the semantics of the respective verbs.

(35) *Der Motor ist sehr am Dröhnen.*
the engine is very at.the droning
'The engine is droning a lot.'

Since the aim of this paper is to provide an explanation for the difference between extent and degree gradation, I will not go further into a discussion of an appropriate deeper lexical decomposition. The central outcome of this section is that degree and extent gradation are realized at two different syntactic layers and that this syntactic distinction is semantically motivated. In the next section, I will come back to the question why expressions used for extent gradation can also be used as adnominal quantity expressions but expressions restricted to degree gradation like German *sehr* cannot.

8 Syntax of adnominal quantity expressions

In the last section, I presented the claim that adverbially used *viel* is a core adverb, whereas *sehr* is a nucleus adverb. In this section, I will argue that the specification of a nominal quantity is also an operation at the core layer. The expression of an adnominal quantity is the nominal equivalent of extent gradation in the verbal domain; therefore it is not unexpected that degree expressions used for extent gradation also show up in the nominal domain.

Role and Reference Grammar proposes a layered structure of the NP analogous to the layered structure of the clause. The three layers in the case of NPs are: nominal nucleus, nominal core, which is the nucleus and the arguments of a complex derived nominal, and NP layer, which corresponds to the clause layer (Van Valin 2005: 24). As in clauses, there is also a periphery for each layer of the NP as well as a nominal operator projection. Van Valin (2005: 24) mentions the following nominal operators: nominal aspect (mass/count distinction, classifiers) at the nucleus layer, negation, number and quantification at the core layer and definiteness and deixis at the NP layer. With regard to core operators Van Valin (2005: 24) states that they are about quantity and NP-level operators are used to integrate the NP in discourse. Crucially, operators at the nucleus layer are taken to be restrictive modifiers, whereas those at higher layers are not (Van Valin 2005: 24).

It matters for the analysis whether we take *viel* to be a quantifier or an adjective. If we analyze it as a quantifier, *viel* would be a $core_N$-level operator. But if we take it to be an adjective, it would not be located in the operator structure but rather be considered part of the constituent structure. With regard to their place in the constituent structure Van Valin (2005: 26) writes: "[...] adjectives are best treated on the analogy of adverbs in the clause: they are constituents of the ($nuclear_N$) periphery whose position is constrained by the iconicity principle – they must occur closer to the nominal nucleus than $core_N$- and NP-level operators and modifiers." This only holds for restrictive adjectives, since in analogy to nucleus operators all restrictive adjunct modifiers are located in the $nuclear_N$ periphery (Van Valin

2005: 24). Nonrestrictive modifiers are considered to be located at the NP-level periphery, whereas the core$_N$-level periphery contains "adjunct setting NPs and adverbials of complex event expressions" (Van Valin 2005: 26). *Viel* is a nonrestrictive modifier and I will claim that it is located in the core$_N$-level periphery, which is – as stated above – concerned with quantity. Starting with an argumentation in favor of *viel*'s status as an adjective, two morphosyntactic arguments supporting this view can be put forward. First, quantity expressions like *viel* can be realized in a different position in the NP than quantifiers such as *einige* 'some'. In (36a) the order of elements in the NP is shown. The quantifier has to precede the definite article, whereas the quantity expressions *viel* can follow the article. Other adjectives like *klein* 'small' follow the quantity expression. Quantifiers are always the first element in the NP (cf., (37)), if the NP does not contain a quantifier, then the definite article is in first position (b). *Viel* can be in the first position of the NP only if the NP does not contain a quantifier (c) or is used in a partitive construction with a definite article in genitive case. Comparing the form of *viel* in (36a, b) with the one in (c, d) shows that the quantity expression has a different form if it is the first element in the NP. This leads to the second morphosyntactic argument for taking *viel* as an adjective.

(36) a. *einige der vielen kleinen Äpfel*
    some the many small apples
    'some of the many small apples'
  b. *die vielen kleinen Äpfel*
    the many small apples
    'the many small apples'
  c. *viele kleine Äpfel*
    many small apples
    'many small apples'
  d. *viele der kleinen Äpfel*
    many the.GEN small apples
    'many of the small apples'

(37) **die einige kleine Äpfel*
    the some small apples

Quantity expressions in German decline like adjectives. German distinguishes between a weak and a strong adjectival declension (there is also a mixed type which is left aside in the following discussion). Table 2 is the paradigm for all four cases in the plural. Each cell shows the inflection of the adjective *alt* 'old' and the quantity expression *viel*. As can be seen, the quantity expression and the adjective inflect the same way. Adjectives exhibit the weak declension if, for example, they are preceded by the definite article. The strong declension is used if the adjective is the first element in the NP or if it is preceded by the indefinite article (cf. Esau 1973 for a discussion of the function of the different adjective endings in German). Quantifiers only show the strong declension, since they are never preceded by the definite article, as shown by the ordering in (36) and (37).

Case	Strong declension	Weak declension
Nominative	alt-e Männer	die alt-en Männer
	viel-e Männer	die viel-en Männer
Accusative	alt-e Männer	die alt-en Männer
	viel-e Männer	die viel-en Männer
Dative	alt-en Männern	den alt-en Männern
	viel-en Männern	den viel-en Männern
Genitive	alt-er Männer	der alt-en Männer
	viel-er Männer	der viel-en Männer

Table 2: Adjective declension in German, plural forms for the weak and strong declension type.

The morphosyntactic and language specific arguments presented above can be supplemented by a semantic argumentation. There is some debate on the semantic status of adnominal quantity expressions, i.e., whether they are quantifiers or rather as adjectives. Usually, quantifiers are taken in the sense of Generalized Quantifier Theory (GQT, Barwise & Cooper 1981). In such a view, they take two set-denoting expressions (type $\langle e,t \rangle$) as arguments and make a predication about the intersection of both sets. They take two arguments and return a truth value, therefore they are of type $\langle \langle e,t \rangle \langle \langle e,t \rangle t \rangle \rangle$. Adjectives, in the semantic sense, are taken as modifiers and modifiers take an unsaturated expression as their argument and return an expression of the same type (type $\langle \langle x,t \rangle \langle x,t \rangle \rangle$).

Adnominal quantity expressions have two different readings, which are called 'proportional' and 'cardinal' readings. The proportional reading of (38) is that a large proportion of the linguistics students signed up for the class or that the number of linguistics students that has signed up for class is large. Partee (1988) argues that only the proportional reading requires a quantificational analysis of *many*, whereas in its cardinal reading *many* is used as an adjective, i. e., modifier.

(38) Many linguistics students signed up for the class.

Following Partee's argumentation for adnominal quantity expressions, there is no need to postulate a quantificational analysis of *beaucoup*. Authors such as Hoeksema (1983), Löbner (1987a, 1987b, 1990) and Solt (2009) argue against Partee's ambiguity analysis of adnominal quantity expressions. Löbner, for example, assumes that the cardinal reading of expressions like English *much/many* and German *viel* is basic and that the distinction between cardinal and proportional readings is merely a pragmatic rather than a semantic one. He argues that information structure affects the interpretation of the adnominal quantity expression and hence there is no need to analyze them as quantifiers. I will not go into the details of the argumentation against a quantificational analysis of adnominal quantity expressions but refer the reader to the literature mentioned above and the references cited within.[15] I follow Löbner's argumentation and assume that adnominal quantity expressions are adjectives rather than quantifiers.[16]

Taken together, there are semantic as well as morphosyntactic arguments in favor of treating quantity expressions as adjectives/modifiers rather than operators/quantifiers. But if they are adjectives, they have to be located at the nominal core layer. The reason is that *viel* is not only sensitive to the mass/count distinction but also to number. As (39a) shows, *viel* cannot combine with a singular count noun but requires a plural noun (b). Mass nouns are transnumeral and license quantity expressions (c). Morphologically *Wasser* 'water' is singular and also *viel* shows singular agreement.

(39) a. *viel   Buch
         much.SG   book.SG

---

[15] The same argumentation as applied to adnominal quantity expressions can be used to show that extent intensifiers function as modifiers rather than quantifiers (cf. de Swart 1993 and Abeille et al. 2004).

[16] The rejection of a quantificational analysis for degree/quantity expressions does not mean that they are modifiers, rather a further option is that they are argument saturating expressions, which saturate a degree argument. Cf. Kennedy & McNally (2005b) for a discussion of this matter. For the purposes of this paper this question need not to be resolved (but see the discussion in Fleischhauer 2016 on this point).

b. *viele   Bücher*
   much.PL book.PL
   'many books'
c. *viel   Wasser*
   much.SG water.SG
   'much water'

Since number is a nominal core operator and *viel* is sensitive to number, *viel* has to be located at the core_N layer too. The resulting tree for the NP *die vielen alten Männer* 'the many old men' is shown in figure 4.

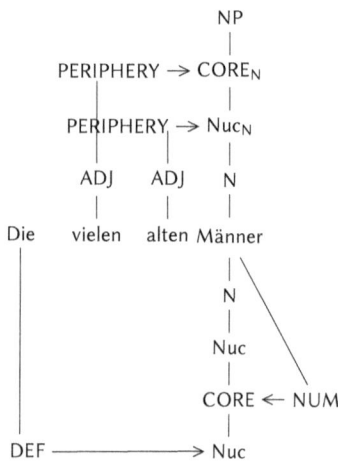

Figure 4: Syntactic structure of the NP *die vielen alten Männer*.

Analyzing quantity adjectives as located in the periphery of the nominal core fits with Van Valin's characterization of core operators as being about quantity. Ergo, we have the adjectival equivalent to those operators located at the same layer as the operators are. Furthermore, by analyzing *viel* as a core adjective we receive a uniform syntactic analysis of *viel* – as located in the core periphery – in its adnominal as well as adverbial uses. This leads to the claim that quantity is syntactically realized in the same way across category borders and also makes it possible to explain the cross-linguistic data discussed in section 3. Languages use the same expressions for extent gradation and the specification of a nominal quantity because it is semantically expressed at the core layer.

9 Conclusion

The general topic of this paper was the distinction between verbal extent and degree gradation. It showed that languages mark extent and degree gradation in different ways. Languages such as English and French use the same degree expression for both types of verb gradation, whereas Polish and German (among other languages) have two different degree expressions for both subtypes. The question emerged whether French and English display the same distinction between extent and degree gradation as German and Polish do. The answer given in the paper is: yes, they do. Degree gradation is expressed at the nucleus layer, extent gradation is realized at the core layer. Adverbially used degree expressions such as English *a lot* and French *beaucoup* are syntactically ambiguous between core and nucleus adverbs. Corresponding degree expressions in German and Polish are syntactically unambiguous.

A follow-up question is why expressions used for extent gradation can also be used as adnominal quantity expressions, whereas expressions restricted to degree gradation cannot. The answer to this question is that quantity in the nominal domain is also expressed at the core layer. Extent intensifiers operate at the right syntactic layer, which licenses their cross-categorical distribution. This leads to the claim that quantity is uniformly expressed at the core layer, irrespective of whether it is a nominal or verbal quantity.

In a next step, the analysis has to be extended to adadjectival uses of degree expressions like in (40). Van Valin (2008) proposes that also modifier phrases have a layered structure and it would be relevant to how the adjectival data fit into the analysis presented in this paper.

(40) a. *Der Junge ist sehr groß.*
 the boy is very tall
 'The boy is very tall.'
 b. *Der Junge ist viel größer als sein Bruder.*
 the boy is much taller than his brother
 'The boy is much taller than his brother.'

Jens Fleischhauer

Acknowledgments

First of all, I want to thank Robert D. Van Valin for very helpful comments on the topic of this paper and on verb gradation in general. In addition to him, many other people made helpful contributions to this paper: Sebastian Löbner, Thomas Gamerschlag, Adrian Czardybon, Albert Ortmann, Anja Latrouite, Sergej Tatevosov and two anonymous reviewers. I also want to thank my informants Aurélien Jarry, Anselm ter Halle, Patrice Soom, Katina Bontcheva and Syuzan Sachliyan for their help. And finally, I would like to thank the participants of the SFB 991 research colloquium, WoSS 8 in Paris and the 2011 Workshop on Modification in Madrid for their comments on several versions of this paper. The work on this topic is financed by the Deutsche Forschungsgemeinschaft through CRC 991 and is part of project B1 on 'Verb frames at the syntax-semantics interface.'

Appendix

I.) Data from Tatar (Turkic, Altaic)[17]

Tatar uses two different degree expressions, which are on the one hand *bik* 'very' for the positive form of adjectives (Ai) and verbal degree gradation (Bi). On the other hand it uses *küp* 'a lot' for grading comparatives (Aii), verbal extent gradation (Bii, iii) and the expression of adnominal quantity (Ci, ii).

(A) i.   *marat bik bijek.*
       Marat very tall
       'Marat is very tall.'

    ii. *marat küp-kä alsu-dan bijek-räk.*
       Marat a lot-DAT Alsu-ABL tall-COMP
       'Marat is much taller than Alsu.'

(B) i.   *kɤɤk bik kurk-ɤt-tɤ marat-nɤ.*
       dog very fear-CAUS-PST.3SG Marat-ACC
       'The dog frightened Marat a lot.'

    ii. *marat küp jer-i kino-ga.*
       Marat a lot go-IPFV cinema-DAT
       'Marat goes to the cinema a lot.'

---

[17] The Tatar data I owe to Sergei Tatevosov.

Degree Expressions at the Syntax-Semantics Interface

    iii. *marat küp jɤkla-dɤ kicäge ten-ne.*
        Marat a lot sleep-PST last   night-ACC
        'Marat slept a lot last night.'

(C) i. *marat küp alma aša-dɤ.*
      Marat a lot apple eat-PST
      'Marat ate many apples.'
   ii. *marat küp šurba aša-dɤ.*
      Marat a lot soup eat-PST
      'Marat ate a lot of soup.'

II.) Data from Bulgarian (Slavic, Indo-European)[18]
Bulgarian uses one and the same degree expression in the adjectival, verbal as well as nominal domain.

(A) a. *Momče-to običa mnogo majka si.*
       boy-DEF loves a lot   mother REFL
       'The boy loves his mother very much.'
   b. *Toj hodi mnogo na kino.*
       he go a lot PREP kino
       'He goes to the cinema a lot.'
   c. *Snošti spah mnogo.*
       last.night sleep.AOR a lot
       'Last night, I slept a lot.' (= long duration)

(B) a. *Momče-to e mnogo visoko.*
       boy-DEF AUX a lot   tall
       'The boy is very tall.'
   b. *Momče-to e mnogo po-visoko ot prijatel-ja si.*
       boy-DEF AUX a lot COMP-tall PREP friend-DEF POSS
       'The boy is much taller than his friend.'

(C) a. *Toj ima mnogo knigi.*
       he has a lot   book.PL
       'He has many books.'
   b. *V kofa-ta ima mnogo voda.*
       PREP bucket-DEF has a lot   water
       'There is much water in the bucket.'

---

[18] The Bulgarian data I owe to Syuzan Sachliyan and Katina Bontcheva.

References

Abeille, A., J. Doetjes, A. Molendijk & H. de Swart. 2004. Adverbs and quantification. In F. Corblin & H. de Swart (eds.), *Handbook of French semantics*, 185–209. Stanford: CSLI Publications.

Barwise, J. & R. Cooper. 1981. Generalized quantifiers and natural language. *Linguistics and Philosophy* 4: 159–219.

Beavers, J. 2011. On affectedness. *Natural Language and Linguistic Theory* 29: 335–370.

Bhat, D.N.S. & R. Pustet. 2000. Adjective. In G. Booji, C. Lehmann & J. Mugdan (eds.), *Morphologie – Ein internationales Handbuch zur Flexion und Wortbildung*, 757–769. Berlin/New York: de Gruyter.

Bierwisch, M. 1989. The semantics of gradation. In M. Bierwisch, & E. Lang (eds.). *Dimensional adjectives: Grammatical structure and conceptual interpretation*, 71–261. Berlin: Springer.

Bohnemeyer, J. & R. D. Van Valin, Jr. 2013. The macro-event property and the layered structure of the clause. Manuscript.

Bolinger, D. 1972. *Degree words*. De Hague: Mouton.

Bosque, I. & P. Masullo. 1998. On verbal quantification in Spanish. In O. Fullana & F. Roca (eds.), *Studies on the syntax of central Romance languages*, 9–63. Gorina: Universitat de Girona.

Cinque, G. 1999. *Adverbs and functional heads*. Oxford: Oxford University Press.

Comrie, B. 1976. *Aspect*. Cambridge: Cambridge University Press.

Doetjes, J. 1997. *Quantifiers and selection*. Dordrecht: Holland Institute of Generative Linguistics.

Doetjes, J. 2007. Adverbs and quantification – degrees versus frequency. *Lingua* 117: 685–720.

Dowty, D. 1979. *Word meaning and Montague Grammar*. Dordrecht: Reidel.

Ebert, K. 2000. Progressive markers in Germanic languages. In Ö. Dahl (ed.), *Tense and Aspect in the Languages of Europe*, 605–653. Berlin: Mouton de Gruyter.

Esau, H. 1973. Form and function of German adjective endings. *Folia Linguistica* 6: 136–145.

Fleischhauer, J. 2013. Interaction of telicity and degree gradation in change of state verbs. In B. Arsenijevi, B. Gehrke & R. Marín (eds.), *Studies in the composition and decomposition of event predicates*, 125–152. Dordrecht: Springer.

References

Fleischhauer, J. 2016. *Degree gradation of verbs.* Düsseldorf: düsseldorf university press.

Fleischhauer, J. & T. Gamerschlag. 2014. We are going through changes: How change of state verbs and arguments combine in scale composition. *Lingua* 141: 30-47.

Gamerschlag, T. 2014. Stative dimensional verbs in German. *Studies in Language* 38(2): 275–334.

Gary, E. 1979. Extent in English. University of California, Los Angeles dissertation.

Hay, J., C. Kennedy & B. Levin. 1999. Scalar Structure Underlies Telicity in "Degree Achievements". In T. Mathews & D. Strolovitch (eds.), *SALT IX*, 127–144. Ithaca: CLC Publications.

Hoeksema, J. 1983. Plurality and conjunction. In A. ter Meulen (ed.), *Studies in model-theoretic semantics*, 63–83. Dordrecht: Foris.

Jackendoff, R. 1972. *Semantic interpretation in generative grammar.* Cambridge, MA: The MIT Press.

Karttunen, L. 1975. On the syntax and semantics of the word *paljon* in Finnish. *Acta Linguistica - Congressus Tertius Internationalis Fenno-Ugristarum*, 227–235.

Kennedy, C. 1999. *Projecting the adjective.* New York: Garland.

Kennedy, C. & L. McNally. 2005. Scale structure, degree modification, and the semantics of gradable predicates. *Language* 81(2): 345–381.

Klein, E. 1980. A Semantics for positive and comparative adjectives. *Linguistics and Philosophy* 4: 1–45.

Levin, B. 1993. *English verb classes and alternations.* Chicago: University of Chicago Press.

Löbner, S. 1987a. Natural language and Generalized Quantifier Theory. In P. Gärdenfors (ed.), *Generalized Quantifiers*, 181–201. Dordrecht: Reidel.

Löbner, S. 1987b. Quantification as a major module of natural language semantics. In J. Groenendijk, D. de Jongh & M. Stokhof (eds.), *Studies in Discourse Representation Theory and the Theory of Generalized Quantifiers*, 53–85. Dordrecht: Foris.

Löbner, S. 1990. *Wahr neben falsch.* Tübingen: Niemeyer.

Löbner, S. 2002. Is the German Perfekt a perfect Perfect? In I. Kaufmann & B. Stiebels (eds.), *More than words*, 369–391. Berlin: Akademie-Verlag.

Löbner, S. (2012). Sub-compositionality. In M. Werning, W. Hinzen & E. Machery (eds.), *The Oxford Handbook of Compositionality*, 220–241. Oxford: Oxford University Press.

Lüpke, F. 2005. *A grammar of Jalonke argument structure*. Radboud Universiteit Nijmegen dissertation.

Maienborn, C. 1996. *Situation und Lokation. Die Bedeutung lokaler Adjunkte von Verbalprojektionen*. Tübingen: Stauffenburg.

Maienborn, C. 2001. On the position and interpretation of locative modifiers. *Natural Language Semantics* 9(2): 191–249.

Mora-Bustos, A. 2009. Epistemic adverbs and mood alternation. In L. Guerrero, S. Ibanez Cerda & V. A. Belloro (eds.), *Studies in Role and Reference Grammar*, 447–467. México: Universidad Nacional Autónoma de México.

Nuyts, J. 1993. Epistemic modal adverbs and adjectives and the layered representation of conceptual and linguistic structure. *Linguistics* 31: 933–969.

Ortigosa Pastor, A. 2003. Temporal deictic adverbs – a constructionist approach. *Annual Review of Cognitive Linguistics* 1: 107–118.

Partee, B. 1988. Many quantifiers. In J. Powers & K. de Jongh (eds.), *Proceedings of the Fifth Eastern States Conference on Linguistics*, 383–402. Columbus: The Ohio State University.

Rappaport Hovav, M. 2008. Lexicalized meaning and the internal temporal structure of events. In S. Rothstein (ed.), *Theoretical and crosslinguistic approaches to the semantics of aspect*, 13–42. Amsterdam/Philadelphia: John Benjamins.

Rappaport Hovav, M. & B. Levin. 2010. Reflections on manner/result complementarity. In M. Rappaport Hovav, E. Doron & I. Sichel (eds.), *Lexical semantics, syntax, and event structure*, 21–38. Oxford: Oxford University Press.

Rice, K. 1989. *A grammar of Slave*. Berlin: Mouton de Gruyter.

Rice, K. 2000. *Morpheme order and semantic scope*. Cambridge: Cambridge University Press.

Roberts, J. 1987. *Amele*. London: Croon Holm.

Sapir, E. 1944. Grading: a study in semantics. *Philosophy of Science* 11: 93–116.

Solt, S. 2009. The semantics of adjectives of quantity. The City University of New York, New York dissertation.

de Swart, H. 1993. *Adverbs of quantification*. New York: Garland.

de Swart, H. 1998. *Introduction to natural language semantics*. Stanford: CSLI Publications.

References

Toratani, K. 2007. An RRG analysis of manner adverbial mimetics. *Language and Linguistics* 8(1): 311–342.

Tsujimura, N. 2001. Degree words and scalar structure in Japanese. *Lingua* 111: 29–52.

Van Os, C. 1989. *Aspekte der Intensivierung im Deutschen.* Tübingen: Narr.

Van Valin, R. D., Jr. 2005. *Exploring the syntax-semantics interface.* Cambridge: Cambridge University Press.

Van Valin, R. D., Jr. 2008. RPs and the nature of lexical and syntactic categories in Role and Reference Grammar. In R. D. Van Valin, Jr. (ed.), *Investigations of the syntax-semantics-pragmatics interface*, 161–178. Amsterdam: John Benjamins.

Van Valin, R. D., Jr. & R. LaPolla. 1997. *Syntax.* Cambridge: Cambridge University Press.

Vecchiato, S. 1999. On the relative order of *beaucoup, guère, peu* and *trop* in French. *University of Venice Working Papers in Linguistics* 9, 255–286.

Vendler, Z. 1957. Verbs and times. *The Philosophical Review* 66(2): 143–160.

Author

Jens Fleischhauer
Heinrich-Heine-University Düsseldorf
Department of General Linguistics
fleischhauer@phil.uni-duesseldorf.de

Volition in Grammar and Lexical Representation of Verbs: The Case of Kabardian Involuntative

Ranko Matasović

1 Introduction

The structure of this paper is as follows. In the Introduction, I present some basic typological facts about Kabardian. In section 2, an interesting morphological feature of NW Caucasian languages is presented, and in section 3 it is discussed how this feature should be represented in the grammar. This leads us to some theoretical questions about the status of lexical rules in Role and Reference Grammar and the inter-relationship of features used in the lexical decomposition of verbs in section 4.

Kabardian (or East Circassian) is a NW Caucasian language spoken mostly in the Kabardino-Balkar Republic of the Russian Federation. Like its NW Caucasian relatives (Abkhaz, Abaza, Adyghe, and the extinct Ubykh), it a polysynthetic head-marking language with very little nominal morphology and a very complex verbal system. It has two grammatical cases: absolutive (-r) and ergative (-m); nouns are case marked only when definite, and personal pronouns do not receive case marking; the ergative also marks oblique arguments, such as the recipient (1).

(1) ś'āł'a-m džāta-r pśāśa-m yə-h-ā-ś
    boy-ERG sword-ABS girl-ERG 3SG.A-carry-PRET-AF
    'The boy carried the sword to the girl'[1]

The verbal complex consists of at least eight prefix slots, followed by the root and at least four suffix slots. Here are the prefix slots: 1. directionals, 2. reflex-

---
[1] My Kabardian examples were drawn from two sources: some were elicited from two informants, Lemma Maremukova and Alim Shomahua, to whom I am very grateful for their help, and others were taken from a collection of Kabardian folk-tales (*Nartxer. Adygey epos.* Nalchik 1999).

ive/reciprocal 3. benefactive applicative 4. conjunctivity 5. potential 6. core negation 7. involuntative 8. causative. Person prefixes can be inserted between these prefix slots (the exact rules for their position are too complex to be discussed here).[2] The prefix chain is followed by the root and the suffix slots: 1. detransitivizers 2. tense/evidential 3. mood 4. illocutionary force.

2 The involuntative in Kabardian

The Involuntative (Russ. *kategorija neproizvol'nosti*) indicates that an action is performed unintentionally. It is expressed by the prefix *ʔaś'a-*, occupying the 7th position in the verbal complex (3).

(2) *ś'āla-m dəġʷə-r yə-wəč'-ā-ś*
boy-ERG thief-ABS 3SG.A-kill-PRET-AF
'The young man killed the thief'

(3) *ś'āla-m dəġʷə-r yə-ʔaś'a-wəč'āś*
boy-ERG thief-ABS 3SG.A-kill-PRET-AF
'The young man (unintentionally) killed the thief'

The only prefix that can occur between the involuntative prefix and the verbal root is the causative prefix *ġa-* and the person marker indexing the Causer.

(4) *ś'āla-m ł'əź-əm   dəġʷə-r ʔaś'-yə-ġa-wəč'-ā-ś*
boy-ERG old.man-ERG thief-ABS INVOL-3SG.A-CAUS-kill-PRET-AF
'The boy made the old man accidentally kill the thief'[3]

In polite questions, the prefix *-ʔaś'a-* can be rendered as "perhaps", or "by chance" (5):

(5) *Šə q'ə-f-ʔaś'a-mə-łaġʷ-ā-wa   p'ara ?*
horse DIR-2PL-INVOL-NEG-see-PRET-GER INTERROGATIVE
'Haven't you seen a horse, by chance?'

---

[2] For discussion, see my online-grammar of Kabardian (Matasović 2011).

[3] Note that, in (4), scope of the involuntative is narrower than the scope of the causative, as the sentence does not mean * "The boy accidentally made the old man kill the thief". This is surprising, since the causative morheme is closer to the root than the involuntative morpheme, so in this case the order of morphemes does not reflect the scope relations of the categories they express.

It is possible that in examples such as (5) the involuntative morpheme has a special use, partly independent of its other functions. Note that the verb łaǧʷən can be translated as 'to watch' in many contexts, as it usually implies that the act of visual perception is volitional/intentional.

Historically, this prefix is compounded of the noun ʔa, 'hand' and the verbal root ś'a 'do'. The logic of this is that to do something unintentionally is to do something 'by hand' rather than intentionally, 'by the mind'. Thus, it was originally an incorporated adverbial phrase, but speakers of the language are not aware of this anymore. The involuntative exists in other NW Caucasian languages, including not only Kabardian's closest relative Adyghe (6) (Klimov 1986: 45), but also Abkhaz (7) (Hewitt 1979) and Abaza (8):

(6) s-ʔač'a-wəč'-ay
 1SGA-INVOL-kill-PRET
 'I killed him unintentionally'

(7) s-amxa-co-jt'
 1SG-INVOL-go-PRET
 'I went unwillingly'

(8) s-amxa-xəčča-t'
 1SG-INVOL-laugh-PRET
 'I laughed unwillingly'

However, the two prefixes expressing involuntative, Kabardian ʔaśa- and Adyghe -ʔač'a- on the one side, and Abkhaz/Abaza (a)mxa- on the other, are unrelated etymologically. It appears as if the involuntative form developed independently in the two branches of NW Caucasian rather than being inherited from the proto-language.

3 What is the Kabardian "involuntative"?

Languages differ in the way volition is encoded in the meaning of verbs. In most familiar European languages there are special lexical roots for volitional actions, distinguishing them from actions unspecified for volition, e.g. English *murder* (which is volitional) and *kill* (which may, but need not be volitional), or *watch* (volitional) vs. *see* (unspecified). However, in many Australian languages, there is "a single lexeme for a type of activity, irrespective of whether or not it is volitional. There is likely to be one verb which covers both 'fall over', which is non-volitional, and 'throw oneself to the ground', which is volitional. Some languages have a single verb covering both 'ignore (someone or something)', a volitional activity, and 'lose (something)', which is non-volitional; and some have one verb covering 'hide' (volitional) and 'lose' (non-volitional)" (Dixon 2002: 57).

In Bats (or Tsova-Tush), many intransitive verbs are unspecified for volition and occur with different case-frames and person/number suffixes depending on the intentionality of their single core argument (or "Subject", Holisky 1987):

(9) *(As)   vuiž-n-as*
    1SG.ERG fall-PRET-1SG.ERG
    'I fell down (on purpose)'

(10) *(So)   vož-en-sö*
     1SG.ABS fall-PRET-1SG.ABS
     'I fell down (accidentally)'

In (9), the subject is volitional, and it is marked by different case-marking and person suffix on the verb than in (10), where the subject is non-volitional.

Finally, in some languages, verbs exhibiting the volitional/non-volitional opposition have the volitional meaning by default. In Japanese, verbs corresponding to English 'kill', 'break', or 'throw' imply that their subject acted intentionally, so that literal translations of sentences like "John accidentally killed the dog", or "Joan unintentionally broke the eye-glasses" (11) are ungrammatical. Rather, one must use a special construction with the verb *simaw-* 'put' (12) in order to get the desired meaning (Van Valin & LaPolla 1997: 118–120):

(11) **Zyoon wa   ukkari-to   megane o   wat-ta*
     Joan TOPIC unintentionally glasses ACC break-PRET
     'Joan unintentionally broke the eye-glasses'

(12) *Zyoon wa   ukkari-to   megane o   wat-te   simat-ta*
     Joan TOPIC unintentionally glasses ACC break-LINKER put-PRET
     'Joan unintentionally broke the eye-glasses'

In terms of Role and Reference Grammar, this means that languages differ considerably in the ways they lexicalize Agenthood. In discussing volition in grammar of any language, one has to establish whether volition characterizes the meaning of the verb itself, or rather the relation of the verb and one of its arguments, presumably the Actor. In the latter case, the verb expresses the will, or desire of the subject that the action or state it denotes be fulfilled, and we are dealing with a grammatical mood, which is usually called the optative. Such a mood exists, e. g., in Classical Greek:

(13) õ paĩ,   gén-oio   patr-òs   eutykh-éstero-s
o boy.VOC become-2SG.OPT.MID. father-GEN.SG. fortunate-COMP.-NOM.SG.
'O boy, may you prove more fortunate than your father' (Sophocles, Aj. 550)

The optative form in (13) expresses the will, or desire of the speaker, but the verb (génesthai 'to become') does not, by itself, lexicalize the will or volitionality (it is not a part of the verb's meaning).

Other languages have different modal forms for expressing volition, e. g. the purposive form which exists in several Australian languages, including Warrongo (Tsunoda 2011: 292):

(14) malan-da nyola   yodi-yal   goyay-ngaL
river-LOC 3SG.NOM swim-PURP across-to
'She intended to swim across a river'

In Role and Reference Grammar, mood markers are represented as operators on the Core of the sentence. However, evidence is plentiful that the involuntative in Kabardian should not be treated as a mood. Mood and modality markers are generally suffixes in Kabardian. The following examples show how the admirative, optative, and permissive moods are formed and used.
The admirative:

(15) sa nawba zə məśa s-łaġʷ ā-ś-yə
I today   1 bear   1SG.A-see-PRET-AF-ADM.
'Why, I saw a bear today!'

The optative:

(16) ā-r   q'a-səžā-śara(t)
he-ABS DIR-come-OPT
'Oh if he would come!'

251

The permissive:

(17) fa-č'a   ś'alā-śa-myə gʷə-č'a   ł'ə-ś
skin-INST boy-AF-PERM heart-INST man-AF
'Although by skin (=judging by the skin) he is a boy, by heart he is a man'

Clearly, then, the "involuntative" does not pattern like the other moods in Kabardian.

If volition characterizes the nature of the action expressed by the verb, then, if it is expressed by an affix, it cannot be represented as a Core operator. Since it characterizes the Nucleus, we might consider introducing a Nuclear operator expressing volition (or the absence of volition). The involutative marker would be parallel to aspectual markers, which are also represented as Nuclear operators in RRG in languages that have aspect as a grammatical category.

A different possibility is to claim that the function of the involuntative prefix ʔaś'a- is to change the logical structure of the verb, and within the framework of Role and Reference grammar this can only mean that it is used to cancel the Agent in the logical structure of the verb.[4] In RRG, this rule would be represented as follows (for intransitive verbs):

DO (x, **do'**(x, [**pred'**(x)]) → **do'**(x, [**pred'**(x)]))

There are two reasons to think that this second hypothesis is preferable. Firstly, introducing a new type of operator into the theory is clearly less economical than analyzing the involuntative in terms of lexical rules affecting the logical structure of verbs, which are posited by RRG in any case, and which are independently motivated in the theory.

Secondly, operators are usually used to express grammatical categories, i.e. they belong to the domain of inflection rather than derivation. Yet the involuntative in Kabardian is clearly a derivational rather than inflectional category. It shares at least seven of the 11 features that may be used to distinguish derivation

---

[4] It would, in principle, be possible to add an operator INVOL ('Involuntative') to the stock of RRG operators and claim that adding the involuntative prefix in Kabardian can be represented as adding of that operator to the logical structure of a verb. This would imply that the prefix ʔaś'a- can be added only to verbs that are lexically not specified as agentive or volitional (i.e. that it cannot be added to the equivalents of English 'murder' or 'watch') but, as will be shown below, quite the opposite generalization seems to obtain in Kabardian: ʔaś'a- may be added only to inherently agentive/volitional verbs to cancel this part of their meaning.

from inflection (Aikhenvald 2007: 36): 1. It is clearly optional (verbs do not have to be inflected for volition, as they do for, e. g., person). 2. The prefix expressing the involuntative is closer to the root than prefixes expressing inflectional categories 3. It is specific to a single word class (verb). 4. It adds a semantic specification to a root (without changing word class). 5. It does not participate in agreement. 6. Its frequency of occurrence is much lower than that of inflectional categories (such as tense, person, or number), and 7. it is expressed by a bisyllabic affix, whereas nearly all of the inflectional prefixes in Kabardian are monosyllabic.

The prefix ʔaśʼa- cannot be used with all the verbs in the language, but the exact restrictions on its use are still quite obscure. The first thing to note is that it is generally incompatible with stative verbs (18–19):

(18) śʼāla-r šantə-m tay-s-ś
boy-ABS chair-ERG DIR-sit-AFG
'The boy sits on the chair'

(19) *śʼālam šantəm ʔaśʼa-tay-s-ś
'The boy accidentally sits on the chair'[5]

However, the involuntative can be used with a number of transitive stative verbs of cognition and perception (20–21):

(20) śʼāla-m pśāśa-r yə-łāġʷ-ā-ś
boy-ERG   girl-ABS 3SG.A-see-PRET-AF
'The boy saw the girl' (also 'The boy watched the girl')[6]

(21) śʼāla-m pśāśa-r yə-ʔaśʼa-łāġʷ-ā-ś
boy-ERG girl-ABS 3SG.A-INVOL-see-PRET-AF
'The boy accidentally spotted the girl'

A reasonable hypothesis would be that the involuntative is restricted to Activity verbs that are specified for Agenthood in their lexical representation. And indeed,

---

[5] The example (19) is ungrammatical rather than just infelicitous, as my informants do not think there could be any circumstances in which one would utter such a sentence (e. g. if someone accidentally sat on a chair not reserved for him/her in a theater).

[6] Kabardian has only one verb corresponding to English 'watch' and 'see', łāġʷən. In most contexts the translation 'to see' is appropriate, but the implication is always that seeing/watching is volitional (see also the example (5) above).

there appear to be quasi-synonymous verbs that seem to differ only in that one has the Agent in in its lexical representation, while the other one does not.

For example, the verb *txalən* 'strangle, kill by biting or cutting the throat' cannot be modified by the involuntative prefix *ʔaśʼa-*:

(22) **ha-m   bāža-r   yə-ʔaśʼa-txal-ā-ś*
    dog-ERG fox-ABS 3SG.A-INVOL-kill-PRET-AF
    'The dog killed (strangled) the fox unintentionally'

However, an intransitive verb derived from the same root, *txaləhən* 'kill (by biting the throat)', may be modified by the involuntative (23):

(23) *ha-r   bāža-m   ʔaśʼa-txaləh-ā-ś*
    dog-ABS fox-ERG INVOL-kill-PRET-AF
    'The dog killed the fox (unintentionally)'

Another indication that the verbs that may take the involuntative prefix contain the Agent in their logical structure comes from their incompatibility with adverbial expressions such as *yəməśʼaxxawə* 'unintentionally'. The verb *wəčʼən*'kill' which may be modified by the involuntative prefix in (3) above, cannot be combined with the adverbial *yəməśʼaxxawə* (24):

(24) **śʼāla-m dəġʷə-r   yəməśʼaxxawə yə-wəčʼāś*
    boy-ERG thief-ABS not.wanting   3SG.A-kill-PRET-AF
    'The boy unintentionally killed the thief'

Thus, it appears probable that verbs to which *ʔaśʼa-* can be added always include the Agent argument in their logical structure. The adding of the involuntative prefix changes the logical structure of the verb by cancelling the agentivity of the verb.

Our analysis predicts that the reverse lexical rule also applies in some languages, i.e. that there are languages in which the Agent can be added to the lexical representation of a verb, thus expressedly characterizing its action as volitional. And indeed, in Amis (Austronesian, Taiwan) we find a suffix (*-en*) which adds the Agent to the lexical representation of activity verbs, while also making them active accomplishments (Wu 2006: 175–177):

(25) *Ca'ay k-u   pataduan n-i   aki mi-curah t-u lumaq*
   NEG-NOM-CN intention GEN-PPN Aki AV-burn DAT-CN house
   'It is not Aki's intention to burn the house.'

(26) **Ca'ay k-u   pataduan n-i   aki curah-en k-u   lumaq*
   NEG NOM-CN intention GEN-PPN Aki burn-UV NOM-CN house
   'It is not Aki's intention to burn the house'

(27) *Patay-en k-u-ra   'oner!*
   dead-UV NOM-CN-that snake
   'Kill that snake!' (the subject must be human)

In (25), with the Active Voice prefix *mi-*, the sentence is grammatical, showing that the verb *curah* 'burn' is compatible with unintentional agents. However, the use of the suffix *–en* in (26) would make the unintentional reading impossible, hence the sentence is ungrammatical. Example (27) shows the regular use of the suffix *–en,* which can only be combined with human, intentional agents. According to Wu (2006: 177) "When suffixed to an activity verb [the suffix *–en*] derives an agentive active accomplishment. The agentive component DO explains why this suffix can only appear with [+human] effector, and why it cannot appear with expressions such as "unintentionally"". Volitionals (or voluntatives) are also reported for some Native American languages – including Klamath and Shasta (Mithun 1999: 450, 499), Chalcatongo Mixtec (Macaulay 1996: 76–78), in the Papuan language Makalero (Huber 2011: 479), and presumably elsewhere. It remains unclear to what extent these formations are the reverse of the Kabardian involuntative, i.e. whether they can be characterized as adding the Agent to the logical form of the verb.

Lexical rules for adding and deleting the Agent in the lexical representation of a verb can sometimes result in zero-affixation, i.e. the operation of the rule does not need to be visible in the morphology. This is the case in Bats (Tsova-Tush), as we saw above. In that language Agentivity is highly grammaticalized, but there is no special suffix for involuntative action, or cancelling of the Agent. In that language, we would say that there is a lexical rule adding (or removing) the Agent from the lexical representation of activity verbs, and the difference in the examples (9) and (10) would be handled by rules of case assignment: the Ergative case is assigned to the Agent argument and the Absolutive to the non-Agent macrorole of intransitive verbs.

4 The broader perspective: operations that cancel parts of the logical structure of verbs

If we agree that adding the involuntative prefix in Kabardian can be represented by a lexical rule, the question arises why this particular type of lexical rule is so rare cross-linguistically. This brings us to the issue of roles played by lexical rules in linguistic theory, and in particular in Role and Reference Grammar. The basic assumption of Role-and-Reference Grammar is that lexical rules operate on logical structures of verbs, which are essentially based on the Aktionsarten and the semantic features that define them. Here is the list of the *Aktionsarten* posited in RRG (Van Valin 2005: 33):

State: **pred'**(x),[7] e. g. *John is ill*
Activity: **do'**(x) [**pred'**(x)], e. g. *John walks*
Achievement: INGR **pred'**(x), e. g. *The baloon popped*
Semelfactive: SEML **pred'**(x), e. g. *The light flashed.*
Accomplishment: BECOME **pred'**(x), e. g. *The ice melted.*[8]
Active accomplishment: **do'**(x, [**pred$_1$'**(x,y)]) & INGR **pred$_2$'**(y), e. g. *Dana ate the fish.*

All *Aktionsarten* have their causative variants, represented with the operator CAUSE, e. g. *kill* ([**do'** (x,0)] CAUSE BECOME [**dead'** (y)]) is the causative accomplishment derived from the accomplishment *die* BECOME [**dead'**(x)]. Moreover, there is a special operator DO that characterizes activity verbs that have an Agent (conscious and willful instigator of an action) in their logical structure, as we saw in the preceding sections.

Van Valin (2005: 41) notes that some patterns of operations cancelling parts of the logical structure of verbs are very common cross-linguistically. In many languages we find a pattern relating states, accomplishments, and causative accomplishments, as illustrated by Van Valin's examples from Yagua, French, and Russian:

---

[7] This is, of course, the representation of a single-argument predicate (or intransitive verb). Other Aktionsarten are also mostly represented by intransitive verbs.

[8] The operator BECOME is actually not a primitive. It is composed of the operator PROC (for 'process') and the operator adding telicity (INGR), but in many languages, including English, BECOME may be used as a shorthand for PROC... & INGR.

Causative accomplishment	Accomplishment	State
(28) Yagua -*muta*- 'open [TR]'	-*muta-y*- 'open [INTR]'	*muta-y-maa* 'be open'
(29) French *briser* 'break [TR]'	*se briser* 'break [INTR]'	*brisé* 'broken'
(30) Russian *razbit'* 'break [TR]'	*razbit'sja* 'break [INTR]'	*razbitij* 'broken'

This pattern can be easily represented as cancelling of the operator CAUSE (i),[9] to make an accomplishment from a causative accomplishment, and the subsequent deletion of the operator BECOME (ii) to make a state predicate from an accomplishment.

(i) [**do'** (x,0)]CAUSE [BECOME **pred'** (y)] → BECOME [**pred'**(y)]
(ii) BECOME **pred'**(x) → **pred'**(x)

So, perhaps this pattern of lexical rules is so common because of the fact that it involves the consecutive cancelling of a single feature from the logical structure of the verb. We can point out that there are other patterns that seem to be rather well-attested in the languages of the world, such as those relating Active Accomplishments to states (31) and to Activities (32, 33), as well as those deriving Activities (34) and Accomplishments (35) from States:

(31) Chukchi: *vak?o-k* 'adopt a sitting position': *vak?o-tva-k* 'sit': **do'**(x) & INGR **pred'**(x) → **pred'**(x) (Active Accomplishment → State, cf. Comrie (1985: 342)

(32) Georgian: *c'er* 'write' : *da-c'er* 'write' (completely): **do'**(x) **pred'**(x,y) → **do'**(x) **pred'**(x,y) & INGR **pred'**(y) (Activity → Active Accomplishment)

(33) Lithuanian: *pa-skusti* 'clean' (completely) : *pa-skut-inė-ti* 'clean' : **do'**(x) **pred'**(x,y) & INGR **pred'**(y) → **do'**(x) **pred'**(x,y) (Active Accomplishment → Activity)

(34) English: *John is stupid*: *John is being stupid*: **pred'**(x) → **do'**(x) **pred'**(x) (State → Activity)

(35) German: *gebrochen* 'broken' : *wurde gebrochen* 'has been broken' : **pred'**(y) → BECOME **pred'**(y) (State → Accomplishment)

---

[9] The approach of Role and Reference Grammar runs contrary to the "Monotonicity Hypothesis", according to which word formation operations do not delete operators from lexical representations. See Koontz-Garboden (2009) for an account of de-causativization in Spanish that argues for the "Monotonicity Hypothesis".

As we see from examples (34) and (35), lexical rules changing the lexical representation of verbs need not be expressed through affixation – they can also be expressed in certain syntactic constructions, or, in other words, constructions may affect the lexical representation of verbs by adding or cancelling elements of their meaning. Obviously, then, many languages have mechanisms for derivation of different Aktionsarten by adding or cancelling parts of logical structures of verbs, but it is still intriguing that some patterns are much more common than others, and there are some patterns that may not be attested at all. For example, why don't we find languages which derive statives, or activities from semelfactives by cancelling the operator SEML?

*SEML **pred'**(x) → **pred'**(x)
*SEML **do'**(x, [**pred'**(x)] → **pred'**(x)

Likewise, there do not seem to be any languages in which accomplishment predicates are derived directly from achievement predicates, or vice versa:

*BECOME **pred'**(x) → INGR **pred'**(x)
*INGR **pred'**(x) → BECOME **pred'**(x)

So, why are some types of lexical rules more common than others? The first thing to note is that, generally, lexical rules cancelling parts of the logical structure of verbs seem not to be less common than lexical rules deriving more complex structures from simpler ones. For example, causatives are just as common, cross-linguistically, as de-causatives.[10] There appears to be no cross-linguistic bias towards iconicity here, so that elements in the logical structure should generally be expressed by affixes. Affixes can just as easily express the absence of an element in the logical structure, e. g. the absence of the CAUSE operator. As Haspelmath puts it, "Variation in the direction of formal derivation can generally be seen as the manifestation of indeterminacy of the conceptual-semantic relation" (Haspelmath 1993: 90). Causative accomplishments are "objectively" more complex than (simple) accomplishments, but that does not mean that this relation must be conceptualized (and lexicalized) in every language so that the former must be derived from the latter by causativization. Indeed, it must not, as we have seen. However, the existence of bi-directional patterns of derivation

---

[10] Nichols et al. (2004) examine 80 languages with respect to valence-increasing and valence decreasing operation. They note that the "reduced" type of valency decreasing (decausativization by means of an affix) is correlated with morphological complexity.

shows that the conceptual-semantic relation exists and that it can be subject to lexical rules.

It transpires from the discussion so far that the types of lexical rules are constrained by two parameters: (1) the frequency of lexicalization of certain concepts, which is the consequence of the overall structure of human cognitive system and the nature of our everyday experiences, and (2) the conceptual distance, measured by the number of shared semantic features, between different types of verbal meanings (or *Aktionsarten*).

The first parameter has to do with economy: certain types of meanings are rarely conceptualized and lexicalized cross-linguistically. This is the case with the change that involves cancelling the Agent, as in the Kabardian "involuntative": languages apparently never have more than a handful of verbs that have the Agent as part of their logical structure, and it would be uneconomical to have a productive lexical operation for cancelling it, if such a rule applied to just a few verbs. Similarly, semelfactive meanings appear to be lexicalized quite rarely (which is why this Aktionsart was not noted in earlier versions of RRG, for example in Van Valin & LaPolla 1997), so having an affix for cancelling semelfactive meanings would be uneconomical.[11]

The second parameter has to do with conceptual differences between different Aktionsarten. In order to measure those differences, we represent the Aktionsarten as sets of features, or semantic primitives. The number of features defining particular Aktionsarten differs, and only those that differ in the presence of a single feature can be easily related by cross-linguistically common lexical rules. The system of features that define the Aktionsarten should be as simple as possible, i.e. we should posit no more features than are needed to derive all six primary Aktionsarten (Semelfactives, States, Accomplishments, Achievements, Activities and Active Accomplishments) plus the two secondary ones (Causatives and Agentive verbs). Here we propose a system of features that is slightly different from the one established in the RRG literature (Van Valin & LaPolla 1997, Van Valin 2005):[12]

---

[11] In languages which do have affixes glossed as *semelfactives*, e. g. the Athabaskan languages, these can be added to verbal stems expressing activities. However, they generally do not mean that an action should be conceptualized as instantaneous, but rather that the action is performed only once, e. g. Koyukon *yeel-t'ut* 'she cut it once' (Axelrod 1993: 73–76).

[12] We do not include the feature [+static], as it cannot be combined with any other feature, unlike the feature [+duration], which serves to distinguish two classes of Aktionsarten. Note also that states

Semelfactives: [-duration, +/-(internal) force, -telicity]
States/processes: [+duration, -(internal) force, -telicity]
Accomplishments: [+duration, -(internal) force, +telicity]
Achievements: [-duration, +(internal) force, +telicity]
Activities: [+duration, +(internal) force, -telicity]
Active accomplishments:] [+duration, +(internal) force, +telicity]
Agentive verbs: [+volition, +(internal) force...]
Causatives: [+external force, +(internal) force...]

The feature [+external force] can be added to all lexical representations to derive the causatives, and the cancelling of that feature would be the equivalent of de-causativization. The feature [+volition], if added to lexical representations characterized by the feature [+force] (i. e. to causatives, activities and active accomplishments) derives agentive verbs from their non-agentive counterparts. The advantage of this system lexical representation is that it operates with features which are independently known to play a significant role in cognitive psychology (telicity, force, and time/duration), and that Aktionsarten that appear to be rarely involved in lexical rules (Semelfactives and Achievements) are separated from the rest in the hierarchy in that they differ in the primary feature [+/-duration]. This should also explain why accomplishments and achievements rarely enter into relationships by means of lexical rules. They differ in two features (duration and internal force) and agree in only one (telicity), so any rule by which one would be derived from the other would have to simultaneously cancel or add two different features.

It is clear from our discussion that all features do not have the same status, but that there is rather a hierarchical organization of features that should be captured by the theory.

An advantage of this system is also that it is hierarchical, so that it reflects our intuition that not all Aktionsarten have equally complex semantic represen-

---

and processes are not easily distinguishable, and should be probably treated as involving a single feature: what they have in common is that they lack the concept of internal or external *force* that is involved in other kinds of events. Thus we would say that both *being dead* and *being heavy* (states) share the same feature with *revolving, flowing,* and *getting old* (processes) because none of those events are conceptualized as result of the application of force. Processes are, in essence, a particular kind of states that cannot be divided into identical parts or periods, e. g. "being white" is a state, and all parts or stages of that state are identical. "Getting old" is a process, hence different stages of that process are not identical.

tation. As a first approximation, we can start with the following representation of features and Aktionsarten. Let us call it the Aktionsart Hierarchy:

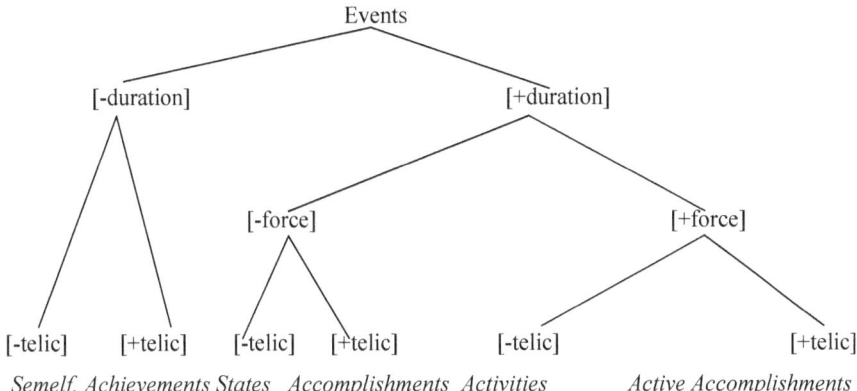

We would predict that those Aktionsarten that are located in different primary branches will be less often related by lexical rules, especially the Aktionsarten that differ in the feature [+duration] and [-duration]. Whether this prediction is borne out by the fact should be established on the basis of a thorough typological investigation, which is beyond the scope of this paper.

Abbreviations used

A = AGENT
ABS = ABSOLUTIVE
ADM = ADMIRATIVE
AF = AFFIRMATIVE
AV = ACTOR VOICE
CAUS = CAUSATIVE
CN = COMMON NOUN
COMP = COMPARATIVE
DIR = DIRECTIONAL
F = FEMININE
GEN = GENITIVE
GER = GERUND
INVOL = INVOLUNTATIVE
LOC = LOCATIVE
MID = MIDDLE
N = NEUTER
NEG = NEGATION
NOM = NOMINATIVE
OBL = OBLIQUE
OPT = OPTATIVE
PERF = PERFECT
P = PATIENT
PERM = PERMISSIVE
PPN = PERSONAL PROPER NOUN
PRET = PRETERITE
PURP = PURPOSIVE
REFL = REFLEXIVE
SG = SINGULAR
UV = UNDERGOER VOICE

References

Aikhenvald, A. 2007. Typological distinctions in word-formation. In T. Shopen (ed.), *Language typology and syntactic Description, III: Grammatical categories and the lexicon*, 1–65. Cambridge: Cambridge University Press.

Axelrod, M. 1993. *The Semantics of time. Aspectual categorization in Koyukon Athabaskan*, Lincoln: Nebraska University Press.

Colarusso, J. 1992. *A grammar of the Kabardian language*. Calgary: University of Calgary Press.

Comrie, B. 1985. Causative verb formation and other verb-deriving morphology. In T. Shopen (ed.). *Language typology and syntactic description*, III, 309–347, Cambridge: Cambridge University Press.

Dixon, R. M. W. 2002. *Australian languages*. Cambridge: Cambridge University Press.

Haspelmath, M. 1993. More on the typology of the inchoative/causative verb alternation. In B. Comrie & M. Polinsky (eds.). *Causatives and transitivity*, 87–120. Amsterdam: John Benjamins.

Hewitt, G. 1979. *Abkhaz*. London: Croom Helm.

Holisky, D. A. 1987. The case of the intransitive subject in Tsova-Tush (Batsbi). *Lingua* 71: 103–132.

Huber, J. 2011. *Makalero. A Papuan language of East Timor*. Utrecht: LOT.

Klimov, G. 1986. *Vvedenie v kavkazskoe jazykoznanie*. Moscow: Nauka.

Koontz-Garboden, A. 2009. Anticausativization. *Natural Language & Linguistic Theory* 27: 77–138.

Macaulay, M. 1996. A grammar of Chalcatongo Mixtec. Berkeley: The University of California Press.

Matasović, R. 2011. A grammar of East Circassian (Kabardian). http://www.ffzg.hr/~rmatasov.

Mithun, M. 1999. The languages of native North America. Cambridge: Cambridge University Press.

Nichols, J., D. A. Petersen & J. Bernes. 2004. Transitivizing and detransitivizing languages. *Linguistic Typology* 8: 149–211.

Piñón, C. 2002. A finer look at the causative-inchoative alternation. Manuscript – Heinrich-Heine University, Düsseldorf.

Tsunoda, T. 2011. *A grammar of Warrongo*. Berlin: Mouton de Gruyter.

Van Valin, R. D., Jr & R. LaPolla. 1997. *Syntax. Structure, meaning and function*. Cambridge: Cambridge University Press.

Van Valin, R. D., Jr. 2005. *Exploring the syntax-semantics interface*. Cambridge: Cambridge University Press.

References

Wu, J. 2006. Verb classes, case marking and grammatical relations in Amis. Ph.D. Thesis, SUNY Buffalo, http://linguistics.buffalo.edu/people/faculty/vanvalin/rrg.html.

Author

Ranko Matasović
University of Zagreb
rmatasov@ffzg.hr

Direct versus Inverse in Murik-Kopar

William A. Foley

1 Definition of direct-inverse systems

Direct-inverse inflectional systems are a common feature among heavily head marking languages (Nichols 1986), i. e. languages which indicate grammatical relations primarily or exclusively through bound pronominal agreement affixes on verbs, being attested in Tibeto-Burman languages, Nilo-Saharan languages, non-Pama-Nyungan languages of northern Australia and many language families of the Americas. Direct-inverse systems fall into a number of typological sub-types, only one of which the data here illustrate, but the crucial definitional point uniting all of them is that the patterns of verbal agreement affixes for the core grammatical relations, subject and object, show alternations according to a relative ranking of the persons involved, first, second or third. Perhaps, the best known exemplars of direct-inverse systems are the languages of the Algonkian family of North America. All languages with direct-inverse inflectional systems make a sharp distinction between local persons, the speech act persons, first and second, and non-local persons, the person absent from the speech act, the third person. These are arranged in a hierarchy such that local persons outrank non-local persons, local > non-local. This hierarchy in turn has been linked to a semantic relations hierarchy, actor > undergoer (Foley & Van Valin 1984, Van Valin & LaPolla 1997). When the two hierarchies are harmonically aligned (Aissen 1999), i. e. the local person is actor and the non-local person, undergoer, the direct inflectional pattern occurs, but when they are disharmonic, the local person is undergoer and the non-local person, actor, the inverse inflectional pattern shows up. These

Jens Fleischhauer, Anja Latrouite & Rainer Osswald (eds.). 2016.
Explorations of the Syntax-Semantics Interface. Düsseldorf: dup.

examples from Potawatomi, an Algonkian language of Michigan (Hockett 1966) illustrate this:

Direct: 1/2 → 3
(1) a. k-wapm-**a**   b. n-wapm-**a**-mun
       2-see-D   1-see-D-1/2 PL A
       'you (SG) see him'   'we see him'

Inverse: 3 → 1/2
(2) a. k-wapm-**uk**   b. n-wapm-**uk**-nan
       2-see-I   1-see-I-1/2 PL O
       'he sees you'   'he sees us'

In Algonkian, the local person, regardless of whether it is actor or undergoer, always occupies the salient prefixal position on the verb (*n-* first person and *k-* second person in the above examples). Its role is indicated by a relator suffix, either –*a* 'direct', which identifies the higher ranked local person as actor and the non-local as undergoer or –*uk* 'inverse', which signals the reverse, the non-local person is actor and the local person, undergoer. In addition, there may be additional markers for number of the local person, as in the (b) examples above.

A dilemma faced by all languages with direct-inverse inflectional systems is what to do when both participants are of equal rank, i. e. either a non-local third person acting on another non-local person or a local first or second person acting on another local person. The former case does not seem to present much of a problem crosslinguistically: they are treated either as a basic neutral pattern or assimilated to the direct system. But the latter do. Languages differ as to what relative ranking, if any, is assigned to first and second person: some languages rank first person over second, others the reverse. Algonkian languages belong to the second class and rank second person over first. This can be seen in the following examples from Potawatomi (Hockett 1966); note that it is the second person in the form of the prefix *k-*, which occupies the salient prefixal position:

(3) a. k-wapm-un   b. k-wapum
       2-see-1 A   2-see
       'I see you (SG)'   'you (SG) see me'

    c. k-wapm-un-um   d. k-wapm-um
       2-see-1 A-PL   2-see-PL
       'I see you (PL)'   'you (PL) see me'

e. k-wapm-un-mun f. k-wapm-uy-mun
   2-see-1 A-PL   2-see-2 A-PL
   'we see you (SG/PL)' 'you (SG/PL) see us'

Many languages employing direct-inverse inflectional systems have further constraints against expressing both local persons via bound verbal agreement pronominals. Heath (1998) provides a useful summary of the twelve solutions that languages have hit upon to avoid precisely this situation. One of these solutions, a zero realization, can be seen in the above Potawatomi data. Note that when the first person is actor, it is expressed overtly, albeit by a suffix (3a,c,e), but when it is undergoer, it is realized as zero (3b,d).

Direct-inverse systems get a brief mention in Foley and Van Valin (1984, 1985) and again in Van Valin & La Polla (1997), but they have not yet been the subject of careful description and theoretical analysis in Role and Reference Grammar. This article is a step in developing a theoretical analysis of the phenomenon and applying it to a description of some typologically unusual direct-inverse systems from two closely related languages of New Guinea, on which I have done fieldwork, Murik and Kopar. These two languages form a small subgroup in the Lower Sepik family, which in turn is a sub-family of the larger Lower Sepik-Ramu family. The Lower Sepik family consists of six languages as follows (the numbers underneath represent a current estimate of numbers of speakers for each language (certainly too high in most cases); as can be seen from the figures, Kopar is moribund, and Yimas is rapidly approaching this state:

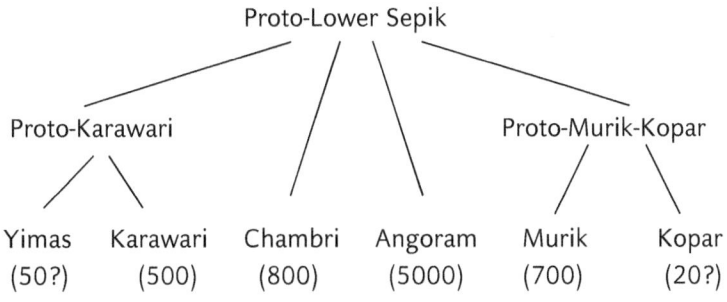

Figure 1: The Lower Sepik Family

2 A theory of case marking

Direct-inverse systems are a feature of the inflection of transitive (and often ditransitive) verbs; intransitive verbs are outside their purview because they only subcategorize for a single argument and so questions of relative ranking never arise. Hence, any theoretical approach to direct-inverse inflectional systems requires first an explicit account of how grammatical relations are assigned to the arguments of transitive verbs, and how any consequent case marking is applied. The following account has been developed from a synthesis of earlier work in Role and Reference Grammar (Foley & Van Valin 1984), Dowty's (1991) theory of proto-roles, Kiparsky's (1997) and Wunderlich's (1997, 2001) ideas about argument ranking, and work within Optimality Theory about case marking systems (Aissen 1999, Woolford 1997, 2001). The principles for the assignment of grammatical relations and case to the two subcategorized arguments of a transitive verb are set out in figure 2:

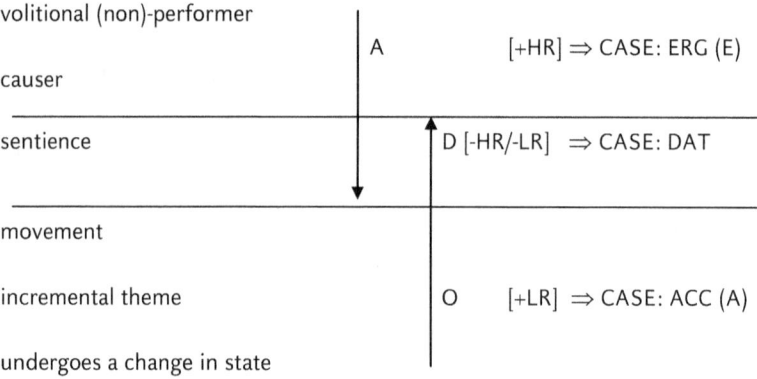

Figure 2: Case Assignment for Transitive Verbs

The semantic parameters down the left side are the various possible entailments held by the two arguments of a transitive verb that are relevant to their grammatical relation and case assignment. Rather than having a separate hierarchy for each proto-role as Dowty (1991) does, I have proposed a single overlapping hierarchy along the lines of Foley and Van Valin (1984), with the overlapping entailments in the middle and the most agentive and patientive at either extreme. The argument of a transitive verb whose entailments are at the upper end of the hierarchy (A in Dixon's (1979) terms) is assigned the feature [+HR] (higher role) and, if relevant, will receive ergative case marking. The argument of a transitive verb whose entailments are at the lower end of the hierarchy (O in Dixon's (1979) terms) is assigned [+LR] (lower role) and will receive accusative case marking. The third argument, the recipient of ditransitive verbs (D), is beyond the concern of this paper, but its entailments are typically in the middle of the hierarchy and those of neither the [+HR] nor the [+LR], hence [-HR/-LR], and will be assigned dative case. Finally, the single argument of an intransitive verb (S in Dixon's (1979) terms) has no argument to be opposed to, so it by definition can be neither [+HR] nor [+LR]. It is simply unspecified for these features, hence [ ], and will be assigned nominative case, as in the following formula:

$$\text{Intransitive verbs: S [ ]} \Rightarrow \text{CASE: NOM (N)}$$

This schema will account for the basic case marking systems, complicated split systems though they are, of the Lower Sepik languages and innumerable other languages. However, Figure 2 on its own does not account for direct-inverse inflectional systems in the Lower Sepik languages or other languages which have these. To generate the direct-inverse systems of Lower Sepik languages, three additional principles are needed:

1. Person Hierarchy
   local > non-local
   first > second > third
   (Generally the ranking of the local persons in Lower Sepik languages is the opposite of Algonkian)
2. Role Hierarchy
   [+LR] > [+HR] > [ ]
   ACC > ERG > NOM
   (This is the constraint that is responsible for generating the inversion in Lower Sepik languages. The ranking of [+LR]/ACC over [+HR]/ERG is contrary to expectation from wider typological considerations, but is crucial to inversion in Lower Sepik languages)
3. Obligatory Nominative
   All verbs must have a nominatively case marked pronominal, and usually only one. This affix should be situated at the left edge (Kopar is the exception here, requiring the nominative pronominal on the right edge).

In Algonkian the higher ranked person always occupies the salient prefixal position and a similar morphological constraint holds for the Lower Sepik languages (again Kopar is the exception). However, these are multiple prefixing languages, and the crucial position is the innermost bound pronominal prefix, the one that immediately precedes the verb theme. Before turning to Murik and Kopar, perhaps it would be best to illustrate the workings of all these constraints and principles with their better described and more transparent sister, Yimas (Foley 1991). Let us consider how one would say 'I hit them' versus 'they hit me' in this language. First of all, for Yimas, like most Lower Sepik languages, there is a person-based case marking split. All local persons have a three way split, ergative versus nominative versus accusative, as for first person singular:

	PRONOUN	ERG	NOM	ACC
1sg	ama	ka-	ama-	ŋa-

Whereas non-local persons simply contrast ergative versus nominative (absolutive is treated as nominative here), so there is no overt accusative, it is formally nominative:

	PRO	ERG	NOM
3PL	mum	mpu-	pu-

The direct form, 'I hit them' (local person acting on non-local person) is straightforward. The local [+HR] is ergative, hence *ka-* 1SG E. The non-local person is [+LR] and should be realized as accusative. But for non-local persons, there are no accusative bound pronominals; their case marking system is ergative-nominative, so any erstwhile accusative is formally realized as nominative, *pu-* 3PL N, simultaneously satisfying the Obligatory Nominative constraint. Because local > non-local by the Person Hierarchy and ERG > NOM by the Role Hierarchy, the first person ergative prefix will occupy the salient immediately preverbal position, and the third person nominative the left edge:

(4) [+HR] =1SG = ERG   *pu-ka-tpul*
    [+LR] = 3PL = NOM   3PL N-1SG E-hit
    'I hit them (PL)'

The inverse form 'they hit me' is a little more complicated. The [+LR] is a local person, and local persons do have overt accusative forms, e.g. ŋa- 1SG A. Note that the local person is higher by both the Person Hierarchy, local > non-local, and the Role Hierarchy, ACC > ERG, so ŋa- 1SG A must occupy the salient immediately preverbal position. The non-local [+HR] would normally take ergative case, and indeed there is an ergative form for third plural: mpu- 3PL E. But the expected form *mpu-ŋa-tpul is ungrammatical because it runs afoul of the Obligatory Nominative constraint: such a verb lacks a nominative prefix on the left edge. So instead, the third plural pronominal is realized by the corresponding nominative prefix, pu- 3PL N:

(5) [+HR] = 3PL = ERG ⇒ NOM   pu-ŋa-tpul
    [+LR] = 1SG = ACC   3PL N-1SG A-hit
    'they (PL) hit me'

These Yimas examples provide a clear and relatively simple illustration of how the direct-inverse system works in Lower Sepik languages. All six languages have such systems, and in very broad outline they are similar and make use of the principles and constraints described above, although the details differ from language to language. It is clear that Proto-Lower Sepik also possessed such an inflectional system, although no two daughter languages are synchronically alike. In many ways, the Yimas system, for all its complications described in Foley (1991) and Wunderlich (2001), actually is the most transparent among the six.

3 Murik

Let me now turn to Murik. The data here are from my own fieldwork on the central dialect of the language. Dialect diversity is extensive in Murik, and in particular, the verbal agreement system of the eastern dialect seems to have been significantly simplified from what will be presented here. Murik is a canonical type of a head marking language: the signaling of core arguments is done exclusively by bound verbal pronominal affixes; there is no nominal case marking and word order is flexible. Murik, like other Lower Sepik languages such as Kopar, Yimas and Chambri (and certainly Proto-Lower Sepik), as well as some adjoining Lower Ramu languages like Watam, distinguishes four numbers in its independent pronominals:

	SG	DL	PC	PL
1	ma	ga-i	ag-i	e < *a + i
2	mi	ga-u	ag-u	o < *a + u
3	min	mindib	miŋgi	mwa

Table 1: Murik Independent Pronouns

Whereas other Lower Sepik languages typically have fewer number distinctions in their bound pronominal verbal affixes than for their independent pronouns, in Murik the same four-way contrast holds. The case marking split for bound pronominals is similar to Yimas. For local persons, there is a binary nominative-accusative contrast, extending to three-way, nominative, ergative, accusative, for the singular forms:

		NOM	ERG	ACC
	SG	ma-	a-	aŋa-
1	DL	age-	age-	ŋe-
	PC	agi-	agi-	ŋi-
	PL	e-	e-	ŋe-
	SG	me-	Ø	ana-
2	DL	ago-	ago-	ŋo-
	PC	agu-	agu-	ŋu-
	PL	o-	o-	ŋo-

Table 2: Murik Local Bound Pronominals

Note that the accusative forms for dual and plural are homophonous. The bound pronominals for non-local persons, again like Yimas, exhibit a binary ergative-nominative contrast. But there is a wrinkle not found in Yimas: the non-local ergative forms in non-singular number make an additional distinction between that used in direct inflection, i.e, third person acting on third person, employing here the sole prefix *bo-* undifferentiated for non-singular number, so that the usual four way number contrast collapses to singular/non-singular, and those used in inverse forms, which preserve the full array of number contrasts:

Direct versus Inverse in Murik-Kopar

	NOM	ERG
SG	o-/ Ø-	Ø-
DL	bo-	bo- (D) / mb- (I)
PC	d-	bo- (D) / ŋg- (I)
PL	g-	bo- (D) / mbu- (I)

Table 3: Murik Non-local Bound Pronominals

The *o-* allorpmorph of the third person singular nominative prefix occurs with intransitive verbs and with transitive verbs when the [+HR] is singular in number; otherwise the Ø- allomorph is found.

Let me start with the most neutral verb form: a non-local person acting on a non-local person. These are of equal rank on the Person Hierarchy, so it will not be relevant here, only the Role Hierarchy and the Obligatory Nominative constraint. With such an argument array, the [+HR] will be realized as ergative and the [+LR] as nominative (there are no accusative bound pronominals for non-local persons, as they exhibit a binary ergative-nominative contrast). This will satisfy the Obligatory Nominative constraint. As ERG > NOM by the Role Hierarchy, the ergative bound pronominal will occur in the salient immediately preverbal position and be the number neutralized form *bo-* 3 nSG E (D), and the nominative, as expected, will be on the left edge:

(6) [+HR] = 3PL = ERG (D)   *do-bo-kɨri-na*
    [+LR] = 3PC = NOM   3PC N-3nSG E (D)-hit-PRES
                                     'They (DL/PC/PL) hit them (PC)

Now consider the possibilities with third person singular arguments, which are always realized as Ø- when functioning as the [+HR] or as [+LR] with non-singular [+HR]s and as *o-* when [+LR] in combination with a singular [+HR]:

(7) a. [+HR] = 3PL = ERG   *Ø-bo-kɨri-na*
      [+LR] = 3SG = NOM   3SG N-3nSG E (D)-hit-PRES
                                 'they (PL) hit him'
   b. [+HR] = 3SG = ERG   *gɨ-Ø-kɨri-na-ra*
      [+LR] = 3PL = NOM   3PL N-3SG E-hit-PRES-3nSG N
                                 'he hit them (PL)'

c. [+HR] = 3SG = ERG   o-Ø-kiri-na-n
   [+LR] = 3SG = NOM   3SG N-3SG E-hit-PRES-3SG N
                                        'he hit him'

Again the [+HR] argument is realized as the prefix closest to the verb, whether it is overt, as with the non-singular forms, or zero as with the singular. The [+LR] is, as expected by the Obligatory Nominative constraint, realized on the left edge overtly, except in the case of third singular [+LR]s in combination with non-singular [+HR]s. But in any case, because of the allomorphy of the third singular prefixes in these combinations, only one affix is ever overt in these forms and that is always the nominative, satisfying the Obligatory Nominative constraint. An additional feature shown in (7b,c) is that when the [+HR] is third singular and hence always realized as zero, the nominative is doubly marked, both by the relevant prefix and two suffixes which indicate further its number: -*n* 3G N and –*ra* 3nSG N. Note this conflated number contrast is exactly the same as that found in the third person direct ergative prefixes.

The direct forms are not too different from the above non-local ones. The main innovation is the possibility of marking the number of second person [+HR] arguments by a set of suffixes, -*na* SG, -*ko* DL/PC, -*ro* PL, which, as we shall see below, come to play a major part in Kopar verb inflection. Murik lacks a corresponding set of first person number suffixes, although Kopar does have these. These second person number suffixes play a role in number disambiguation, something which is not available for first person: ŋo- 2DL/PL A + -*ko* DL/PC ⇒ 2PC A, but ŋo- 2DL/PL A + -*ro* PL ⇒ 2PL A. The corresponding first person prefix, ŋe- 1DL/PL, cannot be so disambiguated. See examples (12b) versus (12c). In direct forms, the ergative [+HR] is also the higher ranked local person, so its bound pronominal will appear in the immediately preverbal slot. The [+LR] is a non-local person, and non-local persons have an ergative-nominative case marking system, so instead of any expected accusative for the [+LR], it will appear as nominative, and, as expected, on the left edge:

(8) [+HR] = 1SG = ERG   o-a-kiri-na
    [+LR] = 3SG = NOM   3SG N-1SG E-hit-PRES
                                       'I hit him'

Direct versus Inverse in Murik-Kopar

Note that if the local person is non-singular, there is no distinct ergative form, as local non-singular bound pronominals have a binary nominative-accusative case schema. Hence any non-singular local [+HR] will be realized as nominative, not ergative. Direct forms with non-singular [+HR] arguments actually have two nominative bound pronominals, the nominative for the [+HR] occurs in the immediately preverbal position as befits its higher rank on the Person Hierarchy, while the non-local [+LR] appears on the left edge. The Person Hierarchy determines the order here, because the Role Hierarchy does not discriminate: both arguments are case marked nominative, the lowest rank, ACC > ERG > NOM:

(9) [+HR] = 2PC =NOM   g-agu-kiri-na-ko
    [+LR] = 3PL = NOM   3PL N-2PC N-hit-PRES-2DL/PC
                                'you (PC) hit them'

Inverse forms in Murik contrast with those of Yimas in having an overt morpheme for inversion, the circumfix, *nV-...-ŋa,* glossed here as I (the V is either deleted or undergoes vowel harmony with the vowel of the following syllable). Inverse forms always entail a non-local [+HR] acting on a local [+LR], and, as noted above, the non-local [+HR] is realized by a distinct set of inverse third person ergative pronominals with a full four-way number distinction. The local [+LR] is higher ranked by the Person Hierarchy, and, as local bound pronominals always have distinct accusative forms, it is also higher ranked by the Role Hierarchy, ACC > ERG > NOM. So the [+LR] will always be realized in the immediately preverbal position in inverse forms. The [+HR] is a non-local person, and its case will be ergative, now realized as a bound pronominal between the initial half of the inverse circumfix *nV-...-ŋa* and the [+LR] bound pronominal. The [+HR] bound pronominal remains ergative; it does not convert to nominative in contravention of the Obligatory Nominative constraint. Presumably this is linked to the fact that it is not on the left edge; the initial half of *nV-...-ŋa* is. In fact, these inverse forms lack a nominative completely. In Yimas the Obligatory Nominative constraint is inviolable: all verbs must have a nominative, and that affix must be on the left edge. Murik seems to have relaxed this constraint somewhat, mainly requiring nominative if the affix is on the left edge, although, as we shall see below, a stronger version of the constraint reappears in one of the local person acts on local person combinations.

(10) a. [+HR] = 3SG = ERG   n-Ø-aŋa-kiri-ŋa-na
      [+ LR] = 1SG = ACC   I-3SG E-1SG A-hit-I-PRES
                                    'he hits me'
    b. [+HR] = 3nSG = ERG (I)   n-mb/ŋg/mbu-ana-kiri-ŋa-na
      [+LR] = 2SG = ACC   I-3DL/PC/PL E (I)-2SG A-hit-I-PRES
                                      'they (DL/PC/PL) hit you (SG)'

There is a further wrinkle in these inverse forms. When the [+LR] is non-singular, number marking for the [+HR] reduces to a simple singular/non-singular contrast. In other words, the distinction between the third person inverse ergative bound pronominals, *mb-* 3DL E (I), *ŋg-* 3PC E (I) and *mbu-* 3PL E (I), is neutralized to simply *mbu-* 3nSG E (I):

(11) [+HR] = 3nSG = ERG (I)   nu-mbu-ŋo-kiri-ŋa-na-ro
      [+LR] = 2PL = ACC   I-3nSG E (I)-2DL/PL A-hit-I-PRES-2PL
                                    'they (DL/PC/PL) hit you (PL)'

As mentioned above, when discussing Potawatomi, transitive verbs with local persons for both [+HR] and [+LR] present especial difficulties for languages with direct-inverse systems, and Murik is no exception. Essentially, there seems to be a reluctance to realize both speech act participants on the same verb. As Heath (1998) points out, languages have resorted to about a dozen methods to resolve this impasse. The one favored by Murik is listed as number five: the 1/2 marker is replaced by a 3 marker, in a word, impersonalization, i. e. realize a speech act participant as if he/she were not, by employing the form for the absent third person participant. This is a common technique in politeness or honorific systems, such as the origins of the polite second person pronoun in German in the third person plural pronoun. In Murik all verbs involving a local person acting on another local person are inverse, marked by the circumfix *nV-...-ŋa*. Further, with the exception of the combination of first person singular acting on second person singular, all local [+HR]s are realized impersonally, The choice of the [+HR] over [+LR] as the target for impersonalization is to be expected in the light of the Role Hierarchy: [+LR]/ACC > [+HR]/ERG. The first and second person [+HR]s are realized as third person, so that these local upon local inverse forms are homophonous with non-local upon local inverse forms. Also, as mentioned above, as these are inverse forms, with non-singular [+LR]s and also second person singular [+LR]s, the number contrast for the [+HR] reduces to a binary singular/non-singular contrast, ie. the contrast between dual, paucal and plural is lost:

(12) a. [+HR] = 2SG ⟹ 3SG = ERG   n-Ø-ŋi-kiri-ŋa-na
          [+LR] = 1PC = ACC   I-2/3SG E-1PC A-hit-I-PRES
                                      'you (SG)/he hit us (PC)'
      b. [+HR] = 1SG ⟹ 3SG = ERG   no-Ø-ŋo-kiri-ŋa-na-ko
          [+LR] = 2DL = ACC   I-1/3SG E-2DL/PL A-hit-I-PRES-2DL/PC
                                      'I/he hit you (DL)'
      c. [+HR] = 2nSG ⟹ 3nSG = ERG nu-mbu-ŋe-kiri-ŋa-na
          [+LR] = 1DL/PL = ACC   I-2/3nSG E (I)-1 DL/PC/PL A-hit-I-PRES
                                      'you/they (DL/PC/PL) hit us (DL/PL)'
      d. [+HR] = 1nSG ⟹ 3nSG = ERG nu-mbu-ŋo-kiri-ŋa-na-ro
          [+LR] = 2PL = ACC   I-1/3nSG E (I)-2DL/PL A-hit-I-PRES-2PL
                                      'we/they (DL/PC/PL) hit you (PL)'
      e. [+HR] = 1DL ⟹ 3nSG = ERG   nu-mbu-ana-kiri-ŋa-na
          [+LR] = 2SG = ACC   I-1/3nSG E (I)-hit-I-PRES
                                      'we/they (DL/PC/PL) hit you (SG)

But when the [+LR] is first person singular and the [+HR], non-singular, there is no neutralization for number, although this does vary among speakers, as some collapse the contrast between paucal and plural here, some between dual and plural, and there may even be speakers who have lost all distinctions in non-singular, so that a first person singular [+LR] behaves identically to second person singular:

(13) a. [+HR] = 2DL ⟹ 3DL = ERG (I)   n-mb-aŋa-kiri-ŋa-na
          [+LR] = 1SG = ACC   I-2/3DL E (I)-1SG A-hit-I-PRES
                                          'you/they (DL) hit me'
      b. [+HR] = 2PC ⟹ 3PC = ERG (I)   n-ŋg-aŋa-kiri-ŋa-na
          [+LR] = 1SG = ACC   I-2/3PC E (I)-1SG A-hit-I-PRES
                                          'you/they (PC) hit me'
      c. [+HR] = 2PL ⟹ 3PL = ERG (I)   nu-mbu-aŋa-kiri-ŋa-na
          [+LR] = 1SG = ACC   I-2/3PL E (I)-1SG A-hit-I-PRES
                                          'you/they (PL) hit me'

Finally, when both the [+HR] and the [+LR] are local persons and singular, both arguments are indicated by bound pronominals on the verb. Furthermore, the Role Hierarchy trumps the Person Hierarchy (or the Person Hierarchy in Murik unlike Yimas ranks second person above first. This may be the case, as there is also evidence in Kopar to support this). The [+LR] case marked as accusative always occupies the salient immediately preverbal position (by the Role Hierarchy ACC > ERG > NOM). This applies vacuously to the form with the [+HR] as second person singular, because the prefix form for this is null (Ø), homophonous with the third person singular ergative prefix, a homophony interestingly that holds throughout the Lower Sepik family, except, curiously, for Kopar:

(14) [+HR] = 2SG ⇒ ISG = ERG   n-Ø-aŋa-kiri-ŋa-na
     [+LR] = 1SG = ACC   I-2/3SG E-1SG A-hit-I-PRES
                                 'you (SG)/he hit me'

The second person singular is overt when it is [+LR]. Now bound pronominals for both arguments are present. Again the Role Hierarchy places the accusatively marked second person singular [+LR] in the immediately preverbal position and the first person singular prefix before that, following the Role Hierarchy (ACC > ERG > NOM) and in contravention of the Person Hierarchy (unless the Person Hierarchy is revised for Murik to place second person above first. This would involve a typological shift between Yimas and Murik). Interestingly, the Obligatory Nominative constraint re-asserts itself here and converts the erstwhile ergatively case marked first person singular to nominative case, in spite of it following the nV- of the inverse circumfix and not being on the left edge:

(15) [+HR] = 1SG = ERG⇒φXΦ   ni-ma-(a)na-kiri-ŋa-na
     [+LR] = 2SG = ACC   I-1SG N-2SG A-hit-I-PRES
                                'I hit you (SG)'

4 Kopar

Kopar, while clearly forming a subgroup with Murik within the Lower Sepik family, as demonstrated by a number of shared innovations, is, in its system of transitive verb inflection, quite different, although it too possesses a direct-inverse system. Kopar was already moribund at the time of my fieldwork and that of

Direct versus Inverse in Murik-Kopar

one of my undergraduate students, Stephen Hill (Hill 1995), over twenty years ago and hardly used at all in daily interactions. This presented some difficulties in collecting full data on paradigms, and speakers were sometimes unsure or varying in judgments as to what were the correct forms. Not unexpectedly in a situation of advanced language obsolescence like this, there was a great deal of variation among speakers. This is not surprising in light of the complexity of the verbal morphology of the language. The analysis presented here is therefore provisional, pending the collection of further data, which may or may not be possible. I am confident the basic data and the analysis proposed is fundamentally correct, although some more subtle details may have been missed. Kopar, like Murik and Yimas, is a canonical kind of head marking language; it signals core grammatical relations by verbal bound pronominals only. Unlike Murik and Yimas, whose bound pronominals are prefixes, Kopar essentially uses suffixes. The pattern of suffixes for number marking for second person, which is somewhat peripheral in Murik verbal inflection, becomes the dominant pattern in Kopar and is extended to both first and third person. The prefixal bound pronominal system has become rather impoverished. Kopar does adhere to the Obligatory Nominative Constraint, but nominative bound pronominals are now found mainly as suffixes and on the right edge of the verb, not the left edge as in Murik and Yimas.

Kopar independent pronouns parallel those of Murik and Yimas in distinguishing three persons and four numbers; indeed most of the forms are cognate with their Murik equivalents:

	SG	DL	PC	PL
1	ma	ke	paŋgɨ	e < *a + i
2	mi	ko	ŋgu	o < *a + u
3	mu	mbi	imɨŋgɨ	mbu

Table 4: Kopar Free Pronouns

Kopar verb inflection like that of other Lower Sepik languages, particularly Angoram, is complicated by the fact that inflectional patterns vary according to tense, aspect and mood. Here I will only consider the present tense forms, which are the most transparent. There are also some additional complications due to conjugation classes, which I will also ignore here and stick to verbs which illustrate regular inflections. The system of bound pronominals in Kopar is quite different from Murik and Yimas. Reduced are the sequences of prefixal bound pronominals. Essentially, Kopar only allows a single argument to be indicated by a bound pronominal (with a couple of minor exceptions noted below), usually just a bound nominative pronominal, although the contrast between intransitive and transitive verbs so central to direct-inverse systems is preserved. The system is easiest to approach from the inflection pattern of regular intransitive verbs; consider the following paradigm of the intransitive verb *ma-* 'eat' in the present tense, marked by *–(r)aŋg*:

(16) 1 SG ma   ma-ma-raŋg-aya
         DL ke   i-ma-raŋg-bake
         PC paŋgɨ   i-ma-raŋg-iya
         PL e   i-ma-raŋg-bwade
      2 SG mi   i-ma-raŋg-aya
         DL ko   i-ma-raŋg-bako
         PC ŋgu   i-ma-raŋg-iya
         PL o   i-ma-raŋg-bwado
      3 SG mu   u-ma-raŋg-oya
         DL mbɨ   mbɨ-ma-raŋg-odɨ
         PC miŋgɨ   ŋgi-ma-raŋg-iya
         PL mbu   mbu-ma-raŋg-odu

Note that only the non-local third persons fully indicate their number by bound pronominal prefixes which are cognate with their Murik equivalents. For the local persons, all contrasts collapse to *ma-* [-addressee] versus *i-* [+addressee]. The language, like all Lower Sepik languages, lacks an inclusive-exclusive opposition, so only the first person singular is [-addressee]; all non-singular first person forms can include the addressee and so occur with *i-* [+addressee]. The prefixal system can be summarized as:

		[-addressee]		ma-		
[+local]						
		[+addressee]		i-		
[-local]	u-		mbi-	ŋgi-	mbu-
	SG		DL	PC	PL

Table 5: Analysis of Kopar Pronominal Prefixes

Compensating for the denuded system of bound pronominal prefixes, there is a full set of bound pronominal suffixes, as seen in (16). Those for second person show cognacy with their Murik equivalents, but there is a parallel set of first person forms in Kopar as well. The contrast between first and second person in non-singulars is marked by the vowel: mid front vowel /e/ for first person and mid back vowel /o/ for second person; this alternative holds for the corresponding prefixes in Murik. It seems that Kopar is conservative here in preserving these first person suffixes that Murik has lost, because outside of the Murik-Kopar subgroup they are also found in Angoram. Also note that the paucal suffix does not distinguish person, being invariably –*iya* PC, so the first and second person paucal forms are homophonous (a similar situation is found in Yimas). The first and second person singular suffixes are also homophonous, the verbal forms are distinguished by the prefixes *ma-* 1SG versus *i-* 2.

The bound prefixes used for the arguments of transitive verbs are essentially the nominative suffixes of (16) and a set of ergative bound pronominals. So unlike Murik and Yimas, which have a split case marking system of nominative-accusative versus ergative-nominative according to local versus non-local persons, Kopar is consistently ergative-nominative across all persons and numbers:

		NOM	ERG
	SG	-aya	na-
1	DL	-bake	-oke
	PL	-bwade	-oki̵
	SG	-aya	-ona
2	DL	-bado	-oko
	PL	-bwado	-uku
	SG	-oya	mbu-
3	DL	-odi̵	mbu-
	PC	-iya	mbu-
	PL	-odu	mbu-

Table 6: Kopar Bound Pronominals for Transitive Verbs

I have inconclusive data for the paucal forms for local persons, so I have omitted these from the table. Note that there is no number distinction in the non-local third person ergative pronominals, and the form used is the prefix for third plural, *mbu-* 3PL. Transitive verbs do not normally allow more than one argument to be indicated by a bound pronominal, essentially because they are competing for the one suffixal position. The exceptions arise when the arguments are of equal rank, i.e. non-local third persons, or when the first singular is indicated by the ergative prefix *na-* 1SG E. But generally only the argument which is higher on the Person Hierarchy is indicated, and that by the respective nominative suffix. When both arguments are equally ranked, non-local third persons, the [+LR] (again the Role Hierarchy [+LR] > [+HR]) is realized by the suffixal nominative bound pronominal, simultaneously satisfying the Obligatory Nominative constraint, but on the right edge. The [+HR] is realized by the number neutralized third person ergative prefix *mbu-* 3PL E:

(17) a. *mbu-timaniŋ-aŋg-oya*   b. *mbu-timaniŋ-aŋg-odi*
       3 E-hit-PRES-3SG N   3 E-hit-PRES-3DL N
       'he/they (DL/PC/PL)' hit him'   he/they(DL/PC/PL) hit them (DL)'

These Kopar suffixes are similar to the suffixal marking of the number of the third person nominative with a third person singular [+HR] in the Murik examples (7b,c), but in Murik these suffixes are in addition to the usual left edge nominative prefixes. However, many Kopar speakers do not mark number for the nominative suffix either and use (17a) for all situations when a non-local person acts on a non-local person, employing free pronouns to make any needed distinctions, i.e, (17a) means for such speakers 'he/they (DL/PC/PL) hits him/them (DL/PC/PL).

With the exception of forms involving a first person singular [+HR], direct forms also only allow one argument to be marked by a bound pronominal. The suffix will always be that of the higher person, i.e. determined by the Person Hierarchy, and because these are direct forms, the suffixes will be drawn from the ergative set, violating the Obligatory Nominative constraint. The [+HR] is actually doubly marked, by the ergative suffix and the [+address] prefix *i-*:

(18) a. [+HR] = 2SG = ERG   *i-timaniŋ-aŋg-ona*
        [+LR] = 3   1/nSG/2-hit-PRES-2SG E
                              'you (SG) hit him/them (DL/PC/PL)'
     b. [+HR] = 1PL = ERG   *i-timaniŋ-aŋg-oki*
        [+LR]= 3   1nSG//2-hit-PRES-1PL E
                              'we (PL) hit him/them (DL/PC/PL)

Direct versus Inverse in Murik-Kopar

But when the [+HR] is first singular, and hence realized by a prefix *na-* 1SG E, it is possible as an option to realize the person of the [+LR] by the pronominal suffix, but not its number: *-oya* 3SG N just marks person in this case, all number contrasts being neutralized. Note that *-oya* 3SG N is both the [+LR] and a nominative pronominal in the salient right edge position, satisfying both the Role Hierarchy and the Obligatory Nominative constraint:

(19) [+HR] = 1SG = ERG   *na-timaniŋ-aŋg-oya*
      [+LR] = 3 = NOM   1SG E-hit-PRES-3 N
                                'I hit him/them (DL/PC/PL)'

The inverse paradigm is marked in Kopar, as in Murik, by an overt inverse marker, in this case *ŋga-* I. The [+LR] local person, which is higher ranked by both the Person Hierarchy and the Role Hierarchy, occurs as a nominative bound pronominal in the salient right edge position, satisfying the Obligatory Nominative constraint, and the prefixal position is occupied by the inverse marker. Again, there is no overt marking of the [+HR] on the verb:

(20) a. [+HR] = 3   *ŋga-timaniŋ-aŋg-bake*
         [+LR] = 1DL = NOM   I-hit-PRES-1DL N
                                 'he/they (DL/PC/PL) hit us (DL)'
     b. [+HR] = 3   *ŋga-timaniŋ-aŋg-aya*
         [+LR] = 2SG = NOM   I-hit-PRES-2DL N
                                 'he/they (DL/PC/PL) hit you (SG)'

This is the standard pattern. However, if the [+LR] is non-singular, there is an alternative reminiscent of what is found in Murik. Instead of invariant *ŋga-* I, special inverse ergative prefixes for the non-local [+HR] can be employed, but in Kopar depending on the person of the [+LR]: *mbi-* for first person and *mba-* for second person. The use of *mbu-* 3 E in examples (17a,b) above could be viewed as part of this system when the person of the [+LR] is third person. These prefixes are obviously cognate with inverse ergative prefixes in Murik, but the principles which determine their distribution are clearly different:

(21) a. [+HR] = 3   mbi-timaniŋ-aŋg-bake
       [+LR] = 1DL = NOM   3 E (I)-hit-PRES-1DL N
                            'he/they (DL/PC) hit us (DL)'
     b. [+HR] = 3   mba-timaniŋ-aŋg-bako
       [+LR] = 2DL = NOM   3 E (I)-hit-PRES-2DL N
                            'he/they (DL/PC) hit you (DL)'

Interestingly, these inverse ergative prefixes can only be used if the [+HR] is singular, dual or paucal. If it is plural, only the ŋga- inverse marker is possible. This, of course, suggests that the inverse marker originated in the third plural inverse ergative pronominal (itself probably cognate with the Murik paucal inverse ergative pronominal) and became an invariable inverse marker by neutralization of number contrasts, a widespread feature of both Kopar and Murik.

In Murik, all combinations of a local person acting on another local person are inverse and commonly subject to impersonalization. In Kopar, these two strategies are split according to person. When a second person [+HR] acts on a first person [+LR], the inflection is necessarily inverse, as according to the Person Hierarchy, and the invariable inverse marker ŋga- is required. The single bound suffixal pronominal indicates the person and number of the first person [+LR], and the second person [+HR] remains unrealized and all its number contrasts neutralized (note these forms are homophonous with inverse forms with third person [+HR]s in (20)):

(22) a. [+HR] = 2   ŋga-timaniŋ-aŋg-aya
       [+LR] = 1SG = NOM   I-hit-PRES-1SG N
                            'you (SG/DL/PC/PL) hit me'
     b. [+HR] = 2   ŋga-timaniŋ-aŋg-bake
       [+LR] = 1DL = NOM   I-hit-PRES-1DL N
                            'you (SG/DL/PC/PL) hit us (DL)'

Interestingly, though, there seems to be some dialectal variation here. The above pattern appears to be the norm, and here the governing principle seems to be both the Person and Role Hierarchy: the first person [+LR] is higher ranked on both these hierarchies and hence occupies the salient right edge position. This outcome is also congruent with the Obligatory Nominative constraint. However, for some speakers, the Person Hierarchy seems to be more important, and in a particular version of it which ranks second person above first. For these speakers, the first person [+LR] is unrealized, and the [+HR] second person singular is realized as the nominative bound pronominal on the right (a re-analysis aided no doubt by the fact that the nominative bound pronominals for first and second singular are homophonous, i.e –aya), so that example (22a) actually means for them 'you (SG) hit us (DL/PC/PL)', although this could all be due to confusion due to the moribund state of the language (again these are homophonous with inverse forms with third person [+HR]s, so that throughout much of the paradigm of transitive verbs in Kopar there is a collapse of the person distinction between second and third; the opposition with first person, however, is generally preserved, except in the nominative singular. This is reminiscent of the other Lower Sepik languages, which collapse the distinction between second and third person singular ergative bound pronominals, a feature surprisingly which is not true of Kopar):

(23) a. [+HR] = 2SG = NOM   ŋga-timaniŋ-aŋg-aya
     [+LR] = 1nSG   I-hit-PRES-2SG N
                            'you hit us (DL/PC/PL)'
   b. [+HR] = 2DL = NOM   ŋga-timaniŋ-aŋg-bako
     [+LR] = 1nSG   I-hit-PRES-2DL N
                            'you (DL) hit us (DL/PC/PL)'

When a first person [+HR] acts on a second person [+LR], the inverse marker is not used. Rather, impersonalization takes place, with the first person [+HR] realized by the impersonal ergative prefix *mbu-*, and again number contrasts for the [+HR] are completely neutralized. In this combination, it appears that the Role Hierarchy [+LR] > [+HR] trumps the Person Hierarchy, because it is the second person [+LR] which is realized as the suffixal bound nominative pronoun on the right edge and the first person is realized impersonally. In other words the pronominal pattern is like that found in (23), so perhaps this could be evidence that the unmarked version of the Person Hierarchy is actually second > first, although then the normative examples of (22) become problematic. In any case, the crucial difference between situations in which the [+HR] is second person and those in which it is first person are that in the latter there is no use of the inverse marker *ŋga-*, but simply impersonalization via *mbu-* 3 E:

(24) a. [+HR] = 1 ⟹ 3 = ERG   *mbu-timaniŋ-aŋg-bako*
    [+LR] = 2DL = NOM   3 E (=1)-hit-PRES-2DL N
                               'I/we (DL/PC/PL) hit you (DL)'

  b. [+HR] = 1 ⟹ 3 = ERG   *mbu-timaniŋ-aŋg-aya*
    [+LR] = 2SG = NOM   3 E (=1)-hit-PRES-2SG N
                               'I/we (DL/PC/PL) hit you (SG)'

5 Conclusion

Direct-inverse systems represent a rather unusual type for the expression of grammatical relations, and while attested on all continents, they are mostly restricted to heavily head marking languages. They also as a class exhibit great typological diversity, for the direct-inverse systems described here for Murik and Kopar are quite different from those of Algonkian languages. Most languages have some version of the Person Hierarchy, but that does not make them direct-inverse languages. What seems crucial to direct-inverse systems of the type exemplified by Murik, Kopar and other languages of the Lower Sepik family, is the Role Hierarchy, and a particular instantiation of this which ranks a [+LR] argument over a [+HR]. This seems counterintuitive, and in fact in many other areas of the morphosyntax of these languages, e. g. nominalization and control, the [+HR] does outrank the [+LR]. But for purposes of the morphological expression of arguments as bound pronominals, it is indeed the case, as we have seen in this paper, that the [+LR] typically outranks the [+HR] and accusative case outranks ergative case, and it is this which determines in particular the inverse alignment. Our grammatical theories, whether formal or functional, have largely assumed or explicitly posited (e. g. Foley 2007) as universal a ranking of actor > undergoer, or rephrased in the terms used here, [+HR] > [+LR], but these data from Murik-Kopar demonstrate that such a ranking cannot be universally upheld, at least not for all aspects of the morphosyntax of languages, as indeed data from deeply ergative languages like Dyirbal (Dixon 1972) or Mam (England 1983) also challenge this ranking. These Murik-Kopar data and rara from other 'exotic' languages show that our theorizing needs greater nuancing, not only to account for the typological diversity across the languages of the world, but also for the variable principles of grammar that differ across constructions within a single language. Typological adequacy was a goal of Role and Reference Grammar right from its outset (Foley & Van Valin 1984), but we need to be typologically adequate within languages not just across them, and this will require much greater attention to the variable principles that inform types of constructions within a language. Data from exotic corners of the world such as these two small languages of New Guinea are essential to such a task, but, unfortunately, these are fast disappearing before our very eyes. Sadly, Kopar is already very moribund, and Murik seriously endangered and, in fact, moribund in its eastern villages. Who knows what other wonders await us in the jungles of New Guinea or the Amazon, but these treasures may be lost before we stumble upon them.

Abbreviations

A	accusative	N	nominative
A	transitive subject	NOM	nominative
ACC	accusative	nSG	non-singular
D	direct	O	transitive object
DAT	dative	PC	paucal
DL	dual	PL	plural
E	ergative	S	intransitive subject
ERG	ergative	SG	singular
HR	higher role	1	first person
I	inverse	2	second person
LR	lower role	3	third person

References

Aissen, J. 1999. Markedness and subject choice in Optimality Theory. *Natural Language and Linguistic Theory* 17: 673–711.

Dixon, R. 1972. *The Dyirbal Language of North Queensland.* Cambridge: Cambridge University Press.

Dixon, R. 1979. Ergativity. *Language* 55: 59–138.

Dowty, D. 1991. Thematic proto-roles and argument selection. *Language* 67: 547–619.

England, N. 1983. *A grammar of Mam, a Mayan Language.* Austin: University of Texas Press.

Foley, W. 1991. *The Yimas language of New Guinea.* Stanford: Stanford University Press.

Foley, W. 2007. Toward a typology of information packaging in the clause. In T. Shopen (ed.), *Syntactic description and language typology*, volume 1, 362–446. Second edition. Cambridge: Cambridge University Press.

Foley, W. & R. D. Van Valin, Jr. 1984. *Functional syntax and universal grammar.* Cambridge: Cambridge University Press.

Foley, W. & R. D. Van Valin, Jr. 1985. Information packaging in the clause. In T. Shopen (ed.), *Syntactic description and language typology*, volume 1, 282–364. First edition. Cambridge: Cambridge University Press.

Heath, J. 1998. Pragmatic skewing in 1 ⟷ 2 pronominal-affix paradigms. *International Journal of American Linguistics* 64: 83–104.

Hill, S. 1995. Kopar fieldnotes. Notebooks in author's possession.

Hockett, C. 1966. What Algonquian is really like. *International Journal of American Linguistics* 32: 59–73.

Kiparsky, P. 1997. Remarks on denominal verbs. In A. Alsina, J. Bresnan & P. Sells (eds.), *Complex predicates*, 473–499. Stanford: CSLI Publications.

Nichols, J. 1986. Head marking and dependent marking languages. *Language* 62: 56–119.

Van Valin, R. D., Jr. & R. LaPolla. 1997. *Syntax.* Cambridge: Cambridge University Press.

Woolford, E. 1997. Four-way case systems: ergative, nominative, objective and accusative. *Natural Language and Linguistic Theory* 15: 181–227.

Woolford, E. 2001. Case patterns. In G. Legendre, S. Vikner & J. Grimshaw (eds.), *Optimality-Theoretical Syntax*, 509–543. Cambridge, MA: MIT Press.

Wunderlich, D. 1997. Cause and the structure of verbs. *Linguistic Inquiry* 28: 27–68.

Wunderlich, D. 2001. How gaps and substitutions can become optimal: the pronominal affix paradigms of Yimas. *Transactions of the Philological Society* 99: 315–366.

Author

William A. Foley
University of Sydney
william.foley@sydney.edu.au

Shifting Perspectives:
Case Marking Restrictions and the Syntax-Semantics-Pragmatics Interface[1]

Anja Latrouite

1 Introduction

This paper deals with case marking restrictions and case marking gaps in Tagalog, one of the languages on which the development of Role and Reference Grammar was based. The language received attention due to its peculiarity to split subject properties between two arguments, the Actor argument and the argument marked by the particle *ang* (Schachter 1976), therefore showing a clear necessity to draw a distinction between role-related and reference-related syntactic properties, according to Foley & Van Valin (1984). Furthermore the language was noted to make a general distinction between core and non-core arguments, the former marked by the particle *ng* in Tagalog, the latter by *sa*, if they are not explicitly selected as privileged syntactic argument (PSA) and marked by *ang*. Foley and Van Valin (1984) and others have suggested that *ang* was formerly a pragmatic marker signalling the topic, which later on got grammaticalized. Up to this day many Philippinists prefer the term 'topic' to PSA for the *ang*-marked argument. The pragmatic origin of the marker *ang* is often evoked to explain why the PSA in Tagalog can be chosen from a much larger array of thematic roles than in

---
[1] The research to this paper has been supported by the Deutsche Forschungsgemeinschaft through CRC 991 and was presented in parts at ICAL 2012 and APPL 2013 based on a chapter in my Thesis (Latrouite 2011). Special thanks are due to the audience at ICAL 2012 and APPL 2013 as well as to Jens Fleischhauer, two anonymous reviewers, and my consultants Royal Panotes Palmero, Redemto Batul and Jeruen Dery for help with Tagalog data.

Indo-European languages (cf. (1a–c)), and why there are referential restrictions on the PSA, i. e. the PSA usually gets a definite or at least specific interpretation, as exemplified in (1b) in contrast to (1a). (Note in the examples given that simple realis verb forms in Tagalog are understood as denoting realized events that are not ongoing at the reference time, here the time of speech, usually resulting in a simple past tense translation.)

(1) a. K<um>ha   ako   ng isda.[2]
       K$_{stem}$<AV>[RLS]take 3SNOM GEN fish
       'I took (a) fish.'
   b. K<in>uha   ko   ang isda.
       K$_{stem}$<RLS>[UV]take 1SGEN NOM fish
       'I took the fish.'
   c. K<in>uh-an   ko   ng konti ang kaniya-ng letse plan.
       K$_{stem}$<RLS>[UV]take-LV 1SGEN GEN bit NOM his-LK leche flan
       'I took a little bit away from his leche flan.'

The debate regarding the so-called *Definite Topic Constraint*, which nowadays is rather thought of as a *Specificity Restriction* on the *ang*-marked phrase (cf. Adams & Manaster-Ramer 1988), has been around in various variations and elaborations since Blancas de San José (1610). Two related, but logically independent claims associated with the *Specificity Restriction* are that an indefinite/non-specific theme argument of a two-place predicate can never be *ang*-marked, while definite/specific theme arguments have to be *ang*-marked. Proponents of this idea base their explanation for voice and PSA selection on it. As there can be only one *ang*-marked argument in a basic Tagalog sentence and as the thematic role of this argument is identified on the verb via a corresponding voice affix, the claim is that the respective referential properties of the theme argument ultimately determine voice selection, or put in other words, the semantics of the theme NP is said to determine the morphosyntactic expression of the verb and the marking of the PSA with *ang*. Note that the reverse claim that theme arguments which are not

---

[2] Glosses: AV: Actor voice; ACC: accusative; BV: beneficiary voice; GEN: genitive; DAT: dative; DEM: demonstrative; IPFV: imperfective; msc: masculin; LV: locative voice; NMZ: nominalizer; NOM: nominative; P: plural; PAST: past tense; RLS: realis; S: singular; UV: Undergoer voice. Infixes are marked by < > and separate the initial consonant of the stem (C$_{stem}$) from the rest of the verb stem. Glosses in subscript and square brackets indicate that a feature is not morphologically marked but implicit to the form.

marked by *ang*, but by *ng*, have to be non-specific cannot be upheld and has been shown to be too strong (cf. Himmelmann 1991, Latrouite 2011 among others).

In this paper I draw attention to a subset of the data that pose a challenge to the *Specificity Restriction*: differential object marking (DOM) and so-called case marking exceptions, i. e. Actor voice sentences in which the referential properties of the theme argument would seem to call for Undergoer[3] voice to arise, but surprisingly do not. Based on these two phenomena it will be argued that the restrictions we find show that it is not primarily the referential properties of the theme argument that determine voice choice. Case marking exceptions can only be explained if event semantics and information structure are taken into account.

The language-specific issues introduced in sections 2 and 4 of this paper have a bearing on the more theoretic question regarding the relationship between morphosyntax and semantics, namely the question whether it is the semantics that drives morphosyntax or the morphosyntax that determines the semantics? As will be laid out in section 3, with respect to Tagalog, both kinds of approaches to the semantics-morphosyntax interplay have been offered, so there is still no consensus as to whether the semantics determines morphosyntax or the morphosyntax determines the semantics with respect to the phenomenon at hand. RRG promotes the idea that linking takes place from the syntax to the semantics (hearer perspective) and vice versa from the semantics to the syntax (speaker perspective), doing justice to the fact that a form may be attributed more than one meaning by a hearer and that a meaning may be conveyed via more than one form or even be left unexpressed by a speaker, only to be derived via certain lines of reasoning on the part of the hearer. Sense disambiguation strategies depending on context as well as implicature calculation obviously fall into the realm of pragmatics, so that this domain also plays a crucial role in such an approach to language. Within RRG the theoretic question asked above would have to be reformulated as 'How do the semantics and the morphosyntax influence each other, and what is the role of pragmatic considerations within this interplay?'

In the last section of the paper, I argue that it is precisely the interaction of the three domains (morphosyntax, semantics, pragmatics) which helps to get a grasp of the Tagalog data, the exceptions and the resulting interpretation of sentences (for the latter see also Latrouite 2014). In line with Latrouite (2011), I suggest

---

[3] Among Austronesianists it has become common to use the notion 'Undergoer' in the sense of 'Non-Actor', so the notion is used in a slightly different sense than in RRG.

that a close look needs to be taken at the different levels at which semantics plays a role: the level of referentiality, the level of event structure and the level of information structure respectively. My main claim is that PSA-selection is a choice based on prominence considerations and that the levels mentioned above are ordered. In short, voice- and PSA-selection is then the result of a number of comparative prominence calculations at different levels which are ranked. It is obvious that the semantic properties which would lead one to judge an argument as comparatively more prominent than another based on the referential properties are not the same as the properties that may lead one to consider an argument as the most prominent one at the level of event structure or the level of information structure. In this sense, the degree of referentiality of an argument is just one out of many criteria that are important for argument linking decisions, and may eventually be ignored if an argument is more prominent on a different level, explaining the case marking and differential object marking patterns that we find.

2 The Specificity Restriction

Bloomfield (1917) is regularly quoted for the observation that in Tagalog Actor voice sentences the logical object (Undergoer) tends to be lacking or 'undetermined'. In Objective/Undergoer voice sentences, however, it is said to be definite (Naylor 1975), specific (Bell 1979, Adams & Manaster-Ramer 1988, Machlachlan 2000, Rackowski 2002, Aldridge 2004b) or individuated (Nolasco 2005, Saclot 2006), as shown in sentence (2b) in contrast to (2a). If the theme argument in an Actor voice sentence is expressed by a demonstrative pronoun, a partitive reading is usually given in the translation, as exemplified in (2c). The partitive reading of the demonstrative pronoun is often taken to be further evidence that definite/specific theme arguments in Actor voice sentences are dispreferred, if not banned.

(2) a. *K<um>ain*   ako   *ng isda.*
    K_{stem}<AV>$_{[RLS]}$eat 3SNOM GEN fish
    'I ate (a) fish.'
  b. *K<in>ain*   ko   *ang isda.*
    K_{stem}<RLS>$_{[UV]}$eat 1SGEN NOM fish
    'I ate the fish.'

c. K<um>ain   niyan   ang bata.
   K_stem<AV>_[RLS] eat DEM.GEN NOM child
   'The child ate (some of) that.'

The observation with respect to the theme argument in Actor voice sentences seems to be true regardless of the semantics of the verb, i.e. a transfer verb like /bili/ 'to buy' in (3) shows the same interpretational pattern as the incremental theme verb /kain/ 'to eat' in (2).

(3) a. B<um>ili   siya   ng libro.
       B_stem<AV>_[RLS] buy 3SNOM GEN book
       'She bought a/some book.'
    b. B<in>ili   niya   ang libro.
       B_stem<RLS>_[UV] buy 3SGEN NOM book
       '(S)he bought the book.'
    c. B<um>ili   niyan   ang bata.
       B_stem<AV>_[RLS] buy DEM.GEN NOM child
       'The child bought (some of) that.'

The question as to what exactly is meant by definiteness or specificity is often answered in rather vague terms in the Austronesian literature. The strongest definition of definiteness would certainly be that the referent of the argument in question is existentially presupposed and uniquely identifiable by both the speaker and the hearer, e.g. via previous mention or due to context and common background. Given that Tagalog happily marks arguments introducing new participants into a story with *ang*, it is more common for Austronesianists to recur to the weaker notion of specificity, e.g. as put forward by Heim (1991) and others. Heim (1991) views specific arguments as those carrying the presupposition of existence (in a given world), without having to have unique reference. This may help to understand the difference between the sentences in (2a) and (2b). Note, however, that based on this definition in terms of presupposed existence, it is difficult to motivate or explain the coerced partitive reading of the Undergoer demonstrative pronoun. If one presupposes the existence of an entity, then one also presupposes the existence of the parts of this entity. In order to explain the coercion, one may have to add Nolasco's (2005) notion of individuation to the definition of specificity. The specific Undergoer in Undergoer voice sentences would then be said to be presupposed and individuated, while it would be less individuated in Actor voice sentences. Stating that the Undergoer argument has to be non-individuated in an Actor voice sentence would be too strong. It would suggest that *Bumili siya ng libro* in (3a) should best be translated as 'she book-bought', indicating that the book cannot be taken up again. However, this claim is too strong; the *ng*-marked participant can easily be taken up in further discourse.

(4) B<um>ili   siya   ng libro   at   b<in>asa   niya.
    B$_{stem}$<AV>$_{[RLS]}$buy 3SNOM GEN book and b$_{stem}$<RLS>$_{[UV]}$read 3SGEN
    'She bought a book and read it.'

There are examples in which demonstrative pronouns do not necessarily receive a partitive reading when expressing a theme argument in Actor voice sentences. Note, however, that in these cases the antecedent very often refers to an abstract concept or a mass concept, i.e. a less individuated concept, as in (5).

(5) a. *Love? Li-limita-han ka   lang niyan.*
       Love? IPFV-limit-LV 2SNOM only DEM.GEN
       'Love? You will just limit it/this!'
       (https://tl-ph.facebook.com/BFLBTPYMNK/posts/318315468216409)
    b. *"K<um>ain   ka   tapos inum-in mo   ito.*
       K$_{stem}$<AV>$_{[RLS]}$eat 2SNOM later drink-UV 2SGEN DEM.NOM
       Buti nag-dala   ako   niyan."
       Good AV.RLS- carry 1SNOM DEM.GEN
       (Sabi ni Mommy sabay lagay ng gamot sa tabi ko.)
       'Eat and afterwards drink this. Good thing I brought it/that.' (Said Mommy placing (the) medicine beside me.)
       (http://www.wattpad.com/23018761-marriage-deeply-in-love-with-my-best-friend-chapter#.UjHPHRzwOQY)

More corpus work on the distribution and interpretation of demonstrative pronouns is certainly desirable and necessary, but the current data clearly point to the fact that theme arguments in Actor voice sentences are preferably understood as less specific, i.e. either as not presupposed or, if presupposed, as less individuated. In other words, theme arguments in basic Actor voice sentences tend to be referentially less prominent.

The question that arises in the face of the examples above is: do the referential properties of the theme argument enforce the choice of Undergoer/Actor voice affixes or is it the voice form of the verb that determines and delimits the interpretation of the theme argument as (+/-specific). In short, is it the semantics that determines morphosyntax or the morphology that determines the semantics?

Note that there are clear and well-known exceptions to the pattern in (2) and (3). In Actor voice cleft sentences, the *ng*-marked Undergoer argument may be understood as either non-specific or specific/definite, as shown in (6a). According to my consultants, the Undergoer may even be explicitly marked as specific/definite by the dative marker *sa*, as shown in (6b). Consequently, it is hard to claim that the case marker *ng* or the voice marking fully determine the resulting reading of the theme argument.

(6) a. *Sino   ang k<um>ain   ng isda?*
       who.NOM NMZ k$_{stem}$<AV>$_{[RLS]}$eat GEN fish
       'Who ate a/the fish?'
    b. *Siya   ang k<um>ain   sa isda.*
       3SNOM NMZ k$_{stem}$<AV>$_{[RLS]}$eat DAT fish
       'She was the one who ate the fish.'

Another set of data that seems to prove the same point comes from Aldrige (2003), who rightly observes that *ng*-marked themes in subordinate sentences may be interpreted as specific. Section 4 provides more examples of Actor voice forms in basic main clauses with specific and even definite theme arguments marked by *ng*. All of the examples just mentioned are viewed as exceptions to the overall pattern, and they all point to the fact that the case form and the voice affix – at least in the case of the Actor voice form – do not by themselves enforce a certain reading of the Undergoer argument. The questions are then: (i) what is the nature of the exceptions we find and how can they be accounted for?, as well as (ii) what is their implication for an analysis of the Tagalog linking system, and more generally for the initially raised question as to the relationship between semantics and morphosyntax?

3 Previous approaches

Rackowski (2002) develops an account in which semantics drives morphosyntax. She views specificity of the theme argument as the driving force for the morphosyntactic patterns in Tagalog. The main idea is that the feature (+specific) triggers object shift. The first step is for v to agree with the specific object. As v is said to carry an EPP (or occurrence) feature (to ensure the right semantic interpretation of the object as specific), the object has to move to the edge of vP to check this feature. Once T merges with vP and the object argument is the closest DP to agree with, the corresponding voice affix on the verb is triggered, i. e. Undergoer voice.

Rackowski's explanation of exceptions like (6) is as follows: In cleft sentences, that is in A'-extraction contexts, T carries one more operator in addition to the case feature and both have to be checked by the same DP. If the object argument were to shift due to its specificity, it would prevent T from checking its operator feature with the operator in the external argument position. Therefore it is blocked from moving and may stay in place despite its specific interpretation. However, this explanation cannot be extended to specific non-subject Undergoers in sentences without A'-extraction of the Actor argument, as in (7). Note that a non-specific or partitive reading is not available nor appropriate in the given example.

(7) *Mag-alis ka   ng (iyon-g) sapatos bago   p<um>asok   ng bahay.*
    AV-leave 2SNOM GEN (2S-LK) shoe   before p$_{stem}$<AV>$_{[RLS]}$enter GEN house
    'Take off (your) the shoes before you enter the house.'
                    (http://www.seasite.niu.edu/Tagalog/.../diction.htm)

Therefore Rackowski suggests that specific readings may also arise belatedly, e. g. through context-induced 'bridging' in the sense of Asher & Lascarides (1998), thereby introducing a second type of specificity, which renders her analysis that the specificity of the object drives morphosyntax a little less compelling and attractive.

Aldridge (2005) takes the opposite approach. In her theory morphology drives syntax, and syntax drives semantic interpretation (SS-LF Mapping). Hence, specificity or the lack hereof is a by-product of the syntactic position an element appears in and results from its LF-mapping. With respect to Tagalog, this means that in a first 'morphology drives syntax'-step the voice affix determines whether a DP raises out of VP or not. Transitive verbal morphology (i.e. the Undergoer voice affix) checks absolutive case and has an EPP feature drawing the object to its outer specifier where it receives absolutive case. Intransitive v (i.e. a verb marked by Actor voice) has no EPP feature, so that the 'direct object' in an antipassive (Actor voice sentence) does not raise out of VP. Based on Diesing (1992), Aldridge assumes for Tagalog that absolutive (*ang*-marked) DPs receive a presuppositional – and thus a specific – interpretation, because they are located outside the VP and mapped to the restrictive clause at LF. Oblique (*ng*-marked Undergoer) DPs, on the other hand, receive a nonspecific interpretation because they remain within VP and undergo existential closure. Note that a very strict version of Diesing's approach would mean that definites, demonstratives, proper names, specific indefinites, partitives and pronouns, i.e. all NPs that are presuppositional, should be located outside of VP. The next section will show that these inherently presuppositional NPs stay in situ depending on the semantics of the verb.

Within this framework, Aldridge's analyses the clefted phrase (*sino, siya*) in (6) as the predicate and the remaining headless relative clause as the subject. The subject is said to raise out of VP and map to the matrix restricted clause at LF; the *ng*-marked Undergoer argument as part of the restricted clause, i.e. as part of the presupposition, may therefore receive a presupposed interpretation at LF. This idea is also inspired by Diesing (1992). 'A DP which remains inside VP prior to spell-out can still undergo QR (Quantifier Raising) at LF and escape existential closure, if it is specific or quantificational. Therefore a specific interpretation should still be possible for an oblique DP in Actor voice' (ibid., p.8). However, this should only be possible if the *ng*-marked Undergoer argument is embedded in the subject phrase which receives the presuppositional interpretation. Based on the examples in (8), Aldridge claims that this is the case: while in (8a) the Undergoer ‚rat' in the relative clause receives a specific (even definite) reading, because it specifies the subject and is thus part of the restricted clause (i.e. of the presupposition), it may not be interpreted as specific in (8b), in which the relative clause does not modify the subject and is thus not part of the restricted clause and the presuppositon. While this is an interesting example, the judgments are not confirmed by my consultants who find a non-specific reading equally plausible for (8b).

(8) a. B<in>ili   ko   ang pusa-ng k<um>ain
       B_stem<RLS>_[UV] buy 1SGEN NOM cat-LK k_st<AV>eat
       ng daga sa akin-g bahay.
       GEN rat DAT 1S-LK house
       'I bought a cat which ate the rat in my house.'
   b. B<um>ili   ako   ng pusa-ng k<um>ain
       B_stem<AV>_[RLS] buy 1SNOM GEN cat-LK k_st<AV>eat
       ng daga sa akin-g bahay.
       GEN rat DAT 1S-LK house
       'I bought a cat which ate a/*the rat in my house.'

(judgments according to Aldridge 2005)

Intuitions and judgments may differ with respect to complex sentences. However, there are also well-known and clear cases of Undergoers in Actor voice sentences that are explicitly marked as specific or presupposed due to their proper semantics without being part of the restricted clause. A first example was shown in (7).

Sabbagh (2012) takes exceptions like these into account and builds on Rackowski (2002). He suggests that in addition to the outermost specifier of vP, there is another intermediate derived object position located above VP, but below vP to which non-pronoun/non-proper name specific themes may move. Objects expressed by pronouns and proper names are said to move to the higher location. His syntactic trees thereby mirror the often-evoked definiteness hierarchy of DPs. Just like Rackowski's and Aldridge's account, Sabbagh's account is purely syntactic. None of them deal with semantic differences beyond the domain of degrees of referentiality. In the next section I give an overview of the types of exceptions to the rule of thumb that AV-forms take non-specific Undergoer arguments and UV-forms specific Undergoer arguments, showing that while referentiality of Undergoer arguments plays a role in the way arguments are case-marked in Tagalog, event structural considerations may overrule referentiality considerations.

4 Exceptions to the Specificity Restriction

In (7) we saw a first example of specific Undergoer in an Actor voice sentence, i.e. an Undergoer modified by a possessive pronoun referring back to the Actor.

Case Marking Restrictions and the Syntax-Semantics-Pragmatics Interface

The sentences in (9a-c) show similar examples of specific, possessed Undergoer arguments.

(9) a. *K<um>a~kain   sila   ng   kanila-ng sandwich.*
k_{stem}<AV>[RLS]IPFV~eat 3pNOM GEN 3P-LK   sandwich
'They are eating their sandwich/ their sandwiches.'
(http://www.rosettastone.co.jp/.../RSV3_CC_Filipino)

b. *Nag-dala   siya   ng   kaniya-ng band.*
AV.RLS-bring 3SNOM GEN 3S-LK   band
'He brought his band.'   (Bloomfield 1918)

c. *Agad-agad ako-ng t<um>akbo   sa banyo at   nag-hugas   ng   akin-g*
At once   1S-LK t_{stem}<AV>[RLS]run DAT bath and AV.RLS-wash GEN 1S-LK
mukha.
face
'At once I ran to the bathroom and washed my face.'
http://flightlessbird.blogdrive.com/comments?id=1

As pointed out in Latrouite (2011) similar sentences are a lot less acceptable with verbs like *tumakot* 'to frighten', *pumatay* 'to kill' or *sumira* 'to destroy', as exemplified in (10) and marked by #.

(10) a. *#P<um>a~patay   siya   ng kaniya-ng anak.*
P_{stem}<AV>[RLS]IPFV~kill 3SNOM GEN 3S-LK   child
'He is killing his child.'

b. *#T<um>akot   siya   ng/sa   kaniya-ng band.*
T_{stem}<AV>[RLS] fear 3SNOM GEN/DAT 3S-LK   band
'He frightened his band.'

c. *#S<um>ira   ako   ng   akin-g banyo.*
S_{stem}<AV>[RLS]hash 1SNOM GEN 1S-LK   bath
'I destroyed my bathroom.'

Latrouite (2011) argues that the verbs in (10) clearly denote Undergoer-oriented actions. The verbstems themselves do not give information on the specific activity on part of the Actor, but only on the result with respect to the Undergoer, here patient arguments. Comparing the verbs in (9) and (10), we can see that the former in (9) denote specific manners of action in contrast to the latter, so that one can conclude that on the level of event semantics the Actor is more prominent than the Undergoer for the events expressed in (9), while it is the other way around in (10). With verbs that denote clearly Undergoer-oriented events, AV-forms with specific theme arguments seem to be limited to sentences in which the Actor is more prominent than the Undergoer on the level of information-structure, as shown in (11). The Actor in (11a) appears in the pragmatically and syntactically marked sentence-initial position in front of the topic marker *ay*, while the Actor in (11b), parallel to the example given in (11b), appears sentence-initially in the contrastive focus position.

(11) a. *Kung ang Diyos ng mga Kristiyano ay p<um>a~patay*
If NOM god GEN PL christian TOP p$_{stem}$<AV>$_{[RLS]}$IPFV~kill
ng kanya-ng
GEN 3S-LK
'If the God of the Christians kills his

mga kaaway bakit hindi ang mga tagasunod niya.
PL ennemies why NEG NOM PL follower 3SGEN
ennemies, why not his followers.'
http://www.topix.com/forum/world/philippines/T8G3JRRR4NPDIV3UU

b. *Siya ang t<um>akot sa kaniya-ng band.*
3S.NOM NMZ t$_{stem}$<AV>$_{[RLS]}$fear DAT 3S-LK band.
'He is the one who frightened his band.'

The conclusion for these data seems to be that specific Undergoers in Actor voice sentences are only acceptable if the Actor can be considered more prominent than the Undergoer on some other level than that of referentiality, i.e. either on the level of event or on the level of information structure.

It is not surprising therefore that verbs that allow for differential object marking are all of the activity-denoting type and do not characterize a property of or a result brought about with respect to the Undergoer.

(12) **Verbs allowing for *ng/sa*-alternation**

a. *Ba~basa ang bata **ng/sa** libro.*
AV.IPFV~read NOM child GEN/DAT book
'The child will read a/the book.'

(DeGuzman 1999, cited from Katagiri 2005: 164)

b. *Nag-ti~tiis   ang mga babae **ng/sa   hirap.***
   AV.RLS-IPFV~bear NOM PL woman GEN/DAT hardship
   'The women bear hardship(s)/the hardship.'
   (cf. English 1986: 1014 simplified)

c. *Nang-ha~harana   ang binate   **ng/sa dalaga.***
   AV.RLS-IPFV~serenade NOM young man GEN/DAT lady
   'The young man serenades ladies/ the lady.'   (Bloomfield 1917)

d. *D<um>a~dalo   ako **ng/sa   meeting***.
   d_stem<AV>[RLS]IPFV~attend 1sNOM GEN/DAT meeting
   'I attend meetings/the meeting.'   (Bowen 1965: 222)

e. *Nag-da~dala   siya **ng/sa   libro.***
   AV.RLS-IPFV~carry 3sNOM GEN/DAT book
   'He is carrying a/the book.'   (cf. Bowen 1965: 221, modified)

f. *T<um>uklaw   ang ahas **ng/sa   ibon.***
   t_stem<AV>peck NOM snake GEN/DAT bird
   'The snake attacked a/the bird.'   (cf. Saclot 2006)

The data seem to show a case of classic differential object marking (DOM) (cf. Dalrymple & Nikolaeva 2006), regulated by the semantic feature of specificity/definiteness. If *sa*-marking in these cases is motivated by a specificity contrast between *ng* and *sa*, with *sa* being explicitly associated with the information (+specific), the following data come as a surprise. Here we are faced with arguments expressed by clearly definite proper names that are neither marked by *sa* nor turned into the PSA, as might be expected.

(13) **Proper Names (of inanimate objects), possible with NG instead of SA**

a. *Na-nood   si Alex   **ng Extra Challenge.***
   MA.RLS-watch NOM Alex GEN Extra Challenge
   'Alex watched the Extra Challenge.'   (Saclot 2006: 10)

b. *Hindi naman puwede-ng p<um>unta   **ng Maynila***
   NEG really can-LK p_stem<AV>RLS]go GEN Manila
   ang kapatid ni Tita Merly.
   NOM sibling GEN TM
   'Tita Merly's sibling really could not go to Manila.'
   (*Aagawin Kita Muli* 1998: 10, modified)

c. *D<um>ating* **ng Saudi Arabia** *ang mga muslim*
d_{stem}<AV>[RLS] arrive GEN S.A. NOM PL muslim
'The muslims arrived in Saudi Arabia

para l<um>ahok sa paglalakbay sa banal na Mekka.
for l_{stem}<AV>[RLS]participate DAT pilgrimage DAT sacred LK Mekka
in order to participate in the pilgrimage to sacred Mekka.'
(CRI online Filipino, 2010-10-21, *Mga Muslim, dumating ng Saudi Arabia para sa paglalakbay*)

d. *D<um>ating kami* **ng Malolos Crossing.**
d_{stem}<AV>[RLS]arrive 1PL.NOM GEN Malolos Crossing
'We arrived at Malolos Crossing.'
(http://www.tsinatown.com/2010/06/see-you-in-paradise.html)

e. *Nag-ba~basa ako sa kanila* **ng Bibliya.**
MAG.REAL-IPFV~read 1SNOM DAT 3PL.NONACT GEN Bible
'I was reading the Bible to them.'

The examples so far show that the specificity of nouns does not trigger, but merely licenses possible marking with *sa* in certain cases. Note that all of the goal arguments in (13b)–(13d) would be good with *sa*-marking as well. This does not hold for the non-goal arguments in (13a) and (13e). The sentences in (14) show some further restrictions we find with respect to *ng/sa* alternation in basic sentences.[4] (14a)–(14b') exemplify that some verbs like perception verbs select exclusively for genitive marked Undergoer arguments, therefore even a clearly definite proper name Undergoer argument has to be marked by genitive in an Actor voice sentence. (14c) and (14c'), on the other hand, show that personal names and pronouns require dative marking, even if the verb otherwise selects for genitive case. For personal names and personal pronouns dative marking is the only option in Undergoer position, it is obligatory.

(14) **Restrictions on *ng/sa*-alternation**

a. <u>*Siya ang*</u> *na-nood* **ng** *Extra Challenge.*
3SNOM NMZ POT.AV.RLS-watch GEN Extra Challenge
'He is the one who watched (the TV show) Extra Challenge.'
(Saclot 2006: 10; modified)

---

[4] Some consultants allow for *ng/sa*-alternations more freely in cleft sentences than in basic sentences.

a.' *Siya   ang na-nood   ??**sa** Extra Challenge.*
    3SNOM NMZ POT.AV.RLS-watch DAT Extra Challenge
    'He is the one who watched (the TV show) Extra Challenge.'
b. *Siya   ang naka-kita   **ng** kaniya-ng   anak.*
    3SNOM NMZ POT.AV.RLS-visible GEN 3S.NONACT-LK child
    '(S)he is the one who saw her(his) child.'
b.' *Siya   ang naka-kita   ***sa** kaniya-ng   asawa.*
    3SNOM NMZ POT.AV.RLS-visible DAT 3S.NONACT-LK spouse
    'S(h)e is the one who saw her(his) spouse.'
c. *Siya   ang naka-kita   *ng/sa akin.*
    3SNOM NMZ POT.AV.RLS-visible GEN/DAT 1S.NONACT
    'He is the one who saw me.'
c.' *Siya   ang naka-kita   *ni/kay Lena.*
    3SNOM NMZ POT.AV.RLS-visible GEN/DAT L
    'He is the one who saw Lena.'

Table 1 gives a summary of our finding: dative obligatorily marks Undergoers expressed by personal pronouns and personal names of animate entities, and optionally marks highly referential common nouns and proper names of inanimate entities, if certain licensing conditions are met.

TYPE OF OBJECT	PROPERTIES		DATIVE MARKING		
			Obligatory	Optional	Dispreferred
Pronoun/personal name	[+animate]	[+specific]	✓		
Common noun	[+ specific]	[+/-animate]		✓	
common noun in possessive phrase	[+/-animate]	[+specific]			✓
proper name	[-animate]	[+specific]			✓

Table 1: Summary of dative marking of objects (cleft sentences)

Based on these observations, the questions (i) what are the licensing conditions for alternations?, and more specificly, (ii) why is *sa* marking dispreferred with NPs denoting possessed objects, if specificity is at the core of DOM in Tagalog?, and (iii) why is the marker *ng* licensed with Goal arguments realized as proper names? can be addressed. The latter phenomenon is especially intriguing as the marker *sa* should be the default marker for two reasons, the specificity of the

303

argument and the fact that goals are usually marked with *sa*. The next section develops answers to these questions.

5 Explaining the pattern

Before we can turn to the exceptions that require explanation a word on the case markers and their distribution is in line, e. g. as described in Foley & Van Valin (1984) and Kroeger (1993). The marker *ang*, called nominative case here, can mark Actor and Undergoer and is not an unmarked case in the sense that the argument marked by it necessarily gets a presuppositional reading. The genitive marker *ng* may also mark Actors and Undergoers, as well as possessors, instruments etc. Due to its wide distribution it is often viewed as the unmarked marker. Out of the three markers, only the dative marker *sa* is exclusively restricted to non-Actor arguments. I take voice marking to serve the function of selecting the perspectival center based on prominence (cf. Himmelmann 1987). Borschev & Partee (2003) put forward the idea of the PERSPECTIVAL CENTER PRESUPPOSITION, namely '*Any Perspectival Center must normally be presupposed to exist.*' This can be used to explain why the PSA, as the perspectival center, is always understood as specific.

With respect to dative marking we need to distinguish obligatory from non-obligatory dative marking. Among the obligatory dative marking cases there is once again a distinction to be drawn between verb-based and property-based assignments, i. e. cases in which dative is required by the verb (cf. 15 a-b, 16 b) as object case, and those where it is required by the nature of the NP, e. g. if the theme argument is expressed by a personal name or pronoun (cf. 14 c-c'), or if the NP has the status of a locative adjunct (cf. 16 a).

(15) **Obligatory *sa*-marking verbs requiring animate Undergoers**

a. *T<um>ulong   ako   *ng/**sa bata**.*
   t$_{stem}$<AV>$_{[RLS]}$help 1SNOM GEN/DAT child
   'I helped a/the child.'

b. *B<um>ati   siya   *ng/**sa bata**.*
   b$_{stem}$<AV>$_{[RLS]}$greet 3SNOM GEN/DAT child
   'He greeted a/the child.'

c. *Um-ahit   ako   *ng/**sa lalaki**.*
   AV$_{[RLS]}$shave 1SNOM GEN/DAT man.
   'I shaved the man.'

(16) **Obligatory *sa*-marking on locative adjuncts and indirect object arguments of ditransitive verbs**

a. Nag-luto   ako   ng isda   **sa kusina.**
   AV.RLS-cook 1SNOM GEN fish DAT kitchen
   'I cooked fish in the kitchen.'

b. I-b<in>igay   niya   ang libro *ng/**sa bata.**
   UV-b_stem<RLS>[UV] give 3SGEN NOM book GEN/DAT child
   'He gave the book to a/the child.'

The cases of non-obligatory dative marking (cf. 12–13), on the other hand, can be divided into default and not-default cases. The former comprise goal arguments of directed motion verbs, which – as we have seen – may happily be coded by *ng* instead of *sa* for reasons that need to be given. The latter comprise theme arguments of manner of action verbs that may be coded by *sa* rather than *ng* as well as all verbs with theme arguments coded by possessive pronouns. For the latter group *sa*-marking is clearly rejected by native speakers. As we can see DOM is restricted to the goal argument of directed motion verbs and the specific theme argument of manner of action verbs, abbreviated and designated as Undergoers (UG) in the graph below.

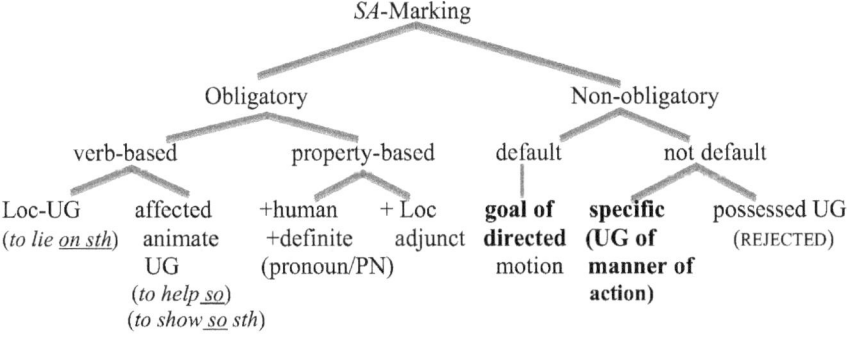

Figure 1

Given this rather complex situation, how can we model the distribution of *ng* vs. *sa*? One possibility is via constraints in an OT-like model. The functional explanation of **obligatory *sa*-marking of animate non-PSA Undergoers** parallels the findings in many languages around the world. It is often suggested that the AVOIDANCE OF ROLE AMBIGUITY (cf. Comrie 1979, deSwart 2007) is the reason for a special morphosyntactic treatment of personal pronouns and personal names. The basic idea is that if both arguments of a transitive verb are animate, then overt or special marking of the animate Undergoer argument as the direct object helps the hearers avoid the potential confusion or ambiguity that may arise due to the fact that the patient argument exhibits a salient proto-agent property, in this sense we are dealing with an expressivity constraint. Recall that *ang*-marking is neutral with respect to thematic roles and that agents and patients/themes are equally good candidates for PSA-choice. One possible objection could be that in Tagalog the thematic role of the *ang*-marked argument is clearly discernable due to the voice affix on the verb. Note, however, that *ang* and *ng* (spoken 'nang') sound very similar, that the *ang*-marked phrase tends to come at the end of the sentence and that voice affixes are quite frequently left out in spoken language. Besides a general tendency of the language to give a special status to animacy (cf. Drossard 1984) these factors may have played a role in the development of obligatory differential object marking.

Expressivity Constraint 1
>**Avoid Role Ambiguity (*Role Ambig.):** Mark the role of the Undergoer argument morphosyntactically, if the Undergoer exhibits the proto-agent properties/logical subject properties [+anim], [+human].

As for the functional explanation of **optional *sa*-marking of specific inanimate Undergoers,** Comrie (1989), Aissen (2003), Primus (2011) and others have stressed the empirical observation from discourse studies that Actors tend to be topical and higher on the referential hierarchy, while Undergoers tend to be non-topical and thus lower on the referential hierarchy. They suggest that – just like animacy – specificity/definiteness is an unexpected property of Undergoers and that role-wise unexpected semantic properties blur the role distinction of the arguments, which is important for processing. The constraint would then be related, in that the explicit marking of the Undergoer role is required to faciliate processing.

Expressivity Constraints 2
>**Mark Undergoer Role/[+spec]'(✓UR/[+spec]):** Mark the role of the Undergoer argument morphosyntactically, if it is definite/specific.

However, we also have to explain the opposite case, i. e. the case of clearly definite Undergoers: (a) proper nouns marked by *ng* (rare) and (b) possessed NP marked by *ng* (obligatory). I suggest that the functional explanation **optional proper noun marking with *ng*** could be as follows: from a functional perspective, the fact that proper names of inanimate entities are not *sa*-marked[5] could be argued to follow from an interaction of the *ambiguity avoidance* constraint with an economy constraint banning (excessive) morphosyntactic marking. The reference of proper names is specific/definite per se, so no additional marker is needed to signal definiteness. Moreover, proper names of inanimate entities, in contrast to personal names, do not run the risk of causing animacy-driven mapping ambiguities. If we think of differential object marking as a means to provide a processing advantage to the hearer (cf. Aissen 2003, Primus 2011), then it is understandable that – in contrast to common nouns – easily identifiable inanimate arguments expressed by proper names do not require *sa*-marking.

Last but not least we need a functional explanation for the **unavailability of *sa*-marking for possessive UG-NPs.** Can possessive marking count as an alternative means to eliminate role ambiguity? There is a point in assuming that the reference of Undergoers is tightly linked to the reference of Actors, e. g. it has been pointed out by Van Valin & LaPolla (1997) that binding of (possessive) pronouns in Tagalog and other languages is indeed better statable in terms of a dependence of the Undergoer on the Actor rather than in terms of positions in a tree. For the data in (14), it thus seems to make sense to assume a third constraint '*Redundancy*' (= Avoid the marking of (role) information that is already deducible from overt morphosyntactic markers).

Economy Constraints 1 and 2
>Avoid marked linkers (*Marked Linker)
>*Redundancy: Avoid the marking of role information that is deducible from overt morphosyntactic markers.

It is clear that the two constraints that are responsible for obligatory *sa*- and *ng*-marking need to be ranked above the other constraints. The tables in (17) and (18) show how the ranking of the constraints yield the correct results for obligatory case marking.

---

[5] In the case of directed motion verbs *sa*-marking is available, as illustrated above, due to the spatial uses of the marker *sa* that go well with these verbs.

(17) **Undergoer: personal name (pronoun)**

UG: personal name [+spec] [+anim]	*Redundancy	*Role Ambig.	*Marked Linker	✓UR/[+spec]
FDAT	✓	✓	*	✓
GEN	✓	*!	✓	*

(18) **Undergoer: animate possessive phrase with pronominal possessor**

UG: CN (PossP) [+spec][+anim]	*Redundancy	*Role Ambig.	*Marked Linker	✓UG/[+spec]
DAT	*!	✓	*	✓
FGEN	✓	*	✓	*

In order to explain free *ng/sa-* alternations the two constraints AVOID MARKED LINKERS and MARK SPECIFIC UGs need to be on a par, as exemplified in the table in (19).

(19) **Undergoer: specific common noun (similar to proper name (inanimate))**

UG: CN [+spec] [-anim]	*Redundancy	*Role Ambig.	*Marked Linker	✓UG/[+spec]
(F) DAT	✓	✓	*	✓
(F)GEN	✓	✓	✓	*

Dalrymple and Nikolaeva (2006) argue that DOM languages can be divided into three types based on the factors that govern the object case alternation.

(20) **Three types of DOM languages** (Dalrymple & Nikolaeva 2006):

Type 1 Languages where DOM is regulated solely by information structure; correlations with semantic features are only tendencies.

Type 2 Languages where DOM is regulated solely by semantic features; correlations with information structure are only tendencies.

Type 3 Languages where DOM is regulated both by information structure and semantic features.

As the discussion of data in the previous section has shown, DOM is more freely available in information-structurally marked sentences like contrastive focus or topic sentences than in basic VSO sentences, where it is clearly restricted to certain verb classes. In this sense, the availability of DOM is regulated by more than just the semantic features of the noun phrases and certain processing considerations in terms economy and expressivity. The availability of DOM also crucially depends on verb semantics and on the respective information-structural prominence of arguments, i.e. on the same aspects that have been identified as important for subject marking in Latrouite (2011). So far we have only hinted at the answer to the question as to why the very prominent theme argument does not turn into the PSA in the cases given above. In the next section we will take a look at how different verb classes and aspects of meaning play a key role in both, DOM and subject marking.

6 Subject marking and DOM in Tagalog:

With certain verbs, Actor voice is not possible at all regardless of the referential properties of the Undergoer argument, as exemplified in (21)–(23a). As we can see these verbs are once again clearly Undergoer-oriented verbs denoting a resultant state of the Undergoer. In basic sentences native speakers insist on Undergoer voice forms as the one in (23b). Actor voice forms seem to be only licensed if the Actor is overtly information-structurally prominent, e.g. in a cleft structure as in (23c).

(21) a. S<um>ira   siya $^{(?)}$**ng** / *sa bahay / *ng kaniya-ng bahay.
    S$_{stem}$<AV>$_{[RLS]}$destroy 3sNOM GEN/DAT house/GEN 3sNONACT-LK house
    '(S)he destroyed a/*the/ *her(his) house.'
  b. S<in>ira   niya   **ang** bahay/ **ang** kaniya-ng   bahay.
    S$_{stem}$<RLS>$_{[UV]}$destroy 3sGEN NOM house/ NOM 3sNONACT-LK house
    '(S)he destroyed the house/ her(his) house.'

(22) G<um>ulat   siya   *ng / *sa bata / *ng kaniya-ng bata.
    G$_{stem}$<AV>$_{[RLS]}$surprise 3sNOM GEN/DAT child/GEN 3sNONACT-LK child
    Intended: '(S)he surprised /*the/ *her(his) child.'

(23) a. *T<um>akot   siya   kay Jose.
    T$_{stem}$ <AV>$_{[RLS]}$fear 3sNOM DAT Jose
    Intended: 'He frightened Jose.' (cf. Schachter & Otanes 1972: 152)
  b. T<in>akot   niya   si Jose.
    T$_{stem}$ <RLS>$_{[UV]}$fear 3sGEN NOM Jose
    'He frightened Jose.'

c. *Siya   ang t<**um**>akot   kay Jose.*
   3SNOM NMZ t_{stem} <AV>[RLS]fear DAT Jose
   'He is the one who frightened Jose.'

Interestingly, however, it is possible to find sentences like those (24).

(24) a. *T<**um**>a~takot   ng mga negosyante   ang rallies.*
   t_{stem} <AV>[RLS]IPFV~fear GEN PL entrepreneur NOM rallies
   'The rallies are frightening (the) entrepreneurs.'
   (simplified from Pilipino Star Ngayon, December 12, 2000, *Mag-rally or tumahimik*)

   b. *Mag- ta~takot   kay Ina   ang abortion ng kaniyang baby.*
   AV-IPFV~fear   DAT Ina   NOM abortion GEN 3S-LK baby
   'The abortion of her baby will frighten Ina.
   (blog, December 12, 2000, *Mag-rally or tumahimik*)

Some speakers only like the Actor voice form in (24b), some also like the Actor voice form in (24a). Note, however, that the sentences have something crucial in common: the verbs are marked for imperfectivity and thus denote an ongoing event, and secondly we have an unexpected reversal of animacy, the Actor is inanimate and the Undergoer is animate. Furthermore the context of both sentences is such that the text is not about the people but about the events, that is the rallies and the abortion respectively. I have nothing to say about the animacy reversal at this point, which may turn out to be coincidental. However, it is fairly well-known fact that imperfective forms tend to put the spotlight on the Actor. Latrouite (2011) lists more examples of basic sentences with Undergoer-oriented AV-verbs that become more acceptable once the verb is marked for imperfective. Why should this be so? I suggest that this is linked to the very general licensing conditions for Actor voice. There are certain contexts and conditions that license or favor the realization of a verb in Actor voice:

- Firstly, the verbs themselves describe activities that characterize the Actor – and not the Undergoer, i. e. not the result with respect to the Undergoer. The Undergoer does not undergo a change of state and no result is implied with respect to the Undergoer. Therefore, the verbs can be analysed as inherently Actor-oriented. Note that this argument also holds for the verbs of directed motion above, which denote a change of location of the Actor and imply no change with respect to the Undergoer.

- Secondly, the imperfective form of the verb focuses on the repetition, iteration or continuation of the activity initiated and pursued by the Actor argument and, therefore, favors Actor-orientation.
- Thirdly, in the absence of realis marking, as in (24), the imperfective verb form is understood in the sense that the event has not yet occurred (but will occur in the future). It is not uncommon in conversational Tagalog to use bare verb stems and still have nominative marking on one of the arguments. Himmelmann (1987) has shown that this marking depends on whether the context is understood as a realis or an irrealis context. In irrealis contexts, i.e. in contexts in which the event has not yet manifested itself, the Actor is viewed as prominent and receives nominative marking, while in realis contexts, it is the Undergoer.[6] This is not surprising, as in the former case we focus on the starting point and the phase prior to the starting point, both of which are more closely related to the Actor than the Undergoer, while in the latter case we focus on the development or end-phase of the event, which is mostly characterized by processes involving a change in the Undergoer and its properties.

Note that for *sa*-marking of the Undergoer to be possible, i.e. for definite Undergoers to be acceptable in Actor voice constructions, we need 'counter-weights' that justify the higher degree of prominence of the Actor in these cases, so that the definite Undergoer does not 'enforce' Undergoer voice. Inherent Actor-orientation of the verb, imperfectivity and irrealis contexts represent such counter-weights that render the Actor event-structurally more prominent. From all that has been said so far, it follows that event-structural prominence is a matter of degree and the result of a rather complex evaluation process. Therefore speakers feel very

---

[6] Examples (Himmelmann 1987: 165 ff.)
(iv) *Um-uwi   na   tayo, Daddy! Uwi   na   tayo!*
    AV:um-go_home already we.NOM D ! Go_home already 1PL.NOM
    'Let us go home, Daddy! Let us go home!'
(v) *Hampas na kayo,   mga bata,sa mga langgam!*
    beat already 2PLNOM PL Kind DAT PL ant
    '(You) beat the ants, children!'
(vi) *Hawak ni Mary ang libro.*   (vii) **Hawak ng libro si Mary*
    hold GEN M NOM book.   Hold   GEN book NOM M.
    'Mary held/holds the book.'   'Mary held/holds a book.' (Schachter 1995: 42-43)

311

certain of the acceptability of *sa*-marked Undergoers in basic sentences whenever the event-related prominence of the Actor is very high with respect to all of the three domains discussed above, but tend to be less certain if this is not the case.

Given that Actor-orientation and Actor prominence play a role in whether or not a specific Undergoer may be marked by *sa* instead of *ang*, it is not surprising that speakers of Tagalog accept *sa*-marking of Undergoers more freely in focused Actor constructions than in basic sentences. This is to be expected, since (as argued in Latrouite 2011) prominence in terms of focus ranks higher than event-structural prominence, while event-structural prominence ranks higher than referential prominence: information-structural prominence > event-structural prominence > referential prominence. The principles for Actor voice selection are given in (25).

(25) Principles for Actor voice selection in Tagalog

Actor voice is chosen

(i) obligatorily, if the Actor is [+focal],
(ii) preferably, if the Actor is strongly event-structurally prominent (verb-inherently & with respect to mood/aspect);
(iii) possibly, if the Actor is event-structurally prominent or if the Actor is more specific than the Undergoer.

In all other cases **Undergoer voice** is chosen.

The most essential point here is that Actor-orientation is a precondition for *ng*-marked Undergoer verbs to be able to take *sa*-marking in special contexts. Note that inherent verb orientation is what distinguishes grammatical from ungrammatical cases of DOM in the introductory part. Result-oriented verbs like 'destroy' and 'surprise' do not denote a specific activity and are therefore Undergoer-oriented, they (almost) always occur with Undergoer voice. In the case of the latter verb, which selects for an animate Undergoer, this requirement is so strong that even the lack of specificity of the Undergoer does not license Actor voice. Note that an emotion verb like *tumakot* 'to frighten' is also strongly Undergoer-oriented, as *takot* 'fear' denotes the (resulting) property of the animate Undergoer, not of the Actor. Therefore, Undergoer voice is strongly preferred with this verb, as could be seen above (23). Actor voice is only found, if the Actor is event-structurally prominent or information-structurally prominent (i. e. in focus) .

Similarly, the perception verb *makakita* 'to see' falls in the category of Undergoer-oriented verbs, given that the stem *kita* means 'visible' and thus denotes a property of the Undergoer, not of the Actor. The example in (26) shows that this verb behaves like a typical Undergoer-oriented verb in that it does not allow for Actor voice in basic sentences, if the Undergoer is specific. Hence, we do not find *ng/sa*-alternations in basic sentences with this verb, but only in focus sentences.

(26) a. *****Naka**-kita   <u>ako</u>   sa aksidente.
         POT.AV.RLS-visible 1SNOM DAT accident
         Intended: 'I saw the accident.'
     b. ***Naka**-kita   <u>ako</u>   ng aksidente.
         POT.AV.RLS- visible 1SNOM GEN accident
         'I saw an accident.'
     c. ***Na**-kita   niya   <u>ang aksidente</u>.
         POT.UV.RLS-visible 3SGEN NOM accident
         'He saw the accident.' (cf. Schachter & Otanes 1972: 383)

Contact verbs like 'to peck', 'to hit' or emotion verbs like 'to suffer from (a disease)' cannot be said to be more Actor- or more Undergoer-oriented, they seem to be rather neutral and, according to a good number of speakers (even if not all) allow for the *ng/sa*-alternation in basic sentences. As Saclot (2006) points out, speakers who allow for this alternation, as shown in (27a) still hesitate to accept sentences like the one in (27b):

(27) a. T<um>u-klaw   ang ahas **ng/ sa**   ibon.
         t_stem<AV>[RLS]peck NOM snake GEN/DAT bird
         'The snake attacked a/the bird.'
     b. *T<um>u-klaw   ang ahas **ng/ sa**   bata.
         t_stem<AV>[RLS]peck NOM snake GEN/DAT child
         Intended: 'The snake attacked a/the child.' (cf. Saclot 2006)

In contrast to the example in (27a), where both arguments are animate but non-human, the sentence in (27b) exhibits a human Undergoer and non-human Actor. According to my consultants, this leads to the judgment that the sentence is awkward, as the human argument should be more prominent than the non-human argument and, thus, should turn into the subject. These fine-grained differences that are often seen as mirroring differences with respect to the hierarchy of animacy (given a human-centered view), only play a role with this small group of verbs.

Finally, we had two classes of Actor-oriented verbs that were discussed more closely in section 2: the first class denoting real activities, the second class denoting results with respect to the Actor (i. e. the change of position of the Actor). Both classes were shown to allow for *ng/sa* alternations in basic sentences in accordance with a number of constraints.

7 Conclusion

It was shown in this paper that DOM in Tagalog is constrained by a number of factors – first and foremost by the principles of voice selection. For DOM to be possible, the Actor has to be the most prominent argument in the sentence in order to become the subject of the sentence. The prominence of an argument was argued to be evaluated on three ordered levels: the level of information structure > the level of event structure > the level of referentiality. Once the preconditions for Actor voice selection are fulfilled and the Actor is information-structurally or event-structurally prominent, considerations with respect to the semantic properties of the Undergoer argument in terms of animacy and specificity come into play. Here it was shown that functional considerations constrain the possible patterns and explain why certain contexts did not trigger DOM although the Undergoer was animate or specific. There seem to be different cut-off points for DOM within the Tagalog community. However, a survey of these language-internal differences must be left to future research.

In terms of the initially raised question regarding the relation between morphosyntax and semantics, the data seem to speak in favour of a non-trivial answer. The way the function of the morphosyntactic markers *ng* and *sa* in Tagalog was described here, we cannot simply come up with a lexical entry consisting of one or two semantic features to account for either their distribution or the readings they yield. Moreover, we have got three dimensions of morphosyntactic marking that need to be taken into account: syntactic marking in terms of preposed arguments in focus (or as contrastive topic cf. Latrouite 2011), morphological marking on the verb in terms of voice marking and morphosyntactic marking in terms of the case markers. The choice of a particular information-structurally marked sentence structure opens up a larger choice of voice forms than acceptable in basic sentences as well as a larger array of interpretations in terms of referentiality for the theme argument in situ. Without special IS structures, the choice of voice forms in basic sentences is more limited, as verbs fall into three classes, two of which tend to come with a certain default. We can distinguish verbs that predicate primarily over the Actor and tend to be AV, those that predicate primarily over the Undergoer and tend to be UV, and those that are neutral with respect to Actor and Undergoer; in the former and the latter case, high referentiality and/or animacy of the Undergoer may influence voice choice; similarly with Undergoer-oriented verbs special properties of the event marked on the verb via imperfective or irrealis markers may influence a deviation from the default voice choice. In this sense, we end up with a system in which morphosyntactic marking licenses an array of interpretations, while at the same time semantic features constrain morphosyntactic options. As there is no simple one-to-one mapping from form to meaning, it seems indeed advantageous to think of language in the RRG-sense as consisting of different layers of structure, which need to be mapped to one another. Given the importance of information structure and verb meaning for the Tagalog linking system more comprehensive corpus work with respect to both domains is certainly desirable.

References

Adams, K. & A. Manaster-Ramer. 1988. Some questions of topic/focus choice in Tagalog. *Oceanic Linguistics* 27: 79–102.

Aldridge, E. 2004. *Ergativity and word order in Austronesian languages.* Cornell University dissertation.

Aldridge, E. 2005. Antipassive, clefting, and specificity. In S. Arunachalam, T. Scheffler, S. Sundaresan & J. Tauberer (eds.), *Proceedings of the 28th Annual Penn Linguistics Colloquium. Penn Working Papers in Linguistics 11.1.*

Aissen, J. 2003. Differential object marking: iconicity vs. economy. *Natural Language and Linguistic Theory* 21: 435–448.

Blancas de San José, F. 1610. *Arte y reglas de la lengva tagala.* Bataan: Tomás Pinpin [typesetter].

Bloomfield, L. 1917. Tagalog texts with grammatical analysis. (University of Illinois Studies in language and Literature, 3). Urbana, Illinois: University of Illinois.

Borschev, V. and B. H. Partee. 2003. The Russian genitive of negation: Theme-rheme structure or perspective structure? *Journal of Slavic Linguistics* 10, 105-44.

Bowen, D. J. (ed.). 1965. *Beginning Tagalog*. Berkeley/Los Angeles: University of California Press.

Bossong, G. 1985. *Differentielle Objektmarkierung in den Neuiranischen Sprachen*. Tübingen: Narr.

Bossong, G. 1991. Differential object marking in Romance and beyond. In D. Wanner & D. Kibbee (eds.), *New Analyses in Romance Linguistics*, 143–170. Amsterdam: Benjamins.

Branigan, H. P., Pickering, M. & M. Tanaka. 2007. Contributions of animacy to grammatical function assignment and word order during production. *Lingua* 118(2): 172–189.

Cena, R. M. 1979. Patient primacy in Tagalog. Paper presented at the *LSA Annual Meeting*, Chicago.

Comrie, B. 1979. Definite and animate direct objects: a natural class. *Linguistica Silesiana* 3: 13–21.

Comrie, B. 1989. *Language universals and linguistic typology*. 2nd edition. Cambridge: Blackwell.

Dalrymple, M., and I. Nikolaeva. 2006. Topicality and nonsubject marking. Manuscript, Oxford University.

De Swart, P. 2007. *Cross-linguistic variation in object marking*. University of Nijmegen dissertation.

Dowty, D. 1991. Thematic proto-roles and argument selection. *Language* 67(3): 547–619.

English, L. 1977. *English-Tagalog dictionary*. Manila: National Bookstore.

English, L. 1986. *Tagalog-English dictionary*. Manila: National Bookstore.

Foley, W. A., & R. D. Van Valin, Jr. 1984. *Functional syntax and universal grammar*. Cambridge: Cambridge University Press.

Heim, Irene. 1991. On the projection problem of presuppositions. In S. Davis (ed.), *Pragmatics*, 397-405. Oxford: Oxford University Press.

Himmelmann, N. P. 1987. *Morphosyntax und Morphologie. Die Ausrichtungsaffixe im Tagalog*. München: Wilhelm Fink Verlag.

Himmelmann, N. P. 1991. The Philippine challenge to universal grammar. *Arbeiten des Kölner Universalien-Projekts* 15. Köln: Institut für Sprachwissenschaft.

References

Himmelmann, N. P. 2005. Tagalog. In A. Adelaar & N. P. Himmelmannn (eds.), *The Austronesian languages of Asia and Madagascar*, 350–376. London: Routledge.

Katagiri, M. 2005. Topicality, ergativity and transitivity in Tagalog: Implications for the Philippine-type system. *Proceedings of the Taiwan-Japan Joint Workshop on Austronesian Languages*, 239–260.

Latrouite, A. 2011. *Voice and case in Tagalog: the coding of prominence and orientation*. Heinrich-Heine-Universität Düsseldorf dissertation.

Latrouite, A. 2014. Event-structural prominence and forces in verb meaning shifts. In B. Copley & F. Martin (eds.), *Causation in grammatical structures*, 372–394. Oxford: Oxford University Press.

Latrouite, A. & R. D. Van Valin, Junior. 2014. Referentiality and Telicity in Tagalog and Lakhota. In Doris Gerland, Christian Horn, Anja Latrouite und Albert Ortmann (eds.), *Meaning and Grammar of Nouns and Verbs*. Studies in Language and Cognition 1. dup, 410-426.

Machlachlan, A. & M. Nakamura. 1997. Case checking and specificity in Tagalog. *The Linguistic Review* 14, 307–333.

McFarland, C. 1978. Definite objects and subject selection in Philippine languages. In C. Edrial-Luzares & A. Hale (eds.), *Studies in Philippine Linguistics*, Vol. 2, 139–182. Manila: Linguistic Society of the Philippines.

Milambiling, L. 2013. Tagalog situation aspect and event structure. Paper read at the Sixth Austronesian and Papuan Languages and Linguistics Conference, 24-25 May 2013. SOAS University of London..

Naylor, P. B. 1975. Topic, focus and emphasis in the Tagalog verbal clause. *Oceanic Linguistics* 16(2): 12-79.

Naylor, P. B. 1986. On the pragmatics of focus. In P. Geraghty, L. Carrington & S. A. Wurm (eds.), *FOCAL 1: Papers from the Fourth International Conference on Austronesian Linguistics*. 43–57 Canberra: Australian National University.

Nolasco, R. 2005. What ergativity in Philippine languages really means. Paper presented at Taiwan-Japan Joint Work shop on Austronesian Languages, National Taiwan University, Taipei, Taiwan.

Nieuwland, M. S. & J. J. A. van Berkum. 2006. When peanuts fall in love. *Journal of Cognitive Neuroscience* 18(7): 1098–1111.

Primus, B. 2011. Animacy, generalized semantic roles, and differential object marking. In M. Lamers & P. de Swart (eds.), *Case, word order, and prominence. Interacting cues in language production and comprehension*, 65–90. Dordrecht: Springer.

Rackowski, A. 2002. *The structure of Tagalog: specificity, voice, and the distribution of arguments*. MIT dissertation.

Ramos, T.V. 1974. *The case system of Tagalog verbs*. Pacific Linguistics, Series B, No. 27. Canberra: The Australian National University.

Sabbagh. J. 2012. *Specificity and Objecthood*. Draft. UT Arlington.

Saclot, M. J. 2006. On the transitivity of the actor focus and the patient focus constructions in Tagalog. Paper presented at the 10th *International Conference on Austronesian Linguistics*, Palawan, Philippines.

Saclot, Maureen. 2011. Event Structure in Tagalog. PhD Thesis. University of Melbourne.

Schachter, P. 1976. The subject in Philippine languages: topic, actor, actor-topic, or none of the above. In C. Li (ed.), *Subject and Topic*, 493–518. New York: Academic Press.

Schachter, P. 1996. The subject in Tagalog: still none of the above. *UCLA Occasional Papers in Linguistics* No.15. Los Angeles: University of California.

Schachter, P. & F. Otanes. 1972. *Tagalog reference grammar*. Berkeley: University of Carlifornia Press.

Silverstein, M. 1976. Hierarchy of features and ergativity. In R. M. W. Dixon (ed.), *Grammatical categories in Australian languages*, 112–171. Canberra: Australian Institute of Aboriginal Studies.

van Nice, K. & R. Dietrich. 2003. Task sensitivity of animacy effects. *Linguistics* 41, 825–849.

Van Valin, R. D., Jr. & R. LaPolla. 1997. *Syntax. Structure, meaning and function*. Cambridge: Cambridge University Press.

Author

Anja Latrouite
Departement of Linguistics and Information Science
Heinrich-Heine-University Düsseldorf
latrouite@phil.hhu.de

Notes on "Noun Phrase Structure" in Tagalog[1]

Nikolaus P. Himmelmann

This paper presents some observations on the syntax and semantics of the Tagalog phrase marking particles *ang*, *ng*, and *sa*. While there is some evidence for the widely held view that the phrase marking particles form a kind of paradigm in that they are at least in partial complementary distribution, they differ significantly in their distributional characteristics. Consequently, it will be argued that *sa* heads prepositional phrases, while *ang* and *ng* head higher-level phrases (i. e. phrases where PPs occur as complements or adjuncts). These phrases may be considered DPs, although they differ in a number of regards from DPs in European languages. Because of these differences, their status as determiners may be open to questions, but there can be little doubt that *ang* and *ng* provide examples par excellence for functional elements displaying (syntactic) head characteristics.

Analyzing *ang* and *ng* as determiners raises the issue of how they relate to other elements which are usually considered determiners, in particular demonstratives. This problem is taken up in the second main part of the article. It is proposed that demonstratives may in fact occur in two different phrase-structural posi-

---

[1] This paper was originally presented at the special panel session Noun Phrase Structures: Functional Elements and Reference Tracking at the Tenth International Conference on Austronesian Linguistics 2006 in Palawan/Philippines. It has been updated slightly, but no attempt has been made to cover more recent developments in the analysis of phrase structure in general, and noun phrase structure in particular. I am grateful to the organisers of the panel, Simon Musgrave and Michael Ewing, for inviting me to this panel. I would also like to thank Jan Strunk for very helpful comments on a pre-conference version of this paper. And I owe very special thanks to Dan Kaufman for detailed, rigorous and challenging comments on a written draft which have helped to clarify some issues and prevented some lapses. Unfortunately, it was not possible to deal with all the challenges in sufficient detail here, a task I therefore will have to leave for the future.

Jens Fleischhauer, Anja Latrouite & Rainer Osswald (eds.). 2016.
Explorations of the Syntax-Semantics Interface. Düsseldorf: dup.

tions, i. e., they occur both as alternate heads instead of *ang* and *ng* and as their complements.

1 Introduction

With a few exceptions (e. g. some temporal adverbials), all non-pronominal arguments and adjuncts in Tagalog are marked by one of the three clitic particles *ang*, *ng* or *sa*.[2] Typical uses of these markers are seen in the following example involving a 3-place predicate in patient voice where *ang* marks the subject, *ng* the non-subject actor and *sa* the recipient:[3]

(1) i\<ni\>abót   **ng** manggagamot **sa** sundalo **ang** itlóg
    handed:PV\<RLS\> gen doctor   LOC soldier   SPEC egg
    'The physician handed the egg to the soldier, ...'

The grammatical category and function of these particles is a matter of debate and there are many different terms in use for referring to them, including *case markers, relation markers, determiners* and *prepositions*.[4] Most analyses, however, agree with regard to the assumption that these markers form a kind of paradigm. There are a number of observations that support this assumption. Most importantly perhaps, as just noted, all non-pronominal argument and adjunct expressions have to have one of these markers. Personal pronouns and demonstratives, which typ-

---

[2] The major exception is personal names (*Pedro, Maria* etc.) which occur with the markers *si, ni* and *kay* (plural *sina, nina, kina*). The distribution of personal name phrases is similar to that of *ang*, *ng* and *sa*-phrases, but there are a number of important differences which preclude the option of simply extending the analysis proposed here for *ang*, *ng* ang *sa* to these markers. The syntax of the personal name markers is not further investigated here, and unless explicitly noted otherwise, the claims made for *ang*, *ng* and *sa* do not apply to them.
Another set of exceptions involves arguments connected to the predicate with the linking particle =*ng/na* as in *pumuntá=ng Manila* (AV:go=LK Manila) 'went to Manila'.

[3] Apart from a few simple phrases used to illustrate basic phrase structure, all examples in this paper are taken from natural discourse. Sources are the author's own corpus of spontaneous spoken narratives, which includes stories from Wolff et al.'s (1991) textbook, Tagalog websites (coded as www) and the texts in Bloomfield (1917). The examples from spoken narratives retain features of the spoken language (in particular common reductions). Glosses for content words are from English (1986). Orthographic conventions follow the standard norm. This is relevant in particular with regard to how the proclitic particles are represented. As they form phonological words with the following item, representations such as *angitlóg* or *ang=itlóg* rather than *ang itlóg* would be more appropriate.

[4] See Reid (2002: 296 f.) for a fuller list of terms used for the elements.

ically are not marked with these markers, occur in three different forms which are known as the *ang*, *ng* and *sa*-form because they have roughly the same distribution as the expressions marked by these clitics.[5] This provides further support for the assumption that they form a kind of paradigm. Furthermore, the markers determine the syntactic distribution of the phrase introduced by them, a point we will return to shortly.

Nevertheless, there are important differences between *sa*-phrases on the one hand and *ang* and *ng*-phrases on the other. Most importantly, *sa*-phrases can be direct complements of *ang* and *ng*. Consequently, it will be argued in section 2 that they occur in different types of phrases while still sharing the essential property of being the syntactic heads of their respective phrases: *sa* heads prepositional phrases, while *ang* and *ng* head determiner phrases.

The proposal that *ang* and *ng* are determiners is not without problems. Among other things, this proposal raises the issue of how they are related to the other main candidates for determiner status in Tagalog, i.e., the demonstratives. Section 3 attends to this issue.

In exploring Tagalog phrase structure, X-Bar theory will be used as a research heuristic, and X-Bar schemata of the type shown in (2) are used as representational devices. The use of X-Bar theory is motivated by the fact that it is a useful tool for investigating hierarchical phrase structure. Furthermore, it provides a representational format which is widely understood. However, using X-Bar theory as a research heuristic does not mean that all universalist assumptions underlying its 'orthodox' uses are adopted here as well. That is, it is not assumed that all major phrases in all languages involve all the positions and functions shown in (2). Instead, every position and function needs to be supported by language-specific, typically distributional evidence. Importantly, no use is made of empty categories and positions simply in order to preserve the putatively universal structure depicted in (2).[6]

---

[5] As in the case of personal name phrases, however, there are a few important differences which preclude a simple extension of the analysis for *ang*, *ng* and *sa*-phrases.

[6] See Kornai & Pullum (1990) for some of the problems created by the unrestrained proliferation of empty categories in X-bar analyses. Note also that much of the following analysis and argument becomes void once it is assumed that the Tagalog phrase markers may be followed by empty nominal heads in all those instances where their co-constituents do not appear to be nominals syntactically and semantically.

(2)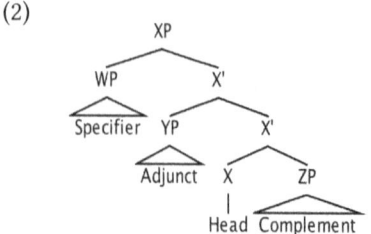

2 On the phrase-structural position of *sa*, and *ang* and *ng*

In form and function, the marker *sa* behaves very much like a (locative) preposition in better known European languages. Apart from some temporal expressions, which may occur without any phrase marker, most adjuncts are introduced with this marker. It also occurs with a number of non-subject arguments, including beneficiaries and recipients. One major difference between European-style prepositions and Tagalog *sa* pertains to the fact that *sa* in Tagalog is the *only* preposition, while European languages typically allow for a broader set of items to function as prepositions. Consequently, *sa* is an obligatory constituent in Tagalog prepositional phrases. Different prepositional meanings and functions are expressed by combining *sa* with a specifier as in *para sa* 'for', *galing sa* 'from', *dahil sa* 'because of', *hanggang sa* 'until', *tungkol sa* 'about', *ukol sa* 'about', or *alinsunod sa* 'according to'. In short, it seems unproblematic to analyse phrases with *sa* very much like prepositional phrases in English, as shown in (3) for the phrase *para sa bata'* 'for the child'.[7]

(3) The structure of PP in Tagalog and English

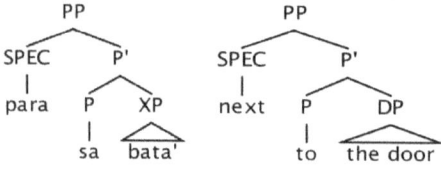

---

[7] I am aware of the fact that SPEC is a highly problematic category (cp. the classic squib by McCawley 1989 and the more recent 'attack' by Starke 2004, inter alia) and that current generative analyses no longer analyse modifiers of prepositions such as *para* and *next* as specifiers (at the cost of an enormous inflation of phrasal heads and categories). The main point here is that despite some differences, phrases marked with *sa* can be analysed very much along the same lines as prepositional phrases in English and similarly structured languages.

Another major difference between Tagalog and English pertains to the category of the complement (the XP in example (3)). In English, this usually has to be a DP (or, if one prefers, an NP).[8] In Tagalog, this is a considerably more complex issue we will return to below.

A third difference between Tagalog *sa* and English prepositions is the fact that *sa* does not allow for intransitive uses (i. e. there are no verb-particle constructions in Tagalog). Consequently, Tagalog *sa* is unequivocally a function word, and it is rather tempting to view it as part of a paradigm of phrase marking function words which would also include the other two phrase-marking clitics *ang* and *ng*. If one assumes that *ang, ng* and *sa* are in a paradigmatic relationship, it would follow that analogous analyses are assumed for *ang* and *ng*. Thus, *ang bata'* 'the/a child' would be analysed as shown in (4).

(4)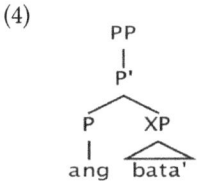

However, the assumption of paradigmatic organisation would imply that *sa* and *ang/ng* are in complementary distribution and occupy the same phrase-structural position. This implication is clearly wrong. While *ang* and *ng* are in complementary distribution, both of them may immediately precede a phrase marked by *sa*, as seen in the following examples:[9]

(5) g<in>agawa   na **ang** **sa** Barangay Catmon
    <in> RDP1-gawá'   na ang sa Barangay Catmon
    <RLS>[UG]-RDP1-made now SPEC LOC Barangay Catmon
    "(the clinic in Barangay Cay Prombo has already been erected,) the one in Barangay Catmon is currently under construction" [www]

---

[8] I am ignoring examples such as *from under the bed* which could be argued to consist of a preposition (*from*) taking a PP (*under the bed*) as complement.

[9] See Reid (2002: 209–211) for a similar argument.

(6) yamang **ang** sa pagóng ay t<um>ubo' hanggáng sa magbunga.
    yamang ang sa pagóng ay <um>tubo' hanggáng sa mag-bunga
    while SPEC LOC turtle PM <AV>growth until LOC AV-flower
    "while that of the turtle grew until it bore fruit."

(7) ang kanilang lagáy ay gaya **ng** sa isang busabos
    ang kanilá=ng lagáy ay gaya ng sa isá=ng busabos
    SPEC 3.PL.DAT=LK position PM like GEN LOC one=LK slave

   o alipin at isang panginoón o hare'.
   o alipin at isá=ng panginoón o hari'
   or slave and one=LK master or king

   'their position was like that of a slave or thrall and a lord or king.'

There are no phrases where *sa* immediately precedes *ang* or *ng* (*sa ang, *sa ng). Consequently, one has to assume a phrase structural position for *ang* and *ng* which is 'higher' than the one for *sa* (i.e. which c-commands *sa*), as shown for the phrase *ang para sa bata'* 'the one for the child' in (8). Recall the remark at the end of section 1 that in this paper no use is made of empty categories in order to preserve putatively universal phrase structures. Hence, given the fact that *ang* and *ng* (like *sa*) cannot occur on their own, the most straightforward assumption is that the PP in examples (5)–(7) is indeed a complement and not an X' or XP-adjunct.

(8)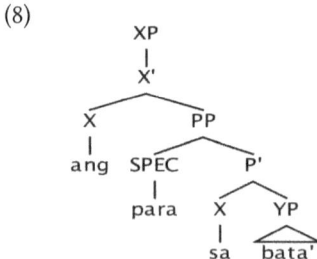

There are other differences between *sa* and the other two markers which make it clear that these indeed belong to different categories. Thus, for example, only *sa* may be affixed with the stative prefix *na*, thereby expressing the meaning 'be in/at/on etc.' as in:

(9) *semantalang   syá 'y **nasa**   tabí ng   ilog*
    samantala=ng siyá ay na-sa   tabí ng   ilog
    meanwhile=LK 3.SG PM RLS.ST-LOC side GEN river
    'When he was close to the riverside,'

There is no **na-ang* or any other combination of an affix + *ang* or *ng*.

Another difference pertains to the possibility of being replaced by a corresponding form of the demonstrative. Both *ang* and *ng* freely allow for this possibility. In the following example, the *ang*-form of the proximal demonstrative *itó* (plus enclitic linker *–ng*) takes the place of *ang*:

(10) *nung   mágising **itong**   iná*
     noón:LK   má-gising itó=ng   iná
     DIST.GEN:LK ST-awake PRX=LK mother
     'When the mother woke up,'

But for *sa*, replacement by the *sa*-form of a demonstrative is impossible. There is no **dito(ng)/diyan(g) Maynila* 'here/there in Manila' as an alternative to *sa Maynila* 'in Manila'.[10] The *sa*-form of the deictic always has to be juxtaposed with a full *sa*-phrase as in:

(11) ***dito**   **sa** kahariang   itó ay merong   isang   sultán*
     PRX.LOC LOC kingdom:LK PRX PM EXIST.DIST.LOC.LK one=LK sultán
     'here in this kingdom there was a sultan'

This also holds for complex prepositions consisting of a specifier and *sa*: **para ditong X* is ungrammatical. It has to be *para dito sa X*.

Furthermore, while *sa* co-occurs with specifying elements such as *para* in the preceding example, there are no such elements which could precede *ang* or *ng*.

Taking now a closer look at *ang* and *ng*, these two markers are identical with regard to their phrase-internal properties. They are clearly in complementary

---

[10] Daniel Kaufman (pc) draws my attention to colloquial examples attested on the Internet, where *ditong Maynila/Pilipinas* occurs in construction with directional predicates such as *puntá* 'go to' or *balík* 'return to'. However, such examples are probably best analysed as involving a clitic positioning of *dító*, the linker linking the predicate to its directional complement (cp. the example *pumuntá=ng Manila* given in footnote 2 above). That is, *kelan balik muh ditong maynila* (when return 2S.GEN PRX.LOC=LK Maynila) 'when will you return here to Manila' (original spelling retained) involves the predicate phrase *balik na maynila* 'return to Manila' with two second position clitics (mu and dító) occurring in between the two elements of this phrase.

distribution, they always occur at the left edge of the phrase they belong to, and they can be replaced by corresponding forms of the demonstratives. They differ with regard to their external distribution: Phrases with *ang* occur in subject function (e.g. *ang itlóg* in (1)), in topic function (see also *ang sa pagong* in (6)):

(12) **ang kuba'** ay ma-hina' ang katawán
SPEC hunchback PM ST-weakness SPEC body
'the hunchback was weak of body' (lit. as for the hunchback, the body was weak)

and as predicates:

(13) **ang langgám** rin ang tumulong sa mga bata'
SPEC ant also SPEC <AV>help LOC PL child
'The ants also helped the children' (lit. The ones who helped the children were also the ants).

The marker *ng*, on the other hand, marks non-subject complements such as *ng manggagamot* in (1) and possessors such as *ng ilog* in (9). When marking non-subject undergoers, *ng* alternates with *sa* in a definiteness alternation: non-subject undergoers marked with *sa* are usually definite; for those marked with *ng* an indefinite reading is preferred, but not obligatory, as demonstrated in (15).

(14) itó ang pusa=ng k<um>ain **sa dagá'**
PRX SPEC cat=LK <AV>eat LOC rat
'This is the cat that ate the rat.' (McFarland 1978:157)

(15) a. itó ang pusang kumain **sa** dagá' unambiguously definite = (14)
 b. itó ang pusang kumain **ng** dagá' indefinite or non-specific preferred, but definite also possible
 c. itó ang pusang kumain **ng isang** dagá' unambiguously indefinite (*isá* = 'one')
 d. itó ang pusang kumain **ng** dagáng **iyón** unambiguously definite (*iyón* = DIST)

Pronouns and personal names always occur in *sa*-form when functioning as non-subject undergoers.

Table 1 summarizes this brief (and not fully exhaustive) survey of the external distribution of *ang*, *ng* and *sa* phrases.

Table 1: :Phrase markers and syntactic functions

ANG	NG	SA
SUBJECT PREDICATE TOPIC	NON-SUBJECT COMPLEMENTS (CLAUSE-LEVEL), POSSESSIVE COMPLEMENTS (PHRASE-LEVEL)	ADJUNCTS, SOME NON-SUBJECT COMPLEMENTS (usually in alternation with *ng*), PREDICATE[11]

Importantly, the distribution of *ang*, *ng* and *sa*-phrases holds *regardless* of what follows the marker in the phrase. As should be obvious from the examples discussed so far, the markers occur with co-constituents of various types and complexity. Thus, for example, *ang* occurs with simple content words such as *itlóg* in (1) or *kuba'* in (12) and with prepositional phrases as in (5) and (6) above. But co-constituents of all three phrase-marking clitics can also be more complex. Thus, they may introduce a verb[12] accompanied by all its arguments and adjuncts except the subject argument as in (cp. also example ?? above):

(16) *at hulih-in ang nag-sá-sabuy sa kanyá ng buhangin*
and catch-PV SPEC RLS.AV-RDP1-spatter LOC 3.SG.DAT GEN sand
'and catch the one who was throwing sand on him'

They may even introduce a complete non-finite clause as in the following two examples.[13] Here the constituents in parentheses constitute full clauses, consisting of a predicate (*manalo* and *talunin*, respectively) and a subject (*tayo* and *ang isang kaaway*, respectively). The predicates are in subjunctive form which is used in non-finite clauses and imperatives. In (18), the clause marked with *ang* (i. e., *ang talunin ang isang kaaway*) itself functions as a (negated) predicate in matrix

---

[11] Predicate uses of *sa*-phrases are not illustrated in the preceding discussion and are not directly relevant for present concerns, but only included for reasons of completeness. Here is a simple example: *sa akin ang Pinas* 'Pinas is mine'.

[12] Verbs are morphologically defined as those content words which are inflected for aspect and mood.

[13] To the best of my knowledge, examples of this type have so far not been discussed in the literature. They are quite rare, but not at all problematical with regard to acceptability in all registers (the first example is from Wolff et al. 1991, the second from Bloomfield 1917). It seems likely that similar examples are possible with *ng* and *sa*, though this has to be investigated in more detail.

construction with a topicalised (= inverted) subject (i.e. *ang hangád ng nagsísipaglaro'*).

(17) talagang nakákatuwá ang [manalo tayo]
talagá=ng naka-RDP1-tuwá' ang maN-talo tayo
really=LK RLS.ST.AV-RDP1-joy SPEC AV-surpassed 1.PL.IN
'It is really fun to win' (lit. when we win).

(18) *Sa sipa' ang hangád ng nagsísipaglaro'*
LOC kick SPEC ambition GEN player

ay hindí ang [talun-in ang isang kaaway]
PM NEG SPEC defeated-PV SPEC one=LK opponent

'In *sipa* the aim of the players is not to defeat an opponent, ...'

The important point for our current concern is that, regardless of the complexity of the constituent following *ang*, a phrase headed by *ang* can function, and can *only* function, as subject, topic or predicate. That is, the syntactic distribution of the phrase is fully determined by *ang*. Similarly, the syntactic distribution of *ng* and *sa*-phrases is fully determined by *ng* and *sa*, except that in some of their uses they regularly alternate in accordance with definiteness distinctions.

Consequently, there can be little doubt as to the fact that *ang* and *ng* like *sa* are the heads of their respective phrases, at least with regard to being the "external representative" (Zwicky 1993) of the phrase, a core characteristic of syntactic heads. Strictly speaking, and unlike demonstratives in both English and Tagalog, these markers are *not* distributional equivalents of their phrases in the sense of Bloomfield (1933) because they cannot form a phrase all by themselves. They minimally need one further co-constituent. Hence, for a phrase such as *ang bahay* we can assume the constituent structure given in (19).

(19)
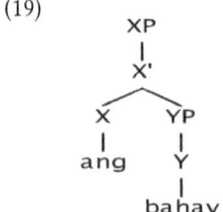

Strictly speaking, *ang* or *ng* as phrase heads instantiate the X-Bar schema only incompletely in that they do not allow for specifiers (which, as noted above, is one of the differences between them and the preposition *sa*).

While it is widely accepted that *sa* is a preposition and hence a phrase headed by *sa* is a PP, there is little agreement as to the category of *ang* and *ng*. I have argued elsewhere (Himmelmann 1984, 1991, 1998: 333–336) that *ang* is best analysed as a specific article and *ng* as its genitive form. If that is accepted, *ang* and *ng* can be considered determiners, and phrases headed by them as DPs, as shown in (20) (and done henceforth in this paper). This categorization would also appear to be supported by the fact noted above that they may be replaced by the corresponding form of a demonstrative. However, this is not quite straightforward support because demonstratives may also co-occur with *ang* and *ng* in what appears to be a single phrase. We will return to this issue in the following section.

(20)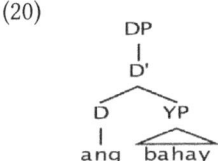

In many ways, Tagalog *ang* and *ng*-phrases are much clearer instances of a DP than the kinds of nominal expressions in European languages that have been hypothesized to instantiate this phrase type. Most importantly, and unlike articles in most European languages, the Tagalog functional elements are obligatory – they occur without exception in all phrases of this type – and they *fully* determine the distribution of the phrase they head. Note that the question of what the actual category of *ang* and *ng* is, is at least in part independent of whether they are phrasal (co-)heads.[14]

I consider it an unresolved issue whether it is necessary and useful to attribute a case function to *ang* and *ng*-phrases in addition to their function as determiners. Calling *ng* the "genitive form of *ang*", as I just did, obviously invites the inference

---

[14] It is clear that functional elements functioning as phrase heads do not show all the head properties usually assigned to phrase heads. Most importantly, they are not heads in semantic terms. I consider it an open issue how the special head status of functional elements is best captured. Possibly, the kind of co-head analysis used in LFG (cp., for example, Bresnan 2001) is more adequate than simply applying the standard phrase structure schema to functional elements as done here.

that at least *ng* is a case marker. However, while this is a convenient gloss giving a rough, though incomplete and in some ways also misleading idea of the distribution of *ng*-phrases (see Table 1 above), it is far from clear whether this form is in any relevant sense similar to genitive case forms in Latin, German or Icelandic, or to phrases marked by *of* in English. Both historically and synchronically, there are good reasons to assume that *ng* consists of the linker *na* plus the specific article *ang*, i. e., that it marks 'linked referential phrases' and thus is but one of the many types of modifiers marked with a linker in Tagalog.[15]

Both *ang* and *ng*-phrases are thus prototypical instances of what Van Valin (2008:168) calls a "reference phrase" (RP). A major advantage of this concept is the fact that it remains noncommittal as to the lexical category of the constituent(s) appearing within such a phrase, thereby avoiding the well-entrenched confusion between lexical categories and syntactic functions enshrined in the classic phrase structure rule S → NP + VP.

The analysis proposed here largely agrees with the analysis in Reid (2002), who also considers *ang* to be a syntactic head. However, Reid provides an analysis in terms of dependency rather than constituency, which makes it difficult to compare the analyses in all details. According to Reid, phrase marking clitics such as Tagalog *ang* or Bontok *nan* are *nominal* heads of their phrases, roughly meaning something like 'the one'. The fact that they cannot form phrases by themselves is accounted for by the feature [+xtns], which means that they obligatorily require a dependent predicate to form grammatical phrases. This is illustrated with the following stemma for the Bontok phrase equivalent to Tagalog *ang malakí* 'the big one' (= example 28 from Reid 2002).[16]

(28) Bontok

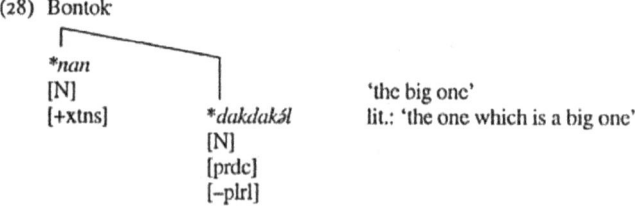

'the big one'
lit.: 'the one which is a big one'

---

[15] The linker itself in all likelihood derives from a (not case-marked!) demonstrative (Himmelmann 1997: 159–188, 2001: 834 f.), which is one reason for not considering *ng* a genitive case marker.

[16] Note that phrase marking in Bontok, and more generally in northern Philippine languages, is quite distinct from the one found in Tagalog. Reid (2006) provides a detailed survey of the systems encountered in the northern languages.

Much of Reid's argument as to why *ang* is a noun rather than a determiner depends on definitions and assumptions specific to the lexicase framework, which need not be further discussed here. Still, even abstracting away from the specifics of the theoretical framework used, there appears to be a major problem with this analysis relating to the fact that it fails adequately to capture the highly grammaticised status of phrase marking clitics such as *ang* and *ng* (but see Reid (2000: 36–42) for a more dynamic version of this analysis, which provides for the possibility that the phrase marking clitics no longer head the constructions but rather become dependents themselves). While the assumption that they are nominals meaning 'the one' may make sense in cases such as *ang malakí* 'the one which is a big one' or *ang bahay*, which in terms of this analysis would have to mean 'the one which is a house', it is difficult to see how one could account for examples such as (17) and (18). In these examples, the complement of *ang* is a complete clause, and it is not clear how this clause could function as the dependent predicate required by the phrase-marking clitic.

Furthermore, in Reid's analysis, it would appear that the phrase-marking clitics are very similar to demonstratives, except that the latter are additionally marked for deictic distinctions. Reid does not discuss demonstratives explicitly, but according to his stemmata (20), (22), (23) and (27), demonstratives are also analysed as the nominal heads of their phrases. As already mentioned above, phrase-marking clitics and demonstratives indeed appear to share some essential characteristics as the latter may replace the former (cp. example (10)). But the relationship between the two classes of elements and the phrase-structural position of demonstratives is more complex than this, as further discussed in the next section.

3   On the phrase-structural position of demonstratives

Demonstratives in Tagalog may be used pronominally, i. e., forming a major constituent all by themselves. An example is the use of *itó* in (14) above where it functions as the predicate in an equational clause. They may also be used "adnominally", that is, as a co-constituent in a nominal expression. In this use, they have to be linked to their co-constituents with a linker as in *itó-ng bahay* 'this house'.

Before looking more closely at the phrase-structural position of demonstratives, it will be useful to briefly look at complex nominal expressions without a demonstrative such as *ang malakíng bahay* 'the big house'. The major observation with regard to these expressions is the fact that there is no straightforward distributional evidence with regard to their heads. Importantly, the order of the co-constituents of *ang* is variable (both *malakíng bahay* and *bahay na malakí* are possible), there is always a linker in between co-constituents of these phrases, and no constituent is obligatory in the sense that only one of them has to be present (i. e. both *ang malakí* and *ang bahay* are well-formed phrases). Note that all of this does not hold true for *ang* (or *ng*): change of its position results in ungrammatical phrases (**bahay ang malaki*, **malaking bahay ang*), and *ang* cannot freely be omitted or occur by itself. Consequently, in a first approximation, we may hypothesize that the structure of phrases such as *malaking bahay* is flat, as shown in

(21)
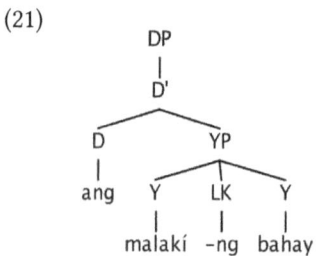

This is almost certainly not the complete story because, on the one hand, very little is known so far with regard to possible constraints on the variable ordering of constituents in these expressions and the pragmatic or semantic correlates of different orders.[17] On the other hand, there may be distributional evidence for identifying the head of such a phrase provided by constraints on the placement of second-position clitics and the plural word *mga*.[18] This, however, is a rather complex issue, which cannot be further explored here. As a consequence, no at-

---

[17] Kaufman (2005: 192 f.) proposes that different orders here correlate with differences in information structure in that the last element in the phrase tends to receive a phrasal accent and to constitute the most salient or contrastive element. A similar suggestion is made by Schachter & Otanes (1972) and Schachter (1987: 944), who, however, limit their claims to demonstratives as further discussed below.

[18] See Kroeger (1993: 153 f.) for some preliminary observations regarding second-position clitics, and Kolmer (1998: 11–18) on *mga* in nominal expressions.

tempt is being made to assign the complement of the determiner in these phrases to a specific category. Instead, the non-specific label YP is used throughout this article.

Returning to demonstratives, there are two major features which have to be accounted for. First, like most other elements in Tagalog nominal expressions, the position of demonstratives is variable. They can appear at the very beginning and at the very end of such expressions, as seen in the following examples:

(22) ***ito**=ng ma-laki=ng bahay*   'this big house'
     PRX=LK ST-size=LK house
     also possible:
     ***itong** bahay na malakí*
     *malaking bahay na **itó***
     *bahay na malaki na **itó***

However, it is not possible to place the demonstrative in between other constituents of a nominal expression:

(23) a. ?**bahay na **itong** malakí*
     b. ??**malakíng **itong** bahay*

Some native speakers consider these examples marginally acceptable (hence the ?) but they then have a clearly different structure: the demonstrative forms a constituent with the word following it, and this sub-constituent is in apposition to the first word. Hence (23)(a) would mean something like 'a/the house, this big one' and (b) sth. like 'a/the big one, this house'. The latter obviously is pragmatically highly marked and thus not liked at all by native speakers (to date, no examples for either (a) or (b) have been found in texts). We will return to this point below.

The second point to take note of pertains to the fact that there can be two demonstratives in what appears to be a single nominal expression, as in:

(24) ***itong** bahay na **itó***   'this house'

(25) ***ito**=ng amáng   sultang   **itó***
     PRX=LK father:LK sultan:LK PRX
     'this sultan-father'

In line with the first observation, both demonstratives have to be at the outermost periphery of the expression. Obviously, it is somewhat unusual to have what appears to be the same element twice in a single expression. I will now try to show that this is in fact not the case. Rather, the two demonstratives in this construction occupy different hierarchical positions and also have somewhat different functions.[19]

There is evidence that demonstratives in the left periphery occur in the same position as *ang* because, in more formal registers at least, *ang* and demonstratives in leftmost position are in complementary distribution. Hence, a phrase such as

(26) ??*ang itong bahay*

is considered ungrammatical in Standard Tagalog (as opposed to *ang bahay na itó*, which is fine). In informal registers, including chat room communication, however, examples such as the following occur frequently enough that one probably has to grant them some acceptability:

(27) *Importanteng-importante **ang ito**=ng ebidensiya.*
    DUP.LK-importante   SPEC PRX=LK evidence
    'This evidence is very important.' [www]

Nevertheless, the fact that *ang* and *ng* are usually missing when a phrase is introduced by a demonstrative suggests that demonstratives in the left periphery in fact occupy the same structural position as *ang* (and *ng* when they occur in *ng*-form). This is not very surprising on the assumption that both *ang/ng* and demonstratives are determiners. In further support of this assumption, it can be noted that a reduced form of the distal demonstrative, i.e., *yung* (< *iyón-ng*), is replacing *ang* in many of its uses in colloquial speech (i.e., it is being grammaticised as a new determiner). Importantly, *yung* shares two of the core characteristics of *ang*, i.e., it cannot form a phrase by itself and it has to occur in leftmost position.

What about demonstratives in rightmost position then? An initial hypothesis would be that they are hierarchically on the same level as the other constituents in a nominal expression, as illustrated in (28):

---

[19] Kaufman (2010: 217 f.) also argues that there are two structural positions for demonstratives, based on the fact that only demonstratives in the left periphery can be case-marked. Demonstratives in the right periphery always take the default *ang*-form, regardless of the case marking of the phrase they appear in (i.e. it is *sa bahay na itó* and *ng bahay na itó*, not **sa bahay na dito* or **ng bahay na nitó*).

Notes on "Noun Phrase Structure" in Tagalog

(28)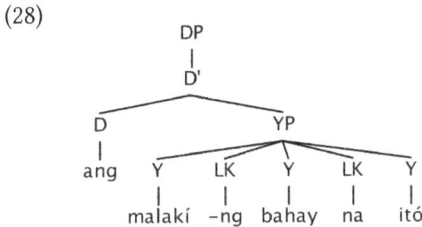

However, such an analysis would wrongly predict that the demonstratives are freely convertible within YPs. One way to ensure that the demonstrative occurs in rightmost position would be to analyse it as being in apposition to the other members of a nominal expression. A possible structure is given in (29).

(29)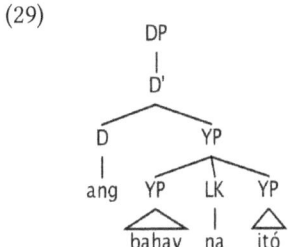

This analysis would also predict that it is possible to reverse the order of the two adjoined YPs in (29), hence creating phrases of the type *ang itong bahay*. As already mentioned in connection with examples (26) and (27) above, such structures are possible in colloquial style, but highly marked in terms of the standard language.

An appositional structure of the type shown in (29) is needed for independent reasons to account for examples such as (30) where a personal name expression (marked by *si*) is in apposition to a common noun expression (*kanyang dalaga* 'his daughter'):

(30) *ang   kanya=ng   dalaga   na si Magayón*
     SPEC 3.SG.DAT=LK young_woman LK PN Magayón
     'his daughter Magayón'

(31)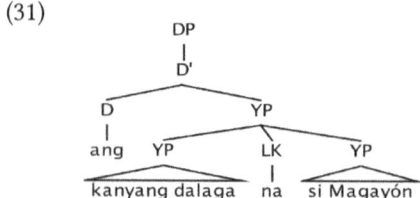

The major alternative to the analysis in (29) would be to consider demonstratives in the right periphery (and also personal noun phrases such as *si Magayón* in (30)) to be in apposition 'one level higher up'. That is, rightmost *itó* could be considered to form a DP by itself which functions as an adjunct to the rest of the phrase, as shown in (32). Since the demonstratives can also be used pronominally, the big advantage of this analysis would be that one could generalize a '(pronominal) head of DP' analysis for all uses of the demonstratives.

(32)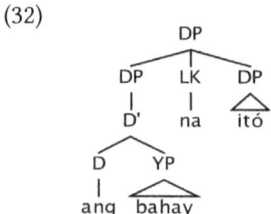

However, there are a number of problems for this alternative analysis. The perhaps least important problem is that it does not allow for structures such as (27) where the demonstrative occurs immediately after *ang*. Furthermore, phrases such as *itóng bahay na itó* would consist of two adjoined DPs headed by the same element, which, while not totally impossible, is not very plausible.

More importantly, demonstratives may form the only other constituent in a nominal expression headed by *ang*. This is necessarily so when demonstratives are pluralized with the plural word *mangá* (conventionally spelled *mgá*) as in (33). But it also occurs when there is no other element in the nominal expression, as in (34).

(33) **ang mga itó** y panghule   lamang ng   mga pare' ng   kwalta
 ang mgá itó ay paN-huli   lamang ng   mgá pare' ng   kuwalta
 SPEC PL   PRX PM GER-a_catch only   GEN PL   priest GEN money
 'these (concepts) were merely a device of the priests for getting money'

(34) *isang   araw ay   inimbita   niyá   **ang   itó***
     isá=ng   araw ay   -in-imbitá   niya   ang   itó
     one=LK   day   PM -RLS(UG)-invite   3.SG.POSS SPEC   PRX

   na tumulóy   sa   kanyang   bahay
   na -um-tulóy   sa   kanyá=ng   bahay
   LK -AV-come_in LOC   3.SG.DAT=LK   house

   'One day she invited this (latter) one into her house.' [www]

Analyzing these examples as appositional along the lines indicated in (32) would imply that *ang* occurs without a complement in these examples. This would be highly unusual since it is nowhere else attested.

I assume that the demonstrative in these examples is identical to the demonstrative which occurs at the right periphery, since all major constituents in a nominal expression may function as the sole complement of *ang*. That is, each of the three main co-constituents of *ang* in *ang malakíng bahay na itó* can be the sole co-constituent of *ang*:

(35) *ang bahay*   'the house'
     ang malakí   'the big one'
     ang itó   'this one'

This, to my mind, strongly suggests that demonstratives, apart from being heads of DPs, also may form phrases of the same type as content words such as *bahay* or *malakí*. Consequently, the analysis given in (29) is to be preferred to the one in (32) despite the fact that it requires a double categorization of demonstratives: they are both (pronominal) heads of DPs and deictic modifiers which occur as adjuncts in the periphery of nominal expressions, preferably in the rightmost position. As heads, they can form DPs on their own or by taking further complements. In the latter case, they are always the leftmost element in a DP.

To further support this analysis, one would expect some semantic or pragmatic differences corresponding to the difference in phrase-structural position. Schachter (1987: 944; see also Schachter & Otanes 1972: 120) notes in this regard

> Although a demonstrative and the noun it modifies may occur in either order, the alternative orderings are generally not in free variation, but are, rather, conditioned by discourse factors. The constituent that comes second typically represents the more salient information and may, for example, be contrastive.

He illustrates this with the following two examples (accents added and glossing modified in accordance with conventions used in this paper):

(36) *Mahal   itong   galáng. (Pero mura itong   singsíng.)*
 mahál   itó =ng galáng pero mura itó=ng   singsíng
 expensive PRX =LK bracelet but cheap PRX=LK ring
 'This bracelet is expensive. (But this ring is cheap.)'

(37) *Mahál   ang   galang na itó. (Pero mura ang   galang na iyán.)*
 expensive SPEC bracelet LK PRX but cheap SPEC bracelet LK MED
 'This bracelet is expensive. (But that bracelet is cheap.)'

In terms of the current analysis, one could further add that in preposed position, demonstratives play a more "determiner-like" role, taking on functions of the phrase-marking clitics *ang* and *ng*, while in postposed position, their function is more clearly deictic.

4 Conclusion

In this paper, it has been argued that the phrase-marking clitics *ang*, *ng* and *sa* in Tagalog are the syntactic heads of the phrases introduced by them. More specifically, *sa* is a local preposition heading a PP, while *ang* and *ng* are determiners heading DPs. While there are sufficient similarities between Tagalog PPs and DPs and their equivalents in European languages to warrant use of these category labels, it should be clearly understood that the former differ from the latter in that the nature of the complements of P and D in Tagalog is still in need of much further research and may turn out to differ substantially. As indicated in section 2, both functional elements appear to allow for a broader range of complements than is usually assumed for Ps and Ds. Most importantly, Tagalog Ds allow PPs and clauses among their complements.

Similarly, Tagalog demonstratives are not just one kind of determiner, interchangeable with the determiners *ang* and *ng*. Instead, they are also adjuncts which have to occur in the peripheral position of nominal expressions, typically in rightmost position, but in some registers also in leftmost position, immediately *after* the phrase-initial determiner.

Abbreviations

AV	ACTOR VOICE
DAT	DATIVE
DIST	DISTAL
DUP	DUPLICATION
GEN	GENITIVE
GER	GERUND
IN	INCLUSIVE
LK	LINKER
LOC	LOCATIVE
NEG	NEGATION
PL	PLURAL
PM	PREDICATE MARKER
PN	PERSONAL NAME
POSS	POSSESSIVE
PRX	PROXIMAL
PV	PATIENT VOICE
RLS	REALIS
RDP	REDUPLICATION (numbers indicate different formal types of reduplication)
SG	SINGULAR
SPEC	SPECIFIC ARTICLE
ST	STATIVE
UG	UNDERGOER

References

Arka, I W. & M. Ross (eds.). 2005. *The many faces of Austronesian voice systems.* Canberra: Pacific Linguistics.

Bloomfield, L. 1917. *Tagalog texts with grammatical analysis.* Urbana: The University of Illinois.

Bloomfield, L. 1933. *Language.* London: Allen & Unwin.

Bresnan, J. 2001. *Lexical-functional syntax.* Oxford: Blackwell.

English, L. J. 1986. *Tagalog-English dictionary.* Manila: National Book Store.

Himmelmann, N. P. 1984. *Linking im Tagalog.* Universität München, Master's thesis.

Himmelmann, N. P. 1991. *The Philippine challenge to universal grammar.* Arbeitspapier Nr. 15. Köln: Institut für Sprachwissenschaft.

Himmelmann, N. P. 1997. *Deiktikon, Artikel, Nominalphrase: Zur Emergenz syntaktischer Struktur.* Tübingen: Niemeyer.

Himmelmann, N. P. 1998. Regularity in irregularity: article use in adpositional phrases. *Linguistic Typology* 2: 315–353.

Himmelmann, N. P. 2001. Articles. In M. Haspelmath, E. König, W. Oesterreicher & W. Raible (eds.), *Language typology and language universals*, 831–841. Berlin: de Gruyter.

Kaufman, D. A. 2005. Aspects of pragmatic focus in Tagalog. In I W. Arka & M. Ross (eds.), *The many faces of Austronesian voice systems*, 175–196.

Kaufmann, D. A. 2010. *The morphosyntax of Tagalog clitics: a typologically driven approach.* Cornell University dissertation.

Kolmer, A. 1998. *Pluralität im Tagalog.* Arbeitspapier Nr. 31 (Neue Folge). Köln: Institut für Sprachwissenschaft.

Kornai, A. & G. K. Pullum. 1990. The X-bar theory of phrase structure, *Language* 66: 24–50.

Kroeger, P. R. 1993. *Phrase Structure and Grammatical Relations in Tagalog.* Stanford: Stanford University Press.

McCawley, J. D. 1989. INFL, Spec, and other fabulous beasts. *Behavioral and Brain Sciences* 12: 350–352.

McFarland, C. D. 1978. Definite objects and subject selection in Philippine languages. In C. Edrial-Luzares & A. Hale (eds.), *Studies in Philippine linguistics*, vol. 2/1, 139–182. Manila: Linguistic Society of the Philippines.

References

Reid, L. A. 2000. Sources of Proto-Oceanic initial prenasalization: the view from outside Oceanic. In V. P. De Guzman & B. Bender (eds.), *Grammatical analysis: morphology, syntax and semantics: studies in honor of Stanley Starosta* (Oceanic Linguistics Special Publications No. 29), 30–45. Honolulu: University of Hawai'i Press.

Reid, L. A. 2002. Determiners, nouns or what? Problems in the analysis of some commonly occurring forms in Philippine languages'. *Oceanic Linguistics* 41: 295–309.

Reid, L. A. 2006. On reconstructing the morphosyntax of Proto-Northern Luzon, Philippines. *Philippine Journal of Linguistics* 37: 1–64.

Schachter, P. 1987. Tagalog. In B. Comrie (ed.), *The world's major languages*, 936–958. London: Croom Helm.

Schachter, P. & F. T. Otanes.1972. *Tagalog reference grammar.* Berkeley: University of California Press.

Starke, M. 2004. On the inexistence of specifiers and the nature of heads. In Adriana Belletti (ed.), *The cartography of syntactic structures*, vol. 3: structures and beyond (Oxford Studies in Comparative Syntax), 252–268. New York: Oxford University Press.

Van Valin, R. D., Jr. 2008. RPs and the nature of lexical and syntactic categories in role and reference grammar. In R. D. Van Valin, Jr. (ed.), *Investigations of the syntax-semantics-pragmatics interface*, 161–178. Amsterdam: Benjamins.

Wolff, J. U., M. T. C. Centeno & V. Rau Der-Hwa. 1991. *Pilipino through self-instruction*, 4 vols. Ithaca: Cornell Southeast Asia Program.

Zwicky, A. M. 1993. Heads, bases and functors. In G. G. Corbett, N. M. Fraser & S. McGlashan (eds.), *Heads in grammatical theory*, 292–315. Cambridge: Cambridge University Press.

Author

Nikolaus P. Himmelmann
Department of Linguistics
University of Cologne
sprachwissenschaft@uni-koeln.de

Integrated and Non-Integrated Left Dislocation: A Comparative Study of LD in Avatime, Tundra Yukaghir & Whitesands

Dejan Matić, Saskia van Putten & Jeremy Hammond

Left-dislocated elements seem to be extremely frequent, if not universal, across languages. Despite their surface similarity, however, they tend to display strikingly different features, both structurally and functionally. Our purpose is to investigate the structural variability of left-dislocation constructions cross-linguistically. The study is based on a fine-grained analysis of naturally occurring instances of left dislocation in three geographically and genealogically distinct languages — Avatime (Kwa, Ghana), Tundra Yukaghir (isolate, north-eastern Siberia), and Whitesands (Oceanic, Vanuatu). The formal parameters of variation investigated include the frequency and type of resumption within the clause, integration within the clause via case/cross-referencing on the verb, recursivity, and connectivity effects such as island sensitivity. We show that the degree of integration of left-dislocation constructions in the sentence can vary from language to language. This variability is used as a basis for a discussion of the notions of *clause* and *sentence*, both within RRG and within general linguistic theory. We conclude that there is no simple formal paradigm (e. g. integrated vs. non-integrated) to satisfactorily explain the diversity we find in this language sample. Instead, we propose to differentiate different degrees and types of integration, which seem to provide a better account of cross-linguistic variation.

1 Introduction

The received wisdom about Left Dislocation (LD) is that it is a structure in which an element of the clause does not occur in its canonical position, but precedes its mother clause; the canonical position of the LD element is occupied by a coreferential pronominal (e. g. Givón 1976, Dik 1978, Haegeman 1991, Alexiadou 2006, Shaer 2009). This is illustrated in (1).

(1) (…) **Bunyan, you know, *he*'s older than the rocks** (…) (Geluykens 1992: 90)

LD raises two major classification problems. First, it is not the only type of structure in which elements in a clause are displaced to the left. On the one hand, there is topicalisation (TOP), in which the left-displaced element is usually considered to reside within the confines of the clause. On the other hand, various types of online production phenomena, such as hesitations, false starts, self-corrections, etc., often do not formally differ from canonical LDs. Second, even if LD proper is somehow disentangled from the rest of detachment structures, there is a considerable variation within the category itself: some instances of LD are restricted as to the type of resumptive expression, while others are undifferentiated in this respect; the presence of a prosodic break between the dislocated element and the clause is frequent but optional; the same optionality characterises the presence of connectivity effects within LD structures.

These issues have bearing on both the practical question of classifying displaced elements in a corpus of any one language and the question of the correct syntactic analysis of LD. The necessity to differentiate LD from both speech disfluencies and clause-level phenomena (TOP) testifies to its perceived status as residing between a syntactic structure proper and a production-level phenomenon. LD displays features of a syntactic template (see Lambrecht 2001, Alexiadou 2006 and Shaer 2009 for recent overviews) and has conventionalised discourse functions (e. g. Prince 1997, 1998), but it does not seem to be fully integrated into the clause to which it relates.

One consequence of this in-between status is that, at the level of identifying and classifying individual instances of displacement in a corpus, there is no principled way of telling LD and speech disfluencies apart. This has to be done on an item-by-item basis with the help of various criteria such as presence of hesitation and self-correction markers, prosodic signals, and the reconstruction of the general intention of the speaker.

The problem of telling apart instances of LD from those of TOP is a more intricate and theory-laden one. The presence of a resumptive pronoun is considered to be the main property by which LD is to be distinguished from TOP, which does not permit resumptives (e. g. Gregory & Michaelis 2001: 1667). There are several other criteria, prosodic and syntactic, that are often adduced as characteristic for LD. It is claimed that LD forms a prosodic phrase marked by boundary tones and/or a prosodic break. However, this does not seem to be universally applicable: special prosodic phrasing is at best optional in a number of languages and can therefore not be used as a definitive criterion to identify LD (see e. g. Geluykens 1992: 92ff. for English, Avanzi et al. 2010 and Avanzi 2011 for French, Feldhausen 2008: 175ff. for Catalan). The syntactic criteria are based on the idea that elements outside of the clause proper cannot be sensitive to clause-internal constraints, while those that are within the clause do not react to discourse-level restrictions. It has been claimed that TOP is sensitive to island constraints, anaphor binding, and similar phenomena, while LD is not; and vice versa, LD is restricted with respect to syntactic contexts in which it can appear (ban on embedding) and with respect to word class (no LD adverbs, due to lack of reference), while TOP does not display restrictions of this kind (Shaer 2009). There are also problems with these types of criteria: first, they do not seem to be universally true (there are differences even between such closely related languages as English and German, Shaer 2009); second, connectivity tests, island tests etc. are applicable only after the fact, i. e. only after a construction has been already identified as an instance of LD or TOP, and are as such not useful in detecting LD structures in naturally occurring speech.

This variability of the properties of LD — the second classificatory problem introduced above — has led linguists to postulate the existence of a number of different subtypes of LD, the major ones being Hanging Topic LD and 'Movement' LD[1], reanalysed as Integrated and Non-Integrated LD in recent research (Shaer 2009)[2]. The non-integrated type is prosodically separated, displays no connec-

---

[1] The latter includes *Contrastive LD* in Germanic and *Clitic LD* in Romance (Anagnostopoulou 1997, Cinque 1997, Alexiadou 2006).

[2] This distinction is often obfuscated by terminological confusion: some authors use the term *left dislocation* only for the non-integrated, hanging-topic type (e. g. Ross 1967[1986], Cinque 1990), while others (e. g. Altmann 1981, Frey 2004) restrict it to the integrated types. In this paper, the

tivity effects, etc., and is therefore clearly extraclausal. The integrated types are prosodically integrated, have a restricted repertoire of resumptives, show connectivity, etc., so that they count as somehow more integrated into the clause. The important point is that the common denominator for the assumed variable types is still the resumptive expression: since all other features are unevenly distributed across LD types, resumptives are the only reliable indicator of the LD structure.

However, this focus on resumptive pronouns is also problematic, as it leaves a number of phenomena outside the scope of LD studies. Firstly, it excludes the so-called Chinese-style topics (Chafe 1976), which share a number of features with typical LDs, but cannot be cross-referenced with resumptive pronouns. Secondly, the status of adjuncts and many types of adverbials is unclear, as some of these kinds of expressions seem to canonically appear in positions which resemble LD but are at best optionally followed by a resumptive pronoun (Lambrecht 2001: 1059). Thirdly, the focus on resumptive pronouns ignores languages which, due to the possibility of zero anaphora, do not need resumptive elements but may still have LD. This paper tackles these issues in some detail.

With respect to its syntactic structure, there is little agreement on how LD should be analysed. Much has been written about LD in the generative framework, and no consensus seems to have been reached. Some approaches seem to assume that LD elements have a specified position in the left periphery of the clause (see Section 3.1 for discussion of this approach). Since this kind of analysis incurs a number of problems, a different analysis has been proposed, according to which LD elements are so-called orphans, i.e. separate sentential fragments that are not part of the syntactic structure but are linked to the clause via discourse-level linking rules (Haegeman 1991). As we indicated above, not all LD constructions are the same, so that integrated LD elements are commonly treated as left-peripheral within the clausal domain, while non-integrated LD elements are analysed as orphans. Some recent proposals (De Cat 2007, Ott 2012) remove integrated LDs from the clausal domain, too, and consider them to be separate referential and/or clausal entities; their intra-clausal properties are explained via ellipsis or adjunction. In effect, these recent approaches bring the two postulated types of LD closer together, treating them both as extraclausal entities. For the sake of brevity, we shall use the term 'orphan' for all types of analysis that

---

term LD is used broadly to cover all types of structures that include pre-clausal elements, as has become common in the literature in the last decade.

assume an extra-clausal nature of LD elements, irrespective of the details of the analysis itself.

In Role and Reference Grammar (RRG), two syntactic domains are recognised: clause and sentence (Foley & Van Valin 1984, Van Valin & LaPolla 1997, Van Valin 2005). For the purposes of this paper, we assume quite simple definitions of these two domains. The clause is the domain that comprises everything that depends on the predicate plus clause-level adjuncts (see Van Valin & LaPolla 1997 on the notion of dependency, and Van Valin 2005 on types of adjuncts). The sentence comprises one or more coordinate or co-subordinate clauses, and/or extraclausal elements which have a determinate position in the syntactic architecture, such as sentence-level adjuncts (Van Valin 2005); in practice, sentences are often coextensive with clauses. The essential point is that the clause is not the only level at which syntactic rules operate, but that there is one more level, not directly bound by the predicate, but still subject to syntactic, as opposed to discourse, rules — the level of sentence. This allows for a dedicated position for LD elements, the left-detached position (LDP), which is, as it were, between integrated and non-integrated: within the sentence but outside of the clause (Van Valin & LaPolla 1997: 36).

The purpose of this paper is to assess the status of LD from a cross-linguistic perspective. We investigate whether LD exists as a grammatical phenomenon in three non-European languages and if so, whether this is the same grammatical phenomenon in each of the languages. The paper deals with LD in three genealogically unrelated and geographically distant languages — Avatime (Kwa, Niger-Congo; spoken in Ghana), Tundra Yukaghir (Paleo-Siberian, Isolate; spoken in north-eastern Siberia) and Whitesands (Oceanic, Austronesian; spoken in Vanuatu). We show that there is no single linguistic property that can reliably identify LD constructions crosslinguistically. Instead, we need a set of criteria which is different from language to language. Furthermore, the contradictory evidence of syntactic tests and morphological clues seem to imply that there might not be one or two right syntactic analyses of LD, but LDs have to be defined on a language-to-language basis. This means that different structures labelled Left Dislocation are in a relationship of family resemblance to each other rather than being mere instantiations of one or two universal syntactic structures.

To make comparison possible, we make use of a heuristic concept of LD, which does not have any ontological pretensions apart from enabling the researcher to find structurally and/or functionally similar structures. This procedure resembles Haspelmath's (2010) idea of comparative concepts which are devised as a *tertium comparationis* for cross-linguistic research defined on the basis of minimal common denominators. Our heuristic concept of LD comprises all structures which include an element that precedes the clause and stands in some kind of relationship to it, excluding those instances which are readily identified as speech disfluencies. Importantly, we do not assume any definition of LD but rather define what LD is for each language and only subsequently try to determine the similarities and differences.

We have identified LD elements in corpora of spontaneous speech which were collected during fieldtrips to the communities where the languages are spoken. In addition, we have done some elicitation to collect grammaticality judgments in order to obtain negative evidence or check whether constructions not found in the corpora are possible. Our corpora comprise various genres, including conversations, public speeches and narratives. Each corpus contains roughly seven hours of text. The examples used in the paper come from these larger corpora. For statistical purposes, a smaller corpus of one to two hours from each language was chosen. The numerical data in the paper refer to the instances of LD found in these subsets of the larger corpora.

The paper is organised as follows. In the next section, we outline the syntactic features required to identify LD in the target languages. We then use the structures identified in this way as a basis for our comparison and discuss structural similarities and differences between the systems in Section 3. Section 4 concentrates on the nature of LD in the three languages. We also consider what additions or changes need to be made in the typology of LD, given the data presented in this chapter. We conclude in Section 5 with remarks on how RRG could best handle an updated typology, and highlight potential areas for future research.

2 Identifying left dislocation in three languages

In this section we describe the defining features of LD in Avatime, Tundra Yukaghir and Whitesands. Before we go into the details of each language, two general observations need to be made. Firstly, all three languages make use of zero anaphora to refer to definite specific referents, usually those that are active or activated in the given context. As the referent of the LD element is necessarily activated at the moment when the clause that follows it is pronounced, these kinds of languages can practically always use NP gaps that are coreferential with the LD element. In other words, if the clause following the displaced element does not contain a resumptive, this does not necessarily mean that it is not LD. Resumptives, even though helpful in identifying LD structures, are thus not sufficient as diagnostics of LD in these languages. Secondly, prosody is not a reliable indicator of LD in any of the three languages: LD can be signalled by a prosodic break, but this is not necessarily the case and, more importantly, a prosodic break does not necessarily indicate LD.

2.1 Avatime

In Avatime, word order is rigidly SVO. Apart from LD, the only displacement construction is the focus construction, in which the focused element occurs clause-initially and is marked with the focus marker, which is a final extra-high tone. There is no topicalisation construction. Subjects are obligatorily marked on the verb (e. g. Avatime is head-marking with respect to the subject[3]) and there is no case marking. The sentence structure in Avatime looks as follows:

(2) LD&AdjunctClause_[Foc_[S_V_O]]

LD is most easily recognized in Avatime by the occurrence of a resumptive element. Of all identified cases of left-dislocated objects (N = 75), 91 % (N = 68) have a resumptive element, as in (3). The other 7 % are identified as LD simply by occurring before the verb (4), which is otherwise not possible for an object (unless marked as focused with the final extra-high tone). Of left-dislocated subjects (N = 58), 36 % (N = 21) are identified as LD by the occurrence of a resumptive element. An example can be seen in (5). This percentage is smaller than that for objects because independent subject pronouns, unlike object pronouns, are optional, due to the obligatory subject marking on the verb. The subject LD cases without independent resumptive element are identified as such because the LD element occurs before a focused element, which forms the left-edge of the clause (6), or because it

---

[3] An issue which we shall not be able to tackle here is the status of head marking. Many languages obligatorily mark arguments on the head of the phrase. The question is: Does head marking count as a resumptive element? If it does, either all arguments are double-instantiated, or all lexical arguments should be treated as LD (see Lambrecht 2001: 1056, and especially Van Valin 2013).

occurs before another LD element, an adjunct clause or a conjunction. Summing up, LD in Avatime is defined as follows:

(a) any phrase followed by a co-referential resumptive pronoun or noun (3), (5);
(b) any non-S argument preceding the subject and/or the verb which is not marked with the focus marker (4);
(c) any argument preceding the focus-marked phrase, an adjunct clause, a conjunction or another LD phrase (5), (6).

(3) **lị̀-fịfḷị̀-nɛ**   ɛ̀ɛ́-sɔlì̀   **lɛ**
    c_{3s}-porridge-DEF $c1_s$.SBJ.PROG-catch c_{3s}
    'The porridge, he was catching it.'

(4) **kpeve tsyɛ** òmonò í-tanu   ze   Ø
    Kpeve too today c_{2p}.SBJ.NEG-be.able be.at
    'Kpeve too, today it (okra) was not there.'

(5) kɔ **li-bí** lɛ́-lɔ́ gì lị̀-kpasí wo li-po-le mɛ̀ kɔ
    then c_{3s}-wound c_{3s}-DIST REL c_{3s}.SBJ-be.in 2SG.POS c_{3s}-stomach-DEF inside then
    lɛ tsyɛ li-tse
    c_{3s} too c_{3s}.SBJ-die
    'Then that wound in your stomach, then that too will heal (literally: die).'

(6) wɔ **tsyɛ** á-dei-lá   wɛ̀ɛ́-ta   wìyàwìyà te
    2SG too c_{3p}-corn-DEF:FOC 2SG.SBJ.PROG-chew ID   like.that
    'You too, you are chewing corn like that.'

2.2 Tundra Yukaghir

Tundra Yukaghir is rigidly head-final, with a relatively free preverbal ordering of elements; the only exception is the focus-marked phrase, which is adjacent to the verb and forms a phrase with it (Matić & Nikolaeva 2014). The argument structure is indexed both on arguments, by means of a rich case system, and on the verb. Verbs are always fully head-marked for subjects; the object marking on the verb is less direct, based on two separate sets of suffixes for transitive and intransitive verbs. Tundra Yukaghir does not allow for centre-embedding of adjunct clauses, formed with converbal forms of the verb, which are clause-initial as a rule. The structure of the Tundra Yukaghir sentence can be summarised as follows:

(7) LD_[AdjunctClause_S&O_[Foc_V]]

In LD, resumptive elements are possible, but relatively rare: 36 % (N = 4) of LD subjects (N = 11) and 40 % (N = 13) of objects (N = 33) are re-instantiated with a resumptive (8). In cases without a resumptive, there are two criteria which can be adduced to identify LD. First, if an element precedes an adjunct clause, it must count as LD (9). Second, if an initial element does not carry the case which is governed by the verb, it can only be left-dislocated (10). In sum, three criteria for LD can be defined on the basis of these structural properties. LD is:

(a) any phrase followed by a co-referential resumptive pronoun or noun (8);
(b) any argument preceding the adjunct clause (9);
(c) any left-peripheral phrase which is not in the case governed by the predicate (10).

(8) **pureː-ńə-j**   rukun, tudel jawul əl=ičoː-čoːn   qajl'-ɣa
berry-COM-PTCP thing   he   road NEG=look-PRIV stone-LOC
jewgeč
stumble.INTR.3SG
'The one with the berries, he didn't look at the road and he stumbled on a stone.'

(9) **mit aruːlək**   l'eː [ńi=joː-r]   Ø   moːrqən ańaː-nun-d'əli
1PL tongue-INST PTL REC=see-SS.IMPF.CVB   only   speak-HAB-INTR.1PL
'Our language, we speak it only when we meet.'

(10) **mit aruː**   könmə-l'ɔ   Ø   əl=kuril'ːː,   met ten
1PL language other-NLZR   NEG=know.NEG.3SG 1SG DEM
ańaː-nun-d'əŋ.
speak-HAB-INTR.1SG
'Our language, some don't know it, and I'm able to speak it.'
(canonical case: accusative **mit aruː-ɣanə**)

2.3 Whitesands

Whitesands is a verb-medial language, with a strict ordering of constituents (SVO). The argument structure is marked by word order, as there is no overt case marking for core arguments. There is no evidence to suggest that topicalisation or any other strategy has any influence on the ordering of constituents, so that LD is the only construction that can alter the SVO order. Verbs are obligatorily head-marked for subjects through a series of agreement prefixes. This agreement prefix alone is often a sufficient argument (i. e. it does not require an additional nominal instantiation), and no referential information can intercede between the prefix and the predicate. All other verbal morphology is either clause operators, or manner/direction information. The Whitesands sentence structure can be summarised as:

(11) LD_[S_V_O_Obl]

LD is often resumed by a pronoun, but this is not obligatory, as there are cases of non-subject LD without resumption (14). For LD of subject arguments, resumption is the only clear criterion for identification, as there are no unique intonational or morphosyntactic cues that indicate that a constituent is no longer in the original pre-verbal position. For non-subject constituents identification of LD is clearer, since any pre-subject phrase must be considered a LD. These can occur with or without a resumptive element. If a non-subject, non-possessive constituent is resumed as a pronoun, this is usually in the special resumptive form *la-* (SG) or *e-* (NON-SG) (12). Thus, LD is:

(a) any phrase followed by a co-referential resumptive pronoun or noun (12);
(b) any non-subject argument that precedes the subject constituent or prefixed verb (13),(14).

(12) **nepien mən u**   kitah kostawafa   anah iien **la-n**
    bait   PL   PROX 1PL   1-PROG.NEG.PL-troll yet   NEG RES-3SG
    'These baits here, we haven't fished them yet.'

(13) **tupunis** t-am-aro   m-ø-ətaɲit   Ø
    tupunis 3SG-PST-why ER-SG-break.by.dropping
    'The tupunis, how did it break?'

(14) **nanmetaw u**   ne-k-ø-ek   Ø
    hook   PROX 2-NPST-SG-touch
    'This (fishing) hook, you touch it.'

2.4 Summary

The positional and morphological criteria for all three languages are summarised in Table 1.

Integrated and Non-Integrated Left Dislocation

	Resumptive element	Non-governed case	Position		
			Pre-Subject	Pre-Focus	Pre-Adjunct-Clause
Avatime	+		+	+	+
Tundra Yukaghir	+	+			+
Whitesands	+		+		

Table 1: Criteria for LD in Avatime, Tundra Yukaghir and Whitesands

What is clear from the above is that there are no reliable criteria to determine LD cross-linguistically. Resumptives do universally indicate LD, but they are merely a sufficient, not a necessary condition for a structure to count as LD, since zero anaphora is frequent across languages. As adumbrated in the introduction, the criteria have to be established on a language-to-language basis, depending on the structural properties of the language, including features such as branching direction, head vs. dependent marking, structural positions for subjects, centre embedding of adjunct clauses, the phrasal nature of the focus, etc. In the next section, we will investigate structural similarities and dissimilarities between LD in the target languages. We demonstrate that all three languages do have a grammaticalised type of LD, i. e. a grammatically defined construction including some kind of extraclausal element occurring before the clause.

3 Similarities and dissimilarities

The investigation of the syntactic properties of the LD structures identified with the help of the criteria described in the previous section yields mixed results: while some of the features occur in all three languages and point to syntactic similarities, others are restricted to only one of the languages and imply underlyingly different structures. In this section, we enumerate the most important similarities and differences between LD structures in Avatime, Tundra Yukaghir and Whitesands and discuss them in an informal way; the results will be analysed in more detail in Section 4.

3.1 Shared features

Features that all three languages share shed some light on the nature of the syntactic positions of LD. First, LD can be iterated: multiple LDs are attested in all three languages, as illustrated in (15), (16) and (17).

(15) Avatime

mɔ   mɛ te   xunyɔɛ, mebi   ţiabà$_i$, bɛ-k$_i̦$ ba$_i$
1SG.CTR 1SG like.this CTR   1SG.POSS:children C$_{1s}$.two C$_{1p}$.SBJ-give C$_{1p}$
ku-plikpa.
C$_{6p}$-letter
'As for me, like this, my two children$_i$, they gave them$_i$ letters.'

(16) Tundra Yukaghir

taŋ ańmil,   taŋ la:mə-p-lə, taŋ či:,   taŋ, tittə   la:mə-pə-γanə
that transport.dog that dog-PL-ACC that people that 3PL.POSS dog-PL-ACC
wa:j tittəl ta:t ńe:d'il ŋo-ri:-nun-ŋa:,   jaqta:-nun-ŋi.
again 3PL thus story be-APPL-HAB-3PL.TR sing-HAB-3PL.INTR
'Those sledge dogs, those dogs, those people, uhm, they tell stories about their dogs, they sing (about them).'

(17) Whitesands

swah u,   in u,   Nalaw t-am-ol   trapol kam lah.
man PROX 3SG PROX Nalaw 3SG-PST-make trouble to   3PL
'This man here, he, Nalaw made the trouble for them.'

The question of multiple LDs has been a part of the discussion on the proper position of LD elements. A long-standing line of (mostly generative) research (e. g. Lasnik & Saito 1992: 78ff, Puskás 2000: 190) considers LD and TOP to occupy the same, left-peripheral position, and to differ only in the type of the movement operation involved. One indication for this is thought to be the alleged impossibility of having multiple LD elements in languages like English, Italian and Hungarian[4] — if there is only one position for LD elements, then there can be only one such element per clause. Our data show that this is not the case in our target languages, and, consequently, no special non-iterative left-peripheral position can be assumed.[5] Instead, the possibility of multiple LDs seems to indicate either a fully

---

[4] The empirical validity of this claim remains to be re-investigated.

[5] It is, of course, possible to construe a special clause-internal functional projection for each of the multiple LD elements in the spirit of linguistic cartography, as first conceived by Rizzi (1997). We reject this possibility on methodological grounds. The procedure of multiplying functional projections whenever a need occurs is, as pointed out by Bouchard (2009), among others, so generous to the analysing linguist that it can generate any surface word order, which makes it practically unfalsifiable.

separate sentential fragment (an 'orphan'), or a repeatable syntactic operation, such as adjunction (see Shaer 2009: 387 on the impossibility of differentiating orphans and adjuncts by way of multiple LDs). In any case, multiple LDs show that LD in Avatime, Whitesands and Tundra Yukaghir is not tied to one dedicated position in the left periphery of the clause.

Second, so-called Chinese-style topics occur in all three languages. We follow Chafe (1976) in using this term to denote preclausal elements which do not play an argument or an adjunct role in the clause, but are interpreted as delimiting the field of relevance of the proposition expressed by the clause, as in *The earthquake, the government was slow to help*. Due to their clear connectedness to the clause and the relevance they have for its interpretation, these elements clearly fall under our heuristic concept of LD (Section 1); furthermore, as we show in Section 4.2, Chinese-style topics have the same syntactic distribution as LD with resumptive elements in at least one of the target languages, Avatime. Examples (18), (19) and (20) illustrate left dislocated Chinese-style topics in Avatime, Tundra Yukaghir and Whitesands.

(18) Avatime

ku-wò=e,   *a-wlakpa-là lɛ-gbí*
C_{5s}-fever=CM C_{3p}-leaf-DEF C_{3p}.SBJ-many
'Fever, there are many leaves (sc. that can be used to cure it).'

(19) Tundra Yukaghir

qajl', *lude*   *ugurčə puń-l'əl-mələ*
stone REFL.POSS leg   hurt-EVID-OBJ.FOC.3SG
'Stone, he hurt his leg.'

(20) Whitesands

mani, *parien t-ol*   *had, ah* **mani,** *(0.5)*
money true   3SG.NPST-make hard HES money

metou sait raha nawanien, kapa
but   side POSS food   no
'Money, it is true that it is hard, money, but in terms of food, no.'

We see Chinese-style topics as a further indication that LD in our three languages is not tied to an argument-like position within the left periphery of the clause, as

LD elements in (18)–(20) are certainly not argument-like entities. The interesting fact is that, in their capacity as delimiters of relevance, Chinese-style topics take scope over the whole clause. This can once again be interpreted in two ways: Chinese-style topics in the three target languages are either separate clausal fragments whose scope-taking properties are a product of pragmatic inference at the level of discourse, or they are adjoined to the clause and are thus structurally high enough to be able to scope over the whole proposition.

Thirdly, in all three languages, LD structures display lack of sensitivity to island constraints, as shown by the dependencies between the LD and an argument of classical syntactic islands, adjunct (examples (21) and (22)) and relative clauses (23). Island violations with a resumptive pronoun in the island are attested in natural discourse in all three languages, and even without the resumptive pronoun, these constructions are still judged grammatical in Tundra Yukaghir and Whitesands and by some Avatime speakers.

(21) Tundra Yukaghir

taŋ kö:d'ədo:$_i$, awja: [eńe:-gi   **(tude-ɣanə)**$_i$ uba:nu-də-ɣa]
that boy   yesterday mother-3POSS 3SG-ACC   kiss-3-DS.CVB
kewečəli.
leave.INTR.1PL
'That boy$_i$, we left while his mother was giving (him$_i$) a kiss.'

(22) Whitesands

John$_i$, niamaha t-em-eru   [mə in **ko**$_i$ k-am-eni nerek i]
John anger   3SG-PST-see COMP 3SG that 3-PST-SAY poison TRNS
'John$_i$ was angry because they said that he$_i$ is poisonous.' [literally: John, the anger saw him because he was said to be poisonous.]

(23) Avatime

ɔ́-dzɛ́   **lɛ́-lɔ́=ɛ**$_i$ mè-te   ó-nyime [gì a-tá-gbanì   **yɛ**$_i$]
C$_{1S}$-woman C$_{1S}$-PROX=CM 1SG.SBJ-know C$_{1S}$-man REL C$_{1S}$.SBJ-INT-marry C$_{1S}$
'This woman$_i$, I know the man who will marry her$_i$.'

The way these island violations are interpreted depends on one's theory of syntactic islands (see Hoffmeister & Sag 2010 and Boeckx 2012 for good overviews). On syntactic accounts of islands, subjacency-based or otherwise, examples like

(21), (22) and (23) entail that the LD element does not belong to the same syntactic domain as the gap/pronoun with which it enters the filler-gap dependency. On a processing account, the LD element is processed separately from the clausal domain, so that its coreference with a gap does not overburden the human parser. On both accounts, the lack of island constraints in LD constructions in Avatime, Tundra Yukaghir and Whitesands shows again that LD elements cannot be considered elements of the clause-internal left periphery. As is the case with the previous two properties, island insensitivity is compatible with both adjunction and orphan analyses of the LD in the target languages. In RRG terms, this means that LD is either within the sentence, but outside of the clause, or that it is a separate sentence fragment.

Finally, all three languages allow noun phrases as resumptive elements. Examples are given in (24), (25) and (26).

(24) Avatime

kipɛ mó-te ki-diyɛ bɛ-kɔ bi̯tɛ
t.o.medicine 1SG.SBJ.NEG-know C$_{4s}$-thing:PROX C$_{1p}$.SBJ-take make

kipɛ xunyɔ
t.o.medicine CTR

'Kipe (type of medicine), I don't know those things they use to make kipe.'

(25) Tundra Yukaghir

la:mə-lək, lewejmədəŋ qańd'əmədəŋ taŋ la:mə-lək
dog-INST in.summer in.winter that dog-INST

ańmil-ńa:-nun-ŋi.
riding-PROP-HAB-3PL.INTR

'With dogs, in summer as in winter, they travel with dogs (sc. on dog sledges).'

(26) Whitesands

penses raha-n, ko penses raha-n t-askilim
pliers POSS-3SG then pliers POSS-3SG 3SG.NPST-hold

'His pliers, then his pliers have grabbed it.'

Note that full NPs that function as resumptive elements are not epithets, which according to some analyses can be bound clause-internally (see Alexiadou 2006).

These examples are therefore problematic for those accounts in which the LD element occurs in the left periphery of the clause in a dedicated position. The problem is that a clause-internal LD element would be co-indexed with an R-expression which it c-commands, in violation of Principle C of the Binding theory (Shaer 2009). If we treat LD as adjoined, the problem of the binding of resumptive NPs could be solved by assuming that adjuncts do not form an obligatory binding domain, as with certain types of English PPs (*They$_i$ hid the money behind them$_{i,j}$*). Of course, no stipulation is necessary if we assume that LD elements are orphans. For an RRG-based account, this does not necessarily follow. LD can be an orphan or an adjunct, but it can also be an element in the left-detached position (LDP) outside the clause but inside the sentence. In this way, it would be outside of the binding domain but still part of a larger syntactic unit.

The evidence of the features that all three target languages share suggests that LD in these languages does not have a dedicated clause-internal left-peripheral position. One possible way to save the clause-internal analysis of at least some instances of LD would be to try and differentiate different types of LD within each language, similar to the analyses that have been proposed for Germanic and Romance languages, so that one type of LD would be clause-internal and derived by some kind of movement, while the other would be of the clause-external hanging topic type (see Section 1). However, we were not able to find any clustering of features that would justify this division. For instance, it is not the case the tokens of LD carrying features that indicate extra-clausal LD, such as multiple LD, Chinese-style LD, or resumptive NPs, are characterised by one set of morphophonological properties (prosodic break, non-restricted resumptives, etc.), whereas those tokens that do not have these features have a different set of properties (no break, restricted type and position of the resumptive, etc.). We therefore assume that each of the target languages has only one type of LD, in absence of evidence to the contrary.

The shared features listed above indicate that the LD structure in Avatime, Tundra Yukaghir and Whitesands can be treated as (a) a sentence-internal element, outside of the clause proper but inside the sentence (in RRG terms) (b) adjoined to the clause at the sentential level (both in generative and in RRG terms), or (c) as an independent utterance ('orphan') connected to the clause inferentially. Options (a) and (c) seem more likely because of the occurrence of resumptive nominal phrases.

3.2 Structural differences

The three target languages differ in a number of respects, which seems to indicate that the position of LD elements in each of them might be similar, but is not identical. In what follows, we address the two most conspicuous differences.

The first diverging feature is the possibility of embedded LD structures. As early as Ross (1967 [1987]), it was noted that LD structures cannot occur within embedded clauses. This has been considered a criterial property of the non-integrated type of LD, which immediately follows from its position outside of the clause proper: if it is the clause that is embedded, than elements that do not belong to it cannot undergo this syntactic operation (apart from some marginal exceptions identified by Ross; cf. Aissen 1992: 68). Among our target languages, Tundra Yukaghir and Whitesands fully conform to this restriction, as shown for Tundra Yukaghir in (27). In Avatime, however, LD elements can freely appear in all complement and some adjunct clauses, as in (28) and (29) (see Van Putten 2014 for more detail).

(27) Tundra Yukaghir

    * awja: [*Ivan, Poːdʼə tude-ɣanə paj-oːl-ɣanə*]   *mə=jöː-ŋ*
    yesterday Ivan   Pod'e 3SG-ACC hit-STAT.NLZR-ACC EX=see-TR.1SG
    Intended reading: * 'Yesterday, I saw that Ivan, Pod'e hit him'.

(28) Avatime

    sị ba sị   [*ì-tsré lɔ gì ɛlɔ̀m a-kɔ̀*   *maní ke-pa*   *mɛ̀*
    tell C₁ₚ COMP C₂ₚ-okra DIST REL Elom C₁ₛ.SBJ-take bring C₆ₛ-house inside
    ba-da   *lɛ kị́ wɔ*]
    C₁ₚ.SBJ.SBJV-sell C₃ₛ give 2SG
    'Tell them that the okra that Elom brought to the house, they should sell it to you.'

(29) Avatime

    blɔ petee kị́à-tsa   [*tɔ kị-bɔ̀-ɛ*   *bị́à-lɛ*   *kɛ kị́*
    1PL all   1PL.SBJ.POT-meet PURP C₄ₛ-money-DEF C₁ₚ.SBJ.POT-share C₄ₛ give
    ɔ̀-ma   *kákaa*]
    C₂ₛ-town every
    'We will all meet so that the money, we share it to every town.'

The obvious conclusion to be drawn out of this is that LD in Avatime is in some way more closely integrated with its host clause than is the case in Tundra Yukaghir and Whitesands. More precisely, it seems to be the case that in Avatime, but not in Tundra Yukaghir and Whitesands, LD and the clause form a unit which is a syntactic object that can be subject to embedding. This means that Avatime LD elements cannot be analysed as orphans, i. e. independent utterances that are linked to the clause via discourse linking.

The second feature in which the target languages differ is the nature of the resumptive expression. It has been noticed before that LD structures can differ in the type of the resumptive expression, both within and across languages. It is usually assumed that the integrated type tends to employ a specialised resumptive pronoun in well-defined positions, whereas non-integrated LD allows for all types of resumptive expressions in all positions (see Alexiadou 2006 and Shaer 2009). All our target languages allow for both nominal and pronominal resumptive elements, as well as zero anaphora (see Sections 2 and 3.1), but only Whitesands also has a specialised pronominal form which occurs only with LD. In Whitesands, this LD-specific pronominal expression is *la-* (SG) or *e-* (NON-SG), as illustrated in (30). Regular independent pronouns can also be used as resumptives, as in (31).

(30) Whitesands

    *ra tiapen mən aha$_i$ n-am-at-ivi   **la**$_i$*
    POSS tuna PL that 2-PST-PROG-SG-pull RES
    'Those tunas, you fish them.'

(31) Whitesands

    *ka-Sauieh$_i$ **in**$_i$ t-apa   m-ø-uven m-ø-ol   tion e*
    DEIC-Sauieh 3SG 3SG.NPST-no ER-SG-go ER-SG-make join DAT
    'But this Sauieh, he didn't want to, so he went and joined in.'

Since syntactic tests yield identical results for both *la* and all other types of resumptives, we assume that Whitesands does not have two or more LD structures on a par with languages like German or Italian (see e. g. Cinque 1997, Grohmann & Boeckx 2004). In other words, Whitesands has developed a specialised marker of coreference with the LD element without concomitant syntactic specialisation. The existence of such a marker seems to imply a closer connection between the

LD and the clause than would be the case if LD were fully syntactically independent, i. e. it points in the same direction as the embedded LD structures in Avatime. Whitesands thus has one signal of closer integration of LD elements with their host clauses.

3.3 An interim summary

The similarities and dissimilarities of LD structures in Avatime, Tundra Yukaghir and Whitesands are summarised in Table 2.

	multiple LD	Chinese-style LD	island insensitivity	resumptive NPs	embedded LD	specialised resumptive
Avatime	+	+	+	+	+	
Tundra Yukaghir	+	+	+	+		
Whitesands	+	+	+	+		+

Table 2: Features of LD in Avatime, Tundra Yukaghir and Whitesands

The evidence of the six criteria applied here is contradictory. On the one hand, the four shared features described in Section 3.1 point to an analysis of LD as non-integrated, be it as an orphan or adjunct (both in RRG and in generative terms) or as a sentential extraclausal element (RRG). On the other hand, embedded LDs in Avatime and the specialised resumptive *la* in Whitesands can be understood only if we assume a more integrated nature of LD in these two languages. In the following section, we shall try to tackle this dilemma from a more general perspective and offer a tentative conclusion.

4 The nature of LD

4.1 Status of LD in Tundra Yukaghir

Tundra Yukaghir provides the only relatively clear case of fully non-integrated LD. The features enumerated in Sections 2.2 and 3 point to syntactic independence of the LD element from the clause. Approaches that recognise only one syntactic level, the level of the clause, must treat non-integrated LD constructions as consisting of a separate sentential fragment (orphan) linked to the remainder of the utterance via discourse-based interpretive rules. If we analyse Tundra Yukaghir LD within the framework of RRG, its non-integrated nature can be accounted for in two ways: (a) the left-dislocated element is an orphan, or (b) the left-dislocated element occurs in the left-detached position (LDP), outside of the clause but within the sentence, following the standard RRG analysis of LD. For the latter analysis to work, we would have to assume that consecutive (non-embedded) LDPs are allowed within one sentence, which is something of a moot point in the theory; we will elaborate on this further in Section 5.

4.2 Status of LD in Avatime

At first sight, most features of the Avatime LD construction characterise it as a non-integrated structure. However, its frequent occurrence in embedded contexts strongly points to an analysis as integrated LD. Importantly, there is no evidence that there are two distinct types of LD in Avatime, an integrated and a noninte-grated one. All the types of elements that can be left dislocated in main clauses can also be left dislocated in embedded clauses. Even Chinese-style LD, which could easily be conceived of as a separate type due to its loose connection to the remainder of the sentence, is subject to embedding, as shown in (32).

(32) Avatime

nítemesį̀ kui-do sị̀ ị̀-kɔ́é lé-yá tete ɔ-bịte lɔ=ɛ blɔ
so 1PL.SBJ-say COMP C_{3p}-custom C_{3p}-PROX like.this INF-do DIST=CM 1PL
ku̧-lị̀ ní committee líyɛ̀ abà ní ɔ̀vanɔ́ yà blɔ petee blɔ
1PL.SBJ-be.at LOC committee C_{1s}:PROX on LOC Vane here 1PL all 1PL
kíà-dzɛ babiakpa
1PL.SBJ.POT-go Biakpa

'We said that the performance of those customs, we who are in this committee here in Vane, all of us will go to Biakpa.'

This means that the integrated and non-integrated features of Avatime LD need to be reconciled within one analysis. To this end, we propose to add another type of LD to the typology: *loosely integrated LD*. The label 'loosely integrated' captures the fact that Avatime LD elements cannot be analysed as orphans. Their occurrence in embedded contexts implies that they form a unit together with the remainder of the sentence. At the same time, they do not behave like other integrated elements.

Integrated and Non-Integrated Left Dislocation

One possible solution would be to analyse Avatime LD as adjunction. We have seen in Section 3.1 that the occurrence of resumptive NPs is a possible problem for this analysis, but that it can be solved by redefining the binding domain in Avatime, i. e. by assuming that adjuncts are outside of the binding domain. If we take a RRG perspective, the syntactic account of loosely integrated LD becomes unproblematic. Avatime LD elements can occur in the left-detached position (LDP). In this way they form a unit with the remainder of the sentence, but are outside of the clause and thus not sensitive to clause-internal syntactic restrictions. The occurrence of resumptive nouns is not a problem on this account, as the LD element is outside of the clause, i. e. of the binding domain. Chinese-style LD is also unproblematic, as there are no restrictions on the semantic connectedness of the element in the LDP to the clause. The only assumptions we have to make are that sentences as a whole can be subject to embedding and again that the LDP can be iterated, both of which are not difficult to accommodate in the theory (see Section 5). In conclusion, the loosely integrated LD of the Avatime type can either be treated as an adjunct (if we assume a redefinition of the binding domain) or, with the assumptions mentioned above, as an element in the LDP within the sentence.

4.3 Status of LD in Whitesands

LD in Whitesands, like in the other two languages, looks non-integrated at first sight. However, like Avatime, it also shows one symptom of integration: the specialised resumptive pronoun. As was shown in Section 3.2, Whitesands has a specialised resumptive pronoun *la-/e-*, which occurs only in LD constructions. This pronoun is optional; regular independent pronouns, nouns and zero anaphora are also allowed as resumptive elements.

This specialised resumptive pronoun leads to a problem under the orphan analysis: how can a separate syntactic fragment trigger a pronoun that is only used with LD and not in other contexts? As mentioned in Section 3.2, there is no evidence that Whitesands has more than one type of LD, such that one has a special pronoun, while the other uses regular pronouns or NP gaps. This seems to leave us with the option to assume that all LD structures in Whitesands are integrated, in the way Italian Clitic LD or German Contrastive LD are integrated into the sentence and trigger specific pronouns (Cinque 1997; see Alexiadou 2006 and Shaer

2009 for an overview of the literature). However, we see no necessity to postulate that LD is of the integrated type in Whitesands because of *la*-resumptives. Given that all other types of evidence point to its lack of integration, we propose a fourth type of LD to account for the Whitesands data: *non-integrated bound LD*. This label is meant to refer to the type of LD in which LD elements can be partially syntactically bound, despite being outside of the sentence. The idea that independent syntactic units can be linked not only via discourse constraints, but also via syntactic rules, is supported by evidence that such clausal phenomena *par excellence* as VP-ellipsis (Van Valin 2005: 231ff) or case assignment (Shimojo 2008) can occur across conversational turns, where the preceding turn controls the syntax of the following turn. We thus presume that in Whitesands, under certain discourse conditions, a certain type of sentential fragment, LD, can trigger the use of the special pronoun *la-/e-* in the clause instead of the canonical personal pronoun. We still have no clear idea of the exact nature of these discourse conditions, but the principle according to which pronoun choice is triggered by previous clauses/sentences is well-attested cross-linguistically (see e. g. Kuno 1987)[6] and thus also a plausible explanation for the use of *la-/e-* in the Whitesands LD construction.

4.4 Expanding the LD typology

As the previous two sections have shown, a simple two-way typology of non-integrated LD versus integrated LD cannot capture all properties of the three languages discussed in this paper. In particular Avatime and Whitesands show properties of both integrated and non-integrated types of LD. There is no evidence in these languages that some LD structures are integrated and some are non-integrated. Therefore, we have proposed to add two more types of LD to the typology, which are between integrated and non-integrated.

The first type is loosely integrated LD. As the name suggests, this is a type of integrated LD that is more loosely connected to the remainder of the sentence than typical integrated LDs. This occurs in the situation in which an LD element is within the sentence proper (integrated), but fails to be sensitive to certain

---

[6] A well-known example is the choice between *er/sie* and *der/die* in German, which is (at least partly) determined by the grammatical role of the antecedent in the previous sentence (see e. g. Bosch & Umbach 2007, Bosch, Katz & Umbach 2007), such that *er/sie* will be preferably used with subject antecedents, *der/die* with objects.

phenomena within the sentence because of being in a position which cannot control them. That is, if an LD construction is not sensitive to some characteristic sentential processes, this still does not imply that it is outside of the sentence. As we have shown in Section 4.2, this type of LD can explain the phenomena we find in Avatime, where LD appears to be have non-integrated properties but is at the same time subject to embedding.

The second type we propose is non-integrated bound LD. This type can account for LD elements that are non-integrated but still control certain phenomena in the sentence. We assume that it is possible for non-integrated LD elements to entertain certain conventionalised, syntactic relationships with the following sentence/clause. This type of LD accounts for the Whitesands data, where LD shows all the signs of being non-integrated, even though there is a specialised resumptive pronoun *la* which occurs only in LD constructions.

Our revised LD typology thus contains four categories: (i) non-integrated, (ii) non-integrated bound, (iii) loosely integrated, and (iv) integrated. These are by no means all possible types that could be envisaged and it may well be that the typology needs to be further refined if data from more languages is taken into account.

5 Summary and conclusion

In this paper, we have investigated the LD constructions in three genealogically and geographically distant languages, Avatime, Whitesands and Tundra Yukaghir, in order to shed some light both on the possible variability of this seemingly simple construction and to contribute to a definition of the category of LD which can stand the test of data coming from languages not belonging to the Standard Average European type.

We limited our exploration only to those cases of LD-like phenomena which are reflected in the syntax, leaving out conversational phenomena such as false starts, hesitations, etc. We show that the major means of identifying LD, resumptive expressions, are indeed a reliable indicator of LD if they are present, but that, due to productive mechanisms of zero anaphora in many languages, their absence is not an indicator that no LD is involved. With this allegedly universal criterion for LD out of the way, the only method of identifying LD remains a definition of the construction on a language-to-language basis.

Once the properties of the structures identified as LD in the target languages are investigated, it turns out that the phenomena which look superficially similar correspond to distinct syntactic structures in each of the languages. Tundra Yukaghir LD seems to be an instance of fully non-integrated LD, most probably a separate syntactic unit, an orphan, lacking any clear syntactic connection to the clause to which it interpretatively relates. While the structure of LD in Whitesands seems to be similar, the connection to the clause is somewhat tighter, as indicated by a conventionalised use of certain pronominal types as resumptives within the clause. Thus, while Tundra Yukaghir LD is of the proper non-integrated kind, the corresponding structure in Whitesands belongs to a transitional category of non-integrated bound LD. The evidence of syntactic tests for Avatime shows that LD in this language belongs to the sentence and is thus of the integrated type. However, LD elements fail to control some syntactic phenomena which they should control if they had a dedicated position in the sentence hierarchy. Reasons for this can be different: LD elements might be sentence-level adjuncts, or have some other property which prevents them from participating in all sentence-level processes. However this phenomenon is explained, Avatime LD can be classified as special, loose integrated type of LD.

We have left our discussion so far at a rather theory-neutral level, assuming merely the existence of LDs separate from the sentence and those somehow integrated into it. The question is what this revised typology means for RRG. How can the distinction between integrated and non-integrated be captured in RRG terms and can the categories of non-integrated bound LD and loosely integrated LD fit in?

The standard analysis of LD elements in RRG is that they occur in the left-detached position (Van Valin 2005: 6), i. e. they are treated as a kind of entity between integrated and non-integrated in the classical generative division. Within RRG, no notion of orphan has been proposed, but the idea of a separate syntactic fragment could be easily accommodated in the theory. However, it is not immediately clear whether this is needed to account for LD within this framework. In the generative theory, the notion of orphan accounts for the extraclausal properties of non-integrated LD, since no intermediate level between clause and discourse exists. However, in RRG, the LDP is already extraclausal. In fact, the LDP has all properties that an orphan is supposed to have and at the same time it has the advantage of being within the syntactic structure. This means that the LDP can also account for non-integrated LD, as well as for loosely integrated LD, as we have seen in Section 4.2. On the other hand, we think that the existence of independent sentential fragments could be a useful addition to the theory, because it would enable it to straightforwardly account for the difference between fully non-integrated LD structures, such as the one in Tundra Yukaghir, and various intermediate types, like the ones we found in Avatime and Whitesands.[7]

Our data can contribute to the theory in three further respects. First, it is unclear whether RRG can deal with multiple LD elements in one sentence. In the RRG sentence architecture, the assumption is usually made of only one LDP per sentence. This would be a problem in the analysis of LD in Avatime, which clearly includes the LDP and can nevertheless host more than one element. We do not see any inherent reason for the assumption that the LDP is not iterative, so that we would like to propose the possibility of multiple LDPs per sentence in RRG. Secondly, RRG does not freely permit sentential subordination, which would be necessary to account for Avatime subordinate LD. Sentential subordination is a part of the RRG architecture, but it is restricted to sentences occurring in the detached position of another sentence (Van Valin 2005: 192). We would propose to extend the possibility of sentential subordination to other types of subordinate clauses (for more details see Van Putten 2014). Finally, our Whitesands data demonstrate that the repertoire of syntactic dependencies across sentences, which has been limited to VP ellipsis and case assignment in the RRG literature (Section 4.3), can be expanded to include specialised resumptive pronouns triggered by LD elements across sentence boundaries, unless, of course, the Whitesands LD elements are also assumed to be placed in the LDP. On the methodological side, we aim to have demonstrated that the identification of LD across languages is no trivial matter, but requires a careful investigation of the potential LD structures on a language-to-language basis.

Our findings, preliminary as they might be, show that neither the simple dichotomy of integrated vs. non-integrated LD types nor the single LDP at the sentential level are sufficient to capture all the various disguises in which LD can occur in natural languages. For this reason we propose to view LD as a type of structure which can occur in three positions – as an orphan, in the LDP and, prob-

---

[7] The fully integrated type is not attested in our target languages, but it seems to be quite well documented in Romance, Germanic, and in Greek (Anagnastopoulou 1997, Cinque 1997, Alexiadou 2006, Shaer 2009), so that RRG would probably have to allow for a clause-internal type of LD, too.

ably, clause-initially (see footnote 7). These various positions are at least partly responsible for the differences we find across languages. We define two types of LD that are intermediate between fully integrated and non-integrated – non-integrated bound and loosely integrated – which help us classify our data. Future research, both on our target languages and on a wider sample of languages, will likely reveal further subtypes and result in a more fine-grained classification.

Abbreviations

A	actor	INTR	intransitive
ACC	accusative	LOC	locative
ASSOC	associative	NEG	negative
AUG	augmentative	NLZR	nominalizer
C-$_{S/P}$	nominal class-singular/plural	NPST	non-past
COM	comitative	PL	plural
COMP	complementizer	POSS	possessive
CONTR	contrast	POT	potential
CVB	converb	PRIV	privative
DAT	dative	PROG	progressive
DEF	definite	PROX	proximal
DEIC	deictic	PST	past
DIST	distal	PTCP	participle
DS	different subject	PURP	purposive
ER	echo referent	REC	reciprocal
EX	existential	REFL	reflexive
FOC	focus	REL	relativizer
HAB	habitual	RES	resumptive
ID	ideophone	SBJ	subject
IMPF	imperfective	SG	singular
INCL	inclusive	SS	same subject
INTJ	interjection	STAT	stative
INST	instrumental	TRNS	transitive
INTSF	intensifier	U	undergoer

References

Aissen, J. 1992. Topic and focus in Mayan. *Language* 68: 43–80.
Altmann, H. 1981. *Formen der 'Herausstellung' im Deutschen*. Tübingen: Niemeyer.

References

Alexiadou, A. 2006. Left dislocation (including CLLD). In M. Everaert & H. van Riemsdijk (eds.), *The Blackwell companion to syntax, Vol. II.* Malden: Blackwell.

Anagnostopoulou, E. (1997). Clitic left dislocation and Contrastive left dislocation. In E. Anagnostopoulou, H. van Riemsdijk & F. Zwarts (eds.), *Materials on left dislocation*, 668–699. Amsterdam: Benjamins.

Avanzi, M. 2011. La dislocation à gauche avec reprise anaphorique en français parlé. Etude prosodiqu. In H.-Y. Yoo & E. Delais-Roussarie (eds.), *Actes d'IDP 2009, Paris, Septembre 2009.* http://makino.linguist.jussieu.fr/idp09/actes_en.html/, accessed September 18th 2013.

Avanzi, M., C. Gendrot & A. Lacheret-Dujour. 2010. Is there a prosodic difference between left-dislocated and heavy subjects? Evidence from spontaneous French. *Proceedings of Speech Prosody 2010, Chicago* 100068. http://speechprosody2010.illinois.edu/, accessed September 18th 2013.

Boeckx, C. 2012. *Syntactic islands.* New York: Cambridge University Press.

Bosch, P., G. Katz & C. Umbach. 2007. The non-subject bias of German demonstrative pronouns. In M. Schwarz-Friesel, M. Consten & M. Knees (eds.), *Anaphors in text: Cognitive, formal and applied approaches to anaphoric reference*, 145–165. Amsterdam: Benjamins.

Bosch, P. & C. Umbach. 2007. Reference determination for demonstrative pronouns. In D. Bittner (ed.), *Proceedings of the Conference on Intersentential Pronominal Reference in Child and Adult Language.* Special issue of *ZAS Papers in Linguistics*, Vol. 48, 39–51.

Bouchard, D. 2009. A solution to the conceptual problem of cartography. In J. van Craenenbroeck (ed.), *Alternatives to cartography*, 245–274. Berlin: Mouton de Gruyter.

Chafe, W. 1976. Givenness, contrastiveness, definiteness, subjects, topics, and point of view. In C. Li (ed.), *Subject and topic*, 25–55. New York: AP.

Cinque, G. 1990. *Types of A' dependencies.* Cambridge, MA: MIT Press.

Cinque, G. 1997. 'Topic' constructions in some European languages. In E. Anagnostopoulou, H. van Riemsdijk & F. Zwarts (eds.), *Materials on left dislocation*, 93–118. Amsterdam: Benjamins.

De Cat, C. 2007. French dislocation without movement. *Natural Language & Linguistic Theory* 25: 485–534.

Dik, S. C. 1978. *Functional grammar.* Amsterdam: North Holland.

Feldhausen, I. 2008. *The prosody-syntax interface in Catalan*. Universität Potsdam dissertation. http://prosodia.upf.edu/aev/recursos/, accessed October 1st 2013.

Foley, W. A. & R. D. Van Valin, Jr. 1984. *Functional syntax and universal grammar*. Cambridge: Cambridge University Press.

Frey, W. 2004. Notes on the syntax and the pragmatics of German left dislocation. In H. Lohnstein & S. Trissler (eds.), *The syntax and semantics of the left periphery*, 203–234. Berlin: Mouton de Gruyter.

Geluykens, R. 1992. *From discourse process to grammatical construction*. ON LEFT-DISLOCATION IN ENGLISH. Amsterdam: Benjamins.

Givón, T. 1976. Topic, pronoun and grammatical agreement. In C. Li (ed.), *Subject and topic*, 149–188. New York: AP.

Gregory, M. L. & L. A. Michaelis. 2001. Topicalization and left-dislocation: A functional opposition revisited. *Journal of Pragmatics* 33, 1665–1706.

Grohmann, K. K. & C. Boeckx. 2004. Left Dislocation in Germanic. In W. Abraham (ed.), *Focus on Germanic typology*, 139–152. Berlin: Akademie-Verlag.

Haegeman, L. 1991. Parenthetical adverbials: The radical orphan approach. In S. Chiba, A. Ogawa, Y. Fuiwara, N. Yamada, O. Koma & T. Yagi (eds.), *Aspects of Modern English Linguistics: Papers presented to Masatomo Ukaji on his 60th birthday*, 232–254. Tokyo: Kaitakushi.

Haspelmath, M. 2010. Comparative concepts and descriptive categories in cross-linguistic studies. *Language* 86: 663–687.

Hoffmeister, P. & I. Sag. 2010. Cognitive constraints and island effects. *Language* 86: 366–415.

Kuno, S. 1987. *Functional syntax: Anaphora, discourse, and empathy*. Chicago: The University of Chicago Press.

Lambrecht, K. 2001. Dislocation. In M. Haspelmath, E. König, W. Oesterreicher & W. Raible (eds.), *Language typology and language universals: An international handbook*. Vol. 2, 1050–1078. Berlin: Walter de Gruyter.

Lasnik, H. & M. Saito. 1992. *Move Alpha: Conditions on Its application and output*. Cambridge, MA: MIT Press.

Matić, D. & I. Nikolaeva. 2014. Realis mood, focus, and existential closure in Tundra Yukaghir. *Lingua* 150: 202–231.

Ott, D. 2012. Movement and ellipsis in contrastive left-dislocation. In N. Arnett & R. Bennett (eds.), *Proceedings of WCCFL 30*, 281–291. Somerville, MA: Cascadilla.

References

Prince, E. 1997. On the functions of left-dislocation in English discourse. In A. Kamio (ed.), *Directions in functional linguistics*, 117–144. Amsterdam: Benjamins.

Prince, E. 1998. On the limits of syntax, with reference to topicalization and left-dislocation. In P. Cullicover & L. McNally (eds.), *Syntax and semantics 29: The limits of syntax*. New York: AP.

Puskás, G. 2000. *Word order in Hungarian*. Amsterdam: Benjamins.

Rizzi, L. 1997. The fine structure of the left periphery. In L. Haegeman (ed.), *Elements of grammar*, 281–337. Dordrecht: Kluwer.

Ross, H. 1967. *Constraints on variables in syntax*. MIT Dissertation (published 1987 as INFINITE SYNTAX! Norwood, NJ: ABLEX).

Shaer, B. 2009. German and English left-peripheral elements and the 'orphan' analysis of non-integration. In B. Shaer, P. Cook, W. Frey & C. Maienborn (eds.), *Dislocated elements in discourse*, 465–502. New York: Routledge.

Shimojo, M. 2008. How missing is the missing verb? The verb-less numeral quantifier construction in Japanese. In R. D. Van Valin, Jr. (ed.), *Investigations of the syntax-semantics-pragmatics interface*, 285–304. Amsterdam: Benjamins.

van Putten, S. 2014. Left dislocation and subordination in Avatime (Kwa). In R. van Gijn, J. Hammond, D. Matić, S. van Putten & A. Vilacy Galucio (eds.), *Information structure and reference tracking in complex sentences*, 71–98. Amsterdam: Benjamins.

Van Valin, R. D., Jr. & R. J. LaPolla. 1997. *Syntax: Structure, meaning, and function*. Cambridge: Cambridge University Press.

Van Valin, R. D., Jr. 2005. *Exploring the syntax-semantics interface*. Cambridge: Cambridge University Press.

Van Valin, R. D., Jr. 2013. Head-marking languages and linguistic theory. In B. Bickel, L. A. Grenoble, D. A. Peterson, & A. Timberlake (eds.), *What's where why? Language typology and historical contingency. A festschrift to honor Johanna Nichols*, 91–124. Amsterdam: Benjamins.

Authors

Dejan Matić, University of Graz
Saskia van Putten, Radboud University Nijmegen
Jeremy Hammond, University of Sydney

www.ingramcontent.com/pod-product-compliance
Lightning Source LLC
Chambersburg PA
CBHW071149300426
44113CB00009B/1134